MIDWEST
Cottage
GARDENING

FRANCES MANOS

TRAILS BOOKS
Black Earth, Wisconsin

Library of Congress Control Number: 2004104306
ISBN: 1-931599-40-8

Editor: Stan Stoga
Photos: James Manos
Project Manager: Mike Martin
Assistant Project Manager: Erika Reise
Assistant Creative Director: Denise Sauter
Designer: Todd Garrett
Cover Photo: Donna Krischan

Printed in China by Everbest Printing Co., Ltd.
09 08 07 06 05 04   6 5 4 3 2 1

Trails Books, a division of Trails Media Group, Inc.
P.O. Box 317 • Black Earth, WI 53515
(800) 236-8088 • e-mail: books@wistrails.com
www.trailsbooks.com

For Jim.

And with thanks to my sister Kathy Voland, my sister-in-law Leah Johnson-Manos, and to good friend Susan Wukitsch for allowing us to photograph their beautiful gardens.

Thanks also to the staff of the Saint Charles Public Library, for so kindly harboring a writer.

And to all the gardeners who have shared their gardens and their gardening hopes and dreams with me—I can't say thank you enough.

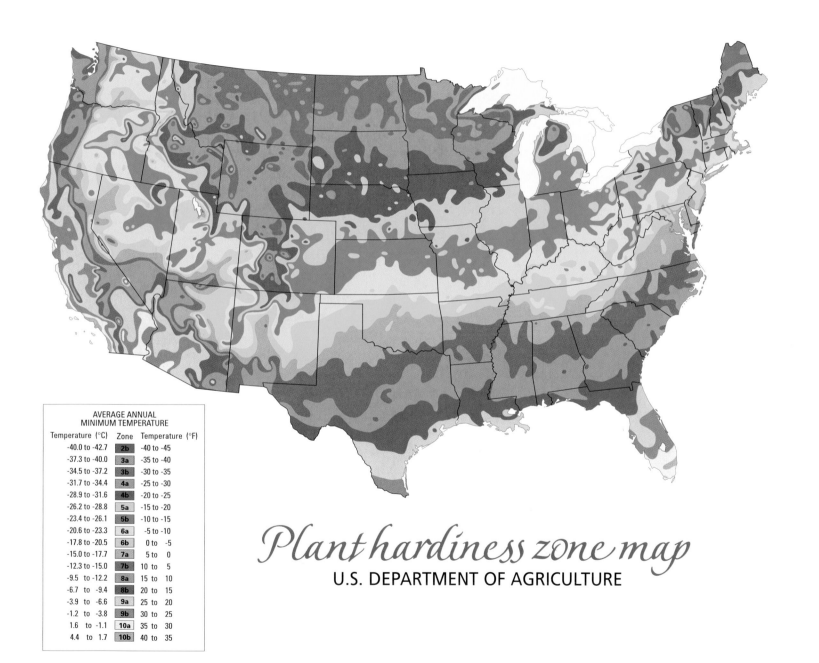

AVERAGE ANNUAL
MINIMUM TEMPERATURE

Temperature (°C)	Zone	Temperature (°F)
-40.0 to -42.7	2b	-40 to -45
-37.3 to -40.0	3a	-35 to -40
-34.5 to -37.2	3b	-30 to -35
-31.7 to -34.4	4a	-25 to -30
-28.9 to -31.6	4b	-20 to -25
-26.2 to -28.8	5a	-15 to -20
-23.4 to -26.1	5b	-10 to -15
-20.6 to -23.3	6a	-5 to -10
-17.8 to -20.5	6b	0 to -5
-15.0 to -17.7	7a	5 to 0
-12.3 to -15.0	7b	10 to 5
-9.5 to -12.2	8a	15 to 10
-6.7 to -9.4	8b	20 to 15
-3.9 to -6.6	9a	25 to 20
-1.2 to -3.8	9b	30 to 25
1.6 to -1.1	10a	35 to 30
4.4 to 1.7	10b	40 to 35

Plant hardiness zone map
U.S. DEPARTMENT OF AGRICULTURE

A cottage
garden can
be beautifully
formal . . .

Table of *contents*

. . . or beautifully casual.

contents

Introduction

I've lived all my life in the middle of the Midwest, about 30 miles west of Chicago, and have been gardening here for almost 20 years, slogging on through hail, drought, powdery mildew, and plagues of earwigs. And I've lived to tell the tale.

Long ago when I was a beginning gardener I quickly noticed two facts that were rarely mentioned in gardening books and magazines: First, gardening can be expensive. Second, gardening can be really hard! I had plunged exhilarated into gardening, intoxicated by the sumptuous color photos in magazines of gardens from all over the world. I'd pored for hours over pictures of lush gardens in the Hamptons, neat vineyards in California, gardens overflowing with roses in Oregon, and gardens arrayed with ranks of foxgloves and lupines in Sussex, England. I was inspired by books such as *Lark Rise to Candleford*, by Flora Thompson, which tells the story of the quaint cottage gardens of England in the nineteenth century, as well as *The Cottage Garden*, by Roy Genders, which describes the delectable old-fashioned flowers of the English country garden. I practically memorized *Vita Sackville-West's Garden Book*, reading raptly of fawn-pink foxtail lilies and her ruminations on alpine lawns. And I was enchanted by a little book named *Cottage Garden Flowers*, by Margery Fish, a book that I still practically sleep with under my pillow. My grandmother had been born on the Isle of Wight, a verdant island dangling from the southern coast of England, and perhaps some of that green heritage flowed in my veins and explained my intense attraction to the idea of a cottage garden. So my early garden dreams were aflame with foxgloves and lupines, cabbage roses and wallflowers. And of course there had to be hollyhocks by a white picket fence.

What I didn't realize at first was how different the American Midwest is, from a gardening standpoint, from other regions of the United States and from England. I was a complete innocent. I hadn't yet wielded a pick axe to break up the clay soil in my yard for a vegetable patch, for instance. I hadn't fought off squadrons of mosquitoes in July while playing tug-of-war with the four-foot-tall specimens of pigweed that had sprouted with lightning speed among black-spotted tea roses. And when I plunked down $25 for three astilbes, and watched them shrivel up and die in a searing August heat wave, I was devastated and began to wonder if having a beautiful garden was even possible where I lived. I dimly began to appreciate that the Midwest is no place for sissy gardeners and, worse, that it was possible to spend a lot of money and still not have the garden of your dreams.

It was that last thing that really nettled me. I did seem to be trotting off a lot to nurseries to buy plants to replace plants that had either withered away or gotten munched down to a nub by earwigs. Or I was buying expensive fertilizers of dubious worth, paying shockingly high water bills, or shopping in a daze for fashionable garden ornaments. I was beginning to wonder: when had gardening become all about buying? And why, for all the money I spent, was I still not satisfied with my garden?

After all, as well as reading gardening books and consulting with the local county extension about planting methods, I also begged advice from the owners of nice gardens in my area: how did they do it? But when I asked a rose grower the secret of her fabulous tea roses, I was taken aback when she escorted me into the dim recesses of her garage, where she showed me an array of bottles labeled with skulls and crossbones, plus what looked like a gas mask. A regular spraying program using malathion for aphids, captan for blackspot, kelthane for the mites, mexachlor for the rose midge, and mercifully I forget what else, was all it took! Oh. I was shaken. "Remember the mask when you spray!" she gaily called after me as I left.

I was learning with growing dismay that it apparently took an arsenal of poisons to have a pretty garden here in the Midwest. The emerald lawns, the roses, the lilies . . . all were dusted, sprayed, and soaked in poison. I felt stymied. Nowadays, many take a sharply political stand regarding the environment, some hugging trees, and others scoffing at environment alarmists. I don't see myself in either camp, though I lean toward the tree huggers, and have, in fact, hugged the wonderful, big horse chestnut in my backyard. I just knew in my heart that I didn't want to garden with poisons.

Meanwhile, I was regularly tossing away six-packs of withered annual lobelia and dianthus and watching foxgloves and delphiniums melt away in the August heat. Once a tea rose actually shrank after I planted it. A pagoda dogwood dropped dead with a groan. Flats of marigolds and an entire clematis were eaten by earwigs. My dream of having a quaint little cottage garden was disappearing literally into the dust along with the delphiniums.

But, I am stubborn, very stubborn, perhaps because my other grandmother was born in Scotland, and the Scots can have a streak of granite running through their souls. It was with the debacle of the shrinking tea rose that I hit bottom with a thud and shook myself free of illusions about Flopsy and Mopsy and chamomile tea in the topiary garden and finally set out to learn how to garden where I actually live, in northern Illinois, not in Connecticut or British Columbia or Sissinghurst, and that's when this book slowly began to evolve.

Another turning point in my evolution as a gardener came during frequent visits to local prairie remnants, which began as just a pleasant way to spend a Sunday afternoon. Rich tapestries of grasses and flowers thrived, shining and alive with birds and butterflies—all without any human intervention at all. Some plants and grasses were seven, eight, nine feet tall and bursting with health—no shrinking tea roses here. And was I seeing things? But wasn't the blue wild indigo (*Baptisia australis*) as elegant as the fussiest delphinium?

I finally began my education by reluctantly facing the realities of our climate. I went to a globe and traced with my finger along the line of latitude (42° N) that passes through northern Illinois and found to my surprise that it also passes through Inner Mongolia, not Sissinghurst, England. Darn. I learned that both northern Illinois and Inner Mongolia have so-called continental weather, which is unmoderated by nearby oceans. So when the temperature climbs, it soars, and when it falls, it drops like a stone. Here in Illinois we shiver helplessly as massive Arctic cold fronts roar down on us via the Canada Express. The temperature falls to -10° F to -15° F at least a few times each winter, and I can recall one winter when it reached as low as -27° F. But on hot summer days, you can almost smell the jambalaya on the warm humid winds wafting up the Mississippi River from New Orleans. Temperatures almost always top a hundred degrees at some point during the summer here.

Then I began looking closely, very closely, at the soil in my garden, which is clay soil. Often hard as a rock with a pallid grayish bloom, some

An early August prairie dotted with purple coneflower (*Echinacea purpurea*).

Sweet autumn clematis (*Clematis paniculata*) graces a white picket fence.

plants did okay in it, while other plants declined. I had noticed that while the soil of nearby prairie remnants was also clay, it was a rich, dark, chocolate brown, very different from the pale gray, dusty soil in my garden. And I looked suspiciously at the long-established trees and shrubs in my garden and began to wonder what part they played in my struggles.

I also started looking more closely at the books I was reading to see where the author actually gardened. Very often, it was in England. The English have given a great gift to the world, which is their perception that gardening is a great art and as such can be taken very, very seriously. But even though Great Britain is at a latitude farther north than the Midwest, it is an island, so the English garden is in a maritime climate, which is temperate and mild and totally unlike our own. So while we can learn much from the English, when it comes down to specifics, their advice needs to be taken with an enormous, boulder-sized grain of salt. Now when I first sit down to read a gardening book, I immediately turn over the title page and look at the publishing information. If the publisher is in the United Kingdom, the author probably is British. Then I begin reading, keeping in mind, literally, where the author is coming from. Even if the book has been reedited for Americans, it may have a fundamentally British slant. I've also come across books originally intended for Australians, New Zealanders, and Europeans, all supposedly modified for American readers. These also must be read with care.

All the while I was clinging to my dream of having a pretty cottage garden. But as I learned more about gardening where I actually live, instead of where I dreamt I lived, my dream of what constitutes a true cottage garden began slowly to change. It dawned on me that the original cottagers were ecologists, though I'm sure they didn't think of themselves that way. They brought native plants into their small land holdings and gardened with knowledge gleaned from their parents and their fellow gardeners. This latter point is significant, for while English gardeners are blessed with a cooperative climate, they also have been gardening in that climate for at least 2,000 years, and you can learn a lot in 2,000 years. (We Midwesterners are just beginning.) The cottagers propagated their own plants and carefully husbanded their resources. Here, then, was a template I could use, a place to start from. I was beginning to see why bringing such a high-strung creature as a tea rose into my clay-soil, high-humidity summer garden was a nonstarter without chemical support, but the Illinois rose (*Rosa setigera*), which has evolved here for tens of thousands of years—why not try that? A radical thought.

So finally I understood. Cottage gardens are not about foxgloves and hollyhocks, thatched roofs and wishing wells, but are all about connections: connections to the land we live on with its native plants and animals and connections to our fellow gardeners, with whom we can share plants and pool knowledge. We can create our own loop, a loop entirely free of commercial interests, if we so desire.

To see where we, as Midwesterners, belong in the long tradition of cottage gardening, let's take a look at the history of the cottage garden.

Our Cottage Garden Heritage

The fashionable, rose-bedecked cottage gardens featured in recent years in glossy gardening magazines are a far cry from the original cottage gardens of the Europe and England of medieval times. In Europe, members of the growing middle class owned small homes with gardens on the outskirts of cities in Germany and Italy and were the original suburbanites. It's with the English cottage gardening tradition that we are most concerned here, though, as it's the English nostalgic vision of the cottage garden that has been exported all over the world, including to New Zealand and Australia, as well as to the United States.

Some suburban plots also appeared on the outskirts of London, but in England, it was the devastation of plague in the fourteenth century that spurred peasants to break from serfdom and to set themselves up as free-living "cottagers" in tiny houses on tiny plots of land. Often these cottagers still worked for the local lord, but as freemen. Most of these cottagers had no money at all and lived by bartering goods and services and by making do with what they had. It was on these little plots of land that we find some of the first cottage gardens.

The cottager was a magpie, gathering plants from the wild, exchanging slips and seeds with fellow cottagers and taking home any plant or seed he could scrounge from the local estate where he worked. Every square inch of ground was devoted to growing something useful, and not a speck of land was left barren or just to grass. Herbs, annuals, perennials, shrubs, fruits, and vegetables grew higgledy-piggledy in exuberant profusion. Wild violets and primroses were among the first flowers in the cottage garden, and honeysuckle and grapes were probably the vines that twined over the door in those long ago days. The simple wild roses of the countryside were often used as hedge plants, and it wasn't until the nineteenth century that some of the exuberantly flowering climbing roses had made their way from Europe to the English cottage garden.

If we could be magically transported back in time to one of these medieval cottages, I think we might get a bit of a shock at what we saw. An old photo in the book *English Cottage Gardens* by Edward Hyams shows a *very* roughly thatched cottage, drowning in a sea of hedge-parsley and hogweed, and Mr. Hyams notes that the picture gives us some idea of the disorder from which cottage gardens were created. So some of the original cottage gardens were probably quite rough and ready and utilitarian, and many of the cottages themselves almost hovels.

The cottager's plot was fenced to keep marauding cattle from trampling on precious plants, as well as to keep his own animals in, and it may be that our traditional white picket fences descend from this practice. The enclosed area was called a "geard," a word that gave rise to both "garden" and "yard." Until the sixteenth century, the English referred to gardens as yards, a practice that made its way to America and the Midwest, where we still garden in our yards. In Britain, a yard is usually a utilitarian outdoor area, as in Scotland Yard, and they garden in gardens. Well, to get back to cottage gardens. The cottager's plot was its own little ecosystem and often included pigs, chickens, and beehives, as well as plants. The herbs he grew were often his only medicine, and his fruit and vegetables were a significant part of his diet. Garlic, onions, mustard, and leeks were grown to flavor the bland and rather meager daily diet of the cottager. Probably many a meal was made of roasted apples and pease porridge, cooked in a seldom-washed iron pot. The profusion of flowers, especially the roses, that we associate with cottage gardens, was a bit of an afterthought.

Most of the plants in the cottager's garden were native to his immediate area. Seeds were gathered from nearby fields, and plants were dug from local woods, hedgerows, or roadsides. Mexico and its marigolds hadn't been discovered, and China was a misty legend. A few flowers, such as poppies, wallflowers, and pinks did make their way from southern Europe in traveler's pockets, and some plants came from even farther afield via returning crusaders, but in general, the cottager didn't have the uncertainty, or admittedly, the fun, of growing a wide variety of plants from all over the world. But the plants he grew were perfectly suited to his garden.

For those of us who are gardening on a budget, note that most of the long-ago cottagers *had no money*. And even if they had a few coins, there was no Wayside Gardens to send them to. The cottager gardened by making do with what he had from local resources, and for hundreds of years, cottage gardens were the gardens of the poor. We can benefit from this philosophy, as some of the greatest creativity flowers under the constraints of monetary limitation.

By the eighteenth century, some of the English gentry had built luxurious cottages out in the country where they could rusticate (with the help of plentiful servants and gardeners). These were some of the first intentionally picturesque and romantic cottages and gardens, and the ideal of the romantic cottage garden appeared at this time.

In the nineteenth century, plant expeditions returned from China, Central and South America, and Mexico, laden with a host of new plants that quickly became fashionable. These were tender plants that had to be raised at great expense in greenhouses and then planted out in elaborate bedding schemes on country estates. Beautiful old Tudor and Jacobean gardens of great houses were ripped out (I shudder when I think of this), but cottagers saved many of the plants from extinction by bringing them into their own gardens and nurturing them there. To this day, old varieties of pinks and primroses turn up in cottage gardens, where they had been banished years ago.

Increasingly torturous bedding plant schemes reached a kind of peak of awfulness in the late nineteenth century, and gardeners and writers such as Gertrude Jekyll and, later, Vita Sackville-West, turned to the relaxed charm of the cottage garden for their inspiration. Their writings, in turn, inspired many gardeners on both sides of the Atlantic. Sackville-West's garden at Sissinghurst, a landmark in the history of gardens, is basically a big, glorious, "cottage garden."

By the early twentieth century, a sea change occurred in the English countryside. Prosperous city dwellers were lured to the beauty of rural areas, and with modern transportation could get there easily, and bought cottages to gentrify. Many poor country people, who had been barely scraping by doing piecework, such as glove or lace making (a few of the many "cottage industries"), journeyed to London to find employment. Whole towns that had once been quite poor in the nineteenth century often had became the province of the upper middle class by the twentieth.

And so the idealized, romantic image of the cottage garden has floated down to us from the past like a brightly lit bubble full of hollyhocks and picket fences, and its appeal to those of us living in this cold and sterile age of technology is more powerful than ever.

WHAT MAKES A
Midwest Cottage Garden Midwestern?

We've looked at the humble origins of the original cottage gardens, but how do we go about creating our own cottage gardens here in the Midwest? Swamped by a culture of commercialized gardening, how do we connect with the original spirit of the cottage gardener? How can we, too, connect with our own environment and use our own ingenuity and ability to create a beautiful garden? That's what this book is all about.

First, we'll look at a core group of plants that grow well here in the Midwest. Choosing plants that thrive in our climate is at least half the battle in creating a beautiful garden, while selecting sulky plants that wish they were in British Columbia or Sussex result in gloom both for the plant and the gardener. The core group contains many familiar plants, along with Midwestern natives that might be new to some gardeners.

Speaking of natives, if there's one thing I hope you take away from this book, it's a heart awakened to the beauty and worth of our native plants. The English cottager turned to the primroses, violets, mallows, and wild roses of his countryside. If we but open our eyes, we can find similar treasures in our own surroundings: the delicate purple prairie clover, the fragile-looking wild petunia, the burning golds of goldenrods and black-eyed Susans, and the elegant pale purple coneflower, just to name a few. The plants are different, but the idea is the same. Bring natives into your garden, and watch the goldfinches appear, and the nuthatches, the hummingbird moths, the dragonflies, and if you're lucky, the bluebirds. Let's caution up front that not every Midwestern native plant is appropriate for every garden; for instance, the nine-foot-tall *Silphium laciniatum*, the compass plant, with its roto-rooter roots auguring down 20-feet into the soil, might be a bit much for the gardener accustomed to petunias. But so many natives are simply waiting for us to recognize their merits and to plant them. There was a moment some years ago when I stood on a low hill overlooking a remnant of prairie, with its shining grasses like rippling silk in the clean wind and the flowers dancing, and realized that we don't need elaborately planned perennial borders in our gardens because we have prairies! The prairie tapestry can be brought right into our gardens, both for our appreciation of its beauty and to provide habitat for local fauna. That moment when I was overwhelmed by the beauty of the prairie, and took it into my heart, was when I finally became a Midwest gardener.

Clouds of black-eyed Susans (*Rudbeckia hirta*) brighten this restored prairie fragment.

The author in her garden.

After learning about plants, we'll learn more about our climate. We'll learn to plant for our two distinctly different growing seasons: the cool, pleasant spring of April, May, and early June, and the hot, droughty season of mid-June onward to fall. Planting without awareness of the heat and drought that comes every summer leads to disappointment. Speaking of heat, how about planning a *shade* Midwestern cottage garden? Shade used to be considered a liability by many gardeners, but I strongly feel that in our climate it's a plus. There are tons of shade plants, including many fruiting shrubs loved by birds, that can be used to create a cool shade cottage garden. Add a water feature, such as a small fountain, and you and the birds have an oasis.

Then we'll take a long look at our soil and the conundrums it poses. Many gardeners really struggle with their soil, which in most gardens is no longer in any sense "natural." If you live in an old house with established plantings, the soil has long ago been sucked dry of moisture and nutrients by fully grown shrubs and trees, leaving you to garden in moist dust. If you live in a newer subdivision, however, the developer has trucked away your topsoil to sell, leaving you with lifeless clay subsoil. And in urban areas, so much land has been paved over that many gardeners have drainage problems. I hope that I'll convince you in the coming pages that time spent in improving soil (which sounds like a hopelessly dull activity) is worth every precious moment in its benefits to your garden.

Then we'll move on to rethinking container gardening. Cottage gardens have always had plants potted up and arranged decoratively throughout the garden. But since potted plants can be baked to a shriveled stalk in a few hours of kilnlike heat of early August here, it takes some special planning to grow a successful container garden in the Midwest, and we'll learn some tricks to make it easier. Finally, to have the abundantly planted garden that is characteristic of the cottage garden—without breaking the bank—we'll learn about plant propagation, including using our cold winters to germinate seeds, thus making our climate work for us, not against us.

Once I asked a very good gardener who grows wonderful roses how one begins to grow such roses. I guess I expected him to give advice on manure, or watering, or, I hoped, a secret fertilizer recipe. Instead, he said the first step to growing wonderful roses was to "become enthusiastic." Once you become enthusiastic, he noted, all else follows. So please come with me, and, I hope, "become enthusiastic" about all the rich and happy possibilities of gardening here in the American Midwest.

My Garden

Before we begin, let me tell you a bit about my garden. I garden in a river town that has been swallowed by the urban sprawl of Chicago. My little wooden clapboard house, on a 50 x 120 foot lot, is pine green trimmed with rose red and was built by Swedish carpenters in 1913. Two evil maple trees parch the soil in the parkway up front, and an angelic Japanese tree lilac blooms in the spring in the front yard. There is a side yard with a crooked pear tree and a copper rose tower and an insane jumble of every plant that I can pack into the best soil in my garden. Passing back along a brick path, we duck under a cedar arch sturdily shouldering a torrent of woodbine and come to a mammoth horse-chestnut tree, as big as something from a fairy tale and as old as the house. It rules the back garden as an implacable master, grabbing its share of water and soil first, leaving little for the lesser plants. During storms, its leaves and branches billow and creak like a schooner tossing on a mighty ocean. Way in the back corner of the garden is a vegetable patch slowly but steadily morphing into a rose garden, and behind the back fence are more roses plus goldenrod, big weeds, and brown-eyed Susans. Wrens, toads, red and gray squirrels, bird baths, a grape vine, and a statue of St. Fiacre, the patron saint of gardeners, also reside in the yard, and the moth-eaten lawn shrinks more and more every year as I think of new things to plant. Of course I have great dreams for my garden—someday a pretty little fountain, or even good soil, but right now, it's a happy place, and on some days I look up from weeding and catch sight of a blurred replica of paradise, garage, weeds, and all.

The traditional cottage garden was a small property filled to the brim with a beautiful profusion of wildly varying plant material. The cottager achieved this by being innocently utilitarian in his plantings. If there was room next to a primrose for a cabbage, in went the cabbage. If there was a spot by the front gate for leeks, then in went the leeks. Broad beans might go in next to a wild rose. If a neighbor handed him a start of honeysuckle, he was delighted and stuck it in wherever; in his judgment, it might do well. The cottager was truly a magpie, or a collector, planting and husbanding everything that came his way. Other than laying a front path that led straight to the door of his home and erecting a fence to protect the plants, the cottager didn't usually consciously plan or design his garden, and in fact, a cottage garden is the polar opposite of an intentionally designed garden. Designed gardens can be beautiful and true works of art. But for those of us who are sentimental and on a budget, the cottage garden is a good answer to the question, What kind of garden should I plant? At least half the plants in my garden were received as starts from friends and neighbors, and others were received at local plant exchanges, so these plants are rooted in my past, as well as in the soil. These plants are a source both of comfort and pleasure for me and mean that my garden is truly unique.

Planning your Midwest Cottage Garden

You might think that devising a cottage garden would be easy for the modern gardener, but I'm not sure that's true. For one thing, most of us aren't innocent like the original cottagers were. We've read too many magazines, watched too many gardening TV programs, seen gardening videos, and gone on too many garden walks to have the "beginner's mind" of the original cottager, and we may feel nervous about our own abilities after being exposed to so many experts. And having seen many great gardens, whether in person or through various media, our standards are high. We aren't just competing with the neighbor down the block, we are competing with Giverny and Sissinghurst! We want something in bloom all the time and for the garden to look

good all the time, something I'm not sure gardeners of the past worried about.

We also don't have the good soil that the cottager may have had, as we live in settled areas where the soil is compacted, impoverished, poorly drained, or totally scraped away. And we can't just walk out into the wilderness to dig up wildflowers, as this would further damage an environment already under stress.

So we need confidence and a few nudges to get us going in the right direction, and that's what the following design suggestions are: nudges. Use these suggestions as guidelines, and if you garden long enough, you may finally get to that innocent frame of mind where you can happily plant the leeks next to the roses and the dahlias next to the tomatoes.

Respect Your Site

One of the first principles of garden planning is to respect your site. Whether you have shade or sun, mature trees or a treeless plain, hard clay soil or, worse, subsoil left by developers—all dictate the nature of the garden, and you violate

Exiled hollyhocks thrive in an alley.

the implacable demands of the site at your own peril. Planting sun-loving annuals in dappled shade or bog plants in dry soil are examples of ignoring site realities.

The Bones of the Garden

While it's fun to go to a plant nursery and purchase flowering annuals and perennials, it's actually a better use of time initially to evaluate the "bones" of a garden. This means the trees, shrubs, and evergreens and pathways, retaining walls, or decks—all the things that remain once winter has come and the flowers and foliage have disappeared. If it means bringing in a professional to remove overgrown shrubbery, plant a tree, or lay a brick path, it's usually a good investment. And if you make a major purchase from a landscaper, such as a group of shrubs, if you ask nicely he may throw in a free design for using the shrubs. It might be just a sketch on the back of an envelope, but it can be quite useful. Good garden "bones" can help it look good even during heat and drought, when some flowers such as roses may stop blooming entirely, or during the dreary days of late February, when nothing is growing at all.

Look Around You

A look at the neighbors' gardens, especially in an established neighborhood, can give you a clue as to what you like and don't like in gardens. If there's a home with landscaping that especially appeals to you, think about why. It might be serene and simple with lots of pachysandra and impatiens or exploding with flowers and ceramic burros. Either way, you have a point of reference for your own garden.

Plant Spacing

When purchasing a plant, consult the label or a gardening encyclopedia for spacing recommendations. I have found that just as humans need their own space, plants seem happier relaxing into the space they need. The better the soil, the more you can crowd a bit. With experience, you will find that some plants look good planted cheek-to-jowl. Clematis, for instance, is happy to clamber over roses and other shrubs. But generally, plants need space, and the garden looks better when you can see the clearly defined shapes of the plants—the mounds, the spires, and the vases. I know this isn't easy because your soil may render spacing recommendations inaccurate, and you don't want to plant so far apart that the planting area looks barren. Our soil can be an unattractive, flat gray color, so unless it's improved or mulched, you'll probably want to keep it well covered.

Another reason to plan your space wisely is that you want to reach all plants in order to care for them. Leave space behind a border, or place stepping stones through a dense planting. Whatever you do, be sure you can get to every plant and have enough space to comfortably weed, prune, and water.

Repetition

Repeating the same plant throughout a garden isn't unimaginative—it's just good design sense. Repetition unifies a garden. Choose a plant you really like and that does well for you, and go ahead and use plenty of it. Beginners, for some reason, seem to think this is cheating, but it's the secret behind many good gardens. I like *Sedum* 'Vera Jameson', lamb's ears, feverfew, and catmint and use them all through my garden's sunny areas. I also have a few fast-growing hostas I use a lot of in shady spots.

Ornamentation

Does your garden have a case of the blahs? I mean, it's nice and it's neat but is a bit bland and boring? A great garden has plenty to look at, and this involves not just plants, but ornamentation. It has a sense of place and is just as much a state of mind as a physical location. Ornamentation can help evoke that state of mind.

Discussing ornamentation can be treacherous, though, as one person's beloved garden ornament can be another gardener's abomination. Just think of pink flamingos, geese wearing little raincoats, and whole families of plaster deer posing on lawns. In England, plaster trolls are controversial—some gardeners love them, others are rendered apoplectic at the sight. I have an inexplicable weakness for plastic swans that I try to keep under control and have noticed little cement bunnies hopping into the garden, and even a plastic whirligig hummingbird has popped up in the vegetable patch. I don't mind, though, because it's fun, and while I take gardening seriously, I don't take it *that* seriously.

This brings us to the first rule of ornamentation: please yourself. It's your garden. Don't worry about fashion and don't be afraid to have fun. Why not have a goose in the garden wearing a raincoat and tam-o-shanter if it makes you smile?

The second rule is, when in doubt, leave it out. During garden walks I've seen more than a few otherwise beautiful gardens marred by one too many fussy plaques, wreaths, and crafty whatnots. Some inspired gardeners can carry off lots of ornamentation, but it does take a sure hand.

As well as being pretty, handsome, or striking, ornaments serve one last important function: they draw the eye through the garden like magnets and then function as resting points. In my garden, first you see the front arch, then the path leads you back to the side garden where you see the rose tower. Your eye pauses there and then is drawn to the archway leading to the rear garden. Once in the rear garden a trellis at the very back fence draws the eye to the end of the garden. Along the way there are smaller ornaments to draw and rest the eye: a cement jackrabbit with big ears, a bench, a birdbath. Without these focal points, the eye would wander a bit aimlessly.

The Odds Are Better

When purchasing or propagating plants for these schemes, remember that it's best to plant in groups of *odd* numbers. For instance, plant in groups of threes, fives, sevens, and up. This prevents a flat-footed, overly symmetrical appearance in the garden. Also, remember that the more of each plant, the merrier. It's better to plant a lot of, say, three types of plants, than a few each of a dozen. Each plant variety has a chance to make an impact this way. Think in terms of drifts and masses. Given the vagaries of our climate, you might hesitate to plant a lot of anything, for fear that it won't thrive, and you'll have a big bare spot. But after you've been gardening for several seasons, start a list of plants that do well for you, and think of ways to use a lot of them. A generous drift of inexpensive marigolds can be more impressive than a spot of one expensive plant here and another over yonder. I remember seeing a picture of a garden of a seventeenth-century chateau in France, where it looked like they could afford anything they wanted. They had planted a river of tall red, orange, and pink zinnias flowing around an emerald green lawn. The caption noted that the seed was especially imported from the United States. Mmm. Sounds like something those of us not living in a seventeenth-century chateau could do for about $1.89.

Having extolled the virtues of using odd numbers, sometimes using pairs of plants is effective. This approach is so simple minded, I'm almost embarrassed to mention it. Paired planters on either side of an arch, or paired trellises along a path, or paired accent plants on either side of a path can define our path through the garden.

What Do You Want from a Garden?

Gardening fads come and go, but I advise to always garden for yourself. The longer I garden, the more I know I want my garden to be a sanctuary, for me, for the people I love, and for birds, possums, toads, bumblebees, dragonflies, squirrels, wrens, raccoons, bluejays, hummingbird moths, chipmunks, lost cats . . . all the creatures with whom I share this little corner of the earth. I'm planting more and more with them in mind, and with the earth in mind, and less and less caring about fashion.

Where Do You Begin?

I have two suggestions: This August, preferably after a terrible drought and a string of humid days with temperatures in the high 90s, go out into your garden in the cool of the evening with a pencil and pad of paper and jot down a list of all the plants that are thriving. Even if you haven't watered enough and haven't weeded for weeks, there's always a hard core of plants that thrive. The list may be disconcertingly short. After a terrible drought some years ago, the list for an area of my front garden under the baleful influence of some Norway maples was as follows: some sedums, including 'Autumn Joy' and 'Matrona', scented geraniums, zonal geraniums, hostas, santivalia, zinnias, *Stachys* 'Big Ears', a white-flowered annual salvia, gloriosa daisies, and *Verbena bonariensis*. So here I had a hard core of plants that were doing fine under the worst conditions, with almost no help from me. This was the list I used to plan for the following year, when I eliminated some annuals that had become mildewed, moved some perennials to the back yard where it's cooler and shadier and where I hoped they would be happier, and pulled up an ornamental grass that had been in tatters. Then I looked at the list to see if I couldn't expand it. If a white-flowered annual salvia had done well, perhaps another color would thrive as well. And there are many different kinds of interesting geraniums to try, and I decided to see if there are any other varieties of santivalia. I decided to add more 'Big Ears' and to encourage the self-seeding of the *Verbena bonariensis*. The idea here is to add more of what works. Simplify. Don't be afraid to use a large quantity of an effective, vigorous plant. My little list might seem positively pathetic to some garden designers, but these plants thrive in a tough spot and almost take care of themselves, and I am grateful to them. You might want to make such a list for each part of your garden that has different conditions.

Why do we do this exercise in August? Because it's easy to think about pretty things to grow in May and June, but it's a whole other story in August, when weather may have already been hot, humid, and drought stricken for weeks. If you are just beginning to garden, take a stroll down the street and see what's happening in your neighbors' gardens and come up with a list that way.

The second suggestion for improving your garden is to take a trip to your local library and check out books by landscape architects James van Sweden and Wolfgang Oehme. They are proponents of the so-called New American Garden Style, in which plants—including natives, grasses, and perennials—are massed in a naturalistic style with an eye to year-round beauty. Another author to look for is Piet Oudolf, who designs gardens emphasizing plant structure, texture, and movement in the wind, rather than focusing on flower color. Ann Lovejoy's book *Naturalistic Gardening* is also informative. If the garden of your dreams is a traditional "cottage garden" with froufrou and rows of pink hollyhocks, this new, natural style, which can sometimes seem more suited to the corporate environment, might not totally appeal to you, but in your plans for next year's garden, you may find yourself loosening up a bit. You might incorporate more grasses, try a few native wildflowers, and look for more drought-resistant plants. You might find your lawn shrinking (along with your water bill), and a year might come when you don't have any hollyhocks at all.

Greenery

The longer I garden, the more interested I become in plant foliage and the less store I place on the often fleeting beauty of flowers. Our hot summers drive the flowering process along at a fast clip so that flowers are sometimes literally here today and gone tomorrow. Attractive foliage, however, is a stable presence in the garden all season long. Just this morning I noticed that the Zepherine Drouhin rose by the front arch had finished its first June flush of flowers. It will go on to flower sporadically throughout the summer, but it's kaput for now, and its foliage is a bit pedestrian. But a nearby hosta, 'Sun Power', with its bold, wavy, chartreuse leaves, will look stunning every day all the way into fall.

The role of foliage in the garden is so important that it's perfectly possible to plant a beautiful all-foliage garden and to omit flowers entirely (though I realize this is a seditious thought for a cottage gardener). I do feel myself moving in that direction. Think of the pale powdery blue of the grass *Festuca glauca*, or the bright chartreuse of the ground cover *Lysimachia nummularia*

The glossy leaves of *Pachysandra* 'Green Sheen' mingle with wild ginger and the spotted leaves of *Pulmonaria* 'Mrs. Moon'.

'Aurea' grown with a rich, purple heuchera. Hostas come in blue, chartreuse, and white, cream, and green variegated varieties. Rue *(Ruta graveolens)* foliage is distinctly blue. There are a number of purple foliage plants in addition to purple heucheras—the herbs purple basil, purple sage, and perilla *(Perilla frutescens)*, as well as the smoke tree *(Cotinus coggygria)*, crimson barberries, and the annual fountain grass, *Pennisetum setaceum* 'Rubrum' are just a few. There are many silver-leafed plants, including lamb's ears, *Lychnis coronaria*, and most artemisias. The metallic, silvery greenness of the Japanese painted fern, *Athyrium niponicum pictum*, contrasts beautifully with warm green leaves. And then there is the golden hop plant, the lovely foliage of Japanese maples, silver lamium . . .

A variety of leaf textures can also vary the garden scene. Think of shiny-leafed plants such as bergenia, European ginger, and *Pachysandra* 'Green Sheen', or of the rough, pebbly texture of sage foliage.

LEAF SIZE

A range of foliage sizes enlivens the garden, and I'm always on the lookout for big-leafed plants that provide relief from too much itty-bitty foliage. Masses of little leaves and flowers can lend an atomized appearance to the garden, with nothing substantial for the eye to latch on to. The hitch here for Midwesterners is that most large-leafed plants either come from the tropics or are found in wetland areas of the temperate zone. Gunnera (this has the largest leaves that can be grown in a temperate climate), rodgersia, petasites, ligularia, and rheum (ornamental rhubarb) are plants for wet or boggy conditions, so if you have such a spot in your garden, be thankful and plant something big!

In a dry soil garden, the list of large-leafed plant candidates shrinks way down, which is why I treasure large-leafed hostas. Large-leafed coleus are also valuable this way, though they need more care and watering than do stolid hostas. And today, while at a garage sale, I couldn't resist peeking into the very pretty garden of the seller, where I spied a big plant with dark green, crinkled, rather shiny leaves, looking somewhat like a rhubarb plant, except I knew it wasn't rhubarb. The owner said it was a "big baby's breath," which hadn't produced a stalk and flowers, though she didn't know why. Well I knew it wasn't even remotely related to baby's breath, and suddenly realized I was looking at the almost legendary *Crambe cordifolia*, a plant famed for its huge size (it can reach seven feet in height) and enormous cloud of little white flowers. There could be a number of reasons why this particular plant hadn't flowered—

perhaps it wasn't getting enough sun or the very good drainage it needs. I've also seen crambe at a nursery, after it had finished blooming, and even its skeletal remains were interesting. All I know is that if I had the sun, I would definitely try crambe to get some large leaves into the garden and would not worry whether it flowered or not.

VARIEGATED FOLIAGE

Variegated plants are striking and extremely popular with gardeners. I was just at a nursery where there was row after row of a variegated hydrangea for sale, almost more of this one variety than all the rest of the shrubs combined. But it's precisely because variegates are so eye catching that they must be sited thoughtfully in the garden to avoid a "busy" look. They are not restful to the eye. And variegated plants can be unstable in their growth habits. I have a *Sedum* 'Frosty Morn' that has been sending up solid-colored shoots this summer, some solid green and some solid white, and apparently other variegates also tend to revert like this. Variegated plants must be well grown and not be sickly or chewed by insects. Some of the spotted pulmonarias, for instance, can look sick, rather than variegated, if they are even slightly withered or tattered.

This is not to discourage any gardener from planting variegates, as they are lots of fun. One of my favorite plants—variegated Solomon's seal—is a variegate. But they do have their "ins and outs" to be wary of.

What other kinds of foliage can we think of? Feathery, swordlike, strappy, stringy, silky, corrugated, velvety, furry, prickly—all of these textures and forms can spark a garden. And let's not forget grasses, whose foliage provides motion to the garden as they sway in the breeze. Foliage can even provide sound—the soft sounds of leaves swaying in the wind can be utterly hypnotic.

So, flowers? What flowers? Who needs them? I'm kidding, of course, but I hope now you'll be seeing foliage in a new light.

Color Is for Free

The hallmark of the traditional cottage garden is to innocently contain *all* colors. It's often the result of years of plant collecting and can be likened to a glorious bouquet of flowers of all colors, sizes, and textures—the proverbial "riot of color." Such gardens remind me of home-sewn quilts—I've never seen an ugly one. Just today (July 15) my husband, Jim, and I drove by a garden so pretty that I yelled "Stop the car!" Jim, who is used to this, stopped on a dime, and I hotfooted it across the street to peer over the fence. The house was a little white cottage facing south, with a white picket fence. In the front yard bloomed larkspur, pink phlox, calendula, all colors of cosmos and zinnias, a low-growing, tough-looking red rose, and a white lily the color of old satin. 'Heavenly Blue' morning glories twined over the fence, and alyssum and marigolds ran along the front path.

I had a feeling that the gardener had planted whatever sounded pretty and easy, and, truly, it was as charming a garden as you could imagine. It was also a casual garden—nothing had been deadheaded, and an old-fashioned sprinkler sat in the middle of the lawn. This detracted not a bit, as the sheer profusion of pretty flowers jostling by the fence and along the front path carried the day.

So a garden with a casual, random color scheme can work, and work well. But I sometimes think that having a predetermined color scheme can be tremendously helpful to a gardener, as color is one of the most powerful allies of the gardener seeking maximum visual impact from plant choices. That includes flower and foliage color, garden ornament color, and color of backdrops such as houses, walls, or arbors.

The painter Claude Monet was one of the all-time great authorities on color in the garden, right up there with Gertrude Jekyll, who studied color as a painter early in her career. Monet painted with plants in his garden, using common flowers such as tulips, irises, peonies, cosmos, and nasturtiums to create a vibrant garden picture. He massed flowers so their color had a powerful effect.

Just a handful of some of his inspired combinations that any of us could try in our gardens include purple perennial geraniums grown amid gold- and purple-bearded iris, pink cosmos with gold sunflowers, "black" tulips with white and dark purple pansies, and purple iris with red poppies. He fearlessly combined such hot colors as orange dahlias with pink and red cosmos, a practice that is just coming back in vogue today. He used purple aubrieta (rock cress) to edge and unite his flower beds, and we might try the same thing using purple alyssum. I'm sure even the white and purple wisteria dripping over the famous bridge spanning the pond in his garden was chosen for its vibrant contrast to the greenish turquoise hue of the bridge. That ineffable color that appears all through the garden at Giverny is available free to all of us for the mixing to use in our gardens. (Try a teal or aqua paint, with a little white mixed in.)

Hemerocallis 'Apricot Ruffles' combines vibrantly with *Platycodon grandiflorus* 'Double Blue'. The goldenrod tones with the yellow in the daylily.

DEVELOPING YOUR OWN
Personal Color Scheme

The yellow of the daylily flower "pops" when paired with this rose-purple allium.

While most of us don't have the large garden, the considerable income, or the unique painter's eye of Monet, all of us can devise an organizing color scheme to pull our garden together. And it can be simple. One gardener I know uses every color in her garden except oranges and orangey-reds. Another gardener uses only pastels. Another uses blue, yellow, and cream with a little pale pink thrown in.

One simple way to decide on a color scheme is to browse through gardening magazines and look for gardens with colors that especially appeal to you. Create a little file of these gardens, and analyze, from the color standpoint, what you like about them.

When planning a color scheme, be sure to keep the big picture in mind. Gardener Elsa Bakalar, in her video *Portrait of a Gardener*, says that her flower garden, which is planted in a flat, open area, is planted to complement the "big, blue bowl of sky" above. Just so, we must keep the color of our surroundings in mind when planting, whether this is a house, an apartment building, or even the surrounding countryside if gardening in a rural area.

Pale yellow hostas, glossy, dark green pear leaves, and the rosy flowers of daylilies create an eye-catching scene.

Personally, I gravitate toward flowers with violet or raspberry undertones—there are lots of pinks and blues like this. For instance, the Gertrude Jekyll rose is the color of crushed raspberries mingling with cream. Any yellow is vibrant when paired with such flowers, though I usually like cool yellows. This scheme goes well with my house, which is a pine green-painted clapboard with a dark rose trim. Brick or orange red, muddy chrome yellows, and neon peach shades set my teeth on edge, so I avoid them.

Important rule: You always have to be ready to make exceptions to prove the rule! I like to have butterfly weed in the garden, even though it is orange, and you might not think it would go with my color scheme. Butterfly weed orange is a pure, translucent orange, though, and it fits into schemes in which muddy oranges would clash.

DON'T FORGET CHARTREUSE AND RED

Whatever your color scheme, consider adding dashes of chartreuse or pure red to the garden. Dashes of chartreuse, such as in the foliage of golden feverfew, golden lamium, some hostas, or the flowers of 'Green Envy' zinnias and lime green nicotianas, make other greens look greener and make the entire garden picture more vibrant. Adding a touch of pure red is an old trick *interior* designers use to add vibrancy to any room, and the same trick works in a garden. An all-yellow color scheme, for instance, looks good with a dash of red. I guess it's kind of like adding a dash of pepper to a stew to liven it up.

I've brought together some color schemes here for you to consider. All of them use easy-care flowers that are happy here in the Midwest.

SCHEMES, SCHEMES, AND MORE SCHEMES.

Let's start with something simple for a dry, sunny spot: Yellow achillea, orange daylilies, and purple coneflowers. Next year add *Sedum* 'Autumn Joy' and Russian sage. This group is a bit cliched, but it does work.

Seen on a local garden walk: While a spectacular pond fully stocked with rare goldfish and surrounded by native plants stood five yards away, all the visitors stood oohing and aahing before a lush planting around a mailbox of baby's breath, *Achillea* 'Paprika', and *Coreopsis* 'Moonbeam'. A *Clematis* 'Jackmani' smothered the mailbox. In full radiant bloom on July 6, the sight was spectacular and couldn't be easier—just give it sun, sun, sun.

Color heaven in early June: white peonies, catmint, feverfew, sweet rocket, coral bells, violas.

Seen on a prairie in July: little blue stem grass (*Andropogan scoparius*), rattlesnake master (*Eryngium yuccifolium*), and purple coneflower (*Echinacia purpurea*). Easy, completely drought resistant, and continues to look great even when the coneflower is finished blooming.

For a warm, glorious, easy posy patch: Gloriosa daisies, purple coneflowers, cosmos, and coral daylilies, along with some little blue stem grass.

Another simple scheme for a sunny spot, cast iron: *Coreopsis* 'Moonbeam', a blue veronica, white balloon flower (platycodan), and *Sedum* 'Autumn Joy'.

An easy-care pink and white scheme, with just a touch of yellow, can be created by using 'The Fairy' rose, deep pink zinnias, fuchsia cockscombs (*Celosia cristata*), ivory-colored feverfew, and white asters with yellow centers.

I once saw a deceptively misty-looking group of butterfly weed, black-eyed Susan, Russian sage, and Queen Anne's lace. I say "deceptively" because these are some really tough customers. Don't give this group so much as a teaspoon of fertilizer. If the Queen Anne's lace makes you nervous, and it does me, try the white lace flower (*Ammi majus*), which is very similar in appearance.

Goldenrod and purple asters are a natural combination for fall.

Some (all?) of my favorite combinations happen by accident, like the delightful combination of *Penstemon* 'Elfin Pink' with *Coreopsis* 'Moonbeam'. Both plants have a delicate, tinkly feeling, and the pale yellow and pale pink look pretty together. Next year, plant something not tinkly with a bold, flat leaf, like *Sedum* 'Autumn Joy', to set them off nicely. And I recently noticed that some *Liatris* 'Kobold', *Asclepias* 'Ice Ballet', and some *Verbena bonariensis* were forming a natural group in the garden. I hadn't intended it, but there they were, united by a crisp, linear feel. Next year, some pale yellow lilies would look great nearby.

Try black-eyed Susan, joe-pye weed, lavender bee balm, purple coneflower, Culver's root, and ox-eye daisy. Here's a nice opportunity to branch out into some prairie natives, using the tall joe-pye weed and Culver's root, along with the more familiar rudbeckia and coneflowers. Once you try these natives, you'll want to try more.

The golden-flowered prairie native *Zizia aptera* and the common garden perennial *Centaura montana* with its intense blue flowers look great blooming together in May and June.

If you've had it with namby-pamby pastels and hunger for deep, saturated color, try the following scheme that I noticed in a magazine article about a house and garden in New Mexico. The porch railings of the house were painted robin's egg blue, and the flowers included purple lobelia, pale yellow petunias, pink and red cosmos, hot orange tithonia, and yellow and red signet marigolds. Wow.

Vivid but low-key: silver lamb's ears, emerald green parsley, purple-leafed 'Vera Jameson' sedum, and *Penstemon* 'Husker Red'. This is an interesting color scheme that could be made even more interesting with the addition of a purple-blue flower such as an annual sage. Offbeat, but pretty.

Speaking of parsley, the intense emerald green of parsley sparks other colors beautifully. I once saw a beautiful window box planted with parsley, different varieties of marigold, and blue salvia.

One of the most beautiful blues there is is red cabbage blue! Just take a look. Many red cabbages are actually pale, dusky indigo blue with a ruby undertone. The degree of blueness seems to depend on the variety. Just think of them as giant indigo roses. You could edge a whole path with these for just a few dollars. Interplant with pale yellow marigold and emerald parsley or lemon thyme for real impact—perfect for a kitchen garden. Even the dreaded scarlet annual sage works in this scheme. And think of all the sweet and sour cabbage you and all your neighbors for miles around can enjoy come fall. Maybe better not think of it!

Cool and silvery: *Artemisia* 'Silver King', lamb's ears, violet perennial sage, pale yellow yarrow. And you could add something pale pink, such as Fairy roses.

The strange, warm pink hue of *Centranthus ruber* makes it an interesting foil for a number of other flowers, including purple coneflowers, coreopsis, orange daylilies, and blue veronica.

Another plant of strange color is the Japanese painted fern, which is ice blue, maroon, and pale green, and which you might think wouldn't go with anything. Actually, as a shade plant, so far it seems to go with *everything*, especially with warm green hostas.

Scheme to disguise a chain-link fence: pink, white, and red cosmos grown up against the fence; morning glories twining over it. Can't suggest anything, though, for the German shepherd.

The golden petals of black-eyed Susans, the misty chartreuse of the heads of dill, and the lacy purples and whites of the self-seeded larkspur create a pleasing color picture.

Be brave and try the globe thistle (*Echinops exaltatus*) in any of the above sunny-site schemes. It provides architecture and focus. Be even braver and try the prairie native rattlesnake master (*Eryngium yuccafolium*).

Easy as pie, and no calories: a happy crowd of *Rudbeckia hirta* and tall zinnias.

Three low-growing, gray-leafed "blending" plants: *Artemesia* 'Silver Mound', lamb's ears (*Stachys lanata*), and catmint (*Nepeta mussini*). Silvery plants can connect and soften even such bright, clashing flowers as butterfly weed and red monarda. So if something is clashing, before you give them the heave-ho, consider bringing in a blender to make peace.

Edge your garden beds and borders with white alyssum—it's like a soft border of lace for the whole garden.

One obvious no-no that I'll mention here, because you do see it in gardens quite often, is to plant two plants of the same color, but different variety, next to each other, unless you have good reason to do so. On a garden walk last week, an otherwise gorgeous garden was marred by a huge mass of 'Stella d'Oro' daylilies planted next to some gold-yellow lilies. Neither plant showed to good advantage, and together they created a strange golden blind spot right in the middle of the garden. There are many exceptions to this rule, though, so tread carefully. I have a lavender-flowered scaevola growing in a pot next to a Persian shield plant, which has metallic, violet-colored leaves. The colors are just close enough to create a pleasant color vibration.

A color scheme to be careful of in the Midwest is the all-white garden. One of the most famous gardens in the world is the white garden at Sissinghurst, England. And it seems so easy. But here in the Midwest in the summer, the sun can shine harshly, especially after the noon hour, bleaching and fading out whites and pastels. I always think of about one o'clock in the afternoon as the "witching hour" in our climate, as even the most beautiful garden can look tattered and flattened under the glaring midday sun. The opposite problem can also occur, with overcast days rendering a white garden dull and brooding. And in planning such a garden, there are many whites available, including bluish whites, cream whites, snow whites, and on and on, and different whites can actually clash. For instance, a flower that is snowy, pure white can make a nearby creamy white flower look dingy. So it takes a sure hand to know what to use where. At any rate, a white garden is not a no-brainer. You might try a small white flower patch consisting of white coneflowers, *Nicotiana alata* 'Nikki White', with some lamb's ears to see how white fares in your garden. Or try white geraniums, petunias, sweet alyssum, vinca, and then some dusty miller.

Pastels can pose a similar problem. The pastels that glow in the mist in an English garden can look faded and flat in the glare of the Midwestern noonday sun, so use with caution. Shade gardens completely circumvent the problem of noonday glare—another reason to plant a tree.

Saturated colors, which are vivid hues undiluted by white, can work well under our intense light. Deep violets, burning orange-reds, fuchsias, chrome yellows, and vivid blues can glow even in the July noonday sun. These colors are not to everyone's tastes, especially those who are incurable romantics, but I find that I like them more and more as I see how well they do in our gardens. To experiment with vivid colors, try a window box planted with fuchsia impatiens, both pale pink and white petunias, trailing ivy, and to finish it off, a deep, glowing red begonia with lime green edges.

Some would say that a very dark green is the best background for flowers, and you might want to keep that in mind when painting trellises or window boxes, for instance. In her wonderful garden video series *The Art and Practice of Gardening*, Penelope Hobhouse notes that she has painted garden benches and the doors of outbuildings *black*, and the effect is quite distinguished.

The bleaching effects of the Midwestern sun on white flowers can be avoided by planting a white *night* garden. You and the moths can enjoy it during the cool of the evening. Consider planting *Datura inoxia* (angel's trumpet), *Brugmansia suaveolens* (also called angel's trumpet), *Oenothera pallida* (white-flowered evening primrose), *Ipomoea alba* (moon flower), and *Nicotiana alata* and *sylvestris* (flowering tobaccos). Candytuft (*Iberis*) is not a night-blooming flower, but its pure-as-the-driven-snow white glows after dark, as do the flowers of white impatiens.

Sedum
'Matrona'
partners with
Hosta 'Sun
Power'.

Himalayan blue poppies, luscious bicolored asters, Pyrenean primroses, towering delphiniums, the rare Chinese foxglove, a pergola dripping with wisteria—when I began gardening, I pored over gardening catalogs and dreamt of the beautiful flowers that would flourish in my garden. Everything I saw a picture of I wanted to plant. I realize in retrospect that my imaginary garden consisted of a cross between an English cottage garden and the Hanging Gardens of Babylon, with a little bit of the Orangerie of Versailles thrown in for good measure.

Six indispensable perennials

Quickly I found that the real world in my backyard was a much different place from the world of my dream garden. There was drought, soil hard as a rock, and also a tree, an ancient horse chestnut that owned the yard, lock, stock, and barrel, though I was pleasantly unaware of this for a year or two. Worms, weather, wilt, and whatever else you can imagine caused me to reassess garden plans as time went on. Maybe I wouldn't have a pergola, after all. I slowly came to my senses and started noticing the gardens of houses nearby with new eyes. Some had been built around 1914, and there were many old, established plantings all around me to be examined. First swimming into my consciousness one late summer day were the warm billows of gold flowers behind our back fence—brown-eyed Susans (*Rudbeckia triloba*). Vibrant color, no bugs, no need for watering, would positively resent staking—the clouds of little flowers bloomed their hearts out, and I fell in love with this native flower. I was later to encounter other valuable members of the rudbeckia family.

Then, at a plant nursery, I noticed an absolutely enormous hosta resting quietly in its pot, and remarkably, it was blue—or at least pretty close to blue. How interesting. Then I noticed that there were chartreuse hostas and white and green hostas—well, if you've ever had the exhilarating experience of having your hosta consciousness raised and expanded, you know what it's like. Before several summers had passed, I had gathered big hostas, little hostas, fountain-shaped hostas, ruffled, fragrant hostas—everything but hostas with feathers—all into my backyard where they thrive happily, except for an occasional slug attack. The siren song of the Himalayan blue poppy was growing fainter and fainter.

Then my sister gave me some peonies, which I planted. Ho hum. My mother had always had peonies in our yard when I was a kid, so it was no big deal. After a couple seasons, though, possibly in a desperate attempt to get my attention and thus save their lives, the peonies didn't just bloom, they *burst* into flower and did everything but sing the Halleluja Chorus and dance the polka. I had never before noticed just how gorgeous, sensual, and fragrant a peony really is. One flower is the equivalent of a whole bouquet of lesser flowers. The Pyrenean primroses were becoming a distant memory.

Then daylilies crept into my consciousness. Well, everyone knows about daylilies. But you look at daylilies with new eyes after wrestling with delphiniums. As with peonies, something musical comes to mind when looking at daylilies, as though you don't have a clump of daylilies so much as a choir. Their upturned flowers seem to sing, and I love them for it. And while I am mad for the newest daylily cultivars, with every new cultivar more tempting, more fabulous, than the last, I also love the plain old orange daylily seen on every street corner and roadside ditch in midsummer.

I came round to the merits of sedum admittedly late, as they seemed the paradigm of all that is dusty, staid, and boring in the plant world, truly old-lady plants. (Sorry, Mom.) I mentally bracketed sedum with the gloomy, sinister yew bushes and prickly barberries that hulked by every bungalow in the neighborhood where I grew up as a child in Chicago. The lady next door to us had sedum in a strip near the driveway, where they were pelted with gravel and dust every time a car pulled in or out. They seemed more like some sort of stoic rock formation than plants. Much time has passed, and an encounter at an arboretum with a stately crowd of *Sedum spectabile* (showy stonecrop) changed my mind. Or perhaps getting closer to becoming an old lady myself has changed my mind. Sedum can have a floriferous, blooming feel, even during the worst of our kilnlike, Midwestern heat. As succulents, sedum store water in their leaves and stems to carry them through drought, so they are made for us. And I learned that while sedum planted in a row can be awkward looking, a bosomy mass of sedum can be quite imposing. Whether in bud, blooming, or

bearing the dried seed heads so much loved by birds in autumn, sedum are totally trouble-free workhorses in the Midwestern garden, and more and more new varieties become available all the time.

For the last of the indispensables, we come to the purple coneflower tribe. Often praised for their robust health and heat tolerance, you rarely hear of coneflowers described as "beautiful," but beautiful they are. The melting purple-violet of coneflower petals combined with the almost iridescent topaz-colored central cone is as beautiful as a late-summer prairie sunset. And *Echinacea pallida*, the pale purple coneflower, is grace itself with its long, drooping flower petals.

These perennials—rudbeckias, hostas, peonies, daylilies, sedum, and coneflowers—are six trouble-free, indispensable plants for the Midwestern garden. They sail right through the lethal Midwestern one-two punch of heat and humidity. Barring a natural disaster or an act of God, you can plant any of these plants with confidence that they will thrive. This doesn't mean that they shouldn't be planted thoughtfully and be well cared for. Every plant needs that. But they are sturdy plants that will dwell in your garden for years, in the cases of hostas and peonies, even decades, rewarding the gardener for time and money spent.

The experienced Midwestern gardener could protest that all kinds of valuable plants are missing from the above select list. There *are* many other plants that do splendidly in Midwestern gardens, but I think the indispensable six are a cut above the rest. We'll take a look at some other good plants a bit later on, but first, let's look at each of the Indispensable Six a bit more closely.

Hostas

There is so much satisfaction to be got out of the contemplation of a goodly hosta clump that it is small wonder that they are becoming so popular.
—Graham Stuart Thomas

Hostas are natives of the woodlands and rocky wilds of Asia and were introduced into this country in the mid-nineteenth century. They are shade plants, though the shade can be dappled, and some hostas can tolerate morning sun.

Most hostas have a mounding, almost sculptural form, and a group of happy hostas can undulate like the waves of an ocean. Some look like giant

flowers, with leaves edged with cream or white. Hosta foliage can be so pretty that sometimes we forget that hostas themselves have flowers. Hosta flowers come in white or shades of purple and lavender, can be fragrant, and look somewhat like lilies. This is no coincidence, as hostas are members of the great family *Liliaceae*. But it's the wide assortment of foliage color and form that make hostas so valuable to the gardener. It's possible to have an attractive shade garden especially devoted to hostas, with other plants as supporting players.

How hardy are hostas? Once I thoughtlessly dumped a 50-pound bag of cow manure on top of a hosta just beginning to emerge during the spring and barely visible. A month later, when I removed the bag, I found the hosta, pale, shaken, and very flat, but growing well. This is one tough plant.

PLANTING HOSTAS

While hostas are easy to grow, when planting, always take time to prepare the soil carefully by loosening it with a spade, removing any stray roots, and evenly digging in plenty of compost. They'll be there for years (I have heard of hostas that are 60 years old), so it's worth taking time to give them a good start. After planting, water the hosta deeply and thoroughly, watering until puddles remain on the soil surface.

There's only one shady location I can think of where perhaps hosta should not be planted, and that's where it would be zapped by direct afternoon sun. At the height of a summer heat wave, this type of sun can actually burn hosta leaves, leaving them with ragged brown holes, a kind of hosta sunburn. I also wouldn't plant hosta in a sun-baked median strip between driveways. I've seen hostas in this unpleasant situation and it makes me want to go in with a hosta swat team, all dressed in green, to rescue them. On the other hand, hostas don't like the stygian depths of total, deep, black shade either—dappled or light shade seems best. And planting them under the eaves of a house where they get absolutely no water is unkind to them, as well, and will result in their decline.

Plant large hostas in the spring or early summer. Large hostas are slow to establish themselves and, if planted in late summer or fall, may not have

Hosta
sieboldiana
'Elegans'.

time to root before winter comes. This is the one time I can think of where you could actually lose a hosta, and I lost a 'Big Daddy' hosta just this way.

Hostas can be some of the last perennials to come up in the spring, so don't worry if you don't see shoots in early spring when other perennials are emerging.

HOSTA TLC

Hostas appreciate regular watering. If there's a drought and you are busy watering other plants, they will grit their teeth and go into a kind of suspended animation and survive, if they have to. But regular watering is best. Well-grown hostas have a lush, cool, billowy appearance that's really beautiful—almost hypnotizing. It's also nice to dig more compost in around each plant every year. One hosta fanatic I know mulches her hostas in the fall with shredded leaves. In the spring she works the leaves into the soil along with a time-released fertilizer such as Ozmacote 14-14-14.

Remove hosta flowers and flower stalks when they become dried and tattered. Slugs are hostas' worst enemies, and in some gardens they are a serious problem. Slugs leave behind big, irregularly shaped holes and sometimes mow down entire leaf stalks, doing their dirty work at night. Mulches provide convenient daytime cover for slugs, so I don't recommend using mulches around hosta if you have a severe slug problem. According to the Shady Oaks Nursery catalog, the "blue" hostas are the most slug resistant as they have the thickest leaves. The hosta 'Sum and Substance' is supposedly the most slug resistant of all the hostas, as it has quite waxy leaves and, indeed, my 'Sum and Substance' has been totally free of slugs. I've also heard that watering your garden in the morning rather than the evening can foil slugs, as they like wet soil and leaves to slither across at night.

I've come across an interesting view of the slug problem in the book *Dream Plants for the Natural Garden*, by Piet Oudolf and Henk Gerritsen. Oudolf says the following:

In nature, hostas will grow in rocky places, mostly facing away from direct sunshine. In your garden, this means that they need a well-drained spot that is semi-shaded, which never gets too wet and whose soil is not too nutrient-rich. A sandy soil with a moderate amount of nutrients is ideal for growing compact, robust hostas that are unpalatable to slugs and snails. All other soil types, especially heavy clay and peat soils, quickly become waterlogged and are too fertile. This will cause them to grow too fast so that the leaves become large (splendid visually) but too thin, providing a delicacy for snail palates . . . We disagree with all other gardening books, which all advise that hostas need a nutrient-rich soil with a lot of fertilizer to produce large leaves. What all those books forget to add is that in so doing you are serving up a snail banquet."

He has a good point about excessive fertilizer, which in many plants can lead to lots of insubstantial top growth. So it's possible that providing good, airy soil with good drainage, but not worrying so much about fertilizer, could be the path to slug-free hostas.

HOSTA DIVISION

Hostas are the ideal plant for a frugal gardener as they are astonishingly easy to divide and propagate. Dig up the clump you want to divide and shake and brush off the dirt. A close look at an established hosta will show that it consists of a number of separate crowns. Pull or cut a clump of crowns apart at their natural divisions, and replant each division. Tugging at clusters of crowns will show where these divisions are. Some experienced gardeners slice off edge portions of well-established hostas with a sharp spade and replant the fragment. This is one plant that can be divided any time during the growing season, though I wouldn't divide one during a severe drought— it would be cruel. And I would wait until after it has flowered.

SOME ALL-TIME GREAT HOSTAS

New hosta cultivars flood the market every spring, but I especially like these classics.

Hosta 'August Moon'. With leaves rounded and pale chartreuse in color, this hosta will illuminate your garden like an August moon. Use it to light up a dark corner, contrast with blue hostas, or team with red coleus or impatiens.

H. fluctuans 'Sagae'. This luxurious variegated hosta is unlike any other. Its frosty green leaves with irregular cream margins undulate in space in a slightly off-balanced fashion, adding motion to the garden. This grows pretty slowly, so try to buy a big one and plant early. Ask for it for your birthday.

H. 'Golden Standard'. A large hosta with light green-gold leaves with darker green margins. This time-tested hosta has beautiful "seersucker" leaves.

H. 'Golden Tiara'. A medium-sized hosta with a demure, rounded leaf shape, almost like petals. The leaves are green with a yellow margin. This hosta lights up a dark corner without seeming garish and has become more popular every year.

H. 'Krossa Regal'. I love this hosta for its graceful vase shape and pale blue foliage. It makes a dramatic contrast to mounding hosta.

H. lancifolia. A case could be made that this is the perfect hosta. One of the smaller hostas, it has shiny, strap-shaped, medium-green leaves. It quickly establishes itself and forms a neat mound. This is a great hosta if you're on a budget, as it's inexpensive and can be divided frequently. It's also extremely drought resistant.

H. plantaginea. A medium-sized hosta famed for its fragrant flowers. It's also known to be slug resistant.

H. 'Royal Standard'. A large, medium-green hosta with moderate ribbing and slightly shiny leaves. This is a classic that always looks good and goes with everything, like a hosta "little black dress."

H. sieboldiana 'Elegans'. This is the hosta to get if you want a big, blue hosta with corrugated, "seersucker" leaves. It's a hulking creature of a hosta, simply magnificent, with enormous, cupped leaves. Leave plenty of room when planting, as it can reach at least three feet across. Hot afternoon sun may burn its leaves.

H. sieboldiana 'Frances Williams'. Similar to the above, but with golden margins that look like they were painted on by a very talented artist. This is one of my all-time favorite hostas, and I've heard a number of other gardeners agree.

H. 'Sum and Substance'. Do you want a big hosta? No, I mean a *really* big hosta. Well, this is it. With its huge chartreuse leaves, you only need one of these. Be sure to plant this early on in the season so it has time to establish itself. This hosta can take a bit more sun than the darker green or blue hostas, but it doesn't like dry soil sapped by tree roots.

H. tokudama. Total hosta elegance. The perfectly pointed leaves are blue and puckered.

H. tokudama 'Aureonebulosa'. This takes elegance a step further, with the leaves streaked and variegated with yellow and green. A stunner.

H. undulata 'Albomarginata'. A big hosta with dark green leaves trimmed with cream borders. I wouldn't plant a lot of these, but they are gor-

The dramatic, swirling foliage of *Hosta fluctuans* 'Sagae' is a perfect foil for other perennials, especially roses.

geous accent plants when used thoughtfully.

H. ventricosa 'Aureomarginata'. Sometimes I think if I were going to a desert island and could only take one hosta, this would be it, though taking a date palm would probably be a better idea. 'Aureomarginata' is large, but not ridiculously large, and has beautiful green heart-shaped leaves casually streaked with cream.

H. 'Wide Brim'. I just planted 'Wide Brim' a month ago, and I already really like the intense cream-gold of its painted-on margins contrasting with the dark green of the leaf center. And 'Wide Brim' is a noticeably fast grower.

One little hosta that makes the rounds from gardener to gardener is what my sister calls "tiny little hosta," and which is the sweetest little hosta you could imagine, with leaves barely three inches long. It may actually be *H. venusta*, which is a very small hosta. At any rate, it's adorable, and whether you get it from another gardener or from a nursery, it's nice to have. And I have just come across a reference to a variegated *H. venusta*. I must have it, I must! Be sure to plant the really tiny hostas up front and center where you can keep an eye on them—it could be fatal if they are heaved up

The undulating leaves of *Hosta* 'Guacamole'.

SUN-TOLERANT HOSTAS

One of the most difficult spots in a garden is one that gets cool shade in the morning and broiling hot direct afternoon sunlight. It's too hot and bright for a shade plant but often not sunny enough for a plant requiring full sun. I have found that the so-called sun-tolerant hostas can work in this unenviable position. Gold, chartreuse, and very light green hostas seem the most sun tolerant. I have H. 'Sun Power', and it's been doing great in a spot that receives rapidly changing shade and direct sunlight conditions during the day. Other possibilities include 'Sum and Substance', 'August Moon', and 'Gold Tiara'. Blue and medium-green hostas with thin leaves are most susceptible to burning under direct sun. Sun-tolerant hostas need good, moisture-retaining soil to thrive.

GROWING HOSTAS FROM SEED

Propagating hostas by division is so easy that you might wonder why anyone would bother to grow them from seed. For that matter, you might be surprised to learn that hostas even *have* seeds. They do, and if you leave the flowers on your hostas this fall, you'll notice brown seedpods forming as the flower petals

by frost in the wintertime and you don't notice what's happened.

If you want the smug pleasure of having some very rare, obscure hostas with which to lord it over other hosta lovers, check out the Heronswood Nursery, Ltd. catalog. They only have varieties collected and propagated from the wild; for instance, *Hosta* sp. HC 970644, collected "from the mountains of the Kei Peninsula [Japan] at 2,503 feet elevation." Unless you know someone with one of these hostas collected at 2,504 feet elevation, you can practice one-upmanship to a satisfying degree.

And a neighbor just gave me starts of H. 'Raspberry Sorbet', which has bright red flower stalks, and H. 'Yakushima mizu', a little hosta with wavy leaves. (It's neighbors like these that restore my faith in humankind.) My current favorite hosta is H. 'Guacamole', a big hosta with glossy leaves that bulge and buckle like a giant blob of, yes, guacamole. And I've also come to like 'Gold Standard' for its unusual inner glow of golden light.

Well, I could go on. How about H. *plantaginea* 'Honeybells', with its fragrant, lilylike flowers, or H. 'Fragrant Blue', with its pale blue foliage, or H. 'Happy Hearts', with its lovely heart-shaped leaves, or . . . *sigh*.

Hosta 'Fragrant Blue' glistens after a rainstorm.

shrivel and fall away. When the seedpods feel dry and papery, snap one off from the stem and open it. You'll find stacks of flat, black, shriveled-looking seeds. This brings us to the "why" of starting hostas from seeds: It's possible to grow loads of hosta from seed for next to nothing in cost.

When I learned this, I immediately ordered seeds for the tiny and very desirable *Hosta venusta* from the North American Rock Garden Society's spring seed list. (You must be a member to do this.) I received six seeds, which I planted in damp, seed-starting mix in a six-pack. This went down into my cool basement. After about five or six weeks, with no visible sign of germination, I wondered if my seed-starting efforts had been a bust. But by the next week, all six seeds had germinated. The first leaves of a hosta seedling are recognizable, sword-shaped hosta leaves. I potted each plant up and placed them out on my back porch to face the blustery March, and from there, they went into the garden. They were like perfect little hosta jewels, and I was thrilled.

I decided to research hosta seed starting further and went on the Internet. Imagine my surprise to find some hosta breeders blasting starting hostas from seed as a total waste of time, saying that the resultant hostas were weak, inferior, and generally useless. Looking at my robust little *H. venusta*, I felt that something here wasn't adding up. The answer suddenly dawned on me: there are species hostas, such as *H. venusta*, and then there are the hybrid hostas that result from crosses between parent hostas. Any seed from a species hosta will be true to the parent. But if you take seed from a hybrid, named-variety hosta, all bets are off. The resulting crew of offspring may look like either parent, or grandparent, or Uncle Fred, for that matter. The hostas sold at local nurseries are almost always named varieties.

So that's why my species *H. venusta* was robust. This year I'm starting *H. yingeri*, which according to Tony Avent of Plant Delights Nursery in Raleigh, North Carolina, has "splendid, spider-like flowers." Further research turned up many other species hostas: *H. lancifolia* (ground cover so vigorous you might not want to bother starting from seed), *H. nigrescens* (tall vase shape), *H. tokudama* (puckered blue leaves), *H. ventricosa* (heart-shaped leaves), *H. plantaginea* (scented), *H. pulchella* (very small—six inches wide), and *H. clausa* (spreading ground cover). Most of these are available from Shady Oaks Nursery in Waseca, Minnesota, or from Plant Delights Nursery. You can buy one plant and take it from there. To learn more about

hosta species, go to the following Web site: www.giboshi.com. Dozens of species are listed, along with their characteristics.

Species hostas are usually various shades of solid green, so if you are looking for hosta excitement, they may not be for you. And hosta hybridizers have taken the species material and run with it, coming up with fabulous and fanciful plants. So I'm not saying here that species hostas are in any way superior to hybrids—just that their seeds are true to the parents.

Speaking of the hybrids, it has occurred to me that just because hosta hybridizers are not crazy about the varied plants that spring from hybrid hosta seeds doesn't mean that you or I might not like them. Some hosta seed starters on the Internet think that the resultant variety is a plus, not a minus, calling each resultant seedling an "original" creation, not identical to either parent.

I started hosta seeds in my cool basement because I have limited indoor seed-starting space. You can get faster germination by starting the seeds at 70°–75°F. Press the seeds onto the surface of moist seed-starting mix, and place the flat into a zip-seal bag. The seeds will germinate in dark or low-light conditions. Once the seeds sprout, some gardeners place the flat five to

The large, chartreuse hosta 'Sun Power' dominates my front garden.

six inches below a fluorescent light, but I have found that, as shade plants, hosta seedlings do well by any bright window. Germination should occur in about ten to fifteen days. Don't panic if some seeds don't seem to be germinating—different species seem to vary wildly in their germination time. Some species that I have started and that germinate quite quickly are *H. venusta*, *H. montana*, *H. capitata*, and *H. yingeri*.

Wait until the seedlings have three leaves before transplanting to small pots. If spring has arrived, you can place flats of these little pots outdoors in a protected spot. Check the pots for dryness occasionally, and water them if needed.

Note that this is not a fast way of growing hosta, and most won't reach full size for several years, depending on the species. But time does fly by quickly, and before you know it, you'll be planting your first group of seed-started hosta into your garden. It's fun!

When you gather hosta seed in the fall, they can be labeled and stored in your refrigerator until early next spring when you start them. I have read that seed can also be frozen in airtight containers and remain viable for years, though I have not tried this.

Peonies

The common garden peony (*Paeonia lactiflora*) is another must-have for the Midwest garden. Peonies love clay soil, so they are right at home here. Whoever coined the term "low-maintenance" had peonies in mind because as well as having beautiful flowers, they are drought resistant and have no significant natural enemies. The latter point really is remarkable, as most plants have *something* that infects them or nibbles on them. The ants that are almost always found on peony flowers and buds are merely feeding on the sugar nectar exuded by buds and don't harm the plant. Ants and peonies go together like bread and butter, or ham and eggs.

The fact that peonies bloom only once during the year in late May through early June is seen as a liability by some gardeners. You can't have Christmas every day, though, and the foliage of peonies remains fresh and handsome all summer. There is even a neat little trick to get around this "liability." Plant magic lilies (*Alstroemeria*) in among the peonies, and by late summer lily flowers will pop up through the peony foliage. Voilá!—a second blooming.

PLANTING

Plant peonies in the fall. If you order a peony by mail, you may get a bit of a shock when you receive a strange, unidentifiable gnarled thing in return. This is the peony plant in bare root form, along with some short stems. It might take some careful study to determine which are the stems and which is the root. Near the juncture of the roots and stem (called the crown) will be some budlike structures that are the peonies' "eyes." When planting, these eyes, which are growing points, should be planted no deeper than about two inches under the surface of the soil. Planting the eyes too deep is one of the main reasons peonies fail to bloom. As with hostas, take time to prepare the soil well when planting a peony. Some garden experts state that after proper planting in good soil, a peony will not need fertilizing for 25 years! Love this plant! Slowness seems to be in the nature of a peony, and most peonies won't bloom during the first couple years of growth.

PEONY CARE

The one danger I can think of concerning peonies is taking them too much for granted. They are amazingly sturdy plants, but they still appreciate regular watering, especially during prolonged drought, and being kept free of encroaching weeds. This is especially important during August and September, when their roots are fattening up to be ready for sending forth growth next May. And they also don't like tree roots honing in on their territory, but then who does?

It's much easier to overfertilize peonies than to underfertilize. Overfertilizing can actually decrease peony longevity. I have never fertilized my 16-year-old peonies and always have more flowers than I know what to do with. How peonies do this, when other perennials such as roses can be so greedy for nutrients, is a mystery to me, but a wonderful one. The Song Sparrow Perennial Farm catalog advises that a little bonemeal can be applied after flowers are finished blooming and have been deadheaded.

Peonies are sun lovers. If your peonies aren't blooming, check to see if they aren't being shaded during part of the day.

Above all, peonies don't like being disturbed, and moving a peony can set it back a good two or three years. They like to sit in one place for decades, waxing fat and happy, getting plenty of water to drink, and enjoying all the oohs and ahs from their gardeners every spring.

PEONY FLOPPING

. . . the peonies lay face down in the earth, drunken with spring . . .

Some peonies have such large, lush flowers that the plant has a tendency to flop over when it rains. There is a way to shore up the plant with some sticks and string that you're welcome to try, but this is one case where I'd forget about saving money and buy some of the metal hoops made specially to support peonies. These can be found at a well-stocked plant nursery or are available by mail. Press the hoops into place in the early spring, and the peony stems will grow up through them.

You might also consider planting single-petal varieties, which have less of a tendency to flop. Check out the Song Sparrow Perennial Farm catalog for 'Pink Princess', 'Krinkled White', and 'Montezuma'. I've seen 'Bowl of Beauty' thriving in several local gardens. This classic peony has dark pink single petals cupped around a large central cluster of feathery stamens.

If you have a particularly lush crop of peonies, you might consider picking some of the bigger blooms as they open and drying the petals to use for potpourri. Removing some of these flower heads can render the bush less top-heavy, and the potpourri makes a nice Christmas present. A simple recipe can be made with equal parts of dried peony petals, dried bee balm (monarda) leaves, and a handful of dried lavender.

Whole peony blossoms can also be dried. Hang them upside down in an out-of-the-way area that has good air circulation. The peonies dry naturally and can be used in lovely dried flower arrangements. A blow dryer can be used to fluff them up a bit.

PEONY VARIETIES

I could go on and on about the many beautiful peony varieties available, as each one truly seems more beautiful than the last. But I think it makes more sense to immediately send away for the Song Sparrow Perennial Farm mail order catalog, in which page after page of gorgeous peonies tempt us.

At local nurseries, peonies 'Sarah Bernhardt' (double pink), 'Karl Rosenfield' (double red) and 'Duchesse de Nemours' (double white) are the usual varieties offered. These are fine peonies and are inexpensive because of their wide availability. Of the three, 'Sarah Bernhardt' seems to have the most trouble holding on to its petals in spring storms, and the petals tend to turn brown as they age. I find it the least satisfactory of this group. The 'Duchesse de Nemours' is fabulous, though. The flowers look like small cumulus clouds that have somehow floated down from the sky and become tethered to a peony bush. The flower heads seem firmer than that of 'Sarah Bernhardt', and though white, they seem to come through bad weather better. On the other hand (I'm aware I'm sinking into a quagmire of peony controversy here), the 'Sarah Bernhardt' flowers are enormous and pretty, and it wouldn't seem like Memorial Day without them. Many gardeners purchase one each of all three.

The fern-leaf peony (*P. tenufolia rubra* 'Flore Plena') is an interesting variety to try. This is a small plant, only about 12 to 15 inches tall. The flower is a bright red double, and the leaves are soft and ferny.

The flowers of most older varieties of peonies have a light, sweet, gentle scent that says "cottage garden," but some modern varieties have no scent at all. It can be quite disappointing to lean over a luscious flower to inhale its scent and smell absolutely nothing. If scent is important to you, try to visit nurseries where peonies are in bloom to smell before you buy. The Song Sparrow catalog indicates which varieties are fragrant.

TREE PEONIES (PAEONIA SUFFRUTICOSA)

It had never occurred to me to try to grow a tree peony, as they seemed exotic and, frankly, prohibitively expensive. But one day my sister brought me a tree peony from the nursery where she works—it had a broken stem, and no one would spend $45 on an unfamiliar plant with a broken stem. It was called 'Pink Hana-kisoi'. I hurriedly read up on tree peonies and gave it a spot with afternoon shade. I half expected it to be a prima donna and drop dead on the spot, but the following May it bloomed, and I was stunned by the beauty of the flowers, which were at least eight inches across. The ruffled petals looked like pale pink silk tissue, and their fragrance curled through the air like incense. Neighbors came to see it, and at dusk I would go out and simply stand and stare. I am now hooked on tree peonies, and if I had the space, I would have a moon garden full of them, along with a tea house.

I've learned that tree peonies are more truly like shrubs than trees and that they may reach four feet in height. At this point, my three-year-old tree peony needs staking, as the large blooms are too much for the woody central stem. I've also learned that tree peonies should be fertilized three times a year: first, after the leaves appear in the spring; second, 15 days after flowering; and third, in late fall. I've been using fish emulsion and also scratch some granular organic fertilizer into the soil. Neither after blooming nor in the fall should the stem be cut back, as this is a woody plant, and next year's buds will appear on the woody stem. If you really become a connoisseur, there is much more to learn, and I have run across a book published in Japan that details tree peony care in minute detail, month by month. Don't be put off by this seeming complication, though, because there is a basic sturdiness to the tree peony that is quite reassuring.

I'm already looking forward to next May and feel that $45 is a reasonable price for such a plant, which is not only beautiful, but very long lived. Tree peonies can reach 100 years in age, and in China, I have heard that there are 700-year-old plants tended by Buddhist monks.

Daylilies

The daylily is the radiant garden star of the Midwest, blooming throughout midsummer. Daylily flowers can be jaw-droppingly beautiful, with heavy, ruffled petals glowing in hues of raspberry or watermelon with pink ribs and gold throats, crimson with veining and shading in burgundy, apricot shaded gold, or the most melting, sugary pinks. Here's the description of *Hemerocallis* 'Dresden Beauty', given in the Gilbert H. Wild daylily catalog: ". . . a cool blend of green to yellow to pink cream air-brushed with rose which deepens in ruffles. Wide raised lavender rib runs deep into lovely lemon lime heart." My goodness. To browse through a daylily catalog is to visualize an ongoing stream of ever-changing color, almost poetic in nature, and it's nearly impossible not to lust for 'Cup of Sugar', described as "cream of primrose with a touch of pink," or 'Only One', described as "cranberry turning to cream before becoming green in heart."

As if this weren't enough, daylilies are almost indestructible (in gardening, we always have to add the *almost!*), and some experts call them "the perfect perennial," tolerating heat and humidity and being easily divided. They are also fairly forgiving as to soil quality but respond enthusiastically to amended soil and fertilization.

The daylily is another of the many garden plants that come from Asia. A daylily flower blooms for only one day, and the name "hemerocallis" come from the Greek word "hemeros," meaning "day," and "kalos," meaning

"beautiful." They are a member of the great lily family (Liliaceae) and are related to "true" lilies such as the Oriental and Asiatic lilies. (But whatever you do, don't refer to a daylily as a "lily" when talking to a daylily devotee. They get very perturbed.) The Chinese have grown daylilies for thousands of years, using them for food and medicine as well as for the garden. Hybridizing the common tawny daylily with related species has lead to an explosion of daylily varieties in a wide range of color, size, flower frilliness, and even scent.

The tawny daylily (*H. fulva*), sometimes called the "orange ditch lily," is the most common daylily—a "weed," I guess, if you want to call it that, though I think it brings a festive air to our streets and country roads as it blooms exuberantly at the height of summer. Like Queen Anne's lace, it's one of those plants that would be considered extraordinary if it weren't so common. And it can be a workhorse in the garden if you have a spot of sloped ground and not-so-great soil. The tawny daylilies will stabilize the slope and grow strongly, choking out potential weeds. Another old-fashioned daylily to seek out is the lemon lily (*H. flava* is the old name; *H. lilioasphodelus*, the new). Sometimes called the custard lily or yellow-tuberose, this sweetly violet-scented daylily has been in English cottage gardens for centuries. It's the first daylily of the season to bloom, in late May, and is lovely planted along with blue bearded iris or with peonies nearby.

I grow the daylily 'Hyperion', a variety first developed in 1925. I enjoy Hyperion as much, if not more, than many of the more modern hybrids, because there's nothing else like its enormous, satiny, butter yellow blooms. The buds are so large they look almost like small bananas. A daylily with large blooms like 'Hyperion' does need to be faithfully deadheaded, however, as the faded blooms can be rather noticeable.

Hemerocallis 'Catherine Woodbury' is notable for the delicacy of its blush pink flower and green throat. 'Cherry Cheeks' is an attractive rose pink. Actually, it's hard to go far wrong with any of the modern varieties. I've seen a few that are a rather harsh red or muddy orange, but in general, anything you come across at a plant nursery has been through a rigorous winnowing process and is among the best that modern plant science can offer.

Some of the most tempting new varieties are the so-called miniature daylilies such as 'Eenie Weenie', 'Little Grapette', or 'Petite Ballerina'. And purple- and plum-colored daylilies are all the rage now, with varieties such as 'Grape Velvet', 'Mountain Violet', 'Prairie Blue Eyes', 'Blueberry Sundae', and 'Wine Time' luring us to our doom.

The 'Stella d'Oro' daylily has been aggressively promoted in the past few years as one of the longest-blooming daylilies, but it can be plagued by earwigs, and I'll admit to loathing Stella. Its rather muddy chrome yellow pops up everywhere at the end of June, and while it is a repeat bloomer, it can fall into a funk in July and look pretty bedraggled. I prefer 'Happy Returns', another repeat bloomer with lighter yellow flowers. My feelings about Stella are probably completely irrational and may stem from when I once worked at a plant nursery where I sold about 100,000 of them, and I guess familiarity breeds contempt.

GROWING DAYLILIES

Planting daylilies is straightforward. If you're lucky, a fellow gardener can donate a clump from her garden for you to plant. And sometimes daylilies pop up at farmer's markets, garage sales, and even rummage sales, so keep your eyes peeled. Daylilies need sun. They can tolerate a bit of dappled shade during the day, but they won't flower as profusely as when in the sun, and shade and our humidity can foster rust problems for the leaves.

Fertilize only as plants just begin to emerge, as heavy fertilization later in the growth cycle can lead to lots of foliage and not many flowers. Some daylily aficionados tinker with the following fertilizer formula, sometimes adding soluble seaweed and other secret ingredients:

1 cup water-soluble fertilizer (15-30-15)

1 cup Epsom salts

1 cup liquid iron

1 cup fish emulsion

15 gallons of water

Don't forget the 15 gallons of water! Or you may opt to make up only a quarter of the mixture, using a bit less than 4 gallons of water. Use about two to four cups of mixture per daylily clump. Speaking of water, while daylilies are tough, be sure to water regularly during drought for best appearance. Plentiful water results in bigger flowers. Other growers use well-composted horse manure, blood meal, cottonseed meal, and agricultural molasses. For

more on organic fertilizers for daylilies, go to the following Web site: www.ofts.com and click on Hemerocallis.

Deadhead daylilies to keep the bloom coming, and for the same reason, cut off seedpods. Deadheading is a bit of a chore, but spent daylily flowers look like limp rags—not a pretty sight. Flower stalks that have finished blooming should be cut back. Regular watering and removal of yellowing foliage should keep the plant as a whole presentable after flowering, but by August you might consider cutting all the foliage back to about eight inches. You can actually cut it back to just a few inches, but this leaves a conspicuous hole. Water well, and new foliage will appear in a few weeks. If tattered daylily leaves late in the summer annoy you, try 'Minnie Pearl', a variety with smooth glossy leaves. At the end of the bloom season, daylilies can be cut back to within a few inches of the ground. When spring comes, new shoots will emerge from the withered foliage, which should be left as mulch until the weather turns reliably warm.

We mentioned earwigs, and they can be a problem with some daylilies. I have heard that daylilies should not be mulched, because damp mulch does attract earwigs. However, I've had earwigs on unmulched daylilies too. My approach lately has been to work on the soil as much as possible before planting, by loosening it and amending it with organic matter. This renders the soil moisture retentive without the use of mulch. I've noticed that yellow daylilies seem to be the most tempting for earwigs. These maddening little creatures may lurk in the flowers of other colors but don't seem to nibble on them as much.

If all else fails, try raising chickens along with your daylilies—chickens will eat the pests and the daylilies will flourish. I say this with a smile, but before dismissing the idea, check out www.chickenlilygardens.homestead .com, a Web site that promotes the joys of raising Bantam chickens among the daylilies. Along with magnificent, inspiring, four-color chicken pictures, the site offers a library of four hundred daylily photos.

Most daylilies can go for years without dividing. But you may wish to divide to give a clump to a friend or to have clumps to plant in other parts of the garden. I have heard that some of the newer daylily varieties mature more quickly than the older and may need regular division. Keep your eye on some of these newer varieties, and if you notice diminished flowering, divide. Daylilies can be divided in late summer. Start by digging up a clump and washing

The luminous daylily 'Minnie Pearl'.

Hemerocallis 'Stuff' paired with swamp milkweed (*Asclepias incarnata*).

away most of the dirt with a hose. Roll the clump of tubers back and forth gently—often they will fall apart by themselves into separate tubers (especially in a mature plant) that can be planted individually. Try not to damage the long daylily roots during this process.

There are early, midseason, and late-season daylilies, and with a judicious selection from each category, you can have daylilies blooming for much of the summer. For instance, I am writing this in early September, and yesterday my sister mentioned that she has *H.* 'Altisima' in full bloom in her garden. 'Catherine Woodbury', that paragon among daylilies, is also a late bloomer, as are 'Dragons Eye', 'Rave On', 'Yaba Daba Doo', and 'Tigerling'.

As companion plants for daylilies, try lady's mantle (*Alchemilla mollis*) or bronze fennel (*Foeniculum vulgare* 'Purpureum'). Bronze fennel works especially well with the common orange daylily. It's a very simple combination but is quite spectacular. Ornamental grasses, such as miscanthus, especially variegated varieties, also blend well with daylilies.

In an article in *Horticulture* magazine, gardener Sydney Eddison recommends *Perilla frutescens, Nicotiana langsdorffi,* love-in-a-mist (*Nigella damascena*), and double, pink poppies (*Papavar somniferum*) as good annuals to plant with daylilies. Perilla is a purple member of the basil family and can be a prolific self-seeder.

"CYBER DAYLILIES"

To explore the many varieties of daylilies available, I recommend that you visit the Web site of the American Hemerocallis Society for their "Daylily Source List." The Midwest is Region 2, so look in that section for local nurseries, but you might also want to check out the Region 1 list, which contains sources for northern grown daylilies. Some of the sources are actually single individuals who are offering their own introductions—the world of daylilies is quite democratic.

Daylilies seem to be a state of mind as much as a flower, and you can lose your heart to them. The kaleidoscopic beauty of some of the newer cultivars, especially, just sucks you in. In addition to the AHS site, there is a universe of daylily Web sites on the Internet, through which you can enter into the world of the cyber daylily. There are personal sites of daylily lovers, daylily poetry, on-line daylily nursery catalogs, and daylily society Web sites. Check out www.daylilies.net to find addresses for personal daylily Web sites. Many sites come with photo galleries of flowers, each more beautiful than the last.

But be forewarned. I've come to think that getting the daylily bug is almost worse then getting the hosta bug. Their compelling attraction is summed up in the name of a new cultivar: *H.* 'Resistance is Futile'.

Rudbeckias

I've already mentioned the wonderful *Rudbeckia triloba,* but there are other equally valuable members of the rudbeckia family for the Midwestern gardener to know about. Rudbeckias are native to the East and the Midwest and are extremely tough, drought-resistant plants. Dry clay soil does not faze them, and while they are basically plants for the sun, they can tolerate some shade during the day.

The most famous rudbeckia is *R. hirta,* otherwise known as the black-eyed Susan, though I have a friend who calls them black-eyed *Susies,* and I like that better. Glowing with color and radiating cheerfulness in the midsummer garden, this plant is truly indispensable. Anyone aiming for a casual cottage or meadow garden look in their garden should plant *R. hirta.* It self-seeds and I always feel thankful for each and every plant, all of which are generally robust and trouble-free. Leaf-miner doodling sometimes appears in the leaves, but this is usually not disfiguring, and if a plant falls victim to a brown wilt, I just yank the whole thing out.

Years ago, plant scientists manipulated the genetic material of *R. hirta* and gave us *R. hirta* 'Gloriosa', or the gloriosa daisy. The flower is almost twice the size of the regular *R. hirta* and has petals of glowing gold, mahogany, and rusty red. If you give it sun, and its very own spot, it will self-seed bounteously year after year, but some of the progeny will probably revert to plain black-eyed Susans. So if you want gloriosa daisies in all their glory, reseed every spring.

Another attractive variety of *R. hirta* is 'Irish Eyes'. The center disc of the flower is green, which sounds odd for a black-eyed Susan, but it's a knockout. A number of gardeners I know have said that 'Irish Eyes' was not long lived in their garden, so be forewarned. And *R. hirta* 'Marmalade' has unusually large flowers, if you want something inescapably eye catching, and *R. hirta* 'Goldilocks' almost looks like a dahlia with its many petals.

A cultivar of *R. fulgida,* a rudbeckia native of the eastern United States, is the famous 'Goldsturm', much used by professional landscapers in modern, low-maintenance planting schemes. 'Goldsturm' is a workhorse perennial and

Hemerocallis 'Juanita' is an elegant three and a half feet in height.

can withstand drought and even a bit of dappled shade. It's nice, but almost a little too perfect and stiff in habit, if that's possible. It doesn't have quite the relaxed, wildflower charm of the plain old black-eyed Susan. It's a good plant, an almost unavoidable plant, though, so don't hesitate to use it.

R. fulgida var. *deamii* is many branched and fairly tall at close to four feet. It makes an interesting and welcome change from 'Goldsturm'. Its smooth, dark foliage stays in good condition throughout the summer, and I have yet to see a plant afflicted with wilt or leaf miner.

R. laciniata 'Golden Glow' is a famous, old-time "passalong" plant that thrives in many gardens all over the United States. One thing it's famous for is falling over—at six to seven feet in height, it usually needs staking. It's considered invasive. Beware.

Brown-eyed Susans *(Rudbeckia triloba)* mingle with seed heads of skullcap *(Scutellaria* spp.*)*.

Sedums

Sedums are remarkable plants, having evolved a metabolism that greatly reduces water loss through their pores, or stomata, during the day. This metabolic system is so unique in the plant kingdom that botanists have given it a name: Crassulacean Acidic Metabolism (CAM). Photosynthesis in sedums is triggered not by light, but by marked temperature change. I'm mentioning this just to give some idea of how special these wonderful plants truly are. Almost completely drought resistant, they are precious assets in the Midwestern garden. Sedums are sometimes called "stonecrops," because in old cottage gardens they were planted between the mortared stones of houses and walls and so were "crops" that seemed to grow from stone.

Sedums such as *Sedum* 'Autumn Joy' are so low care that I almost can't think of anything to say about them. They need sun, though they are willing to have a go at dappled shade for part of the day, and will endure blasting heat, drought, earthquake, and poor, rocky soil with cheerful indifference. Large animals can dash through them; gardeners can neglect them—nothing fazes

R. nitida 'Herbstsonne' (shining coneflower) is a way-underused rudbeckia that more gardeners should know about. It's beautiful, with pale green cones and large, gracefully drooping yellow petals. It's tall, at about six or seven feet, but if kept well watered and grown in full sun, it won't need staking for most of the season. By September, it will be sagging, along with the rest of the garden, and for that matter, with the gardener, so it should either be deadheaded and staked or cut back. 'Herbstsonne' is notable for its healthy, attractive foliage that stays in good condition throughout the summer, right to the bitter end.

One last rudbeckia to take note of is *R. subtomentosa*, the sweet black-eyed Susan. Sometimes called the fragrant coneflower, its petals are held horizontally, giving the flower a starlike appearance. The petal scent is sweet anise. Found in low meadows and stream banks, sweet black-eyed Susan doesn't like extremely dry soils, and its height can vary from three to six feet, depending on soil moisture. Loved by birds and butterflies, this is a fine native plant for the home garden.

The rudbeckia species tends to self-seed, so the gardener needs not expend any effort in their propagation. If you wish to increase your supply of a cultivar such as 'Goldsturm', though, you must dig up and divide the plant.

Here *Rudbeckia nitida* 'Herbstsonne' has reached its full height of six feet and has not needed staking.

them. They snap back quickly even if pulverized into green dust by hail, as I have learned from personal, horrible experience. Sedum is another example of a plant group that actually seems to like poor, or "lean," soil. I wouldn't waste a smidgen of compost on them—they wouldn't appreciate it.

As for variety, there are mat-forming, creeping sedums and upright forms. Botanists have placed the upright forms, sometimes called "border sedums," into a separate genus, *Hylotelephium*. I mention this for your information only, as I think no one but a botanist will go to the trouble of using this tongue-twisting name. Some people make fun of sedums because they are not always graceful looking, and some upright forms do have more than a passing resemblance to broccoli. You *could* say they are the nerds of the flower world. Personally, I think many varieties of sedum are truly handsome, and then there's the fact that *you don't have to worry about them* at all. You come to appreciate this the longer you garden. Sedums don't complain and don't pout and can be used as the backbone of many planting schemes. Showy stonecrop (*S. spectabile*) has pale green buds in the spring, pretty lavender pink flowers in the summer, and distinguished golden brown seed heads in the fall and winter. It is often at the peak of its magnificence late in late August and early

Sweet black-eyed Susan (*Rudbeckia subtomentosa*) blooms in early August.

September, when other perennials are begging for mercy. I really can't think of another plant that has such an attractive appearance through all four seasons of the year. Sedums are extraordinary plants.

Usually a neighbor will be able to give you a cutting, which just needs to be stuck in the soil, tamped down, and watered. Even just a sedum leaf will root, if given the opportunity. Water it regularly, and it will go on from there. The above-mentioned 'Autumn Joy' is a good choice, though I have heard S. 'Brilliant' also highly recommended. I have a nameless variety that came from my grandmother's garden: it's lighter green and has smoother leaves than 'Autumn Joy'. A trade via the Internet netted me a sedum called "Butterfly's Feast," which looks like my grandmother's. And I have a S. 'Mini Joy', a low-growing version of 'Autumn Joy' that has proved to be infinitely more useful than I initially expected. It's a crisp, steady-state, front-of-the-border edger—not as floppy as some of the shorter sedums such as 'Vera Jameson'. It forms a neat little hedge, and I am only beginning to think of ways to use it.

Don't get all excited like I did when I found a sedum named S. 'Indian Chief' at a local nursery. I was delighted to find what looked like a new cultivar.

Lining the garden path is the dark pink flowered *Sedum* 'Mini Joy' and a passalong *Sedum spectabile* with light pink flowers.

A fall flock of Painted Lady butterflies stops to gather nectar from *Sedum spectabile* flowers.

It looked like 'Autumn Joy' but was much taller and more columnar. Imagine my disappointment to learn later that 'Indian Chief' is an old name for 'Autumn Joy' and that it was tall and columnar probably because the grower had grown a bunch of them too close together. Oh, well. Live and learn.

A hybrid named 'Vera Jameson' is a lovely sedum and one of my favorite perennials. It's lower (10 to 12 inches tall) and more graceful in habit than 'Autumn Joy' and has a charming, floriferous feel all summer. The plant is a variegated light gray, green, and purple and combines beautifully with many other perennials. Do you want to know what it's really wonderful for? It's for planting in a sunny spot with wretched soil where you want flowers, but flowers won't grow. My front garden has been zapped of all moisture and nutrients by two nearby horrible Norway maples, a duo of doom. Nothing short of ripping out the trees, back hoeing all the soil out to a depth of about ten feet, and trucking in all new soil will fix it. Nothing thrives in this spot, except, thank goodness, for pretty 'Vera', purple coneflowers, hostas, and daylilies. One thing I've noticed about 'Vera' is that its color varies markedly from nursery to nursery. I think the amount of sun it gets determines how purple or green it is. The classic combination for S. 'Vera Jameson' is to plant it with the soft blue grass *Festuca glauca*. This pretty planting is extremely drought resistant, and very easy.

If you like dark purple, consider growing S. 'Mohrchen', with its handsome, mahogany foliage and pale raspberry pink flowers. Like all deep purple-foliaged plants, it needs careful siting so that it won't visually disappear into the soil: it needs to be nestled in with lighter-foliage plants. With thoughtful sighting, though, 'Mohrchen' is a knockout. It seems a bit less vigorous to me than other sedums, and I don't recommend buying gallons of it before you have evaluated it in your garden.

Two newer sedums are S. 'Frosty Morn' and S. 'Matrona'. 'Frosty Morn' has pale green leaves iced with white and flowers dainty as snowflakes. It has a cool, delicate appearance in the garden and goes with everything. S. 'Matrona' is statuesque and purple stemmed, and its magnificent, creamy, raspberry-colored flower heads drive the bees mad. Just looks great.

A small, upright sedum is S. *telephium*, called live-forever or orpine. This pretty little plant has long been found in English cottage gardens, as it is a British native. Another smallish sedum is the October daphne (S. *sieboldii*). It is low lying and has sprays of bluish leaves on arching stems.

Several years ago during a late June heat wave, I ripped out the fainting, dusty alyssum in my garden and planted creeping sedums instead and have never looked back. Creeping sedums function as drought-resistant ground covers and edgers and are valuable workhorses for the Midwestern gardener. And while a faintly dull aura glumly hovers over the word "sedum," and the word "creeping," doesn't help matters, I have more than once been asked by admiring gardeners about the creeping sedums in my garden. They can have a neatness and crispness that is truly attractive, especially when everything else is wilting in 95-degree heat. There are many, many varieties of creeping sedum, some higher, some lower, some smaller, some larger, but all expressing the same general theme of mat-forming succulents, often with starry flowers. *Sedum ternatum* 'Shale Barrens' was my first creeping sedum and has attractive, small, round leaves. Other low-growing sedums include *S. album* (chubby, fingerlike leaves, white flowers), *S. kamtschaticum* (coarsely toothed leaves, yellow flowers), *S. rupestre* (narrow leaves, yellow flowers), and *S. spurium* (oval leaves, pink flowers). A variety of *S. spurium* called 'Dragon's Blood', with blood red flowers blooming in July is widely available. The Plant Delights catalog speaks very highly of Chinese sedum (*S. tetractinum*) as being "a spectacular attention getter in the rock garden!" And if you really hear the call of creeping sedums, check out the Arrowhead Alpines catalog for a spine-tingling assortment. Yes, spine tingling! Or type in "sedum nurseries" as a key word to search the Internet for sources for more varieties. Sedums are ideal plants to order via mail, as they can easily survive shipping delays.

Creeping sedums can tolerate a surprising amount of dappled or light shade during the day. The only condition that truly spells total doom for them is soggy, poor-draining soil.

Beware of *S. acre*. It's widely available and oft recommended, and in photographs it looks nice, but in my garden it's been a weedy, flabby-looking pest. It's possible that my hard clay soil doesn't agree with it. Also, there are interesting cultivars of it that might prove better behaved, including 'Mini Green' and 'Mini Blue', both of which have very small leaves.

One last interesting use of creeping sedums is as topiary plants. If you've ever struggled with a wire topiary form and dried up ivy, consider these sedums. The people at the Black Cat Nursery in Chehalis, Washington, recommend using a small variety of *S. album* for topiary, as it is fine textured and fast growing. There is also a large variety of *S. album*, but small is what you want.

I tend to scoop up any new sedum that I see, so useful are they in the gar-

Sedum 'Matrona'.

den, and last summer I hit a bonanza, finding *S. cauticola*, *S. middendorfianum*, and *S. aizoon*. *S. cauticola* is a mounding plant, about eight inches tall, with blue-gray leaves, purple stems, and pink flowers blooming in September. Its color scheme is both the good and the bad news, as the pink flowers/blue leaves all on the same plant are startling and won't work just anywhere. A plant with warm green foliage might bring *S. cauticola* back to earth, but I haven't yet figured out just what plant that might be. *S. middendorfianum* is a very small, mat-forming sedum with tightly packed maroon leaves. Its stems need to trail over something, so place it at the front of a raised bed. It's a native of the stony soils of Mongolia and Manchuria. *S. aizoon* is upright with long stems that reach 12 to 16 inches. Its yellow flowers bloom June through August. This isn't a graceful plant, and the flowers are rather homely, but there's something endearing about it. It's doing its best, and I like it. I've read that it combines well with *Euphorbia dulcis* 'Chameleon', and since I have both plants at opposite ends of the garden, it looks like a spring project to bring them together.

S. 'Autumn Joy', although sometimes scorned as commonplace, is particularly useful to us, as it is widely available and can be a workhorse in many very easy-care and good-looking plantings. Try it with a golden spirea or with grasses such as calamagrostis or penisetum. Pair it with asters such as 'Purple Dome' and then add a threadleaf coreopis such as *Coreopsis* 'Moonbeam'. The lavender blue mists of Russian sage or caryopteris also look good with 'Autumn Joy'. And I've seen it planted with salmon-colored dahlias.

One way to enhance the appearance of sedums such as 'Autumn Joy' is to cut them back in midsummer. Wait until they're about 18 inches tall, and then prune them back to 15 inches tall. Flowering is not affected, and the plants are more compact, with straighter stems.

While sedums are as close to indestructible as a plant gets, they do like sun, good drainage and good air circulation. If they are overcrowded, consistently watered overhead, or growing in poorly draining soil, a fungus may rot the stems.

Echinacea

Extra! Extra! Coneflower Explosion in Midwest!

Is there such a thing as a perfect perennial for the Midwest? I nominate *Echinacea purpurea*, the purple coneflower, and its related cultivars and species. What a wonderful flower. ("Echinacea" derives from the Greek word *echinos*, meaning "hedgehog.") In late July, radiant stands of blooming purple coneflowers appear in Midwestern gardens and natural areas everywhere next to black-eyed Susans, monarda, butterfly weed, daylilies, wild asters, and joe-pye weed—little meadows for our delight. This plant is exceptional for many reasons, not the least of which is its big, bold scale in the garden—it's definitely not a shrinking violet. The flowers of some coneflower varieties can reach six inches in diameter.

Why else is it so wonderful? How about long bloom period, sometimes as long as three months, and this in addition to its attractive appearance when in bud and later on as the flower dries on the stalk. Then there are the flower colors. Depending on the species or cultivar, the blooms range from a vibrant ruby purple to dusky purple to pale pinky-purple, contrasting beautifully with the iridescent, coppery-colored central cone. Coneflowers make attractive and exceptionally long-lasting cut flowers. There's even a yellow purple coneflower for the contrarions among us. Then there's the sturdiness of the plant with its stout stems, so well suited to surviving heat, drought, and summer storms. Coneflowers have no problem with clay soil—quite the opposite. So there's no maddening prima donna drooping or flopping from this spunky plant. The word for this plant is "durable."

Another reason for their deserved popularity is that they look good with so many other perennials. I've mentioned a few good companions above, but the big, simple scale and vibrant color of the flowers makes coneflowers work well with almost anything, so they are great perennials for beginners. (They also look good with many annuals. Somehow, some volunteer bachelor buttons came up next to the purple coneflowers by my back fence this summer, and this coneflower/cornflower combo looks great, with the blue in the cornflower picking up the blue undertone of the coneflower.)

Do you want another reason why coneflowers are so great? You don't have to deadhead them. The cones and petals dry nicely, and birds, especially goldfinches, love to eat the dried seeds come early fall. Hummingbirds are also said to like purple coneflowers. And speaking of beautiful flying creatures, butterflies love coneflowers. I have read that they're a favorite plant of the red admiral butterfly, though I've seen only the monarch around ours. Not that I'm complaining. I would love to see what those iridescent central cones look like through the eyes of a butterfly!

There's a simple reason why coneflowers do so well here: they're genuine Midwestern natives and have evolved in our climate for tens of thousands of years. There's very little, up to and including buffalo stampedes and tornadoes, that seriously bothers these plants. Their only serious dislike is damp, boggy, wet soil. They evolved on the open prairie and on woodland margins, so they can tolerate a bit of shade, but don't overdo it.

There are a number of different types of purple coneflowers, including, of course, the species itself, plus cultivars. Purple coneflowers used to be lumped together with black-eyed Susans by botanists—they were all thought of as yellow coneflowers, with the purple just being a variation of the yellow. Today, purple coneflowers are grouped by themselves in the genus *Echinacea*, leaving the black-eyed Susan in the genus *Rudbeckia*. Both groups have the prominent central cone and drooping leaves that separate them from a closely related group, the sunflowers, of the genus *Helianthus*.

At first glance, the purple-flowered coneflowers can look quite similar to one another, but I've found that just as a connoisseur of wine can detect and appreciate minute differences in their favorite beverage, a lover of coneflowers (an echinaceaphile?) can delight in the gradations of purple in the flower petals, the angle of the petals, the color of the cone, the smoothness of the foliage, and other such coneflower minutiae.

Some philistines describe coneflowers as "coarse," even—I'm shocked to say—weedy, and an old common name for them is hedgehog coneflower, but I truly disagree with this judgment. A coneflower may seem coarse to some when compared with, say, a delphinium, but then where are your delphiniums come mid-August? Groveling in the dust, that's where. And I think you could turn this perception around and criticize other plants for looking spindly and namby-pamby in comparison with the robust coneflower. So the coarseness issue is definitely in the eye of the beholder. The sheer healthiness of the coneflower seems to offend some gardeners, who may feel that a flower should be hard to grow or it's not worth it.

Most coneflowers grow to be about three feet in height, but height seems to vary according to soil richness. *E. paradoxa* routinely reaches five feet. Be prepared for *E. purpurea* to self-seed, though not obnoxiously.

I've gone into some detail about purple coneflowers, simply because these are such good plants for Midwest gardens, and once you try one type, you may want to experience the delights of the others. Beautiful, healthy, and versatile: you can't ask for much more.

ECHINACEA CARE

I don't think of purple coneflowers as plants you care for, exactly, as they have lived for eons on the prairie without any care from gardeners at all. Still, keep in mind that they like sun and decent soil. They can weather drought but look happier when watered regularly. Japanese beetles are also fans of coneflowers, but I notice that they seem to stay on the cone of the flower and nibble that, not the petals, where it would be more noticeable.

As with the above rudbeckias, species coneflowers will seed around the garden and can be considered borderline invasive. If this is a problem for you, clip off the seed heads as they mature. Echinacea cultivars must be divided to propagate.

Before we leave these remarkable plants, did you know that Native Americans used to use the dried flower heads as hair combs? Try one—it works.

The proud blossoms of purple coneflower (*Echinacea purpurea*).

A self-seeded *Agastache*,
its exact name lost in the
mists of history.

The six indispensables are the backbone of the Midwestern garden. A lushly blooming peony can be one of the highlights of the gardening year, and a unique hosta, a gardener's pride and joy. It's easily possible to have a beautiful, drought-resistant, low-maintenance garden using only the six indispensables. But there's another important group of perennials that are vital garden players, though they may play more modest roles. Familiar hard-workers such as feverfew, lamb's ears, bee balm, perennial geraniums, cat-mint, silver artemisias, Virginia creeper, and lily of the valley, as well as less familiar amsonias, euphorbias, and eupatoriums, can tie a garden together, freshen it, twine over it, layer it, and weave it together, all the while staying healthy and happy. They contribute richly to the garden but don't ask for much in return from the gardener. I'll admit that some of these plants could be called "old chestnuts." And like any gardener my attention sometimes wanders and I am drawn to planting the newest plant on the block. Often I get a pleasant surprise, but usually I return to my old friends. Whenever I am tempted to dismiss these plants, I think of Monet's garden. He filled it with lamb's ears, tulips, cosmos, hollyhocks, iris, asters, and daisies—nothing unusual at all. But what he did with them . . .

Perennial support players

Before saying one more word about the support players, though, I have to mention that some of these plants could be considered borderline invasive, and I'll point out situations where they shouldn't be used. If you have really good soil, for instance, feverfew will self-seed like mad and be a nuisance. They *are* strong growers, but I like to think their strong growing habits are an asset to the Midwestern gardener, not a liability. We have tough growing conditions here, and I think we need to harness the power of tough plants that don't have to be coaxed into performing. You could even say that invasiveness

is the fuel that powers a bountiful cottage garden.

One more thing: if you know any other gardeners at all, they might be able to provide you with starter plants for some of the above, as "passalongs." Most gardeners would be glad to dig up a clump of lamb's ears or a pot of feverfew for you, to share the wealth.

Agastache foeniculum
(ANISE HYSSOP)

Anise hyssop is a plant loved by both bees and Midwestern gardeners. With clean, licorice-scented, green foliage shadowed with purple and stiff spikes of lavender flowers, anise hyssop stands sturdily upright like a garden candelabra, never needing staking. Disease and insects pass it by, and it sails through the worst summer heat and humidity. By winter, its skeletal remains are dramatically silhouetted against the snow. It can be plunked in a pot and grown as a container plant and moved anywhere in the garden where you need height. It likes sun but accepts dappled shade with equanimity. It's not quite perennial in our zone, and in my garden only a few plants actually pull through a cold winter, but there are plenty of seedlings. These seedlings seem to appear in mid- to late-June, when the weather is reliably warm, so don't panic if you don't see them first thing in the spring.

This quickly brings us to what some gardeners don't like about the agastaches: they are self-seeders. So be forewarned. But the seedlings are large and easy to pull out or transplant to a spot of your choosing. I find the self-seeding reassuring rather than annoying, because I know I'll have a reservoir of healthy, good-looking plants to fall back on if a weak sister plant poops out and I need something to plant in its place.

From midsummer on, anise hyssop plants are softly humming with bumblebees. Don't let this alarm you—these gentle bees are much more interested in the flowers than they are in you.

I am hovering on the brink of sending for seeds of A. *nepetoides*, the 'Giant Yellow Bubble-Mint', advertised in Plantworld Seeds, a British seed catalog. It purports to be "an enormous monster for the back of the border. Massive, chunky square section stems carry nine-inch spikes of creamy yellow-green flowers much loved by bees." Sounds like fun!

At nurseries, agastaches can be found with either the annuals or the perennials and are sometimes grouped with the herbs, so you might have to search a bit for them.

Amsonia tabernaemontana
(EASTERN BLUE STAR)

Hardy, insect and disease resistant, can be grown in sun or light shade, not invasive—you might wonder why this shining, graceful, North American native isn't grown more widely. I honestly don't know. The probable answer is that while a truly beautiful plant, it doesn't have giant pink flowers the size of dinner plates or any of the other usual attractions and/or afflictions of more popular plants. I only know that the longer I have it, the more I like it, and suddenly, last year, I fell madly in love with it. (Nongardeners may raise eyebrows at the notion of falling madly in love with a plant, but I know fellow gardeners will understand!) Amsonia stands about two and a half feet tall, and produces small, starry, steel blue flowers in late spring. The blue is elusive, and sometimes I can only see the blueness out of the corner of my eye. In some lights the flowers are a cool white. The willowlike leaves remain attractive all season long, turning gold in the fall.

My plant is thriving in dappled shade, so I was surprised a few years ago to see my sister's plant thriving in full sun. Her plant is larger, has self-seeded (decorously), and blooms earlier and longer. It's a tribute to this plant that it has done so well, so uncomplainingly, in shade in my garden. Amsonia needs decent soil on the moist side—it's not a plant for depleted, dry soil. It spreads, but very slowly, and it can grow for years without needing division.

Amsonia goes well with butterfly weed, sundrops, black-eyed Susan, or white wild indigo. My shade-dwelling plant thrives among wood asters and hosta.

There are at least ten species of amsonia that I am aware of, and while not all are suited to our soil, I am looking forward to tracking down A. *ciliata* (downy blue star) and A. *illustris*, which has shiny leaves. Right now on order from a mail-order nursery is so-called Arkansas amsonia, which I am hoping is A. *hubrichtii*, or threadleaf blue star. Its fine-textured leaves will turn bright yellow in the autumn.

I am writing this in January and have only to look out the window to see the graceful golden stems of amsonia arching above the snow.

Artemisia ludoviciana
('SILVER KING' AND 'SILVER QUEEN')

'Silver King' artemisia is a member of the great plant genus *Artemisia*, which includes such other famous members as tarragon, sweet Annie, southernwood, and mugwort. It's grown for its silvery foliage, which goes with everything, not for its flowers. 'Silver Queen' has wider leaves but is otherwise very similar to 'Silver King', and many a gardener gets them completely confused, myself included.

'Silver King' is definitely on the invasive side, and I would not plunk it down into a bed of prized perennials growing in rich soil. It will soon muscle its way to the front and begin taking over the whole bed, and soon you will have a bed of Silver King. But if you have a sunny, difficult spot, and I think we all have difficult spots, Silver King might be the answer. It swells up into a silver cloud and is quite beautiful. The secret to Silver King's strength is that it's not quite as picky about drainage as some other more choice artemisias such as *Artemisia* 'Powis Castle'. 'Powis Castle', a celebrity among artemisias, might hang around for a couple of years and then vanish, I think because of drainage problems. Silver King has no such compunction. Silver King is, of course, drought, insect, and disease resistant. It's not at its best in really hard, compact, clay soil, though. Loosening the planting-site soil well with a spade and perhaps digging in some sand or even gravel will make Silver King pleased as punch.

Plant breeders have come up with a silvery artemisia called *A. ludoviciana* 'Valerie Finnis'. This is a shorter version of Silver King, with broad leaves as jagged as a bolt of lightening. I find it to be an nice change from plain old Silver King, and it seems to be just as hardy.

Chrysanthemum parthenium
(FEVERFEW)

This is a perfect plant for cottage gardens, whether American or British, although it can be invasive in rich soil. It's low growing, with pungent-smelling, ferny leaves and little white button flowers. There are a number of varieties of feverfew—some have single flowers, some double, some have golden centers, and some have golden centers and no petals. There's even a variety known as golden feverfew that has chartreuse foliage. Golden feverfew can light up the dullest corner of the garden and it goes with almost everything.

Feverfew has long been used as a medicinal plant, and modern research shows that a chemical compound in its leaves may help alleviate migraines. In my garden, though, feverfew's main function is to be a reliable, pretty little plant that's fresh as a daisy, a plant to which it is related. Feverfew only becomes a problem, in my experience, if you have very rich soil. If you have this, feverfew might self-seed more than you'd be happy with. But since my soil is not

super-rich, feverfew never gets very far.

By the heat of midsummer, feverfew flowers and foliage dry up and turn brown. Cut off the crispy stalks right down to the deep green basal foliage using sharp clippers. If you have a lot of feverfew, this might take a while, but it's one of those gardening chores that can be pleasantly mindless and that yields big dividends. Keep the sheared feverfew watered, and a whole new crop of flowers will spring up in two or three weeks.

Convallaria majalis
(LILY OF THE VALLEY)

Here's another common plant that we take so much for granted but that can be so beautiful. Lily of the valley is a ground cover for a shady corner with moist soil. It will happily increase in that corner year after year, crowding out weeds. Lily of the valley has been cultivated since at least 1000 B.C.—talk about an heirloom plant! It can be invasive in rich, moist soil. My own experience, however, has not shown that lily of the valley is invasive, but I do have it in rather mediocre soil.

Lily of the valley always reminds me of my younger sister Janet's wedding. Her bouquet was simply a huge handful of lily of the valley. It remains the most beautiful wedding bouquet I have ever seen.

I'll admit that lily of the valley is a sentimental choice for this section and that perhaps it's not a garden blockbuster. It's not even difficult to grow. But the flowers . . . the scent . . . I simply couldn't have a garden without them.

And the maid-like lily of the vale,
Whom youth makes so fair and passion so pale,
That the light of its tremulous bells is seen
Through their pavilions of tender green.
　　　　　　—Percy Bysshe Shelley

Eupatorium purpureum
(JOE-PYE WEED)

If you need height in your garden, consider joe-pye weed. It grows up to 10 feet tall and yet remains erect without staking. Domes of fluffy, pale purple flowers are proudly held aloft in late summer and are popular with nectar-seeking monarch butterflies. This is a robust plant with a slightly coarse appearance and might not work in a highfalutin garden with hoity-toity tea roses, for

Self-seeded purple joe-pye weed (*Eupatorium purpureum*) emerging rather unexpectedly from between the branches of the Asian pear tree.

White snakeroot (*Eupatorium rugosum*) blooms in the shade in early fall.

instance. But for a casual country garden, it's absolutely perfect, and the longer I know joe-pye, the more I like him, er, it.

Don't be afraid of the size of this plant. In soil of average moisture, it doesn't flop, and it doesn't spread. And in seven years of growing joe-pye weed, I've found exactly two little joe-pye weed seedlings, so it's not exactly a rampant self-seeder.

E. maculatum 'Gateway', a cultivar of spotted joe-pye weed, is another handsome member of the eupatorium family. At five feet in height with pink flowers, smooth, dark stems, and attractive foliage, this is a slightly more elegant version of joe-pye weed, and if you can find it, grab it. And the beautiful *E. rugosum* 'Chocolate' (chocolate leaf snakeroot) has handsome maroon-green foliage and is taking European gardens by storm.

Another interesting member of this family is *E. coelestinum*, called perennial ageratum or mist flower. It's a heat- and drought-resistant plant whose blue flowers, similar in color and appearance to annual ageratum flowers, bloom through late summer and fall. The White Flower Farm catalog recommends *E. coelestinum* 'Cori' as having an especially bright, clear blue. Some gardeners have noted that perennial ageratum can be invasive in good soil, but so far, clay soil is putting the breaks on it in my garden. Asters, boltonia, brown-eyed Susans, and goldenrod are good companion plants.

Boneset (*Eupatorium perfoliatum*) is an attractive wilding with white flowers, supposedly reaching about four feet. Mine is growing in soil of average moisture and is less than two feet tall! (Sometimes I hate to admit these things!) We'll see what happens next year. Otherwise, its greyish foliage is good looking and the flowers pretty.

The genus *Eupatorium* is native to eastern North America. Joe-pye weed was long used by Native Americans as a remedy for typhoid fever. The native American word for that fever was "jopi," so that's how joe-pye weed got its name. Please don't be put off by the word "weed" in its name—this is an entirely garden-worthy plant that is indispensable for Midwestern gardeners.

Euphorbia (SPURGES)

The genus *Euphorbia* seems strange to me, as it contains a polyglot of plants that seem like they couldn't possibly be related: cactuslike things, tropical trees, and our Christmas poinsettias are in this group, as well as a Midwestern member of the family, *Euphorbia corollata*. Some euphorbias thrive in dry, stony fields in Turkey, and others cling precariously to cold mountainsides in Nepal. Most have a milky sap running through their veins as well as colored, showy bracts instead of flower petals. Bracts are leaves modified by nature to protect buds. For our purposes euphorbias have a sterling virtue: drought resistance, and this is where we Midwesterners come in. A vein of gold runs through this jumble of plants, a vein that we can mine.

Let's don our mining helmets and start with flowering spurge (*Euphorbia corollata*). This is a delicate-looking, pretty little wildflower (about a foot in height) with sprays of small, white flowers that remind me of little white collars on dresses. I've seen it growing on dry, gravelly ridges, but it is doing fine in my dry, clay soil. Flowering spurge is not for shade or moist soil.

I also have *E. cyparissias*, the cypress spurge, which has feathery stems and small yellowish bracts. I bought it at a church rummage sale, which is perhaps a very dangerous place to purchase plants. Soon after planting, it I found it referred to in a garden encyclopedia as a "vicious spreader" for sunny banks, and I did see it later at a neighbor's garden—a 16-by-16-foot area of solid cypress spurge. In my garden it does have that unnaturally perky look of an invasive plant, and a six-week drought hasn't bothered it in the slightest, so we'll see what happens. If you have a thoroughly rotten, hellishly dry spot, this could be your plant. It might be wise to seek out the available cultivars, such as *E. cyparissias* 'Fens Ruby', and 'Orange Man', whose bracts turn orange at maturity.

Follow-up note: A year after planting, my cypress spurge formed an attractive, low hummock covered with chartreuse bracts by the first week of May. Fighting off pussytoes to the right, and a brick walk to the left, it has spread, but not far.

A euphorbia found in many local gardens is *E. polychroma*, the cushion spurge. This is a plant I've always meant to get but somehow has eluded me. I have seen it in several nearby gardens, and just down the street it grows in the alley, so it must be quite hardy. Cushion spurges are low mounding plants with neon yellow bracts. They can take some light shade. I've read of an interesting variety, *E. polychroma* 'Candy', which has purple foliage and yellow flowers. And an old-fashioned garden combination is cushion spurge grown with bleeding hearts (*Dicentra spectabilis*). Their bloom times overlap in May.

My sister gave me a start of donkey-tail spurge (*E. myrsinites*), a plant with trailing, foot-long stems that does well placed at the front of a mounded border with good drainage. My plant is draped over some paver bricks along the front sidewalk and thrives in punishing summer heat and drought.

Euphorbia dulcis 'Chameleon' is an up-and-coming euphorbia, as more and more Midwestern gardeners discover its attractive whorls of maroon and pale red foliage. It's doing beautifully in my garden, and next spring I will plant something silvery nearby for contrast.

Just tantalizingly out of our reach is Robb's euphorbia (*Euphorbia amygdaloides* var. *robbiae*), often mentioned as a stellar plant for dry shade and as one of the finest euphorbias of all. The hardiness zones assigned to it vary wildly: some say Zone 6 and others Zone 8. I'm thinking it would be worthwhile for us to try this in our gardens in a sheltered spot to see what happens—maybe it isn't out of our reach after all! And *Euphorbia griffithii* 'Fireglow' is often mentioned as a superior euphorbia, with attractive, reddish "flowers" and very dark green foliage.

I've read in *Classic Plant Combinations*, by David Stuart, that the euphorbias and sedges (*Carex.*) "are made for each other," so here is yet another avenue to investigate.

Euphorbias can self-seed, and my donkey-tail spurge has somehow sent seeds across the sidewalk to a mulched area, where half a dozen small plants have popped up. Some euphorbias can tolerate light shade, and the amount of light a plant receives can influence its coloration.

The foliage of cypress spurge (*Euphorbia cyparissias*) and sweet everlasting (*Antennaria* spp.) add texture to the garden scene, even when not in bloom. Both are highly drought resistant.

Geranium
(HARDY GERANIUMS)

Don't confuse hardy geraniums, sometimes called perennial geraniums, or cranesbills, with pelargoniums, the very popular, tender annual so many of us grow on our windowsills in terra cotta pots. They are distantly related botanically, but for gardening purposes, they are entirely different plants. Here, we consider true geraniums.

When we moved into our circa-1913 house in 1985, I found not one, but two hardy geraniums growing in the garden. My gardening consciousness at the time was pretty low and Neanderthal-like, and I murmured, "How pretty," and foolishly turned back to reading about heather gardens and wallflowers. Well, it was a long time ago.

Meanwhile, the taller of these deceptively demure-looking little plants was desperately trying to tell me something: "Forget about those stupid wallflowers, and look at us, Fran." It wasn't until the next spring that I noticed the shimmering iridescence of the lavender flowers covering these plants and—hey—these are really pretty! What are they? A quick trip to a perennial guidebook revealed that they were *Geranium maculatum*, or wild geranium. They are spring-blooming natives, and I later saw swaths of them growing in the woods at a nearby forest preserve. My eyes were slowly opening: grow what grows. The other geranium, which I later found to be a variety of *G. sanguineum*, or bloody cranesbill (a violent name for a plant as inoffensive as a sleeping lamb), looked so unlike the wild geranium that I didn't connect the two at first. It was a low, mounding plant growing in poor soil in full sun by the concrete back steps, steps you can bake pizza and grill sausage on, come August. Its little magenta flowers bloomed well into summer and have done so for years, even in dry, windy springs and through sudden, early summer heat waves.

Perennial geraniums comprise an enormous and problematic family for the Midwestern gardener to choose from. A good perennial geranium can be very, very good, but a bad one can be pretty horrible. The good ones are the ones that have earned a place on this roster. They are dependable, drought-resistant perennials whose flower colors have an iridescence and candylike sweetness that's really pleasing. Many perennial geraniums are just a hair's breadth from being out-and-out wildflowers, and they bring that kind of charm to the garden. I am writing this in late May, and I've placed a handful of wild geraniums in a big old tin can on the kitchen table. It's as pretty as can be.

G. *macrorrhizum* is not only one of my favorite perennial geraniums, but it is also one of my all-time favorite perennials. First and foremost, it looks good through the worst drought. And its low mound of dense, neat foliage makes it a perfect, though unusual, ground cover. The foliage is fragrant, with a scent of resinous apples, and is touched with russet in the fall. I have G. *macrorrhizum* 'Album', which has white flowers with prominent pink stamens—*very* pretty—as well as 'Ingwersen's Variety', which has pink flowers and is taller than the species. 'Bevan's Variety' has magenta flowers. The Herronswood nursery catalog, of course, has the last word on G. *macrorrhizum*, by offering a number of unusual cultivars, including a variegated one that you have to actually go to the nursery (in Kingston, Washington) to purchase, perhaps to seek an audience before purchasing. I am almost tempted. A hybrid of G. *macrorrhizum* and G. *dalmaticum* is G. *cantabrigiense* 'Biokovo', an eight-inch-tall mound of neat foliage with pink flowers. Like G. *macrorrhizum*, it is extremely drought resistant and has reddish fall foliage.

Any of the G. *sanguineum* cultivars are worth a try. I have G. *sanguineum* var. *striatum*, which has pretty pale pink flowers, as well as the species. There are at least eight other cultivars available. This species needs more water to stay presentable than G. *macrorrhizum*, but if kept watered and sheared back, it usually will reflower.

Other hardy geraniums for Midwestern gardeners to consider include G. *cinereum* 'Ballerina' (pink with red veins), G. *endressii* 'Wargrave Pink' (pale pink), G. *magnificum* (blue-violet), and G. *psilostemon* (cherry pink with black-veined centers).

Two that haven't worked for me are G. *pratense* and G. 'Johnson's Blue', though it may be that I haven't given them the sites they need. G. *pratense* is quite tall and floppy, with spindly stems, and probably needs to be grown supported by grasses, like a wildflower. But its leaves become crispy and brown by midsummer, so I feel unenthusiastic about it. The tempting 'Johnson's Blue', with its extraordinary blue flowers, has G. *pratense* in its parentage, and you can tell by the way it flops. If you attempt to grow it, it needs support from surrounding grassy plants and doesn't work as a specimen. My sister notes that 'Johnson's Blue' used to be sold everywhere here five years ago and is seen less often nowadays, a sure sign that it's slinking back to Portland. There are tons of other perennial geraniums available, but I urge you to proceed with caution, and I am thinking of my G. *pratense* lying in a tangled heap right now, desperately in need of shearing.

Follow-up note: In desperation, I moved G. *pratense* to a spot in the back of the garden with some Miss Lingard phlox and bouncing bet. The three of them get along famously, and now, in July, I see the purple flowers of G. *pratense* held up high.

Monarda
(BEE BALM)

Monardas are North American native flowers found at the sun-dappled edges of woodland areas. They grow up to three feet in height and bloom in late June and July. Most monardas have a distinctive flowery, minty scent that is pleasant, and traditionally the leaves are used to make tea. The flowers are unique in form, with a mop-head look, and sometimes are two tiered, or even three or four tiered. Monardas are susceptible to mildew, but quite a few modern mildew-resistant varieties have been developed. Growing them in full sun can limit mildew development. Monardas have no problem at all with our heavy clay soil—quite the opposite, in fact. I would say they were invasive—well, they are invasive—but since they form shallow rooted mats with runners, they are easy to pull out. The worst spot for monarda is in dappled shade and dryish soil. It can't quite surmount these two deficits and responds by becoming skeletal and mildewed.

Wild bergamot (M. *fistulosa*) is a good monarda for us, because as a native prairie plant, it has a high tolerance for drought and heat, and bees and butterflies are wild about it. To see a prairie alive with delicate clouds of this pale lavender flower, sharp violet spikes of liatris, soft hummocks of prairie dropseed, dots of pale purple coneflower seedheads, and with butterflies dancing above all, is to see one of the great wonders of the natural world.

Bee balm (M. *didyma*), is a wild red monarda and not quite as drought tolerant as M. *fistulosa*. Many common cultivars are derived from M. *didyma*. 'Croftway Pink' has fluffy, deep pink flowers, and M. 'Cambridge Scarlet' has vivid, true red flowers. I happen to be partial to purple monardas and especially like M. 'Mahogany', which has gorgeous, indigo purple flowers.

My favorite monarda is M. *fistulosa* × *tetraploid*, which has rose-scented leaves. The flowers are purple, underlaid with indigo shadows. When this is in bloom, I visit it every day along with the bees to inhale its sweet fragrance.

M. 'Lambada' is a lavender monarda with four tiers of flower heads and is a wonderfully gay, frivolous-looking plant. Who says Mother Nature doesn't have a sense of humor? Dr. Seuss could have designed this plant.

Monardas are good perennials for beginners to try, as they are easy to

Wild bergamot (*Monarda fistulosa*) and black-eyed Susans (*Rudbeckia hirta*) bloom on the late July prairie. The sweet, dry scent of wild bergamot perfumes the summer air.

grow, very pretty, and have great presence in the garden. At three feet tall with those fluffy flowers, they don't get lost in the shuffle and can pretty much take care of themselves in a casual garden. In very good soil they are spreaders, and I can't help but notice that in springtime everyone seems to be giving away clumps of red monarda. Still, they aren't unstoppable garden thugs, either, and I think their value outweighs their downside. Don't be scared off by mention of mildew; they'll be fine as long as they're in full sun, and even in partial shade they will usually only get a touch.

Nepeta faassenii
(CATMINT)

Not to be confused with cat*nip* (*N. cataria*), cat*mint* is a low-growing plant with soft gray, minty-smelling leaves and panicles of delicate amethyst flowers. A blooming catmint plant is a misty cloud of blue floating idly in the garden. Catmint is a sun-loving plant that is drought, pest, and disease resistant, and I feel you can't ask more of a plant. After the initial flush of bloom in June, the stem and flowers start to dry up. Swoop in with your shears, cut it back at least by half, and water thoroughly. Within three or four weeks, it will be back, blooming again, and will bloom on and off for the rest of the summer. Catmint reminds me a little of peonies, in that it is so reliable that it's easy to take for granted. Left unsheared and unwatered after blooming, cat-

The large, tubular flowers of *Nepeta* 'Souvenir d'Andre Chaudron' provide contrast to the satiny white petals of an Asiatic lily.

mint becomes frowsy and shapeless. A bit of pampering results in a well-defined mound of flowers.

You might come across a variety of catmint called *N. mussinii*. According to the book *Perennials for American Gardens*, this is "much less desirable than *N. × faassenii*, although good selections have their place."

There are a number of other catmint varieties available, including *N. sibirica* and *N.* 'Six Hills Giant'. My sister highly recommends 'Six Hills Giant' as a good variety to grow with roses—at three feet in height, it hides their knobby knees. And I've just read of *N. parnassica*, purporting to be one of the biggest catmints, topping six feet. I also have *N.* 'Dawn to Dusk', whose flowers supposedly are pink, but it's a very pale pink, almost white, and it seems a bit wishy-washy to me. My sister is growing *N.* 'Souvenir d'André Chaudron', whose long, graceful stems bear large, amethyst blue flowers. This is rapidly becoming a favorite for many gardeners, as it looks wonderful with roses.

Does catmint attract cats? Yes, but they have to accidentally brush against it or crush it to release its oils in order to know that it's there. Otherwise, they walk right by it and are none the wiser. So much for cat intelligence. A big tabby rolled back and forth over one of my catmint plants, leaving it permanently shorter than the others. But it was so funny to see the cat, who was in a state of complete bliss, that I didn't mind. I always think a garden should be used, whether it's by humans or cats, and that the most interesting plants have a story to tell.

Parthenocissus quinquefolia
(VIRGINIA CREEPER)

I hesitated to include Virginia creeper in this list because some gardeners would argue that it is invasive, particularly in good soil; I have to admit, some gardeners are right. It can clamber up and over fences, up trees, hoist itself up onto your porch and grab your wicker rocking chair by a leg, and then, with underground stems like telephone cables, try to stealthily invade your perennial beds. However—and this is a big *however*—Virginia creeper has beautiful leaves that turn a warm red in autumn and has attractive berries. It also looks nice in flower arrangements. And ultimately, it can't move faster than you or I can. In spring, I spend an hour ripping it out, and that keeps things under control. It's a small price to pay for having such a lush, drought-resistant vine that leafs out and cools down a garden even in the throes of a drought and that will grow in shade or in blasting sun.

Stachys byzantina
(LAMB'S EARS)

With silvery leaves as soft as a baby lamb's ears, this is another "you-can't-garden-without-it" plant for the Midwestern gardener. The leaves feel like flannel cloth—the plant used to be called Savior's flannel or Jesus flannel. Legend says that it was used by Mother Mary on the wounds of Jesus. Lamb's ears is also known as woundwort, reflecting its past function as an ad hoc Band-Aid.

In our day, lamb's ears is an attractive, low-growing ground cover. You can try to grow it along a path, but it doesn't seem to like being planted in a row and soon sets to forming attractive clumps here and there in the garden, tactfully showing you how it should be done. It needs full sun and doesn't like rich soil. Later on in the summer, lamb's ears sends up flower stalks with lavender flowers. I like the stalks, but not all gardeners do, and there is a variety called 'Silver Carpet' that is sterile and doesn't produce stalks.

Lamb's ears grows so well and easily that all beginning gardeners should have it in their garden, as it makes the gardener look skillful. The silvery-bluish color goes with everything, and the plant is especially pretty in an herb garden.

By the end of the summer some of the leaves may have dried up and matted under the living part of the plant. I just pull this stuff out, throw it in the compost heap, and then cut back some of the stems if the plant is wandering too far afield.

Some gardeners insist that lamb's ears can be grown in the shade, and it's true: it will *survive* in the shade for a summer or so and then will slowly begin moving toward the nearest available sun, doggedly plowing through grass if need be.

Another good variety is S. *byzantina* 'Big Ears' (also called 'Helene von Stein'), which has big, rather rounded leaves. I've gotten to like 'Big Ears' almost more than the smaller-leafed variety, as it remains in good condition right through the end of the year, and the big leaves aren't fussy looking.

There are other plants in the *Stachys* genus that are also useful to the Midwestern gardener, including the betonys, S. *grandiflora* and S. *officinalis*. S. *grandiflora*, big betony, is the showier of the two, with spikes of violet flowers. This is a hardy and attractive plant that can take some light shade. S. *officinalis*, betony has a long history of use as a medicinal herb. It's not as showy as big betony, but is a nice plant with a pleasantly old-fashioned feel to it for a casual cottage garden.

Rosa 'Iceberg' underplanted with *Stachys byzantina* 'Big Ears'.

41

Sweet autumn clematis (*Clematis paniculata*) smothers an archway in early September.

I've noticed that some gardeners are preoccupied with perennials and seem oblivious to annuals, while others stick to easy annuals such as marigolds and feel nervous about making the "big jump" to perennials. As a practical gardener, I try not to be prejudiced one way or the other, as both annuals and perennials have their strong and weak points. On the face of it, perennials might seem the better buy because they are supposed to come back year after year. Buying a little six-pack of marigolds is a one-shot deal and could be seen as wasteful.

Gardening, though, is often more complicated than you might think at first. Some "perennials" only come back for a year or two and then disappear. The plant might not like the drainage in your garden or might need some nutrient that your soil can't provide. If you have many plants in your garden, you might not even notice at first that the plant is gone—you suddenly notice a bare spot and think, "Didn't I have a *Rapaciousnungulus* plant there a year or two ago?" It will simply have vanished, and you may not at first remember what it was, which shows there's a good reason to keep some sort of planting record. It will also tell you that to have this plant in your garden regularly, you're going to have to keep buying it every few years. Shasta daisies and columbines are good examples of "perennials" that can be short-lived in Midwestern gardens.

Dictionary of perennials

On the other hand, there's a large assortment of annuals that self-seed. Plants flower and go to seed; the seeds ripen and fall onto the soil, and next year, sprout. These annuals may pop up in your garden for years, and for all intents and purposes are "perennial." Please see the chapter on self-seeding annuals for more info on these helpful flowers.

Having mentioned above that some perennials can peter out and leave us in the lurch, I would like to spotlight perennials that *are* what the name implies and are good choices for the Midwestern garden. These sturdy plants will come up year after year and are worth the investment in time and money by the gardener. Ultimately, though, the quality of your soil and gardening care, and the intrinsic nature of the plant itself, will determine which goes and which stays for the long haul.

ACHILLEA (YARROW) Achilleas are sun-loving, drought-tolerant plants growing about two to three feet in height and are fine plants for the Midwestern garden. They do best in ordinary, even somewhat poor, loose, garden soil. Rich, humus-y soil causes lax growth and inferior flowers. Some horticulturists regard yarrow as one of the best perennials for dry soil, whether clay or sand. It blooms from June through September, and some varieties will bloom all the way to frost, especially if you remove old, dried flower heads. Yarrows are vigorous growers, and clumps should be divided at least every two or three years. About the only thing that spells doom for yarrow is soggy soil.

Common yarrow (A. *millefolium*) has been used as a medicinal plant for a long time; there's evidence that the Neanderthals used it 60,000 years ago. For all the wonderful medicinal properties and historic associations of common yarrow, I don't recommend including it in your garden, unless you specifically are trying to create a garden of historic or medicinal herbs. It's invasive and has a slightly weedy feel to it, though some gardeners come staunchly to its defense. If you want a white yarrow, try A. *millefolium* 'White Beauty', whose large flower heads are a nice creamy white. And it's not invasive, at least not like common yarrow. There are some pink and crimson varieties that are also superior in appearance and habit to the common yarrow, such as A. 'Cerise Queen', 'Rosea', and 'Fire King'. A. *millefolium* 'Paprika' is one of my favorite yarrows, having a warm red flower that blends smoothly with other perennials in the garden. Be sure to cut it back after blooming to encourage a fresh flush of growth. A. 'Moonshine' is also very popular, with flowers of a haunting, pale, sulphurous beauty. The pale yellow flowers of A. 'Anthea' are a warmer pale yellow than 'Moonshine', and some gardeners find it easier on the eyes than the truly lunar yellow of 'Moonshine'. And German hybridizers have come up with some pretty pastel yarrows, though I've noticed they tend to fade and turn brown during extreme heat.

Fernleaf yarrow (A. *filipendulina*) is another good yarrow to try, with its soft, ferny foliage. It's the tallest of the yarrows, reaching three feet or more. A. *filipendulina* 'Gold Plate' is recommended by some gardeners, though some

horticulturists say A. *filipendulina* 'Coronation Gold' is the best yarrow of all, as it's not floppy.

There are even low-growing yarrows that can be used as ground covers. Bluestone Perennials offers A. *tomentosa* 'King Edward', a six-inch woolly yarrow, and Busse Gardens offers hybrid 'Maynard Gold', also six inches. Remember, keep in average dry soil for best effects. My 'King Edward' vanished, I think because of so-so drainage and compacted soil.

A. *ptarmica* 'The Pearl', with its rosettes of white flowers so unlike the "plates" of the other achilleas, is often suggested as an alternative to baby's breath, though it has a softer feel. I recommend seeking out a plant (not seeds) of this particular variety as opposed to settling for plain A. *ptarmica*, whose common name is sneezewort. Sneezewort is usually what's handed over the fence by a nice neighbor, but 'The Pearl' is a genuine improvement, with nicer flowers and better habit. Sneezewort is nothing to be sneezed at, though, as it is a pretty plant for the cottage garden and has been grown in American gardens at least since the eighteenth century.

One last interesting thing about yarrow: some organic gardeners feel that when its chopped leaves are added to a compost heap, it speeds up decomposition. It's worth a try.

ADENOPHORA CONFUSA (LADYBELLS) Ladybells are a member of the ubiquitous bellflower tribe, but according to the White Flower Farm catalog, they are more durable and long lived than bellflowers. I find that they have the casual charm of a wildflower. The long, drooping, blue-violet flowers, which bloom in late June through July, give the plant a winsome look. It grows to about three feet and looks best when planted in clusters—you want a fine stand of ladybells, not a few planted here and there. This plant combines nicely with black-eyed Susans. Ladybells do well in ordinary, well-drained soil and like sun but don't mind a bit of late afternoon shade.

Ladybells are a perfect flower for the cottage garden, as they spread slowly but surely and are completely hardy. They're nice to bring to plant exchanges, as many gardeners have never heard of them and are charmed by the name.

I've heard that ladybells don't really like being divided and transplanted—they sulk. It's true. I've had a perfectly healthy ladybell clump sulking in my garden for most of the summer after being transplanted. I've noticed that it has sent up a few shoots lately, though, so perhaps it realizes it has no alternative but to grow.

AEGOPODIUM PODAGRARIA 'VARIEGATUM' (BISHOP'S WEED OR GOUTWEED) This is a heroic member of the parsley family that has *saved lives*, at least many Midwestern gardeners' lives, as it's *the* plant for a shady spot with terrible soil where all else has failed. Perhaps some experienced gardeners will read this and think I have lost my mind for including this invasive plant among other respectable perennials, but it does have a place in the scheme of things. Just don't put it in good soil with your "good" perennials, or I agree, you may, no, you *will*, regret it. But if you have a dry, shady, poor soil spot where nothing else will grow, bishop's weed is a perfectly decent solution to the problem. It has attractive light green and white foliage and blooms from late May through July with flowers that resemble those of Queen Anne's lace, also a member of the parsley family.

If it gets shabby and seedy looking late in the summer, mow it with a lawnmower and water deeply; it will regenerate and look refreshed.

I have bishop's weed in a spot that had been a driveway for about 50 years. Cars drove back and forth over this spot for a long time, compacting not just the molecules, but the atoms, of the soil ever closer together each year. A few inches below the surface, the compacted, Styrofoam-like soil peters out into cinders and gravel. A bit farther down, it turns into solid clay. The first time I tried to sink a spade into this, honestly, the spade made a clanging noise and *bounced back*. This wouldn't happen in England, I thought grimly. My heart sank at the thought of renting a jackhammer to break it up, and my wallet quivered at bringing in truckloads of new soil. What would Penelope Hobhouse do? I had no idea. So I planted bishop's weed. It's bustling around busily taking over the area, much to my intense relief, and I won't have to give it another thought. There's something to be said for this plant.

There is a solid green version of bishop's weed, but in my opinion, it's possibly the most boring plant God ever created. Not only is it boring, but it looks like poison ivy, and people back away when they see it. So it's boring *and* terrifying, unfortunate qualities for a garden plant. I am afflicted with ennui every time I see it and can't even bring myself to dig it up. So there it stays. Zzzzzzzzzzzz.

AJUGA (BUGLEWEED) This is a common, fast-growing ground cover for shade that flowers in April and May. The flowering represents either an advantage or disadvantage over pachysandra, ajuga's main competitor, depending on your perspective. The carpet of amethyst flower spikes in spring is beautiful, but the spent stalks left after flowering are not. It's easy

enough to shear them off, of course. Ajuga can be invasive and can grow rather spottily into nearby lawn.

There are a number of ajuga cultivars available, and most have mottled, purply, rough, shiny leaves. Recently, I planted *A. genevensis*, or Geneva bugleweed. This is a solid, dark green ajuga, the color of a Girl Scout uniform. Someone asked me why I would plant a green ajuga, when ajuga's claim to fame is to be mottled and purple. For one thing, it's a free country. For another thing, I don't totally like the mottled, purply color of most ajuga. I only uneasily tolerate it and think the solid green species is quite handsome.

I hem and haw about ajuga and right now am in an anti-ajuga phase. There are other shade-loving ground covers that I like so much more than ajuga. This year I've planted a giant ajuga, in the hopes of giving this plant one more chance. I'm hoping it will look less straggly than the smaller version and will leave my lawn alone. We'll see.

ALCHEMILLA ERYTHROPODA AND ALPINA (DWARF LADY'S MANTLES) While lady's mantle (*Alchemilla mollis* and *A. vulgaris*) is frequently recommended as easy to grow in the Midwest, am I the only one who thinks it gets terminally frowsy and limp and dusty looking as the summer progresses? I don't think it's quite as versatile here as it may be in English gardens, as I think hot temperatures are stressful for it. Dwarf lady's mantle (*A. erythropoda*) is a compact, much fresher, greener-looking version of *A. mollis*. It always looks

In a neglected corner of the garden, a daylily is overtaken by a sea of bishop's weed (*Aegopodium podagraria* 'Variegatum').

bandbox fresh and cool no matter what the weather. By late June, shear off the chartreuse flowers and give it a good watering to give it strength for the rest of the summer. Come spring, I carefully pull off the old foliage, revealing the fresh green leaves beneath. In twelve years my plant has self-seeded sparingly, inscrutably, and I now have six or seven plants, each of them welcome.

Alchemilla alpina is another diminutive lady's mantle, and I've been growing it for the past several years. It's proving to be as hardy and attractive as *A. erythropoda*. The leaves of *A. erythropoda* are fan shaped, while the leaves of *A. alpina* comprise five separate, shiny lobes. Even the backs of the leaves are like shiny silk. This is a lovely little plant, and I hope it self-seeds once it becomes more established.

Speaking of *A. mollis* and *A. vulgaris*, I've seen the plants together side by side, and the difference is minute. *A. mollis* seems to have slightly more defined leaves. Both are at their best in moist soil.

Lady's mantle is a classic companion of daylilies, as its low, mounding form goes well with the long, curving daylily leaves.

ALLIUM CERNUUM (NODDING WILD ONION) This lovely little (12 to 18 inches) native plant definitely deserves a spot in the cottage garden. It's tough, adaptive, and beautiful. Gracefully drooping pink flower heads appear in late July though September. How adaptable is it? I have one plant in dappled shade and one in full sun, both in fairly dry soil and doing well. Then a few weeks ago I saw it growing in the wild in really deep shade on a moist river bank. Versatile!

ALLIUM SENESCENS VAR. 'GLAUCUM' (CURLY GARLIC) I'm not sure why curly garlic is such a well-kept secret, as it's a neat and attractive plant that can be placed in front of a border and looks good all times during the growing season. Its turban of leaves curls and swirls around in a whorl of bluish green. It's wonderful for contributing a sense of motion and pattern to the garden picture. It reseeds, but only modestly, unlike some alliums, and the tiny, curly seedlings are cute. I have several of these plants, which are totally pest and disease free, and would recommend them to anyone. Just keep them down in front where they can be seen. In some publications I have seen the plant listed as curly onion and even curly chives. I guess the operative word here is "curly."

Curly garlic slowly grows out from the center over the years, developing a bald spot, and eventually needs dividing.

ANAPHALIS MARGARITACEA (PEARLY EVERLASTING) Pearly everlasting is an old-fashioned perennial bearing clusters of white, buttonlike flowers and gray, felty foliage. Anaphalis tolerates heat and drought perfectly. Robert S. Hebb, in *Low Maintenance Perennials*, states that Japanese pearly everlasting (*A. yedoensis*) is the preferable anaphalis for the garden. I got my plant, labeled only "pearly everlasting," at the Dane County Farmers Market in Madison, Wisconsin. Little white button flowers bloom from late July through September.

In my garden, anaphalis has had one drawback, and it's a pretty big one. Every early spring, it's plagued with little black worms. They appear out of nowhere like winged monkeys and weave webs over the flower bud and leaf tips, which shrivel. Last year the obvious solution to this problem finally occurred to me, and I snipped the afflicted bud from each plant with a pair of scissors. Not only did this completely eradicate the worms, but the plants leafed out beautifully. I have the feeling that these worms are peculiar to this type of plant, as I've also seen them on curry plants, which have similar, downy, silvery foliage.

ANCHUSA AZUREA I mention anchusa because if you see it in bloom at a nursery you will want to buy it, and it's perhaps not a good idea. The intensely blue flowers are sensational, almost as blue as Mel Gibson's eyes. But after blooming, the plant degenerates into a horrible, scraggly mess. My sister gave me a little rhyme to remember: "Always refusa a gift of anchusa."

ANEMONES (JAPANESE ANEMONES AND WINDFLOWERS) I love Japanese anemones, as they look far more exotic than most plants at home in the Midwestern garden. Anemones look like they could grow in a garden on the moon, with their perfectly circular little buds, stiff, wiry stems, and flower petals of flawless, other-worldly satin. Another nice thing about anemones is that they flower for a lengthy period from late summer through early fall, a time when much of the excitement in a garden is over and most other flowers tend to be a rather monotonous chrome yellow color.

A. tomentosa 'Robustissima' (grape-leafed anemone), with pink flowers, is one of the hardiest anemones and in moist soil can be a spreader. The species and cultivars of *A. × hybrida* are among some of the loveliest anemones but are a bit more picky about growing conditions than *A. tomentosa*, not liking drought or soggy winter soil. They are definitely hardy enough to be considered for this area, though, and perhaps can only be considered picky in comparison to *A. tomentosa*.

Take the time to dig in plenty of humus or compost when planting anemones; otherwise, they need only routine care. They don't like to be

ANTHEMIS (GOLDEN MARGUERITE) In a nutshell, anthemis is a yellow-petaled daisy with floppy stems and feathery foliage that *must* be placed at the front of a border. There's no use in placing it any farther back, as it will simply march forward. A raised or mounded bed is very much to its liking, and it can take sun and some drought. It begins blooming by early July and will need deadheading.

AQUILEGIA SPP. (COLUMBINE) Surely there's a shady corner somewhere in your garden for *Aquilegia canadensis*, the wild columbine. It's sometimes called "wild honeysuckle," though it's not related to honeysuckle at all. It is in the buttercup family. Blooming from mid-May through late June, as described in the Thompson & Morgan catalog, it has "nodding blossoms of long, delicately pointed, red spurs around yellow petals that drift above dark green maidenhair fern-like foliage." The red and yellow color scheme may sound grating, but the colors have a delicacy that's actually very pleasing. Growing it next to a white-flowered or silvery plant might soften the brightness if it bothers you. There's also an all-yellow variety called *A. canadensis* 'Corbett'.

Pests called leaf miners enjoy tunneling through columbine leaves,

The distinctive round buds of the Japanese anemone. This is *Anemone hupehensis* 'September Charm'.

stranded in a site that receives blasting sun and heat and prefer dappled shade part of the day. Depending on the variety, anemones range in height from two to four feet. These beautiful flowers definitely deserve a place in more Midwestern gardens. I have some nestled next to a birdbath by the back fence, and they are lovely. I've heard that fall anemones look well planted with England asters, and since both plants are tough perennials that can tolerate less than perfect soil, they make a natural combination.

There is one amusing phenomenon I have noted with these anemones—if you're transplanting a clump, it's almost impossible to do so without breaking the root, and the broken root will generate another clump of anemones. I have tried three times to move a clump of anemones that long ago was inexplicably planted in the middle of the vegetable patch. The result? I now have *four* clumps of anemones. So if you want to transplant a clump, dig down *deep*.

While I have just indicated that anemones are fall bloomers, there is an exception: *A. sylvestris*, or snowdrop anemone. This lovely little white-flowered anemone blooms in the shade in spring during early May. It's hardy, pretty, and tends to spread via rhizomes, but it's so pretty that you (probably) won't mind.

Anemone hupehensis 'September Charm' in bloom in early September.

leaving winding white trails visible on the leaf surface. Picking off the worst affected leaves and removing leaf litter from around the plant can help control leaf miner. Sticky yellow whitefly traps and applications of neem oil have also been found effective.

Another species of columbine is *Aquilegia vulgaris,* or European columbine, sometimes called granny's bonnet. A native of Europe, granny's bonnet comes in a wide range of soft purple, blue, and crimson flowers. Granny's bonnet has been grown forever in English cottage gardens and does well in our Midwestern gardens. It self-sows in my garden, and that's okay with me. Sometimes a double-petaled sport appears, but I prefer the single-petal variety.

The fact that there is only one wild columbine native to the Midwest indicates that columbines aren't thrilled with our climate, and I think this is true. Clay soil drainage may not be to their liking, and hot summers stress them. I just sadly removed a beautiful white columbine (*A. flabellata* 'Alba') this year that had been run into the ground by leaf miners and a nameless virus.

The upshot of all of this is that I have only the two species columbines in my garden, but no cultivars, though I sense the cultivars might not be impossible if close attention is paid to their soil, shade, and drainage requirements. My darker suspicion is that you might have to replace the plants every year or so to have success.

ARISAEMA ATRORUBENS (JACK-IN-THE-PULPIT) I just received a jack-in-the-pulpit plant this spring in a plant exchange and planted it in a shady spot. It's about a foot tall. Jack-in-the-pulpits are a bit unnerving to me—yes, they are beautiful, but they are also scary looking, like they eat chipmunks when your back is turned. This amazingly complex-looking plant is native here in rich, moist woodlands. I have read that it is an adaptable plant and can reach "prodigious proportions" in rich soil, perhaps not a sight I want to see. It flowers from April through June, and then a cluster of scarlet berries forms. A friend of mine has a colony of these in fairly dry soil, and the plants are quite small.

Green dragon (*A. dracontium*) is another arisaema native to this area. I have only seen pictures of it, but the flower, if you can call it that, and you probably can't, is long and elegant.

Having read that green dragon can tolerate somewhat dryer soil than jack-in-the-pulpit, and having seen the extensive colony of the latter in my friend's dry soil, these plants may be tolerant of soil of medium moisture.

ARTEMISIA SPP. I'm going to pause here and take a deep breath, because there's a lot to say about artemisias. With their often aromatic, silvery foliage, ease of cultivation, and drought resistance, artemisias have much to offer to the Midwestern gardener. The silver color of their foliage, with its undertone of icy green or pale blue, has a neutral, cooling quality that has a place in almost any garden color scheme. Frederick McGourty, in *The Perennial Gardener,* entitled his chapter on artemisias, "If in Doubt, Use Silver," and this gives some idea of their importance in garden design schemes. Artemisias flower but in most cases do so dully and inconspicuously—their beautiful foliage is their main attraction. 'Silver King' artemisia, *A. ludoviciana,* has already been discussed in chapter three.

Combining artemisias with other drought-resistant plants such as yarrows and sedums creates a section of garden that needs little watering. This self-sufficient section will look better and better to the gardener as the summer moves on.

Let's immediately rule out growing mugwort (*A. vulgaris*) in our gardens: I have found out the hard way that this plant is so invasive, it's scary. It's a pungent-smelling herb with a long history as a medicinal plant and in the practice of magic, but, however interesting, I remain content to see it in other herb gardens than my own. At least I don't *think* I have it in my garden any more, but you never know.

One nice artemisia is *A. lactiflora,* called white mugwort or, sometimes, ghost plant. This has been called the aristocrat of the artemisia family and is the only artemisia grown for its flowers. It grows from four to six feet in height and has plumes of little white flowers and dark green foliage. The undersides of the leaves are silvery. This artemisia is unique in that it needs soil more moist than other artemisias and that it can tolerate a bit of shade.

A. schmidtiana, or silver mound (also called angel's hair), is one of the most commonly grown artemisias in our area. Forming a decorative little tuffet or "bun," about a foot tall and a foot wide, silver mound looks good edging a border or snuggling up with other plants, flattering them with its finely divided, silvery blue foliage. Silver mound grows best in poor, dry soil and must have total sun. If grown in rich soil, it can get floppy. Silver mound is another one of those plants that's so common that we forget it needs care to look its best. By midsummer, it has flowered and may look unkempt. Steady your nerves and shear it back by half. It will look stunned, but it recovers and is back to a pretty mound shape in a couple of weeks. Silver mound is sometimes suggested as a ground cover, but this can be expensive, as it doesn't spread or reseed. Remember, though, when thinking of using it as a ground cover, that silver mound needs sun, sun, sun, and great drainage.

A. absinthum, or common wormwood, is another venerable plant long grown in herb gardens. The variety 'Lambrook Silver' is the one to grow. At about three feet in height, its foliage creates a feathery cloud of silvery white. The White Flower Farm catalog lauds 'Lambrook Silver' as "one of the finest and most easily grown foliage plants for the border."

A. 'Powis Castle' is the fashionable artemisia of the moment. Growing to about 30 inches in height, it forms a dense, very silvery-looking mound and has attractive, finely cut foliage. 'Powis Castle' lived for two years in my garden and then vanished, the victim of pretty good, but not wonderful, drainage.

Another nice artemisia is *A. stelleriana* 'Silver Brocade,' a variety of dusty miller. This low-growing silver plant has leaves divided into softly rounded and curved lobes. The patterning of the leaves really does remind me of baroque brocade fabric—beautiful *A. stelleriana* is very drought resistant.

Let's not forget *A. pontica*, or Roman wormwood (also called old warrior). This is like a miniature artemisia, as it's very low growing and has soft, feathery foliage. Be aware that as pretty as this little plant is, in good soil it can be invasive. I have it on a leash and collar in a border with so-so soil, where I admire it greatly, but that's about as far as it's going in my garden. It can be used as an edging like silver mound, but it's foliage is more feathery and is more light blue-green than silver. I actually like Roman wormwood better than silver mound, as it has a more relaxed, feathery feel, but because of its invasive tendencies, I can't recommend it without qualification.

A. annua is the so-called sweet Annie of herb garden fame and is actually a self-seeding annual. It's a tall, fragrant artemisia used to make herbal wreaths and is sometimes called sweet mugwort. It's another strong growing plant, one that I have growing behind our back fence, along with tansy and heliopsis. The three duke it out, and so far, it's a draw. Warning: it's an aggressive self-seeder. I've seen it growing in gravel and between the cracks in sidewalks.

A. abrotanum (southernwood) is another herbal artemisia that has been grown in cottage gardens for ages. It has greener, juicier-looking foliage than other artemisias and forms a clump about 30 inches tall. Its leaves are soft and finely divided. Its fragrance, which is often praised, smells like Lysol to me. So while some herbalists recommend tossing southernwood leaves in your salad, I wouldn't dream of serving such a thing, at least not to my friends.

An unnamed artemisia, received as an Internet trade, with the chartreuse-leafed *Agastache foeniculum* 'Aurea'.

This is definitely a subjective perception, though, because many gardeners think it smells lemony. I have heard of an interesting use for this plant. Bunches of leaves and branches can be simmered in water, and the liquid can be strained off and used to rinse or bathe cats and dogs. Apparently, it's a natural flea repellent. I have to ask a reader to try this, though, as my cat would kill me if I tried it. There is a tangerine southernwood also available. It's considerably taller and more columnar in shape than plain southernwood, and this time, I agree with other gardeners that it does smell somewhat like tangerines. Both the plain and the tangerine southernwoods lasted in my garden for about four years and then disappeared, again, drainage victims.

Some of the larger southernwoods can get woody quickly and need to be cut back hard every fall. One last use for southernwood is to plant it around rose bushes as a natural insect repellant. The pretty, soft green foliage of southernwood combines naturally with roses.

One last artemisia to mention (honest!) is the herb tarragon. This is the culinary artemisia and, to my mind, the greatest artemisia of all. It grows perfectly here in the Midwest but is not at all ornamental and should skulk in an inconspicuous spot in the workaday vegetable patch. Culinary tarragon must be purchased as a plant. Any so-called tarragon "seeds" you come across are actually from Russian tarragon, a variety that has no flavor, and why it is offered anywhere, I don't know.

Dwarf goatsbeard (*Aruncus aethusifolius*).

I mention these many species and varieties of artemisia because it represents an interesting mother lode of plants for the Midwestern gardener with her or his drought-prone garden to investigate and experiment with. Artemisias originated in the American prairies, the Siberian steppes, the mountains of Japan, and the deserts of Turkestan. What this means to us as gardeners is that they don't like or need rich soil and can withstand drought. A sunny spot in dry, well-drained soil suits them just fine.

Artemisias can be rooted in water and then planted. Just let the slip develop some roots and then plant. Don't let the roots become too long and tangled, as they are easily injured in potting.

Whew—finally time to leave the artemisias.

ARUNCUS DIOICUS (GOATSBEARD) Attention, attention: this is a large plant. For a shady border, this wonderful North American native grows up to six feet tall and at least three, sometimes four, feet around. If you can imagine a cream-colored astilbe the size of a large shrub, that's aruncus. It flowers in mid-June and (usually) does not require staking. It likes light shade and is not fussy about soil.

The word "dioicus" in its name refers to the fact that an aruncus plant is either male or female. Some sources state that the male is the more attractive of the two, but others say the seedpods of the female are prettier. I don't think I'd worry about this too much, one way or the other. Anyway, this may be a moot point, as the plants are seldom identified by sex at plant nurseries.

I've just purchased a dwarf aruncus named *A. aethusifolius*. My sister-in-law grows it in her garden and raves about it. Under a foot in height, it grows into a plump mound and is covered with feathery flowers in midsummer.

ASARUM CANADENSE (WILD GINGER) A truly choice, hardy, wonderful ground cover, and a merciful change from the usual pachysandra, wild ginger is amazingly easy to grow. It grows wild in Midwestern woodlands in spots where the soil is moist in the springtime. The heart-shaped leaves are smooth textured, and the crushed root smells like ginger. While it likes rich, moist soil, it easily tolerates drier conditions. Wild ginger sports truly bizarre flowers that look like something from a Dr. Seuss book and that hide beneath the petals in April and May. Another good variety, *A. europeum*, European wild ginger, has glossy foliage but tends to be more difficult to find at local nurseries. I find it grows much more slowly than *A. canadense*. There are other gingers—the Heronswood Nursery mail order catalog offers 14 gingers, and it would be fascinating to try all of them, though I suspect not all are hardy here. At any rate, if you're stuck in the pachysandra rut, wild ginger will blast you out.

ASCLEPIAS TUBEROSA (BUTTERFLY WEED) Butterfly weed is a sun-loving, native American plant that grows to about two feet in height. This is a plant of meadows and woodland margins. The flowers are orange, but wait, before you move on, it's a wonderful orange, being clear, clean, and almost translucent. Some oranges, as in orange zinnias, can be rather muddy, but butterfly weed orange is the orange found in a rainbow. By the end of the summer, its elegant, spindle-shaped pods are packed with seeds attached to their silken parachutes, all ready to venture out on the wind.

The only slight worry concerning butterfly weed plants is that they are slow to come up in spring, and it's easy to forget they are there. This is an often repeated garden caution, and it's absolutely true. The plant seems to wait until it's sure you've forgotten about it before emerging. Definitely keep its spot identified with a marker. And butterfly weed can't tolerate damp, rich, heavily mulched soils, where it will languish and rot. This spring I planted a butterfly weed cultivar in such soil (What was I thinking of? Not much, apparently), and it simply melted away with a sigh.

Monarch butterflies eat only plants from the milkweed family (Asclepidacae), of which butterfly weed is a member. They use the flat flower heads as landing pads and drink the flower nectar. Toxic substances in the milkweeds accumulate in the body of the butterfly, rendering it poisonous to predators. So if you want to attract monarch butterflies, be sure to include butterfly weed and its relations in your garden. For more on this, check out a wonderful Web site, www.monarchwatch.com, which tells all about monarchs and the milkweed family.

There are other less-famous members of the milkweed family that are worth growing as well. Cherry red–flowered *A. incarnata*, swamp milkweed, can tolerate moister soil than butterfly weed. It doesn't *demand* moist soil, though, and does well in ordinary garden soil. At three feet tall, it's taller and more graceful than butterfly weed. Any plant with both "swamp" and "weed" in its name has a bit of an uphill battle when it comes to acceptance by gardeners, but this really is an elegant, gardenworthy plant, and I've found that it's just as attractive to monarch butterflies as *A. tuberosa*. Like all the milkweeds, spindle-shaped seedpods form after flowering. One drawback: it's a self-seeder, and you might want to gather the pods before they open and discard them, to forestall the problem.

An exotic member of the wild ginger family, Chinese wild ginger (*Asarum splendens*) peeks up through autumn leaves. This clump persists on sloping ground, indicating that it likes water passing over its roots, but does not like sitting in damp soil.

The bursting seed heads of swamp milkweed (*Asclepias incarnata*). Be sure to remove them if you don't want self-seeding.

51

Whorled milkweed (*A. verticillata*) has feathery leaves and delicate white flowers. Its diminutive seedpods are exquisite. Whorled milkweed spreads, not horribly or perniciously, but it definitely spreads.

The Prairie Moon Nursery catalog offers *A. viridiflora,* the short, green milkweed, which has been described by Dick Young, in *Kane County Wild Plants and Natural Areas,* as "a treasure that should be perpetuated." I am also tempted by an offering in the *Prairie Moon Nursery* catalog for *A. tuberosa* "for clay." Regular butterfly weed likes well-drained soil, so a clay-loving variety would be interesting to try.

One summer in my garden, a white-flowered *A. incarnata,* 'Ice Ballet', got bright orange aphids on its stems. No other plant in the garden was affected. I washed the aphids off with water, and the plant was fine, but it left me wondering, "What was all *that* about?" The bugs did not return the following summer. The species *A. incarnata,* though, has never been touched by bugs or disease.

Don't be tempted to plant butterfly weed's close wild relation, *A. syriaca,* or common milkweed. There's plenty of it growing out on the prairie to look at, and it's invasive with a capital "I" in the home garden.

Wild asters blooming on an early October prairie.

ASTER SPP. Asters are hardy, sun-loving, fall-blooming plants (from late August on), and it's been noted that they are becoming increasingly used as substitutes for fall chrysanthemums, which are not always winter hardy. Spring is the best time to plant asters.

A good wild aster for the casual garden is the New England aster, *A. novae-angliae*. At five feet in height, it has rich purple flowers with golden centers. A rough-and-ready plant fine for ordinary garden soil, it's best in full sun. This aster and goldenrod, of course, are the classic fall combination. There is an attractive red variety of the New England aster called 'Septemberrubin' that's worth investigating. A dwarf variety of the New England aster is *A.* 'Purple Dome'. This long-blooming plant is smothered in flowers from August through October.

There are so many interesting wild asters available (there are at least two hundred species in North America) that I tremble at the thought of enumerating them. Some wild asters can be rather tall, undistinguished plants with weedy looking flowers. Some gardenworthy species, however, are *A. oblongifolius* (aromatic aster, two feet tall, violet flowers), *A. laevis* (smooth aster, two feet tall, blue flowers), and *A. ptarmicoides* (upland white aster, 18 inches tall, white flowers). *A. divaricatus* (wood aster, one to two feet tall, white flowers) and *A. macrophyllus* (big-leafed aster, two feet tall, white flowers) are both gems that tolerate dry shade. So there's an aster for everyone!

Plant scientists have been busy, too, and new aster varieties seem to come on the market every year. Cultivated asters, often low growing and domed in habit, come in lovely shades of purple, blue, and rose, as well as white. I'm growing 'Professor Anton Kippenburg' and can testify that its intense blue flowers are really stunning.

ASTILBE SPP. Astilbes are often highly recommended in gardening magazines and books as "easy," long-blooming perennials for the shade garden, but I think they need careful soil preparation and siting to succeed in the Midwestern garden. In the wild, astilbes grow by moist ravines and by streams in slightly acidic soil that borders on being boggy. Heavy, dry, cold clay soil doesn't hold enough moisture to make astilbes happy. So it's a good plant, but it's more picky to grow than other plants on this list. Thoroughly turn over the soil where it's to be planted, and carefully remove any stones or roots. Then, dig plenty of moist, leafy compost and peat deeply into the soil. Water well and mulch. Also, the ideal site for astilbes is in dappled shade, not deep dark shade.

You might want to start with *A. chinensis* 'Pumila', which is somewhat tolerant of dry soils, or *A. taquetti* 'Superba', which is fairly tolerant of heat and drought, but even these varieties don't like dryness.

Star astilbe, (*A.* 'Dunkellachs'), is only 14 inches in height with dark pink flowers and has been increasing in popularity. Another star astilbe is 'Sprite', with bronze leaves and pink flowers. Both make good ground covers, but I would perfect my astilbe-growing technique before investing in a bunch of them.

The following astilbes have been rated by local experts as especially suited for Midwestern gardens: 'Bridal Veil' (snow white), 'Cattleya' (rose pink), 'Pumila' (light magenta), 'Deutschland' (creamy white), 'Europa' (pale pink), 'Fanal' (ruby red), 'Feuer' (red), 'Straussenfeder' (pink), 'Peach Blossom' (rosy pink), 'Rheinland' (soft pink), 'Superba' (magenta purple), and 'Weisse Gloria' (white).

An unusually beautiful (and tall—it's three feet in height) astilbe is *A.* 'Straussenfeder', which has fine, filigree-like pink tendrils that arch decoratively in the air.

Astilbes should be divided every three to four years to keep them vigorous. Divide in early spring or in late July to mid-August, allowing three or four "eyes" per division.

Astilbe advice: If you've never grown an astilbe before, buy one and try it before investing a lot of money in a whole bunch. I know a number of good gardeners who have problems with astilbes, finding that they get a bit brown and crispy by late summer.

BAPTISIA AUSTRALIS (BLUE WILD INDIGO, RATTLE-BUSH) Here is an easy-to-grow member of the pea family that I predict will become more and more popular with Midwestern gardeners as time goes on and word of the beauty of this plant spreads. Even its name—blue wild indigo—is as beautiful as a poem. Growing to about two to four feet, depending on soil moisture and richness, the plant has tall spikes of blue-purple and lavender pea blossoms (resembling lupine flowers) in late May and early June. Its leaves somewhat resemble those of clover. The blossoms of this North American native attract butterflies. Ornamental black seedpods develop after flowering. It goes well with ornamental grasses, other prairie flowers, and common perennials such as Siberian irises and peonies.

Being completely cold hardy, drought resistant, tolerant of either sun or a touch of dappled shade, and requiring (usually) no staking, baptisia is as close

to a carefree plant as Midwestern gardeners will find in our solar system. If it had its druthers, it would like to be planted in soil on the moist side, so dig in plenty of humus such as leaf mold when initially planting. It will tolerate dry soil, though. And as a member of the pea family it "fixes" its own nitrogen from the atmosphere and so needs no fertilizer from the gardener. Any perennial that fertilizes itself deserves to be high— *high*— on our list of desirable plants.

Site baptisia carefully, as it doesn't like disruption once it becomes established. As a matter of fact, I wouldn't divide or move baptisia ever, as its root system doesn't lend itself to division. The White Flower Farm catalog says, "They can hardly be pried out of the garden once established."

Baptisia grows very slowly at first, so buy the largest plant you can find at the nursery. Otherwise, if your plant is very small, you may forget you have it after a while. This happened to my sister-in-law. One day she showed me a mysterious plant that had popped up in the middle of a stand of monarda. What could it be? It was *Baptisia australis,* and since *B. australis* isn't the sort of plant that pops up just anywhere for the fun of it, we guessed that she had planted it at least three years before, forgotten about it, and then planted the faster growing monarda right on top. Now, slowly and stubbornly, the wild blue indigo was making its appearance.

B. LEUCANTHA (WHITE WILD INDIGO) This is a lovely prairie plant with all the good qualities of the above blue wild indigo but has white flowers tinged with purple and is taller (up to six feet in height). It blooms in May and June and needs sun and good drainage.

There is also a cream wild indigo, *B. leucophaea,* that is more low and mounding than the blue. I recently had the good fortune to see a cream wild indigo flowering in a remnant of prairie just a few miles from our house. It was startlingly beautiful, and I felt I was seeing something really rare and extraordinary, like a panda or a white tiger. This plant had actually disappeared from the wild in our county and had been reintroduced by a local conservation group. Flowering nearby were prairie shooting star (*Dodecatheon meadia*) and a lovely little plant named Seneca snakeroot (*Polygala senega*). It had neat, glossy leaves and little white spires of flowers. Seeing Seneca snakeroot brought home to me that gardeners have barely scratched the surface of what nature offers in the Midwest.

BELAMCANDA CHINENSIS (BLACKBERRY LILY) I'm planting blackberry lilies this summer and am greatly looking forward to their flowering next July. Received through the GardenWeb in exchange for some iris, they have amazing, squiggly, saffron yellow roots, and I have the feeling that you get with some plants that they will do well. Seedpods came along with the plants and look exactly like blackberries, which explains the plant's common name. Blackberry lilies are actually related to iris, though, not lilies. So I've put them in a sunny spot, crossed my fingers, and await next summer.

Next summer: They have bloomed, and they are simply beautiful. The flowers have the same beautiful, translucent orange color of butterfly weed, and the petals are freckled. With its clean, irislike foliage, this is a very nice plant.

BOLTONIA ASTEROIDES 'SNOWBANK' (WHITE BOLTONIA) As the species name suggests, boltonia is similar in appearance to asters and is in the aster family. And it flowers at about the same time, in the late summer and fall. So why not grow asters, you ask? I hate to be disloyal to asters, but *Boltonia* 'Snowbank' is a bit like a superior aster. It's less susceptible to mildew, has a more compact, rounded habit, has masses of flowers, and doesn't need staking. Now, come to think of it, why grow asters? Boltonia does need sun. There is a variety with pink flowers called 'Pink Beauty'.

BRUNNERA MACROPHYLLA (SIBERIAN BUGLOSS) In spring, brunnera swells the ranks of other blue-flowering perennials such as pulmonaria, forget-

The lovely, pure orange-colored flower of the blackberry lily (*Belamcanda chinensis*).

me-nots, Virginia bluebells, and polemonium. But you can't have too many pretty blue flowers this time of year, especially with all the tulips and daffodils in bloom. Brunnera can be thought of as a large (about 18 inches tall), perennial forget-me-not, but it has the added charm of pretty, rather leathery, heart-shaped leaves that stay in good condition during summer and is altogether a more substantial plant than the forget-me-not.

Brunnera likes shade and will tolerate average soil but appreciates it if you dig in some extra organic matter when planting. This is a tough plant, but be sure to water it during a prolonged drought. I came late to the charms of brunnera but now am won over. I think it gets lost in the shuffle with all the other charming, blue-flowered spring plants, but its durable, attractive foliage gives it the edge over some of its competitors.

BUDDLEJA (BUTTERFLY BUSH) Here is the pathetic sum total of my experience with a butterfly bush: For three years I have had the smallest butterfly bush that anyone has ever seen. It's a 'Black Knight', and while seemingly healthy, it is only two feet tall. I'd given it everything I could think of to make it happy when my sister pointed out that it needs sun, and lots of it. My tricky front yard, with its shifting light dapples of sun and shade, was just too shady for it.

So give it plenty of sun and good soil, and butterflies will come in droves. Our winters are a bit cold for it, and it will die back to the ground at winter's end. It takes its time coming up in the spring, so don't be quick to assume it's dead and yank it out. In England, butterfly bushes apparently don't die back in the winter and get much larger and bushier than they do here. Still, if yours is only two feet tall, you might consider moving it to a sunnier location.

CALAMINTHA OFFICINALIS (CALAMINT) Calamint is a "darkhorse" perennial on this list. Usually categorized as an herb, it functions as a decorative, drought- and disease-resistant perennial in my garden. Many gardeners are not aware of it as either herb or perennial. This *is* a modest plant, but it has charm. The common calamint plant, such that you might find at a well-stocked plant nursery, is less than a foot high and has small white flowers. One calamint plant is nothing to get excited about. A cluster of calamint, though, forms a soft little cloud of white flowers, looking almost like a little snow storm. It's pretty and adds a soft, misty touch to the garden. After flowering, calamint still looks pretty as a lacy little cloud of tan seedheads. Calamint has a minty scent, so I suppose you could use it for tea, but with so many other excellent herbs that can be used for tea, I wouldn't rush to use this one.

Calamint self-seeds to the point of being annoying, but I just take a shovel and turn over what I don't want.

C. *grandiflora* 'Variegata' is another fine calamint, with striped light green and cream leaves and violet flowers. I've had my plant for three years and, to my joy, it has self-seeded twice. No mildew, no bugs, just pretty.

Two other calamints bear investigating: C. *grandiflora* and C. *nepeta nepeta* are listed in the *White Flower Farm* catalog. "If we had world enough and time . . . "

CALLIRHOE INVOLUCRATA (WINECUPS) This low-growing member of the malva family has translucent, wine-colored flowers that bloom in June and July. Winecups need full sun and very good drainage, and the soil can be poor and dry. I suspect that good soil might even work against callirhoe. This is a tough but beautiful plant that deserves a home in more Midwestern gardens. It sprawls a bit and can be used to cover a sunny sloping area. Removing spent flowers will prolong bloom.

CAMPANULA SPP. (BELLFLOWER) It's hard to imagine a garden without at least one representative of the bellflower tribe, as it's a group that has something for everybody, including flowers famous in history and folklore. Both the blue bells of Scotland and Canterbury bells are campanulas, and the peachleaf bellflower grew in the gardens of Tudor England.

There is even a black-sheep, nefarious member of the campanula family named C. *rapunculoides*. This is a plant that would fester in a witch's garden in a fairy tale, and I am somewhat taken aback to find how much I like it. Some gardeners would rather eat poison than have this plant in their garden, but I feel that if you have a truly desolate spot where nothing else will grow and that isn't usually seen close-up, C. *rapunculoides* would probably be glad to help. It has pretty violet flowers and coarse-looking foliage. Another nice thing about this plant from the standpoint of money-saving is that you don't have to buy it—you probably already have it. One gardener has said, though, that if you let C. *rapunculoides* into your garden, you will never know peace again, so if in doubt, leave it out. Also, beware of this plant at neighborhood plant sales. I came across what was obviously a campanula at such a sale, which the seller called "purple flags." How pretty sounding, and it cost only a quarter, so I bought it. I actually had it planted and had sat down to read the newspaper when I suddenly realized it was *rapunculoides*. I jumped out of my seat as though goosed with hot pincers and ran outside and tore it out of the ground. So beware.

Variegated calamint (*Calamintha* 'Variegata').

The peachleaf bellflower (C. *persicifolia*) grows to about 24 to 42 inches in height and is almost unanimously acclaimed as one of the best of the bellflowers, both for it's beauty and robust growth. It comes in both white and pale amethyst blue, and both are pretty. After blooming, cut it back at least by half, and it will bloom again in a month, though it won't be as tall.

The blue bells of Scotland (also called harebells), C. *rotundifolia*, are commonly found growing wild in the upper Midwest, often along the roadside. It grows in gravel or sandy soils of dry or well-drained woods, slopes, and meadows. It's a delicate little plant with wispy leaves and fragile, violet bell flowers that bloom midsummer through to fall. In our climate, C. *rotundifolia* needs some shade during the day. I haven't personally grown this plant, but several Chicago-area gardeners have specially recommended it to me as one of their favorites.

A low-growing, purple-flowered bellflower often pops up at plant sales and exchanges, and I believe it is the Serbian bellflower (C. *poscharskyana*). It's quite pretty in bloom, in mid-June, but becomes rather seedy-looking by the time July comes along, and it's tedious to deadhead. If you have a large garden where it can sink back into anonymity after blooming, give it a try, but if you have a small garden where every plant must look its best at all times, pass it by.

Campanula 'Kent Belle' has been highly recommended to me by my sister-in-law. About two feet in height, it has rather large, cobalt blue bell-like flowers. Its main flowering is in early summer, but it then goes on to flower quite heavily on and off for the rest of the summer.

Campanula glomerata, the clustered bellflower, sends up bouquets of deep purple flowers atop erect stems. This is a tough plant, reputed to be somewhat invasive in the shade, and since I got my plant at a local garden club's plant sale, this is probably true.

Among the natives, C. *americana* has pale, purple-blue flowers on a tall stalk. It doesn't have as many flowers per stalk as the garden varieties but is still very pretty and delicate, with the nice fairy-tale quality you find in many campanulas. It also blooms for a long time—July through October. I've seen it growing in the wild in moist spots with grasses. Books say it's three feet tall, but the plants I've seen are closer to five feet. It's ultimate height may depend on soil moisture.

At a plant exchange this spring, I was *very* surprised to see pots of C. *lactiflora* 'Prichard's Variety' amid the many pots of ribbon grass and chives and immediately pounced on a pot and scuttled away with it, along with a yellow aster and a clump of purple Siberian iris. This campanula variety apparently has amethyst blue flowers on three-foot stems, and I am looking forward to it blooming this summer. At another sale, I came across C. *takesimana* 'Elizabeth' and pounced on it, as well. This should reach two feet and has rather large, dusky rose bells. Thompson & Morgan sells seeds for the species C. *takesimana,* which was discovered in Korea. T & M refers to it as "a cracking good border plant." I've always wanted a cracking good border plant and am happy to have 'Elizabeth'.

The word I would use to describe the cultivation of campanulas is "average." They need average soil, average water, and don't like blasting-hot sun but can't deal with deep shade, either.

Campanulas are quite tough plants and definitely have a role in the Midwest garden. Is there a campanula downside? As the end of the blooming period approaches, blooming flowers, brown drooping petals, and seedpods may all be on the plant at the same time, and the gardener must make a judgment call as to when to cut back.

CASSIA HEBECARPA (WILD SENNA; SOMETIMES CALLED SENNA HEBE-CARPA) I first heard about wild senna, a member of the bean family, in *Low Maintenance Perennials,* by Robert S. Hebb. He described the plant as being about three to five feet in height (depending on soil richness and moisture), with clusters of yellow flowers with black anthers appearing July through September. Hebb noted that "some large border plants have a coarse appearance, but Wild Senna is extremely fine-textured and the compound leaves remain in attractive condition throughout the season. If the plant did not bloom at all, it still would be valuable on this account." He went on to mention that it's completely drought resistant, can grow for years without division, has no insect or disease problems, and never has to be staked. So last year I went out and got a wild senna plant, and I wish I had planted it sooner. The foliage is very clean, the plant perfectly upright, and my dry, clay soil is not fazing it even a little bit. The foliage has the lacy look of honey locust tree leaves, and the plant has the presence of a shrub.

There has to be *something* wrong with this plant, though so far I haven't found out what it is. A possible problem is that in moist soil, it may reach seven or eight feet in height and then topple.

I've seen wild senna planted with other wildings such as black-eyed Susans, Queen Anne's lace, yarrows, bee balms, purple coneflowers, and ornamental grasses. Once established, you wouldn't have to water this crew at all, unless faced with horrendous drought conditions. Cassia is an up-and-coming Midwestern native, soon to be much more well known than it is now.

This spring, delighted with the wild senna, I decided to try another member of the bean family, milkvetch (*Astragalus canadensis*). This is a more delicate plant than wild senna and is much floppier. As it sagged over, I felt a bit disappointed until I suddenly realized that in the wild it floats among grasses and doesn't need to stand up on its own. Just yesterday I came across a picture of it nestling with little bluestem (*Andropogon scoparius*). So now I must mull over what to plant for its support next year. I'm also curious about a group of western milkvetches mentioned in *The New England Wild Flower Society Guide to Growing and Propagating Wildflowers of the United States and Canada,* by William Cullina. They apparently are beautiful plants, as well as being extremely drought resistant and adaptable. These are much lower-growing plants than A. *canadensis,* all under a foot tall.

CENTAUREA SPP. (PERENNIAL CORNFLOWERS) I have gradually gotten less and less enthusiastic about the genus *Centaurea,* though it includes some classic cottage garden plants that are commonly grown here in the Midwest. I started out liking the perennial cornflower, C. *montana,* which does have pretty blue flowers, but my liking has slowly but surely run downhill. Perennial cornflower needs space to spread out, and the flowers, while a pretty blue, are rather wispy, and the entire plant becomes ratty looking as summer wears on. The fact that it perks up in cool fall weather tells me it's not a hot weather plant. Add to this the fact that it needs frequent division and occasionally gets little black worms, and my enthusiasm has dwindled away almost to nothing.

I did recently see *C. montana* grown with a clump of *Zizia aurea*, a delicate, yellow-flowered prairie perennial. The indigo blue and light yellow flowers made a nice combination, I must admit.

I've grown two other perennial centaureas—*C. macrocephala* (globe centaurea) and *C. dealbata* (Persian centaurea). Without fail, both plants gear up to bloom and then are knocked over by storms—every summer. The globe centaurea was banished from the garden, and the Persian centaurea is hanging on by its toenails behind the back fence. Are these good plants? Don't know.

CENTRANTHUS RUBER (JUPITER'S BEARD, RED VALERIAN) This is one of the most old-fashioned of the old-fashioned plants, having grown in cottage gardens and monasteries for centuries. It needs sun, average, but good-draining, soil, and is about three feet in height, though mine is rather floppy

Wild senna *(Cassia hebecarpa)* blooms in late August.

and settles down to about two. As well as having an interesting history, centranthus's other claim to fame is that it has a long blooming period, the rosy flowers appearing from June through autumn. If it starts looking bedraggled, cut it way back—it will bloom again. In the wild, centranthus grows on limestone cliffs, and this is a clue to the gardener that it can benefit from having some lime dug in the soil when planting.

Centranthus is one of those perennials that I've heard may vanish after one or two years. I think our drainage is not quite up to snuff for it. On the other hand, I've been waiting for my plant to vanish for eight years now, and so far it's still here. But it *could* vanish. I love its unusual, warm, pinky red flower, healthy foliage, and old-fashioned charm. I once saw a photo of centranthus grown along with some misty blue catmint. It made a pretty picture and would be easy to grow in a Midwestern garden. I also have a white centranthus, which has lovely lacy white flowers. I hope it, too, doesn't vanish. All in all, centranthus is a winner and deserves to be in more gardens.

CERASTIUM TOMENTOSUM (SNOW-IN-SUMMER) This low-growing plant with silvery leaves and snow white flowers is good for growing on sunny, sloping areas with poor soil. It blooms in late spring and has invasive ten-

The seedpods of wild senna *(Cassia hebecarpa)*.

dencies. To be honest, I tore out the cerastium I had and replaced it with *Gypsophila repens*, which has a cooler, less seedy and blasted look than cerastium once it has finished blooming. However, the White Flower Farm catalog offers a species named *C. biebersteinii* that apparently is an improvement. It's possible I just caught cerastium on a bad day—actually, many bad days—and may give the *C. biebersteinii* a try one of these decades.

CHELONE (TURTLEHEAD) A North American native, chelone is a wild-flower member of the snapdragon family that has found a place in home gardens. Growing to about three feet in height, its tubular flowers resemble turtle heads. The word "chelone" (ke-LOH-nee) is from the Greek for "turtle" or "tortoise."

Of *Chelone glabra*, Dick Young, author of *Kane County Wild Plants and Natural Areas*, says, "This is a perennial of classic elegance with its smooth, neat foliage and clean, white, turtlehead blossoms peeking out of a late August and September fen."

C. lyonii, or pink turtlehead, is sometimes thought to be the most desirable of the chelones for the garden because of its lustrous foliage, neat habit, and tolerance of dryer soils, though in light of Young's opinion of *C. glabra*,

Chelone lyonii 'Hot Lips', a fall bloomer for shade.

this may be debatable. I recently saw a cultivar named 'Hot Lips'. Its rose-pink flowers will appear later in the fall, but I was impressed by its clean, dark, glossy foliage, attractive even without bloom. It was about 18 inches tall and two feet across and almost looked like a little shrub.

C. obliqua has rose-purple flowers, is heat tolerant, and is the longest-blooming chelone. Claims are made that *this* is the most ornamental of the chelones, and I guess we gardeners will have to leave the horticulturists to squabble and make our own decisions as to which is the prettiest.

That chelones are naturally found in fens (marshy areas) tells us that they like moist soil. I have seen chelone in bloom at a local fen. Its elegant, cream-colored flowers were standouts among the orange jewel weed and the lacy green umbels of cow parsnip. All three stood knee-deep in squishy soil. But it's an adaptable plant, and if you have a spot of moist, average soil with light shade, it will prosper. It is not a plant for dry shade. Chelone blooms from late July through September and partners well with hostas, asters, phlox, and goldenrods.

One last bit of turtlehead lore. According to Sylvan T. Runkel in *Wildflowers of Illinois Woodlands*, "When a bumblebee enters the flower and disappears inside after nectar, his movements and the resulting vibration of the flower give the appearance that the bee is being chewed up by the turtle-head blossom." Be sure to tell any little boys you know about this—they'll be right over.

CHRYSANTHEMUM × MORIFOLIUM (GARDEN CHRYSANTHEMUM)

The chrysanthemum is the emblematic flower of autumn, and come September, pots of it grace gardens everywhere. Its rich hues of gold, purple, and russet blend warmly with the falling leaves. By late October, the perennial questions arises: can my pot of chrysanthemums be planted in the garden, to come up next year? The short answer is "no." Fall chrysanthemums have been bred for floriferousness, not winter hardiness. They have come from protected greenhouse conditions to sit on your front porch, where they have endured heat, wind, cold, and drought. By the time you are wondering if they can go into the garden, they have just about had it. A friend of mine did mention in August that she had just planted some chrysanthemums in the ground and said that in her experience they would return next year. So perhaps early planting is a key to wintering over.

But to have perennial chrysanthemums flourish in the garden, buy small chrysanthemum plants in the spring. They often are available in jumbo six-packs. Plant them in sun and average soil, enjoy the flowers, and then cut back and water. By fall, they will put on another lovely floral display and will bloom every fall thereafter. I have lemon-yellow chrysanthemums, originally retrieved (with permission) from a discount nursery's dumpster, and a purple variety purchased in wretched condition in the first week of May for 97 cents. These plants have been indestructible and bloom in almost three-foot mounds every fall.

I have another perennial chrysanthemum, C. rubellum 'Clara Curtis'. Pink, single-petaled flowers, almost like daisies in appearance, bloom in September and October. My one reservation about Clara is that it seems vigorous almost to the point of being invasive. It's not an uncontrollable thug, though, and is fine for the casual cottage garden. Two other cultivars are 'Hillside Pink Sheffield', which is apricot-pink in color, and 'Mary Stoker', which is a pale apricot.

As noted in The Complete Garden Flower Book, "Chrysanthemums have been renamed and moved to the genus Dendranthma, though the name has yet to catch on."

CIMICIFUGA (SNAKEROOT) Some flowers are cheerful, and some are perky, but cimicifuga in bloom is purity and elegance personified. If you can imagine a white, six-foot-tall bottle-brush arising from fernlike foliage, you are close to imagining what cimicifuga looks like. It works well in the back of a shady border and is notable in that it doesn't require staking. When planting, take the time to work in plenty of humus and leaf mold. While cimicifuga is always called a shade plant, it does best in light or dappled shade, not deep, dark, dank shade.

In fall, the plant goes to seed, and the seed head is ornamental. The long stems should be cut down before winter, though, as they will break and topple over in cold and wind.

Cimicifuga is a really beautiful plant—its spires almost remind me of choir music rising up into the air in a cathedral.

COREOPSIS (TICKSEED) Coreopsis is a deservedly popular staple in many Midwestern gardens. Drought resistant, heavy flowering, and fresh and perky even in severe heat, coreopsis is an easy-to-grow winner of a plant. Some cultivated varieties are fairly low in height, growing only up to about two feet or less. The daisylike flowers are usually butter yellow, some having double petals, and some streaked with red. Coreopsis needs a full day of sun, so don't try to finesse it in where it would get dappled shade—it won't like it. It does fine in

A thriving, spring-planted chrysanthemum.

average, light-textured soil. I have C. 'Sunray', and in my rather heavy clay soil it tends to flop over.

Most varieties begin blooming in June. Deadheading coreopsis will keep it blooming for much of the summer, but you will need patience for this. At a certain point, it's best to just shear the whole plant back by two-thirds and water it so it can bloom again. If you don't have patience for deadheading coreopsis at all, try the verticillata varieties such as 'Moonbeam' or 'Zagreb'—they bloom steadily from late June on and look good without deadheading.

'Moonbeam', a variety of thread-leaf coreopsis, is my favorite coreopsis. Its pale yellow flowers work well in many color schemes. C. verticillata 'Zagreb' is another attractive thread-leaf coreopsis variety, and I would probably be growing it right now if I hadn't seen 'Moonbeam' first. Its flowers are a bit of a more ordinary shade of golden yellow than the creamy, buttery yellow of 'Moonbeam'. In Perennials: How to Select, Grow and Enjoy, by Pamela Harper and Frederick McGourty, the C. verticillata group is not only praised as a good variety of coreopsis, but is lauded as some of the best all-around perennials, period.

59

Bugbane
*(Cimicifuga
racemosa)* lights
up the shade
in August.

You might come across another verticillata coreopsis, C. *rosea*, at a nursery—this is similar in appearance to 'Moonbeam', but the flowers are pink with yellow disks. The similarity is a bit deceptive, since C. *rosea* needs more moisture than C. *verticillata*. Be sure to dig in plenty of moisture-retentive organic matter when planting it. I've heard a number of gardeners expressing disappointment with C. *rosea*, but I think if you give it moist soil, it's fine. I've even read that C. *rosea* can be invasive, and it may be one of those plants that could "take off" if it found conditions to its liking. In my dryish soil, however, it took one look around, packed its bags, and left.

There's a dwarf coreopsis—C. 'Nana'—that I haven't grown but have only heard the highest praise for from all quarters. It's about six inches tall, is mat forming, and has gold-orange flowers.

The species coreopsis is C. *lanceolata*, known as tickseed or sand coreopsis. Tall coreopsis (C. *tripteris*) and stiff coreopsis (C. *palmata*) can, in dwindling numbers, be found in prairie remnants in the Midwest. Sadly, C. *lanceolata* might be extinct in the Midwest wilds. Dick Young, in *Kane County Wild Plants and Natural Areas*, describes C. *palmata* as "a warm and appealing plant nestling in prairie grasses," and C. *lanceolata* as "a beautiful perennial." C. *tripteris* is worth investigating if you're up for a tall (up to six feet), back-of-the-border plant. Young describes it as "an aristocratic plant with a mellow, waxy sheen and graceful flowering heads."

Coreopsis seems to have the plant equivalent of a fast metabolism, and depending on the soil it's grown in, may need dividing at least every two or three years. If left crowded, the base of the plant can rot.

CORYDALIS LUTEA (CRESTED LARK, YELLOW FUMITORY) *Corydalis* is a genus that's starting to become better known and appreciated in the Midwest. A mounding, shade-loving little plant of about a foot in height, it has fernlike foliage, and its small, snapdragon-like tubular yellow flowers bloom from late May through September: this is a *long*, long-blooming plant that also tends to self-seed. Corydalis is related to bleeding hearts (*Dicentra*), and there is a resemblance in the leaves and flowers, especially between it and the fringed dicentra, *Dicentra eximia*. There are at least six wild varieties of corydalis native to Illinois, so this gives us Midwestern gardeners a clue that the garden variety, C. *lutea*, will work for us. Corydalis does well in shade but not dry shade with poor soil. Dig in some compost or leaf mold when planting to help the soil retain moisture.

There are two blue-flowered varieties, one named C. *flexulosa* 'Blue

Panda', the other *C. flexulosa* 'China Blue'. I'm most familiar with 'China Blue', which is a beautiful, beautiful plant. Note that only one "beautiful" doesn't adequately describe it! Not only are the flowers a translucent, delphinium blue, but the foliage has a blue cast, making the entire plant exceptionally attractive. Like *C. lutea*, 'Blue Panda' blooms most of the summer. I must mention that lately I have heard murmurs of discontent with the blue-flowered corydalis—that they are short lived and finicky. So proceed with caution.

Several years ago, I received a damp, newspaper-wrapped plant in the mail as part of a plant trade at Gardenweb.com. It was labeled *C. heterocarpa*. I found no reference to it in any of my perennial encyclopedias, and after an exhaustive search on the Internet, the only mention I found was in a garden forum, where gardeners were excitedly gossiping about what a great plant it is. The gossip was that it looked like a big, yellow-flowering bleeding heart and thrives during heat and humidity. As it grew in my garden, *Corydalis heterocarpa* looked nothing whatsoever like a big, yellow-flowering bleeding heart, but it did resemble a very big version of *C. lutea*. This is fine with me, as it is a handsome plant, with the typical tubular yellow corydalis flowers borne aloft like flags. Each flower was prettily shaded at the petal base with pale green.

But later that autumn, the plant simply dropped dead. Dead as a doornail. The only conclusion I can draw from this sad state of affairs is that it does not like dry shade, though whether it was the dryness or the shade that particularly bothered it, I don't know. I had enriched the soil, but perhaps the two-month drought that summer was too much for it. I know it was too much for me. I took another look on the Internet and this time found several more references to it. It was on a "List of Flora of a Subtropical Forest in the Islands off the South-east Seashore of Korean Peninsula." Oh. At another Web site it was referred to as "False Bleeding Heart" and was mentioned as part of a rhododendron garden. This clue tells me that *C. heterocarpa* may need acid soil. Someday, I'll try again.

Please see the section on shade later in the book for information about another corydalis: *Corydalis cheilanthifolia*, a corydalis that thrives in dry shade.

DELPHINIUM No, delphiniums are not impossible to grow in the Midwest, and yes, I have seen them in local gardens. But as plants that like brief summers with cool evenings, delphiniums face tough going here. The best approach seems to be to grow them as annuals, and I know of one local gardener who does this successfully every year. They are pretty easy to start from seed in early spring and then can be planted out with the first warm

weather. Then, you must genuflect before them and kiss their leaves. And they need staking. Apparently an inconspicuous truss made by hammering three pieces of one-by-two-inch lumber, each five feet tall, with the help of several muscular gardening assistants, does the trick. And they need protection from the wind. And protection from slugs and snails. And don't get any moisture on their leaves, and keep their soil moist at all times, but *not soggy*. And don't forget the fungicide and insecticide applied at ten-day intervals. Mulch well. Look out for cyclamen mites. And what they really like is a foundation bed along an east-facing wall where they get morning sun only, but they don't like the shade of large trees (pout, pout). Be sure to dig out the subsoil to a depth of two feet and backfill with humus plus the well-rotted manure of Jersey cows (*not Holsteins!* What were you thinking of?). Dust with sulfur, and don't forget the wood ashes. They are not adverse to having their ears tickled, and their favorite bedtime story is "Miss Rumphius."

So I grow larkspur. I also *thought* I was growing D. 'Blue Butterflies', a tough, miniature delphinium, but I just went out to take a look at it and could see no sign of the plant. Perhaps it has "bloomed itself out" as the experts say. Like I say, I grow larkspur.

DIANTHUS CARYOPHYLLUS (CLOVE PINK); D. BARBATUS (SWEET WILLIAM) The first perennial I ever grew from seed was *Dianthus* 'Clove Pink', and it remains a sentimental favorite. The flowers have an intensely sweet yet spicy aroma that floats through the garden on a warm June day. Mesmerized, I sometimes follow the fragrance to its source and inhale. It could make your head spin.

The clove-scented pinks represent a direct link with the flowers of the oldest English gardens, whether it be the nineteenth-century cottage gardens, the Tudor gardens of the sixteenth-century, or even farther back, to the medieval castle gardens of the fourteenth-century. Someday I hope to track down a source for 'Fenbow's Nutmeg Clove', dating from the fourteenth-century, and reputedly one of the oldest garden plants still in cultivation.

Before I grew a pink, I was under the impression that they might not grow well in our clay soil, as they are said to like light, sandy, sweet soil and good drainage, and in general this is true. Many of the flats of annual dianthus sold at garden centers every spring are destined to decline and die in our heavy soil. Perennial pinks such as *D. deltoides* and *gratianopolitanus* face an uphill battle here, as well. Clove pinks do well, though, as long as you grow them on mounded soil or in raised beds. Pinks form low mats of grassy,

The ferny-looking *Corydalis lutea* will bloom on and off all summer if there is rain.

blue-tinted foliage and bloom in early summer. My clove pinks lasted for years before an unusually wet spring caused rot in some of the mat of leaves and stems. I have since read that these plants should be lifted and divided every three or four years.

It's also possible to take a "slip" from a pink plant to propagate it. Hold on to a main stem with your left hand, and yank a side stem away with your right hand. The side stem will come off with a "heel," which is a part of the main stem. This slip can be potted up and grown into a new plant.

Another wonderfully old-fashioned member of the pink family is sweet William, *D. barbatus*. There's a lot of confusion in garden literature as to whether sweet William is a perennial or a biennial. After reading that it is a hardy annual, I pretty much gave up worrying about it. Whichever it is, sweet William comes back in the same spot year after year, blooming heavily in mid-June. Its little pink, white, and rose blossoms look like flowers from an old English chintz fabric, and the entire plant is about 18 to 24 inches tall. Once sweet William is finished blooming, shear off the spent blooms, water and fertilize, and it will bloom again profusely by late July. Sweet Williams are sur-

prisingly tough plants, and they will tolerate drought and heat quite well. I have even found that once the flowers are sheared off once and for all by August, the tightly packed, dark green basal foliage can serve as a very presentable ground cover.

There are many, many, many more species in the pink and carnation family to investigate, but I have remained so enamored of my clove pinks and sweet Williams that I prefer to dally with them, enjoying their sweet, old-fashioned charms, and to leave the other types to other gardeners.

DICENTRA SPECTABILIS (BLEEDING HEART, LYRE FLOWER) Bleeding heart is the queen of the cottage garden and the plant personification of sentiment. Growing about two-and-a-half feet in height, little heart-shaped pink and white flowers like lockets dangle along gently arching stems. Bleeding heart is a spring perennial, blooming in late May and early June along with the peonies and irises. It's a shade-loving plant that likes nothing better than nestling among hostas and ferns. Because of its unique appearance, you can grow one bleeding heart as a specimen plant, but I have also seen in a neighbor's large garden a spectacular drift of bleeding hearts planted among hostas. The many arching stems with their dangling lockets was an unforgettable sight.

Dig in plenty of humus when planting bleeding heart, as it likes rich, moist soil. As the summer heats up, the plant may die down and disappear, but growing hostas and ferns nearby will fill the gap. This year, after a long, cool spring, the bleeding heart in my garden didn't die back, and the foliage remained good looking all summer. So weather conditions may determine whether it stays for the summer or goes dormant.

Postscript: After twelve years, my bleeding heart disappeared, leaving behind one self-seeded plantlet. The winter had been rough, and the spring long, cold, and rainy, and apparently it was all too much for an old plant. To my knowledge, it had never self-seeded before, and I am keeping a close eye on its descendent.

While *D. spectabilis* is the most commonly grown bleeding heart, *D. eximia*, or the fringed bleeding heart, is also well worth growing. It may seem traitorous to say so, but I almost like it better than the common variety. Its finely divided leaves are pretty and soft looking. Look for a white variety, *D. eximia* 'Alba' as it's fresh as a cloud in June. Be particularly on the lookout for the choice *D. eximia* variety 'Stuart Boothman', with its ferny, light blue-green foliage and pale pink flowers—it's one of my favorite dicentras.

D. formosa 'Luxuriant' is renowned for its long bloom time, which is May through September, but having observed the plant in a nursery, I find the cherry pink flower color to be a bit harsh, at least compared with the delicate pink flowers of 'Stuart Boothman'. I'm of two minds about this, though, and since I'm a big dicentra fan will probably someday fall for 'Luxuriant' and include it in my garden.

Bleeding hearts are in the same family, the fumitory family, as *Corydalis lutea*, mentioned above, and you may notice a resemblance between the two. Squirrel-corn (*D. canadensis*) and Dutchman's-breeches (*D. cucullaria*) are two wild relatives of bleeding heart and can be found blooming profusely in Midwestern woods in the spring.

DICTAMNUS FRAXINELLA (GAS PLANT) Dictamnus is a venerable cottage garden plant that deserves to be much better known in the Midwest. It has the presence of a small shrub and is about two feet in height. It has resinous, lustrous foliage smelling of citrus. Dictamnus grows slowly and will not bloom the first year it's planted. Once established, though, it's in for the long haul and is considered a fine, low-maintenance perennial. In *Perennials: How to Select, Grow and Enjoy*, the authors mention that a dictamnus plant will probably outlive the gardener who planted it. Dictamnus likes sun or partial shade, ordinary soil, and needs no staking. Its flowers come in white, pink, or purple. *Everyone who has this plant likes it.*

To grow dictamnus, seek out the largest nursery-grown plant you can find, plant it in decent soil and sun, and then busy yourself with other things for the next few years. It is slow. But it's worth it.

DIGITALIS AMBIGUA OR GRANDIFLORA (YELLOW FOXGLOVE) This is a modest little foxglove that's happier in Midwestern gardens than the towering biennial foxgloves of English cottage garden fame. At about two feet in height, this perennial foxglove has soft creamy yellow flowers that are lightly spotted with cinnamon brown at the throats. It blooms in June through July and likes being in a shady, woodland setting. Some gardeners, perhaps blinded by visions of six-foot-tall, raspberry-colored foxgloves, complete with attendant elves, are not impressed by the gentle charms of *D. ambigua*, but I just love it. It's a trouble-free plant that happily blooms away in its little shady corner in June, asking for nothing and being so charming in return. It does prefer moist soil, though. I have the feeling that my crew of perennial foxgloves would expand more than it has but is hemmed in by hulking hostas.

Another interesting foxglove is *D. ferruginea*, or rusty foxglove. I haven't grown it myself but have seen it while on several local garden walks. The flowers are much smaller than those of *D. ambigua*, with rust-colored markings.

One last word before leaving perennial foxglove territory: they really do need moist, light soil with good drainage, which puts them at odds with our clay soil, and they don't like our hot weather, either, which limits their bloom time. A hot spell in late June could leave your foxgloves blooming for barely two weeks. While cutting them back usually results in another flush of bloom later in the summer, giving them good soil will maximize the length of the first bloom period. I must mention, though, that my perennial foxgloves have come back year after year, and I have even divided them several times, so conditions here are pretty good for them, just not optimal.

DODECATHEON MEADIA (MIDLAND SHOOTING STAR) It's hard to think of a more charming prairie plant than this delicate, late-spring perennial. Shooting star is a member of the primrose family and has clusters of white, pink-streaked flowers whose petals are swept back, giving the impression that it's joyously hurtling through space.

Shooting stars are considered to be fairly straightforward to grow in the garden. They need spring rains and decent soil to flourish. The soil I've seen them growing in out on the prairie is dryish, fibrous, and even a bit sandy. Shooting stars are spring ephemerals and will die back and disappear completely after flowering—be sure to mark their location.

Dodecatheon is available at nurseries offering woodland and prairie flowers and can be purchased through mail order from Prairie Moon Nursery: www.prairiemoonnursery.com; Prairie Moon also offers plants for *D. amethystinum*, amethyst shooting star. Doesn't that sound like the most beautiful plant in the world? Next year.

DORONICUM CAUCASICUM (LEOPARD'S BANE) Doronicum is a lemon yellow member of the daisy family that, surprisingly, comes up in May with the tulips. I have only had it in my garden for two years, but so far it's been absolutely delightful. It has the gaiety of a parasol on a beach on the French Riviera. This is a low-growing plant, only about a foot or a bit more in height. Doronicum's quirk—and let's face it, most plants seem to have a quirk or two—is that it dies down and disappears completely after blooming. This sort of thing unnerves gardeners. I like it well enough to not mind this quirk, at least so far. It was originally a woodland plant and likes dappled shade. I once saw a picture of a doronicum massed beneath a crabapple tree, and the effect was breathtaking. My plant gets some shade in early morning and late afternoon, and so far so good. Stay tuned. If nothing else, if a leopard slinks into your yard, you'll be prepared.

Update, a year later: Well, it didn't return this spring, so maybe that's why some gardeners avoid it—it may be short lived. Still, doronicum has a delightfully gay, sweet character to it, and if I see it at a good price, I will probably plant it again. Also, my sister's doronicum is a venerable three years old, so it may persist if it's in a spot to its liking.

ECHEVERIA (HENS-AND-CHICKENS) Hens-and-chickens is another English cottage garden favorite that does well in the Midwest. It's a low-growing succulent that thrives in heat, drought, and poor soil. Our kind of plant! In my garden, the hens-and-chickens crowds up to and slightly over a path made of old paver bricks for a nice, bountiful, cottage-gardeny feel. The "hens" part of hens-and-chickens are green rosettes of succulent leaves. The plant increases in size when a runner from the main rosette grows out over the soil and sends down roots where it touches the earth to grow a little "chicken," or a small green rosette. It's easy to propagate this plant—just cut off a chick with part of its stem and dig a shallow depression where you want to plant it. Snug the chick down into the hollow and cover the stem with soil. Water it, and it will

Perennial foxgloves (*Digitalis ambigua*).

pretty much take care of things from there on. Hens-and-chickens spreads steadily but slowly in a spot it likes, but it's easy enough to control the spread. A number of colors and varieties of hens-and-chickens (also known as sempervivum) are available at various nurseries. There is a brown variety available, but be sure to plant it in among some green varieties, or it will blend right in with the soil and be less than impressive.

ECHINOPS (GLOBE THISTLE) Echinops is not exactly a household word, and it *is* a plant of strange beauty, like a plant of the atomic age, with indigo blue flower clusters like giant molecules, held aloft at odd angles on stiff stems with prickly leaves. It's about four feet in height. The unearthly beauty of the plant and the glowing soft blue of the geometrically perfect flowers make it a striking foil for billowy, pale pink phlox or pale yellow daylilies. Echinops is not demanding, wanting average, even lean, dryish soil and sun. It blooms in July and August. I am most familiar with *E. bannaticus* 'Blue Glow', with flowers the color of faded blue jeans, but the cultivar 'Taplow Blue' is also frequently recommended.

EPIMEDIUM As an attractive, trouble-free ground cover for dry shade, epimedium belongs to a small and select group of plants. For years, experienced gardeners urged me to *get epimedium*. Authors of many books advise readers to *get epimedium*. Yes, it looks a bit spindly in the pot at the nursery, and yes, it's slow growing, says the chorus, but still, *get epimedium*. So four years ago, finally, I got epimedium, and now I'm wondering why I waited so long. The original plant has tripled in size and has clean-looking, heart-shaped leaves untouched by pests. And no one mentioned the delightful flowers in spring, so much like tiny daffodils. It's only slow growing in comparison to, say, lamium, but otherwise it increases at a stately and steady rate. Now I'm scouring catalogs for other varieties and have joined the chorus: *Get epimedium!*

ERYNGIUM YUCCIFOLIUM (RATTLESNAKE MASTER) I'd heard about rattlesnake master and had seen it at a plant nursery, but it took a trip to Crabtree Nature Preserve in Barrington, Illinois, to see it in action. My husband and I, after hotfooting it through a shaded path where sandflies attacked without mercy, rounded a bend and found ourselves overlooking a prairie in full bloom, with wave after wave of little bluestem grass covering the low rises and hosts of silvery rattlesnake master and purple coneflower as far as the eye could see. As usual, nature is the best garden designer of all, and the combination of the silky grass with silvery, rigid, eryngium, and the black seed heads of the coneflower looking like polka dots, was simply magical.

Rattlesnake master is a member of a group of plants known as sea hollies. It's about four feet tall and its silvery, thistlelike appearance is attractive for its architectural presence among more conventional flowers. Rattlesnake master is perfect when combined with butterfly weed, black-eyed Susans, and purple coneflowers. Other eryngium species are used in English gardens all the time, again, for their structural interest and striking, silvery color.

Designers at The Natural Garden perennial nursery in Saint Charles, Illinois, include rattlesnake master on their list of "well-behaved prairie plants for the perennial garden."

ERYTHRONIUM ALBIDUM (WHITE TROUT LILY, DOGSTOOTH VIOLET) A common sight in spring woodlands, this little plant is easy to identify with its mottled leaves and lilylike flowers. It is, in fact, a member of the lily family. *E. americanum*, the yellow trout lily, is also very pretty. Trout lily is a woodland ephemeral and will die away completely come summer. In the home garden, it thrives in dry shade. Although common in woodlands, be sure to purchase trout lilies through a nursery. The passenger pigeon used to be common, too, and we can never be too careful about protecting these woodland treasures.

EUPATORIUM (SEE CHAPTER 3)

FILIPENDULA RUBRA (QUEEN-OF-THE-PRAIRIE, MEADOWSWEET) Stand back! Filipendula needs space. This regal plant with fernlike foliage can top six feet, its rose-pink flowers fluffy as cherry-flavored cotton candy blooming in mid- through late summer. *This is not a plant for hot, dry sites.* Its natural habitat of moist prairies, fens, and damp meadows tells us that it likes moist, even wet, soils and partial shade. If you can provide the moisture, try it with bee balm, joe-pye weed, turtleheads, and mallows.

I have *F. vulgaris*, also known as dropwort, in my garden. *F. vulgaris* is a very different animal from *F. rubra* (if you can say that about a plant), as it does well in fairly dry soil and can take sun as long as it doesn't have to face blasting afternoon sun. It has low, ferny foliage and a cloud of fluffy white flowers in mid-June held aloft on stiff, slender stems. Some nurseries offer an improved variety of this named *F. vulgaris* 'Plena', or double dropwort. This is a very satisfactory and attractive plant, and I've noticed it popping up in more and more Midwestern gardens, as it mingles nicely with a wide variety of other garden perennials, and its ferny foliage makes it something a bit different. If you try only one filipendula, try dropwort.

FRAGARIA 'PINK PANDA' The first time I ran across *Fragaria* 'Pink Panda' was at a local garden society's plant sale. Members had dug up extra plants from their gardens and were selling them at the local VFW hall. One thing I know about such sales is that the plants do well locally, sometimes too well, or they wouldn't be there. The sale was crowded—I hesitated at the 'Pink Panda' table, moved on, and when I came back, all the 'Pink Panda' was gone. Next year I won't hesitate.

'Pink Panda' is an ornamental strawberry with pretty pink flowers. It sends out runners, and I have seen in it hanging baskets as well as covering areas of sloped ground.

GAILLARDIA ARISTATA (BLANKET FLOWER) What's the deal with gaillardia? After all, this North American native perennial is hardy in zones 3 through 10, drought and heat resistant, flowers continuously throughout the summer, likes poor soil, and is considered to be "easy" to grow by many experts. And with its vibrant yellow petals, streaked with gaudy red shading to purple at their bases, it easily stands up to our bleaching summer sun. Perfect for us, right? Maybe. Gaillardia needs *very* well-drained soil, can't tolerate a smidgen of shade, wants to live in Arizona, and for some of us, perennial gaillardia will bloom one summer and then won't return. I've noticed that it seems happiest in raised beds and on retaining walls, where it gets the perfect drainage it needs.

My friend and coworker Jeff does grow gaillardia successfully, and here's how he does it: He took bags of top soil and worked the soil into an area bounded by his front walk and driveway, mounding the soil. The site gets blasted with sun all day and all summer long. Then he went to a local mass market nursery and asked for *purple coneflowers.* (This may be the secret.) He planted what they gave him, and up came tons of gaillardia. He regularly beats back the mounds of gaillardia with hedge clippers and brings in bouquets of big, beefy blooms. I am jealous, as my gaillardia are hanging on by their toenails, though they do look pretty this year growing alongside the sky blue of tall annual ageratum and pale yellow Boston daisies.

Given the "ins-and-outs" of gaillardias, you might wonder if they're worth it. Since they do well in poor soil and blistering heat and bloom steadily throughout the summer, which is so unusual for a perennial, I think they are candidates for the Midwestern garden, though perhaps not if you're on a strict budget. Other perennial varieties such as *Gaillardia × grandiflora* 'Goblin' have dark red seed heads and orange-red petals tipped with yellow, creating an interesting "bull's-eye" appearance. These are brilliantly colored, vivid flowers—just be prepared for "perennial" gaillardia to behave as an annual, and you won't be disappointed.

GALIUM ODORATUM (SWEET WOODRUFF) Whorls of the little, dark green leaves of sweet woodruff nestle in shady nooks in my garden and I enjoy each and every plant. If you like the neatness of pachysandra but want to try something different and feel suspicious of the rampageous untidiness of ground covers such as ajuga, check out sweet woodruff. It's a neat and tidy little plant that is very tolerant of shade and dry soil, placing it in a select group of plants. It has pretty white flowers in May and June that turn to a mist of tiny seed heads for the rest of the summer. Some of my sweet woodruff grows amid hostas, and the rather busy little leaves make a nice contrast to the big, smooth hosta leaves.

I don't recommend giving good soil to sweet woodruff. My sister-in-law has wonderful soil and cannot get sweet woodruff to grow. In my poor soil, it grows bountifully.

There is another, lesser known member of the galium family that is also wonderful here. This spring, my sister and I simultaneously came across a mention of G. *aristatum*, or tall sweet woodruff, in a gardening article. We were on the phone to each other immediately: where could we find this gem? It had been described as the type of plant gardeners pass over the fence to one another, and as not commonly available. I looked in my catalogs—my sister in hers—we searched on the Internet, and I came up with one source, somewhere in northern Canada. G. *aristatum* became the Great White Whale of our gardening existence, and we planned a trip out to a nursery near Rockford, which we heard tell sold G. *aristatum*. So it was G. *aristatum* this, and G. *aristatum* that, for quite a while. My sister works at Spring Bluff Nursery, near Sugar Grove, Illinois, and one day a customer brought in several plant tags, looking for further plant recommendations. One of the tags was for G. *aristatum*. My sister nearly shook the lady's brains out to find out where the tag had come from. The lady wasn't sure, she couldn't remember—had it been . . . maybe it was . . . Then she remembered, fortunately for her life. This led us pronto to Prestige Nursery in Bloomingdale, Illinois. We were fearful. What if they only had one plant? Families have been torn apart for less. Fortunately for us, they had plenty, and so we both were able to bag our own *aristatum*. And yes, it is a simply wonderful plant, with its soft cloud of tiny flowers that have steadily sailed on all summer. So we are satisfied. I grow mine in a spot with sun and shade alternating throughout the day, and it's thriving; my sister grows hers in full shade, where it's a bit shorter but also thriving. Of course, though, imagine my surprise when I received the latest

Bluestone Perennial catalog and found, big as life, an entry for G. 'Victor Jones', described as false baby's breath. Could it be? Yes. It's the same thing. So now we have a backup source.

Galium aristatum postscript: Several years after planting, tall sweet woodruff is about four feet in height and is a bit floppy, but in a billowing, attractive way. I think its great strength is that it looks good with everything, especially purple coneflowers and dayflowers, enveloping these rather sturdy plants in ghostly clouds of tiny flowers.

GAURA LINDHEIMERI Gaura is the subject of much teeth gnashing among some Midwestern gardeners, as it's an absolutely lovely plant with a nice long bloom time (July through September), but it's not reliably hardy here. And there's nothing quite like gaura flowers, which are frivolous looking, white petaled, and red spotted with long, delicate stamens. 'Whirling Butter-flies' is the name of the most commonly available cultivar, and the flowers *are* like fluttering butterflies or pinwheels held aloft on graceful, wiry stems. I've even seen gaura grown in an urn as a container plant, and it looked fabulous. Not only is it pretty, but you know that any plant native to Louisiana and Texas, where I've heard the climate is almost as bad as ours, is tolerant of extreme drought and heat. So gaura has a lot going for it. This plant is so lovely that gaura lovers everywhere in the Midwest plunk down good money every spring for the plant, *when they can find it*, which, to their horror, is not always. Every spring, members of the Gaura Fan Club dangle helplessly above the chasm of a summer without gaura, and they don't like it.

I was mentioning the sad plight of gaura lovers to my sister, who expressed surprise, saying that her mother-in-law had gaura in her garden for years and that she had it as well. I was perplexed. What was their secret? It turns out that while gaura itself is not always hardy here, *it is a self-seeder*. So gardeners who have been conscientiously mulching around their gaura have unknowingly short-circuited the self-seeding process, and not mulching could be the answer to having gaura in the garden every year. Also, gaura likes deep, well-draining soil, not heavy clay or moist, rich soil. Digging in some grit, sand, or even pea gravel to raise the bed might make things more to the liking of this charming southern native. Of course, if you start out with a gaura cultivar like 'Whirling Butterflies', the self-seeded plants might not be exactly like the parent, but the plants in my sister's garden looked identical to 'Whirling Butterflies', so if you like gaura, encourage self-seeding.

GEUM TRIFLORUM (PRAIRIE SMOKE OR LONG-PLUMED PURPLE

AVENS) Geums are related to potentillas, apples, roses, and strawberries, and all are in the rose family. G. *triflorum* is about 15 to 18 inches in height and has light pink-maroon flowers that are very pretty. As pretty as they are, though, the flowers aren't what's exciting about this plant. The "oohs and ahs" start when the flower petals fall away, leaving a silky mop of fine hairs extending from the blossom cup. These shiny tendrils dance in the wind, like a plume of smoke.

Prairie smoke grows wild on dry prairies, blooming in May. Its silky seed heads remain on the plant until mid-June, then the leaves form a low-growing ground cover. It does self-seed, but not obnoxiously, and is a perfect flower for the Midwestern cottage garden in spring.

My neighbor Mary has prairie smoke growing along with *Anemone sylvestris* (snowdrop anemone) in her front garden, and it's a wonderful sight come May.

GYPSOPHILA PANICULATA (BABY'S BREATH) Baby's breath *looks* soft and delicate with its billowing clouds of tiny white flowers, but is actually tough and easy to grow. That is, *if* you plant it in a sunny, well-drained spot. The name "gypsophila" derives from the Greek words for "lime loving." Most Midwestern soil is more on the alkaline than the acidic side, though, so gypsophila is happy here. And this is where that box of seashells you brought back from Florida could prove useful. You can crush the shells with a mallet and dig the shards into the soil to help lighten and sweeten it. Boggy, moist, low spots in your garden, rich with leaf mold, will kill this plant. But in the right spot, baby's breath is rock solid. It also self-seeds, and I usually have two or three nice new little plants every year.

Baby's breath will billow to about three feet in height and begins blooming in July. Plant it near oriental poppies, so when they have bloomed and disappeared, it can billow into the hole they left behind. Some gardeners complain that baby's breath not only billows, but flops, and devise elaborate staking strategies. I guiltily and lazily let it be supported by surrounding plants, as it doesn't mind crowding.

G. *repens*, creeping baby's breath, is another tough, pretty plant for the front of a border or path edging. Its little white flowers bloom in early summer, and it lifts its head up only to about eight inches. My creeping baby's breath has bloomed year after year with little care other than shearing it back hard after blooming to keep it neat. As a matter of fact, this plant has been so reliable I almost forget I had it until I came to this entry. I much prefer it to

Purple coneflowers and tall sweet woodruff (*Galium aristatum*).

cerastium (snow-in-summer), a similar-looking plant that can get seedy looking after blooming.

HELENIUM AUTUMNALE (SNEEZEWEED) Now we arrive in the *Hs* and to a slightly confusing group of plants. It's easy to mentally mix up *helenium* with *helianthus* and *helianthus* with *heliopsis*. Not to even think about *hesperis* or, God forbid, *helianthemum*. We shall try, here, to sort them out.

Helenium is a daisylike flower that blooms in late summer and early fall. It's a close relation to sunflowers and black-eyed Susans. It likes full sun and moist soil. There are a number of varieties of helenium, ranging in height from two to six feet, and having flowers in warm, rich shades of yellow, orange, or bronze, the colors of old tapestries. None of this rather dry data conveys the real value of this flower, which is that it's a cheerful, richly colored, sturdy, easy-to-grow plant that blooms at a time when other perennials have pooped out. The center button of the helenium flower is very pronounced, giving the flower a distinctive appearance, as if it had a nose. I feel duty-bound to report that not every gardener likes the species helenium. In rich soil, it can become lanky and need frequent division. To avoid the height problem, pinch back plants by a third when they are about a foot tall. Also, purchasing shorter cultivars would help. It's the species that can get to be six feet tall; cultivars such as 'Moerheim Beauty,' 'The Bishop', and 'Brilliant' are in the three-foot range.

Also, if you dream of starting a prairie garden, helenium would be a good plant to include. Its tall, vigorous growth will be an asset, not a liability, grown among tall grasses. It also looks nice grown with Russian sage (perovskia).

HELIANTHUS MULTIFLORUS (PERENNIAL SUNFLOWER) If I had to choose between species helenium, heliopsis, and helianthus, to be honest, I would give helianthus the booby prize. It teeters on the brink of being invasive and has coarse foliage. So why do I mention it at all? Well, if you want an unpretentious, trouble-free, tall, strong-growing perennial with yellow flowers that attracts bees and that has been grown in cottage gardens for a long time, this could be for you. Also, I have to be honest—I have a big clump of it growing behind my back fence, and I don't think I'll be getting rid of it soon. Growing along with some tansy and sweet rocket, it has what I hope is cottage garden charm. And it's not a horrible plant. Well, not really horrible. Heck, it *grows*—what more can I say. The White Flower Farm catalog offers two cultivars, including the frightening-sounding *H. giganteus*, which can grow to 10 feet, and *H.* × *multiflorus* 'Flore Pleno', which is appar-

ently loaded with flowers. Unfortunately, these won't be what you get when a neighbor hands you a clump of helianthus over the fence. Don't say I didn't warn you!

HELIOPSIS HELIANTHOIDES (FALSE SUNFLOWER) This sun-loving, North American native is closely related to the above helianthus. It's what I think of as a sturdy, uncomplaining, trouble-free, long-blooming perennial. It has golden yellow flowers and, depending on the cultivar, can grow anywhere from two-and-a-half to four feet. Some cultivars have greenish or brown centers, and others have double petals. Heliopsis blooms late in summer. Its fault, if you can call it that, is simply that its yellow flowers bloom at a time when so many other yellow flowers are blooming, and by September, a lot of gardeners are tired of yellow flowers. However, if *you* don't have any such flowers in your garden, you might consider heliopsis.

H. helianthoides is the native prairie species and is also called oxeye. It should be grown in poor soil to avoid lankiness.

HELLEBORUS ORIENTALIS (LENTEN ROSE) For years I never gave hellebores much thought, though come to think of it, this didn't make me any different from about 99.99999 percent of the rest of the human race. They sounded . . . hard, like something Lady Fernwood-Snoot would specialize in. "I had Chaps the gardener give the family hellebores three-year-old ox manure and aged rainwater the other day and they're reaaally quite lovely," she would trill at the Hellebore Society Symposium in London. "And would anyone like some of this absolutely lovely sherry? It's been in the family for yeaaars." "Oh, how lovely," murmur the members. "Here, here."

Meanwhile, back in the Midwest, I kept hearing that *Helleborus orientalis*, the Lenten rose, would grow here and could actually be considered "easy." This is a plant I haven't grown yet but have heard from so many credible quarters that it *will* grow here that I am mentioning it here and planting it this autumn. I keep hearing that it's a lovely, very early blooming plant with foliage tough as leather. They bloom so early in April that they could well be considered late-winter-blooming perennials, which makes them unique. The nodding flowers are a cream color tinged with rose with an undertone of green, and the plants are about two feet tall. A fellow gardener advised me to plant them in fall in good soil along with bulbs in a shady spot—even though the trees may not have leafed out when they are blooming, the shade will later protect the plant. She also says that the foliage of the Lenten rose is so tough that it persists through all but the coldest winters.

Hellebores are in the buttercup family, which could explain their toughness, or at least the toughness of *H. orientalis*. The other hellebores remain obscure to me, and I would be interested to hear from gardeners who have grown any.

Follow-up: Last fall I finally obtained and planted *Helleborus* 'Niger', the Christmas rose. I was thrilled when it sent up shoots in late January but crushed when a spell of bitter weather shriveled the shoots to the ground. It is now May 6, and the plant is up and looks fine. I am waiting with bated breath for flowers.

Later: I'm still waiting. But the foliage is leathery and lustrous, and the plant is holding its own. Maybe next year. And my sister has a hellebore with long, thin leaves that is also doing well.

HESPERIS MATRONALIS (SWEET ROCKET) If you've ever gone for a drive on a mellow evening in late May, you may have noticed billows of pale purple flowers everywhere in gardens, waste areas, alleys, and on country roads. This is *Hesperis matronalis,* a plant named after an evening star. Its common name is sweet rocket. Hesperis is a European wildflower that has found a home in cottage gardens both abroad and here in America. Because it *is* everywhere, I don't cultivate it in my garden, though it has found a foothold in the alley behind our house. (It has since sneaked into the garden, front and back.)

Hesperis is about 30 inches tall and has soft clusters of pale purple and sometimes white flowers. The flowers are especially fragrant in the evening. Once it's finished blooming, rather skeletal-looking stalks are left behind that become mildewed and which should be cut back. If you water, there may be another blooming.

While hesperis was purportedly the favorite flower of Queen Marie Antoinette, I feel honor-bound to report that some Midwest naturalists are not so enthusiastic about it. Its spread has crowded out worthy native plants. Dick Young, in *Kane County Wild Plants and Natural Areas,* says, "Their pervasive fragrance and gaudy color suggests an overdressed matron wearing too much cheap perfume, as these plants soon become too much in the landscape." Whew. I think Young is being a bit harsh, but keep his words in mind when thinking about bringing it into your garden.

HEUCHERA SANGUINEA (CORAL BELLS) Coral bells has long been one of my favorite garden perennials. This North American native is easy to grow, neat and tidy in habit, and looks good all times of the year, even after flowering. You can feel confident that almost any variety of heuchera you run across at a plant nursery is a good buy for your garden.

The distinctive look of its slender, wiry stems rising from a mound of foliage and its cloud of tiny flower "bells" flowering in June and July adds a delicate, airy touch to any garden. You can almost hear its little bells tinkling in a breeze. One nice thing about coral bells is that it's hard to tell when it has finished blooming, as the flowers and stems stay neat looking for some time even when blooming is finished. They will eventually topple over or break off, but you don't have to hurry to cut them back. So as you lie in your hammock reading a potboiler, you can look over to the coral bells and idly think "I wonder if the coral bells need deadheading?" and then go right back to reading. I like coral bells so much that I have dotted them all through my garden. They are perfect "front of the border" edging plants and can be used in groups as ground cover.

Coral bells grow well in a variety of situations. In our climate they appreciate some afternoon shade but must have at least three hours of sun during the day to bloom. They do fine in ordinary soil amended with some humus. They do not like poor, dry soil—there are limits to their perfection! So far I have a number of varieties of heuchera, including one I bought a long time ago at a plant nursery, one from my mother, one from a neighbor (H. 'June Bride'), several plants of H. 'Palace Purple', and a new variety

The dark green fingers of foliage of a bear claw hellebore (*Helleborus foetidus*).

purchased this year called 'Mint Julep', which has pale green scalloped leaves veined with dark green. I love it.

The slight downside to this plant is that it tends to heave up out of the ground as the soil alternates freezing and thawing during winter and spring. Don't hesitate to just press the plant back in with your hands, but even if you forget, the plant will survive. It also helps, when planting, to plant a bit lower in the soil than is usual. Also, lots of rain tends to make the stems a bit soggy, especially if blooming is finished, causing them to fall over. Just cut them off. Heucheras are quite easy to divide. As the clump gets older, some of the stems get a bit woody and "satellite" plants form. Every three or four years in the fall, dig the whole plant up, divide, and replant the divisions. Discard any dried up, woody material. (I have also done this in the spring successfully.)

Plant breeders have been busy developing different varieties of heuchera, including many purple varieties. *H. micrantha* 'Palace Purple', with its rich purple foliage, has become a classic. Although this popular plant is sold as being for both sun and shade, in our gardens it needs shade. In the sun, its leaves become dull. The pretty little white flowers provide just the right finishing touch to this lovely plant.

Before we move on, let's not forget our native heuchera, *H. richardsonii*, or alumroot, found blooming in May with mayapples in Illinois oak woods. Some gardeners profess disappointment with alumroot as being drab, and it is kind of a government-issue olive color, but I think it's a handsome and neat-looking plant with lots of interesting detail, and the longer it's in my garden, the more I like it. Alumroot is similar in appearance to coral bells, but the stems are thicker, and the flowers, instead of pink, are greenish brown. Well, *everything* doesn't have to be pink, does it? The stems undulate sinuously like the arms of a Spanish dancer. This is a plant used for its structure and crispness of its foliage in the garden picture. I've been growing my alumroot in the sun for about five years now and have only recently discovered that it's a shade plant. So it's adaptable as well as attractive. It has been pointed out that this native has grown in this area for thousands of years, so it's probably a good bet for our gardens! I guess I just like heucheras, with those airy little bells, no matter what color.

HYDROPHYLLUM VIRGINIANUM (VIRGINIA WATERLEAF) A pretty, late spring–early summer woodland bloomer, Virginia waterleaf is not easy to find at local nurseries, but I'm mentioning it because if I don't, it will continue to languish in oblivion, and it's too fine of a plant for such a fate. It's a grace-ful one and a half feet tall and has delicate, pale lavender flowers with long, decorative stamens. It blooms prettily among the brunnera or forget-me-nots in May and June. It needs moist shade but will also make a go of quite dry shade, and I have some growing amidst lamium with no problem.

HYPERICUM KALMIANUM (KALM'S ST. JOHN'S WORT) This is technically considered to be a shrub, but it's a small one (18 inches), so I'm slipping it in here with the perennials. This is a nice, woody plant with pretty golden-yellow flowers. It's notable for its exceptionally long bloom time: June through October. The flowers have fluffy stamens, and the leaves are smooth and attractive. All in all, this isn't a spectacular plant, but it is a *good* plant, and there's an uncomplaining quality about it that I really like.

There are a number of hypericums that grow wild in the Midwest. I just planted *H. punctatum*, or spotted Saint John's wort, this spring, and a local nursery also sells *H. pyramidatum*, great Saint John's wort.

HYSSOPUS OFFICINALIS Hyssop is an obscure plant usually relegated to the herb garden, where it languishes unnoticed by perennial enthusiasts, but I think it is an attractive, hardy, trouble-free addition to any Midwestern flower garden. This is a modest, not spectacular, plant of a quiet charm. The dwarf variety of hyssop is especially nice, remaining as crisp looking as a woodcut from an old herbal all summer. Hyssop's tiny flowers are amethyst blue, and the leaves are minty smelling. It blooms in August. Hyssop, whether dwarf or not, is perfect planted with white or pink antique roses. Hyssop attracts bees and butterflies like mad. It also purportedly attracts hummingbirds, but since our yard is alive with cats, I've never had a chance to verify this. On a warm summer's day, though, watching the bees fly to and from the hyssop flowers is pleasantly mesmerizing, and what other, unlucky bees do in a garden without hyssop, I'm not sure.

IBERIS SEMPERVIRENS (PERENNIAL CANDYTUFT) Iberis is another one of those modest, old-fashioned perennials that do very well in the Midwestern garden. At barely a foot tall, if even that, iberis is a perfect front-of-the-border edging plant. It's fine in well-drained, ordinary soil with some lime added and likes sun but can tolerate some shade late in the day. To make it really happy, though, give it dry, chalky soil and full sun. It flowers in May. The flowers of candytuft are a pure and intense white, a truly beaming white that is the standard by which I judge all other flower whites. On a misty late-spring twilight, the white all but glows in the dark.

The only slight bit of controversy regarding perennial candytuft is whether or not to shear off the spent flower stalks. If only all world controversies were so momentous. Some, including me, consider the flower stalks to be ornamental, but others feel that they should be removed. See what you think. Some books mention that the plants will bloom again after shearing, but in our climate this is wishful thinking. For the rest of the summer, however hot, iberis foliage remains fresh dark green, and I don't ask for more than that. Iberis sprawls if not cut back hard in the fall.

The 14-year-old iberis in my garden probably gets a bit more shade than it really likes, and it certainly doesn't get chalky soil, so it has spread only a little, and I haven't had occasion to divide it. Seeds from *I. sempervirens* can be used to start new plants, but if you have one of the varieties such as *I.* 'Purity', you will need to take a stem cutting.

KALIMERIS PINNATIFIDA, ALSO KNOWN AS ASTEROMOEA MONGOLICA (JAPANESE ASTER) I never would have known about kalimeris if I hadn't run across it in my sister-in-law Leah's spectacular garden. She has at least three clumps scattered throughout her front border. It looks like a neat, upright-growing aster, with small (one-inch) blossoms like chrysanthemums. Since I had never seen an aster look that pristine and tidy, I asked what it was. All Leah could remember (the plants were *18 years old*) was that it began with a K and was Japanese. This sent me scurrying home to look through my files and then to the Internet, where I tracked it down: *Kalimeris pinnatifida,* the Japanese aster. Several years ago, *Better Homes and Gardens* magazine rated kalimeris as a "great garden perennial" that's underused here in the United States. It has no serious insect or disease problems and, as the 18-year-old plants in Leah's garden would indicate, is rock-solid hardy and happy here. It also has a long bloom time, from midsummer to fall, and doesn't need staking.

So why isn't it grown more here? For starters, you won't find it at many local nurseries. And local nurseries don't have it because gardeners don't ask for it. So there is a chicken and egg problem. This is one plant that might best be obtained through mail order, or perhaps we should all start nagging our local nurserypeople to stock it.

I've run across tantalizing references to other kalimeris species in Internet English nursery catalogs, all sounding hardy and gardenworthy.

KNAUTIA MACEDONICA This plant is known in some circles as *Scabiosa macedonica,* which gives an idea as to how closely knautia and scabiosa are related; knautia does look just like a big scabiosa. Several years ago via the Internet, I traded some purple coneflowers for knautia and was very excited when a really big box of knautia was dropped off at my door by my ever-patient mailman. I was amazed to open it and find dozens of knautia crowns and thought, wonderingly, "How generous." In retrospect I should have been totally suspicious, because nobody trades that much knautia unless they have a football field covered with it in their backyard. I planted it, and it had the bright, perky, manic look of an invasive plant that has at last achieved a foothold in your garden. It didn't miss a beat and started blooming right away. Knautia flowers come both a deep purple-red and a light lavender blue, and I got the lavender blue, which was disappointing, because the violet red was its main attraction for me. It has continued to bloom each July and August since, hemmed in by brick edging and a rose bush.

In some ways, though, knautia is a perfect cottage garden plant. It's pretty, vigorous, and you'll have plenty of new crowns to give away every few years. Just keep in mind that while not rampageously invasive, it's no shy violet, either. It will take sun or some dappled shade late in the day and is not particular as to soil.

LAMIASTRUM GALEOBDOLON (YELLOW ARCHANGEL) Yellow archangel is an attractive ground cover whose light-colored foliage and yellow flowers light up a shady corner in late spring. I have the variety 'Herman's Pride', a nice, neat little plant whose pointed white leaves are veined in green. A lot of lamiastrum might seem busy, but a little is striking in the garden, and everyone always asks me what it is. I say "*Lamiastrum* golly . . ." cough, cough, cough.

LAMIUM MACULATUM (DEAD NETTLE) The common name "dead nettle" doesn't do justice to this useful ground cover. It's an easy plant for dappled shade and can withstand drought once established. The green and silver leaves are prettily scalloped and mound softly. 'Beacon Silver' has lilac flowers, 'Pink Pewter' has pink flowers, and 'White Nancy', not surprisingly, has white flowers. I've heard that *L.* 'Chequers' does particularly well in dry shade. And *L.* 'Beedham's White' has golden foliage and is good for brightening dark corners. Keep an eye on it, though, because I have found that golden lamiums seem slightly less vigorous than other varieties.

Since lamium tolerates dry shade quite well and is not pachysandra, it is especially valuable to shade gardeners who are bored silly with pachysandra. Lamiums can be sheared back after flowering and will bloom again. Lamium can also be rooted in water in late spring and used as an inexpensive, vining filler for container plantings.

Pink hyssop mingles with the tiny pink flowers of the mosquito flower *(Lopezia cordata* 'Pretty Rose').

If you are seeking an unusual lamium, check the Arrowhead Alpines catalog for their lamium from Iran, which apparently is *the* source for "fantastic" lamium.

LATHYRUS (PERENNIAL SWEET PEA) Annual sweet peas get a lot of press in garden magazines these days, but annual sweet peas don't like the Midwest very much—they sulk in our hot summers and refuse to flower, and this even includes a variety I tried that was supposedly tolerant of hot weather. They really want to be in Vermont or Oregon. Failing that, they want to be planted very early in the spring like garden peas and treated as spring flowers. All is not lost, though, if you yearn for sweet peas later in the season, as there is a perennial sweet pea *(Lathyrus latifolius)* that will exuberantly clamber up just about any lattice or fence if given decent soil and dappled shade in the afternoon. It has pretty pinky lavender flowers, curlicue tendrils, and interesting winged stems. The flowers morph into skinny little pea pods that dangle decoratively in late summer. When summers are hot, it will flower only moderately and then really swing into action with cooler early autumn days. In cooler summers (in my experience, below the 80s), it's covered with pinky lavender flowers for weeks and weeks on end. This is a big, spineless plant (it has hit eight feet in my garden and is waving its tendrils around looking for

new worlds to conquer) that tends to sprawl. You can take advantage of this tendency by using this vine as a ground cover. A friend of mine who has just come back from a vacation in Pennsylvania said she saw piles of perennial sweet pea growing up the side of a mountain, so it would seem that nature uses it as a ground cover as well.

I recently planted another member of the lathyroid family: *L. vernus*, or spring vetchling. It's small (12 inches tall) and blooms in the spring along with the pulmonarias and primulas. Its flowers in mid-April are charming and jewellike, like little earrings. This spring was cool, but still, the flowering of *L. vernus* was rather brief—barely two weeks. But as the two-tone violet-colored flowers faded, their color turned to amethyst blue, making the little plant quite colorful. Tiny brown pea pods formed and were held high above the foliage. The summer's heat dried them, and they opened and shattered, leaving the curled husks on the plant. I had heard that the plant's appearance suffers in the heat, but while not quite as fresh looking as it was in the spring, it was still decent looking after a long, hot summer.

LAVENDER Sometimes new gardeners ask if you can grow lavender in the Midwest. I guess it looks so delicate that it seems as if it wouldn't survive our winters. Actually, English lavender, *Lavandula angustifolia*, with its varieties Hidcote and Munstead, grows quite well here and is a surprisingly tough plant. It won't tolerate one single dapple of shade, though. Lavender needs full, blasting, uncompromised sun, as well as lean soil with very good drainage. Rich soil will eventually lead to lavender decline. Cut it back hard when fall arrives or it can get woody.

There's one caveat about lavender. If you've ever seen pictures of big, bushy hedges of lavender growing in English cottage gardens, I'm afraid it's not going to grow that large and lush here. Our cold winters limit its growth. Hidcote reaches only 12 inches and Munstead, 18 inches.

Another lavender regret: some very lovely species of lavender, including *L. heterophylla,* sweet lavender, and *L. stoechas,* Spanish lavender, are not hardy here. This is really too bad, as they are beautiful plants that thrive in our hot summers—it's the cold winters they can't handle. If you're a lavender lover, these plants are worth buying every spring. I am trying *L.* 'Goodwin Creek' this year, which has interesting, felted stems. Supposedly it's hardy here, but I'm not holding my breath.

Postscript: 'Goodwin Creek' looked as if it couldn't wait to drop dead, and, sure enough, it did not survive the winter.

Several years ago I grew *L. angustifolia* 'Lady', a lavender that was supposed to bloom the first year it was started from seed. It did, much to my surprise, but then the next year quickly declined due to rot. So the garden gods giveth, and they taketh away. I wonder if the vigor necessary to cause such quick blooming exhausted the plant, leaving it unable to cope with our winter dampness.

It's quite easy to propagate lavender plants. Simply select one of the stems that's drooping slightly on the outside of the plant and pluck off the lower leaves. Press the stem to the ground and anchor it there with a stone or even a bobby pin. In about six weeks, roots will have formed, and you can clip off the new plant and replant elsewhere.

LEUCANTHEMUM VULGARE (OXEYE DAISY) This is the old-fashioned daisy, essential for saying "He loves me . . . he loves me not." The oxeye daisy is a strong grower and in rich soil can be invasive. But for most of us Midwestern gardeners, it's a good alternative to the short-lived Shasta daisy. It surprises many gardeners that the Shasta daisy is said to not do well in the Midwest, but the soil isn't well drained enough here for its liking, and the summers are too hot for it. Most Shasta daisy plants will last for only a year or two and then will vanish. For some reason unknown to me, my Shasta daisy clump has been going gangbusters now for eight years. I've had to divide it several times, and I've just gone outside to take a look at it on this grey, January day, and it looks ready to spring into life at the slightest breath of spring. It's plants like this that make life difficult for garden writers! If you have trouble with Shasta daisy, you'll look with new interest at the oxeye, which is a perfectly decent daisy, though it does have a smaller flower than the Shasta.

LIATRIS (GAYFEATHER) I would like to say that liatris is one of my favorite flowers, except I'm aware I've said this about a lot of flowers and my opinion is perhaps becoming suspect. Nevertheless, liatris *is* one of my favorites. As a prairie native, liatris is perfectly adapted to our Midwestern climate. Its long spike of gorgeous flowers, rose-purple with an undertone of raspberry, adds a dramatic exclamation point to any garden when it blooms in August. Liatris is unusual in that the buds at the top of the spike start blooming first and work their way down, so the spike looks like it has a pom-pom at its tip. It's a sun lover and grows well in ordinary soil on the moist side—this is not a plant for poor, dry soil. It's drought, disease, and pest resistant. And, it attracts butterflies. For instance, the White Flower Farm catalog says, "*L. ligulistylus* is a butterfly's dream." On that basis alone, I'm sure we will all want

this plant in our garden—isn't it nice to know what butterflies dream about? There are at least nine varieties of liatris, ranging in height from a dwarf *L. spicata* 'Kobold' that's about two feet in height, to other varieties ranging from four to six feet tall.

If you have a large garden or meadow area, there's an easy way to dramatically increase your stock of liatris. Just wait until the entire liatris spike is finished blooming and the seed heads are dried and ripened (usually by October). Cut off the spike and lay it down in soil, covering it with about a half inch of soil. Mark the spot, and by next spring there should be a clump of seedlings, which can be pulled apart and replanted.

LIMONIUM LATIFOLIUM (SEA LAVENDER) For a mist of lavender in the garden in mid- to late summer, try sea lavender. It's quite graceful, with its sinuous stems undulating as though in lazy undersea currents. It goes beautifully with other rather misty plants such as artemisias as well as bright annuals such as zinnias. *Limonium latifolium* is related to the annual *L. sinuatum*, much used in dried flower arrangements. Sea lavender grows to about two feet in height and needs full sun, though it's doing well in my garden where it doesn't quite get six hours. It's a nice, hardy plant. I like it much better than another everlasting I have named German statice (*Goniolimon tartaricum*), which is stiff and prickly looking and which may get accidentally run over by a lawn mower one of these days.

LINARIA (TOADFLAX) Toadflax is a deceptively wispy-looking little plant bearing spikes of flowers like tiny snapdragons and is known to some gardeners as perennial snapdragon. *Linaria vulgaris*, also called butter-and-eggs, has yellow and orange flowers and is pretty, but quite invasive. It has naturalized as a weed in the wild, and a gardener should think twice before bringing it into the garden. I have seen it out on a piece of dry wasteland duking it out with milkweed, so it's no weak sister. In good soil, it could definitely be a problem. In mediocre soil, it's a cute little plant that could be the answer to your prayers, so judge accordingly. Toadflax likes sun.

Several years ago I started seeds for *L. purpurea* 'Reverend Bowring', and it has established itself well in my dry, clay soil. Spires of little white flowers bloomed the first summer, and the plant held its own against several larger plants encroaching upon it. This has emboldened me to try another linaria, and next spring I will start seeds for *L. purpurea* 'Canon Went'. My aim is to establish it with my pink centranthus plant, as I've heard they make a good combination. Pictures of 'Canon Went' show its upright stems of pink flowers, and it's quite pretty. If you want to try a toadflax, probably 'Canon Went' or the 'Reverend Bowring' would be the better choices than the scrappy *L. vulgaris*.

LINUM PERENNE (PERENNIAL FLAX) The charm of this wispy plant lies in its very wispiness, which creates a pleasant contrast to the more substantial foliage of other sturdier plants. Flax's delicacy is a bit deceptive, though. A native of the open grasslands of Europe and Asia, its central stem is wiry, and it can withstand heat and a fair amount of drought. Try *L. perenne* 'Saphir', dwarf blue flax. Its pretty, clear blue flowers appear from May through August, so it can be said to bloom nearly all summer. A new batch of flowers comes into bloom every day.

Flax self-seeds, and I'm always surprised how this little plant holds its own year after year against the bigger plants. Some flax even came up this summer amid some tomato vines in the vegetable patch. It's not supposed to do that, but it looks absolutely charming.

LOBELIA SIPHILITICA (GREAT BLUE LOBELIA) At this point in my gardening career, I am a lobelia neophyte, having planted this variety just this spring. It's doing beautifully in average soil with some late-afternoon shade. Its flowers, which bloom from August through early September, are a sky blue of startling purity. I've looked longingly at its relative, the cardinal flower (*L. cardinalis*) at nurseries, but with its nonnegotiable need for moist soil, I've had to pass it by. Its flowers are a *scarlet* of startling purity, truly the color of a cardinal's feather. There's something so pure in the color of both flowers that they seem almost to burn in ether.

The Heronswood Nursery catalog lists ten recent lobelia cultivars, most hardy to Zone 4, and apparently tolerant of average soil. I say "apparently" because what the people at Heronswood think of as average soil might not be what you or I think of as average. Those of us with some good, moist soil might want to have a go at *L.* 'Monet Moment', described as "truly sensational," with "intensely shaded flowers of vibrant rose-pink," or *L.* 'Grape Knee-Hi', a dwarf lobelia with rich purple flowers.

Lobelias are odd in that they are not true perennials. According to *Growing and Propagating Wildflowers*, by William Cullina, lobelias form offsets near the base of the plant, and it's these offsets that root. The original flowering stem dies after setting seed. Whether the offsets make it through the winter or not apparently decides whether you have lobelia year after year or not. So, we'll see.

LUNARIA ANNUA CRUCIFERAE (MONEY PLANT, HONESTY) Money plant is a long-time cottage garden favorite famous for its seed packets, which look like silvery, translucent "coins." The common name "honesty" refers to seeing the seeds clearly through the skin of the packet. Others have thought the packets resembled small, luminous moons, hence the name lunaria. Folk wisdom says that gazing at a lunaria plant in the full light of the moon enables the gardener to fly, but please don't blame me if it doesn't work for you!

Lunaria is just beginning to flower in my garden today, May 1, and has royal purple, cross-shaped flowers and is about two feet tall. Its seed packets are so striking that sometimes we forget about its beautiful flowers. A classic garden combination is to grow lunaria with either English or Spanish bluebells (*Hyacinthoides non-scripta* or *hispanica*).

Lunaria is a biennial, but I'm placing it here among the perennials because once its presence is established in the garden, it functions as a perennial, never leaving your garden for a moment whether you want it to or not. My lunaria is a stickler and stays on a strict biennial schedule, being all green leaves one year and flowering the next. It has gone on like this for years, and you would think that a plant or two might slip up, but no.

Not everyone, including myself, is totally convinced as to the charms of money plant. When finished blooming, the plant has a skeletal look that I find unattractive, even with its silvery "coins." You almost feel obligated to use the coins in some sort of dried flower arrangement, whether you like such things or not. At any rate, I wouldn't buy a lunaria plant, because somewhere, somehow, you will probably run into a fellow gardener handing out the "coins." It's that kind of plant.

LUPINUS PERENNIS (WILD LUPINE) Stately ranks of lupines tower magnificently in many an English cottage garden, and the Midwestern gardener may be tempted to give them a try. And many local nurseries do sell lupines. Lupines need cool summers and acidic, well-drained, moist, sandy soil, though. Many of us have slightly alkaline, okay-draining, dry, clay soil, so as you can see, we have a problem lupinewise. If you're sure you have good drainage, especially in the winter, and you can dig in lots of organic matter and sand, you might make a go of lupines, but an especially hot summer or soggy winter could be their death knell. I have seen lupines grown locally, and my sister-in-law successfully grows lupines, but she lives only a few miles from Lake Michigan, with its moderating effects on temperatures. And, she has wonderful, light soil and a bona fide green thumb. She has actually had lupines self-seed. But for the rest of us, I guess what I'm trying to say is that I would pick other flowers to grow before attempting lupines.

There is one lupine native to the upper Midwest, *Lupinis perennis*, or the eastern wild lupine, the only wild lupine growing east of the Mississippi. It's found naturally in dune areas and blooms May through June. If you can give it nice, light, sandy soil, you might give it a try.

If you are still pining for stately ranks of lupines, consider the Midwest's answer to lupines, Culver's root (*Veronicastrum virginicum*). The tall (two to five feet), white spires of this elegant plant are truly lovely, and more and more gardeners, including British gardeners, are using it. There is also a pink variety, *V.* 'Roseum'.

LYCHNIS CORONARIA (ROSE CAMPION) I include rose campion here as a perennial even though there is a chance it will disappear from your garden after a year or two if it doesn't find conditions to its liking. If it's happy, though, it will self-seed in perpetuity and can survive in less than perfect soil. The flowers of the rose campion can more accurately be described as neon, day-glo magenta rather than rose, and combined with its silvery white leaves, it's a color scheme that raises the hackles of some gardeners. Frederick McGourty, in *The Perennial Gardener*, opines that "It has a color that because of its vulgar loudness appeals mainly to people with tin eyes." Well, excuse me. I enjoy the over-the-top brilliance of its flowers and sometimes get tired of quiet good taste. And, interestingly, though the neon magenta/silver color scheme might seem modern to our eyes, rose campion, a member of the pink family, has been grown as a garden flower in Europe since the mid-fourteenth century. It has long been a popular cottage garden plant, so let's go ahead and enjoy it.

I've just come back inside from cutting rose campion back (July 16). It bloomed beautifully for more than a month in severe drought conditions. Deadheading the plant extends its bloom time, but this was a month when I barely had time to fix supper and comb my hair, much less deadhead lychnis every day. There are still some flowers on the plant, but it's time to cut it back, as yellowing seed heads have formed, and some of the stems are flopping. The stems rise up from rosettes of leaves growing at ground level, and I cut the stems all the way down to the rosettes. Amid the rosettes I found quite a few damp, yellowing leaves and removed those also. I split open a seed head and found it full of small brown seeds. I could have salted the ground with these seeds then and there if I wanted more lychnis, but the one clump is all I need.

Rose campion grows to about two and a half feet in height, is a sun lover, and likes well-drained soil. Its unique color demands that the plant be thoughtfully sited in the garden. As much as I like it, I agree it doesn't go with everything. Nearby warm green foliage tones it down nicely, and I've seen it grown mingled with blue veronica, *Heuchera* 'Purple Palace', and baby's breath for an unlikely sounding, but successful, combination. If you just can't bear the thought of a neon-magenta flower in your garden, there is a more tasteful white version available named *L. coronaria* 'Alba'.

I've had *L. chalcedonica*, or Maltese cross, for years, but I find its intense, fire-engine red flower hard to take. It seems to clash with everything, and I can never find quite the right spot for it, though I keep trying.

I also grow *L. viscaria*, German catchfly, in two varieties: 'Snowbird' and 'Firebird'. I've come to simply love these little plants, as they are perfect for the cottage garden. About a foot and a half tall, they flower through mid-May into June and are perfectly charming in a totally unassuming way. They are easy to grow and easy to divide, and their foliage remains unmarred even during our humid summers. The stems have the stickiness of Velcro, hence the name "catchfly."

There is one pitfall to watch out for with the lychnis tribe. Both 'Snowbird' and 'Firebird' developed crown rot after several years in my garden, I

Great blue lobelia (*Lobelia siphilitica*) grows among the variegated leaves of *Lysimachia punctata* 'Alexander'. They are in quite dry soil, with light shade for most of the day.

think because they were planted in dense clay soil of average drainage and were crowded by other plants. They need sun, excellent drainage, and their own space. I managed to dig up both plants before they totally succumbed to the rot and potted them up. Then, I am ashamed to say, I completely forgot about them. Several weeks later, I found that after sitting high and dry in black plastic pots they were in vibrant health. So drainage is key.

The genus *Lychnis* gets more and more interesting to me and has many members that used to be common cottage garden plants. Someday I hope to track down *L. vespertina,* also known as white campion or night-scented campion. Roy Genders, in *The Cottage Garden and the Old-Fashioned Flowers,* refers to it and a double form that used to be common in English cottage gardens. Apparently, it was fragrant like its relation, the pinks. *L. coeli-rosa* (rose-of-heaven) and *L. flos-jovi* (flower-of-jove) sometimes appear on seed lists, and I hope to find them and grow them.

Lychnis is closely related to the silenes, a group of low-growing sun-lovers often grown in rock gardens, and for those gardeners with sun, this could also be an interesting group of plants to investigate.

LYSIMACHIA CLETHROIDES (GOOSENECK LOOSESTRIFE) Gooseneck loosetrife is known for its sinuously curving clusters of flowers resembling goose necks and beaks. The whole plant can somewhat resemble a flock of geese. This is a really beautiful, elegant plant, but be forewarned that it's a strong, potentially invasive grower, spreading via underground runners. Growing up to about three feet in height, it could go on a rampage through your garden if the soil is rich and moist. But if you have a spot with some ordinary soil where it's usually sunny, gooseneck loosestrife can be grown as a trouble-free perennial that has a wonderful, casual "cottage gardeny" feel to it. The flowers bloom in July and August and are beautiful as cut flowers in bouquets—everyone will want to know what they are. This is a cue for you to get out your spade and hand out clumps to your fellow gardeners, *warning one and all,* though, about its invasiveness. Most of us casual gardeners are happy to have such a plant.

Another lysimachia to consider is *L. punctata,* or yellow loosestrife. It's sometimes also called the "circle plant" because of the whorls of yellow flowers that circle the center stem when the plant blooms in June and early July. This bushy plant is three to four feet tall. And as with gooseneck, it can become very invasive in moist soil. *L. punctata* is closely related to *L. vulgaris,* or great yellow loosestrife, a plant with long cottage garden associations in

Britain. The plant is reputed to repel flies and so was grown in many gardens, dried, and hung from the cottage rafters. This is an unassuming, pleasant plant, fine for the Midwestern cottage garden.

A lysimachia that I received in a trade on Gardenweb.com is *L. punctata* 'Alexander'. Its pale green and cream variegated foliage looks great, and its whorls of yellow flowers appearing in midsummer are quite pretty.

If you can find it, *L. ciliata* 'Purpurea' with purple-green-brown leaves (I can't think of any other way to describe their color—there's actually a blue undertone in the leaves, as well) and yellow flowers blooming in midsummer is a striking addition to the garden. Not everyone likes *L.* 'Purpurea', as its brown and yellow color combination, admittedly unusual, strikes them as peculiar. The attractiveness of this plant in the garden is revealed when grown with plants having emerald green foliage or yellow, pink/maroon, lavender, or sky blue flowers. It also looks good with *blue* grasses. I think of *L.* 'Purpurea' as a "designer's secret" plant—they know that its strange darkness serves as a fabulous foil for so many other perennials.

There is even a groundcover lysimachia, *L. nummularia* 'Aurea'. This is a bright chartreuse creeper, which is quickly finding a spot in many gardens as a companion to *Heuchera* 'Purple Palace'. So far in my garden 'Aurea' has been a strong grower but not as invasive as I had heard. I have it growing among some double buttercups, no shy violets themselves, and both plants seem locked in a stalemate, keeping each other in bounds.

LYTHRUM ALATUM (WINGED LOOSESTRIFE) If you feel disappointed about not being able to grow lythrum, you may wonder if the related species *Lythrum alatum* might be a good substitute. *L. alatum,* a native of moist prairies, doesn't look anything like purple loosestrife, though. It's barely two feet tall and is more multibranched and graceful than *L. salicaria* and has tiny pink-purple flowers that bloom much of the summer. It's actually a very charming little plant but is nothing like its big, bad cousin. *L. alatum* is worthy of being grown for itself, not as a substitute for anything. This is a diminutive plant, and you need to grow a crowd of it—one, two, or even three plants won't make much of an impact.

LYTHRUM SALICARIA (PURPLE LOOSESTRIFE) Purple loosestrife is that pretty, long-stemmed violet flower blooming in broad swathes in damp areas by country roads. It may be pretty, but it's a terrible plant thug, one of the worst, a European native that's been spreading rampantly throughout American wetland areas, crowding out native plants. The decimation of native plants also means that some species of wildlife are deprived of their usual food sources, leading to a decline in their numbers. It's a serious enough problem that some states have banned the sale of lythrum within its borders, and you will find that most plant nurseries and catalogs don't sell lythrum. If you do find it—don't buy it. Under the Illinois Exotic Weed Act, it's illegal to sell or plant *L. salicaria* and its cultivars, 'Happy', 'Robert', 'Firecandle', 'Brightness', 'The Beacon', 'Lady Sackville', 'Atropurpureum', *L. s. roseum superbum*, and *L. s. tomentosum*. The controversy is not whether purple loosestrife itself is a problem—everybody agrees that it is. But there are also questions about sterile cultivars of a related species, *L. virgatum*, such as 'Morden Pink', which can only spread slowly by runners and would be unlikely to spread outside the garden. Nevertheless, until more is known on this, I would avoid this plant.

MACLEAYA CORDATA (PLUME POPPY) Macleaya is a big plant with great presence that should be placed in the garden with thought and care, because of both its unusual appearance and its extreme invasiveness. Some years ago I had initially placed it with some shrub roses and rudbeckias, where its unique character quickly became muddled and lost. For that matter, the shrub roses and rudbeckias got muddled and lost as the plume poppy soared. Give macleaya a prominent position as a specimen plant, where visitors can admire its stately architecture and where you can keep an eye on it. There's much to admire in this plant, though, with its beautifully shaped leaves with their silvery undersides. The leaves cover the plant almost from the ground up, so that unlike some plants with barren stems or knobby knees, the entire macleaya plant is presentable for viewing. Strong stems that don't need staking give rise to the feathery "plumes" of tiny petalless flowers that bloom in August. Macleaya likes full sun with a touch of shade and is not demanding as to water. Actually, macleaya will probably like just about anything you give it, up to and including the stygian darkness of Hades, and would probably grow on the surface of the planet Venus.

In *Low Maintenance Perennials*, Robert S. Hebb says, "It should not be considered for a small garden or a low maintenance situation." I agree. There's an exuberant energy to this plant that would seem cramped and constrained in a small garden, not to mention the havoc it could create in spreading.

Macleaya, originally from China, is a big, lumbering, Uncle Lurch member of the poppy family.

Lysimachia punctata 'Alexander' sports whorls of yellow flowers.

A member of the malva family, the perennial rose mallow (*Hibiscus moscheutos*). This is one of the Disco Belle series.

MALVA ALCEA (HOLLYHOCK MALLOW, GARDEN MALLOW), M. MOSCHATA (MUSK MALLOW) If your hollyhocks are attacked by rust, and if hibiscus flowers are too tropical looking and gaudy for your taste, investigate another branch of the mallow family—the malvas. From summer through fall, if you give them what they want, these bushy plants will be covered with blooms that resemble hollyhock flowers.

M. *alcea* 'Fastigiata' is a variety particularly well suited to Midwestern gardens, as it can tolerate heat. Experts regard 'Fastigiata' as superior to the species, being a neater, less-sprawling plant. The word "fastigiata" means "upright." It grows from three to four feet tall and has rosy pink flowers. The White Flower Farm catalog shows this malva variety paired with our old friend, *Coreopsis* 'Moonbeam,' and it's a nice-looking and easy-to-grow combination.

I mentioned, a few paragraphs back, that malvas are long flowering "if you give them what they want." In my experience, malvas are not substantial plants and tend to self-sow here and there in the garden and get lost. To remain established in the garden, they need their own space with good soil and a steady water supply. So they are not really low-care plants.

Another good malva to investigate is M. *moschata* 'Alba', or musk mallow. Referring again to the White Flower Farm catalog, it says 'Alba' is "great planted with Antique Roses in the cottage garden, where it will self-sow freely and add its casual charm." M. *moschata* 'Alba' grows from about two to three feet in height and has pure white flowers. It blooms from June through September.

This spring I started seeds of another malva named M. *sylvestris* 'Mauritiana', and every seed came up. But if the flowers look half as good on the seed packet (like rippling purple panne velvet), that's okay. How often we are seduced by the picture on the packet.

Follow-up note, July 10: The flowers look as good as on the seed packet, and I am astounded. Each plant—and I'm afraid that after giving away plants to everyone but Mike the mailman, I still have at least a dozen—is covered with lovely, glossy, purple blooms. However, the plants tend to flop, and the lower leaves tend to yellow, and the spent blooms hang like rags on the plant while the new blooms flower. So if you stay microscopically focused on the flowers themselves, you'll like M. 'Mauritiana'. But the plant itself is—how do I say this delicately—a "dog." It needs to be nestled in closely with other, shorter plants to look good.

On a walk down a nearby picturesque alley, I came across a pretty crowd of self-sown *Malva sylvestris* 'Zebrina', its white flowers streaked with purple. At about two feet in height, it was like a small hollyhock.

I'll mention the genus *Sidalcea* here, because it and *Malva* are so closely related and have a similar feel in the garden. These are like delicate, resolutely upright miniature hollyhocks, with shallow, cuplike flowers. They are very pretty, like hollyhocks you would invite to a fairy's tea party.

The genus *Malva* is an interesting group of plants, containing not only the above garden perennials, but also wild mallows (including marsh mallows), cotton, and okra.

Postscript: I am so ashamed. In my rush to describe the malvas, I'm afraid I trampled over their relations, the hollyhocks (*Alcea rosea*), and this will not do, because today (July 18) I have seen the light about hollyhocks. I was just at my friend Susan's inspirational cottage garden, which could be called "Hollyhock Garden" because hollyhocks were everywhere. They posed by Susan's white picket fence, they swooped up into apple trees, and with bland insouciance they lay prone among dill and larkspur. The hollyhocks owned the garden and they knew it. One even leaned over and blew smoke in my eyes. Susan was way across the garden, of course, and didn't witness this.

Yet another member of the malva family: hollyhocks (*Alcea rosea*). These bloom in my friend Susan's garden in July.

She was looking at her Manchurian apricot tree, heavy with ripening fruit. But the hollyhocks—they had seeded themselves, here, there, and everywhere. Some were pale lemon yellow, some were rose pink, some the ivory white of elephant tusks. Right then and there, I fell in love with hollyhocks. I also learned an interesting thing about hollyhocks: rust doesn't matter. At least not in a casual cottage garden, where the plants nestle amid other flowers. If planted by themselves in a stilted row, rust-inflicted hollyhocks are an unpleasant sight. So hollyhocks are gregarious, one could even say flirtarious! They can also take a surprising amount of shade, and as I write this, I think of the stands of hollyhocks growing happily amid Susan's apple trees.

Yes, hollyhocks are biennials, but I am sneaking them in here with the perennials because once they establish a presence in your garden, plants will appear every year.

MELISSA OFFICINALIS (LEMON BALM) A member of the mint family, lemon balm has fresh green foliage in late spring and flowers from June through September, though the flowers are insignificant. In our summer heat, it tends to get a bit crispy looking. I like lemon balm because its lemon-scented foliage can be used to brew a truly delicious, tranquilizing tea. Plant lemon balm in average or poor soil in sun. Lemon balm self-seeds, and some gardeners might consider it a nuisance.

But back to the tea. It does have a genuine calming effect, which can be so helpful to the rattled gardener after finding a prize hosta eaten by slugs, for instance, or after an earwig has popped out of a daylily as the gardener bent to take a closer look. So I like to always keep a few plants at the ready. To make a nice cup of lemon-balm tea, harvest a cupful of fresh leaves. Lay them flat on a piece of paper towel and microwave for about two and a half minutes. Crumble the leaves into a tea ball and immerse in a cup of boiling hot water. Allow to steep for about five minutes. Tastes delicious with a few drops of clover honey. There, there, don't you feel better already?

MERTENSIA VIRGINICA (VIRGINIA BLUEBELLS) This dependable, pretty plant with true blue flowers appears in late April and early May along with the daffodils. Tuck this in a shady corner among the bleeding hearts, wild ginger, or hostas, as it is a spring ephemeral and will die back totally with the approach of summer. As it fades, it turns a brown at the edges, and you might be tempted to water it. Don't—nothing will bring it back except next spring.

There's nothing spectacular about this plant, but it is charm itself, and spring wouldn't be spring without it.

MYOSOTIS (FORGET-ME-NOT) Forget-me-nots are members of the borage family, a family famous for the sky blue flowers of some of its members, such as Virginia bluebells. Forget-me-not blue is one of the bluest blues there is, almost as blue as Paul Newman's eyes. This delicate, low-growing spring flower has a wildflower feel to it. While often pressed into duty to grow amid rather pompous-looking ranks of red or pink tulips, I think its shy, fragile beauty looks best scattered here and there under trees and in hollows in the spring garden. In nature, forget-me-nots can be found growing in moist areas near rivers, and this gives us a clue that they will appreciate moist soil in our gardens as well. Forget-me-nots are generally disease and insect free. They are not happy in scorching sun, and they can get easily crowded out by other nearby, beefier plants such as hostas. My forget-me-nots almost dwindled away to nothing after some newly planted hostas took over their space, but I caught them just in time.

OENOTHERA BIENNIS (SUNDROPS, EVENING PRIMROSE) Sundrops, with their glowing, lemon-drop yellow flowers, are hardy, easy-to-grow North American natives fine for the Midwestern cottage garden. Most sundrop varieties range from about eight inches to two feet in height and are drought resistant and long flowering. To become acquainted with this group of flowers you might want to begin with O. *fruticosa*, or common sundrops. The plant, which grows in clumps up to two feet in height, flowers profusely in June and continues through August. It likes sun and is not fussy about soil.

Some gardeners think bright, fluorescent yellow sundrops are a jarring note in the garden. But I think they are just the sort of cheerful, easy-to-grow plant that many of us love to have in our casual gardens. Still, if you're looking for garden color tranquility, sundrops may not be for you.

If you are up for it, evening primrose, or O. *biennis*, is five to six feet tall with flowers that open at dusk. A night-flowering plant might seem useless, but actually a nocturnal stroll through a garden redolent with the eddying fragrances of four-o'clocks, moon flowers, and evening primroses can be an almost mystical experience. It's no coincidence that many night-flowering plants are so fragrant, as pollinating insects such as moths are lured by their fragrance rather than through sight.

And I've just planted O. *speciosa*, or showy primrose, in my garden. The moment I laid down the trowel, I felt uneasy, as showy primrose is reputed to be invasive. But the picture on its tag was so pretty! So we'll see. I put it in poor, dry soil and hope that that will rein in its spreading proclivities. What have I done?! (As it turns out, nothing horrible, but *don't put this in rich soil*.)

There is even a marauding primrose of rumor, called the spinning primrose, an ominous-sounding name if I ever heard one. My sister said that a friend of hers got a small plant from *her* friend and that since last year it has spread *20 feet* in her garden. Crowds of neighbors gather to watch it in the evening because the flowers open at exactly 8:15 every night. I don't know about you, but a plant that spreads 20 feet in one year makes me uneasy, and if a neighbor tries to pass a slip of a spinning primrose, I'll probably decline.

PACHYPHRAGMA MACROPHYLLUM This plant is a real find, and it came to my garden via a wonderful mistake. My sister had made a pilgrimage to Herronswood, the famous nursery in Kingston, Washington. Apparently having left her glasses at home, she reached for what looked like a really unusual pachysandra and came home with several plants, one for each of us. With our glasses on, we read the label: *Pachyphragma macrophyllum*. Oh. This drew a total blank from both of us, but there was nothing to do but plant, in my case in rather dry shade in the back garden. This spring, lots of juicy new foliage appeared, then in the first week of April came a soft cloud of lovely white flowers. The flowers looked familiar, and I had only to stride to my front garden to find an arabis in bloom, with almost identical white flowers. As it turns out, both plants are in the Crucifereae family. Arabis is mat forming with rather small, dull-textured leaves, while pachyphragma has a looser, more mounded form and shiny leaves. My rather elderly arabis is a nice plant but somehow not as exciting as the pachyphragma, which so far is working beautifully in dry shade. (And it has continued to work even during drought.)

I did some research and was delighted to find that pachyphragma (we're going to have to find an easier name!) is closely related to *Cardamine*, a species of which is lady's smock, that most English of English spring flowers and a traditional cottage garden favorite. (At one point pachyphragma was named *C. asarifolia*.) So now, of course, I will have to locate some seeds of *C. pratensis* to see how lady's smock might fare in my garden. Then, on to *C. pratensis* 'Flore Pleno', a double-flowered lady's smock. What delightful, flower-strewn vistas are ahead! Cardamine may need moister soil than I have, but I will never know until I try.

I've also learned that pachyphragma spreads by stolons but is easy to control and that it can be used as a ground cover. The word "stolons" makes my gardening antennae quiver, but so far, after three years, it's shown no sign of being invasive.

PACHYSANDRA TERMINALIS 'GREEN SHEEN' There's not a lot to be said about plain old pachysandra, *Pachysandra terminalis*, except that it's green, it grows, it's everywhere, etc. My sister has been tantalizing me with tales of the *P. terminalis* 'Green Sheen' she has in a secret nook in her garden, saying that the shiny dark green leaves are great looking. I am pondering what I can do to gain an audience with 'Green Sheen' and how, perhaps, even to get a clump. I have nothing as tantalizing in my garden as 'Green Sheen' to trade, so perhaps out-and-out bribery would work. Jewels, brownies . . . something.

Follow-up: A stroll through my sister's garden shows that 'Green Sheen' grows as willingly as plain pachysandra but is much more interesting looking, its shiny leaves effortlessly lighting up the darkest corners. It was my luck to try a variegated pachysandra, which proved rather weak and listless and disappeared after one year.

PACHYSANDRA PROCUMBENS (ALLEGHENY SPURGE, AMERICAN PACHYSANDRA) This is the American cousin of the pachysandra (Japanese spurge) growing in so many of our gardens. *Pachysandra procumbens* is taller than the common pachysandra by a few inches, more relaxed looking, and has slightly serrated, downy leaves. It spreads slowly and needs good, moist soil, so it's not the carefree workhorse that common pachysandra is. Still, it's pretty and provides an interesting contrast to the same old, same old . . . snooze . . . pachysandra found in so many gardens.

I had planted *P. procumbens* in a fairly dry spot several years ago, and it seemed gradually to fade away. I notice it's back this year, so it's tougher than I first thought. But it does need decent soil, a dapple or two of sun, and is not for compacted, poor soil or dry shade conditions.

PAPAVER ORIENTALE (ORIENTAL POPPY) I always think of the oriental poppy as being a bit of a prima donna. It's not that it's difficult to grow—quite the contrary—it's an "easy" plant. And it is incredibly spectacular when in bloom, the flower looking like a translucent goblet held high on a graceful stem. But when it's done, it's done. It disappears with a swirl of its capes and without a backward glance, leaving a gaping hole in a border. As long as you are forewarned on that account and have the space, I wouldn't hesitate to grow it. Classically, baby's breath is grown nearby and encouraged to fill in the gap, and larkspur or catmint might work as well. I'm not that organized to grow a plant specially to fill in a poppy's gap and find that with some nudging and arranging, the surrounding plants can be rallied to fill the hole.

Oriental poppy plants like sun and good drainage and grow from two to three feet in height. They bloom in late May and early June. Their foliage is attractive and thistlelike, but it disappears too, along with the flower after it's bloomed. The flowers are traffic stoppers with their silky petals and sooty black centers. If the flower is really large, the plant may have to be staked. The foliage returns, come fall, and that's when the plant may be divided.

Perennial poppies are among my favorite flowers—there's an ephemeral, fragile quality to them that's haunting. And they are dramatic. Once my husband and I were standing by a poppy plant, when he noticed that sepals of a poppy bud were opening and the crumpled, damp flower petals were emerging. As we stood and watched, the flower opened completely, as if through in time-lapse photography, and it was one of the most miraculous things I've seen in the garden.

PARTHENIUM INTEGRIFOLIUM (WILD QUININE, AMERICAN FEVERFEW)
A crisp-looking, three-foot-tall prairie perennial, wild quinine has clusters of stubby little white flowers blooming for most of the summer. It's drought, pest and disease resistant. It likes sun and good drainage but otherwise asks for nothing but a good home. This is another of the wonderful, up-and-coming prairie perennials on its way to becoming a Midwestern gardening classic.

PATRINIA SCABIOSIFOLIA (GOLDEN VALERIAN, YELLOW PATRINIA)
Patrinia has been hovering at the edge of plant stardom for a number of years now, and such is the innate conservatism of many gardeners that it may take still more years before it gets its big break and appears in local gardens in its best role as a sturdy, long-blooming cloud of chartreuse flowers in borders. Just last fall at a local nursery I saw a cart laden with gallons of patrinia—it was on special for $2.00 a gallon—as many gardeners apparently had passed it by. It's too bad, because as well as being long blooming (some claim all the way from June to September) and pretty, it's very tolerant of our heat and humidity.

Patrinia is clump forming, with basal foliage a bit like scabiosa leaves, hence the name. In summer and fall, its tall stems (the plants I have seen have reached about four feet, but it may get taller) hold aloft plates of sulfurous yellow flowers. It needs decent soil on the moist side and is tolerant of shade in the afternoon, as it is a native of lightly shaded woodlands. It reminds me a bit of a very sturdy dill. In my garden I have white patrinia (*Patrinia villosa*) but haven't grown it long enough to pass judgement.

Patrinia is an airy cloud of little yellow flowers when in bloom and is a perfect partner to *Verbena bonariensis*—both are airy screens that you can see through to other plants. I've also heard it suggested that Russian sage is a good companion.

A little cloud is hovering over patrinia: daylily rust has surfaced on our shores, and patrinia may be an alternate host for it. The rust does not kill daylilies, but it does disfigure their leaves. The rust has popped up in Iowa but is so new to the Midwest that horticulturists don't know if it will survive our cold winters or if it even will be a serious problem. But if you have lots of daylilies, I wouldn't risk bringing patrinia into your garden until more is known about it.

Patrinia is in the family Valerianaceae and is closely related to common garden valerian (*Valeriana officinalis*). Valerian just appeared in my garden a few years ago, unannounced and unasked-for, possibly via bird droppings. It has relaxed stems about three feet in height and rounded white flower heads that have a complex scent, being both sweet and a bit skunky at the same time. I like valerian (fortunately). It is a classic cottage garden plant—a bit on the coarse side, but attractive.

PENSTEMON DIGITALIS AND P. BARBATUS This varied group of plants belongs to the snapdragon family. Penstemons can be a bit treacherous for the Midwestern gardener because, while many are North American natives, some are native to the West, especially the West Coast, and only a few are natives to the Midwest and the Plains states. It makes a difference which goes into your garden. *Penstemon barbatus*, a Midwestern native, and its selections, 'Elfin Pink', 'Prairie Dusk', and 'Prairie Fire', can withstand our moister, denser soil. All penstemons need good drainage. I initially had trouble with P. 'Prairie Dusk'—for two years it didn't bloom. Then I transplanted it into a site where I'd mounded up soil to improve drainage. That did the trick, and since then it has bloomed beautifully. Its thick foliage remains shiny and attractive even in heat.

Two other native penstemons are *P. grandiflorus* (large-flowered beard tongue), which has two-inch purple flowers, and *P. pallidus* (pale beard tongue). Both of these originally came from prairies a bit farther west than our area, but I have seen them sold at local nurseries. The flowers of *P. grandiflorus* are strikingly big and beautiful, and *P. pallidus* is quite elegant. And I've just recently run across a rave review in the *Plant Delights Nursery* catalog for *P. hirsutus* var. *pygmacus*. Apparently it has "hundreds of tiny bell-like flowers, each with light purple petals with white tips." *Penstemon hirsutus* is an Illinois native, a rarity growing on gravelly hilltops.

One of the most commonly available penstemons here in the Midwest is *P. digitalis* 'Husker Red'. It has deep ruby-purple leaves and white flowers and blooms in late May through early July. It needs full sun.

If I sound a bit hesitant about penstemons, it's because I am. It seems that if you're going to be a penstemon fancier, you'd better be prepared to move to Utah. In bloom, they wave pennants of pretty flowers, but the entire plant is boxy looking. And you really need to do your research when you come across an unfamiliar penstemon and be prepared to mound the soil. 'Husker Red' can become mildewed and tattered looking after blooming, and I've never been enticed into planting it. It may be that I haven't seen the light yet, penstemonwise, and that there may be a revelation yet to come.

PERSICARIA VIRGINIANA (FLEECE FLOWER) I've been growing *Persicaria* 'Painter's Palette' for four years now and feel it's on its way to becoming a cottage garden classic. It's easy to grow, striking to look at, and drought resistant. It's about two and a half feet tall. It's grown mainly for its leaves, which are handsome ovals marked with a jagged red V, but don't forget that in late September and early October, sprays of tiny red "beads" appear that are really lovely. If I have any vague feelings of unease about the plant, it's

Common valerian (*Valeriana officinalis*).

because it's a member of the polyganum family, which contains some noxious weeds. So far, this persicaria has self-seeded, but not horribly. There were about six new little plants this spring. I have it in dappled shade and mediocre, rather dry, soil, however, so I hesitate to recommend planting it in rich soil: proceed with caution. I have also come across high praise for *P. microcephala* 'Red Dragon', which has leaves marked with burgundy diamonds framed in pale green.

Persicaria dies down completely in the fall. Cut the withered foliage back, leaving only a couple of inches of stem, and it will completely reemerge in the spring.

I haven't grown it, but *Persicaria polymorpha* is a favorite of famed landscape designer Wolfgang Oehme. Quoted in a magazine article, Mr. Oehme calls the plant an "incredible perennial," which blooms from May until frost and is very hardy. He says it's six to seven feet high, with fluffy white flowers and pointed leaves. Definitely something we should try.

Postscript: My sister-in-law Leah has *P. polymorpha* in her front border, and the plant *is* spectacular. She warns, however, that it is preyed upon by Japanese beetles.

The stately plumes of *Persicaria polymorpha* in late June.

PEROVSKIA ATRIPLICIFOLIA (RUSSIAN SAGE) Perovskia is a relative newcomer to the Midwestern garden and has instantly become an irreplaceable classic. In bloom, it's a graceful sweep of misty blue-purple flowers and silvery, aromatic foliage and is a perfect foil for almost any other plant you can think of. In some ways, it reminds me of a big, misty lavender plant, and it would be at home in an herb garden. Perovskia is a sun lover and blooms in midsummer, but it looks good even when past bloom. While it likes well-drained soil, I have found that it's pretty tolerant of a variety of soils and situations, and clay soil doesn't faze it. It grows to about waist high or taller and should be cut back to the ground in fall to prevent it from becoming woody.

The White Flower Farm catalog refers to perovskia as "one of the great garden plants of all time," and I agree that for beauty and versatility it's hard to beat. There are three additional varieties of perovskia: *P. atriplicifolia* 'Blue Spire', 'Filagran', and 'Longin'. I just planted 'Longin' last fall and have been watching it emerge this spring. The leaves are broader and less lacy than the species and look just as attractive in their own way. Any cultivar of this fine plant is worthy of consideration for your garden.

PETALOSTEMUM PURPUREUM (PURPLE PRAIRIE CLOVER) Here's a delicate, pretty prairie plant for smaller gardens, growing from one to three feet high. It sports fingers of tiny rose-purple pea blossoms for most of the summer and has finely divided foliage. From 8 to 10 stems may emerge from one root. The authors of *Illinois Wild Flowers* have this to say on this lovely flower: "The entire plant lacks any suggestion of weediness. It is clean-limbed and fine, reminiscent of the beauty of the old prairie when flowers for miles covered the grassy sod."

The natural habitat of purple prairie clover is the dry prairie. I haven't had much luck with it in my heavy clay soil, but I think if you have a sunny spot with good drainage for it, it could be a fine plant.

PHLOX I can remember as a child plucking a phlox flower from its stem and tasting the sweet nectar at its base with the tip of my tongue. That long ago, pale lavender phlox from my mother's garden was probably *Phlox paniculata*, or the common garden phlox, a North American native that long ago found a home in our gardens. Horticulturists developed colorful varieties from it that are some of the most popular summer-blooming perennials today.

There are problems, though, with *P. paniculata*, and some garden experts actually advise *against* its use in a low-maintenance garden. Part of the problem is that because phlox *is* so common, gardeners are unaware that it needs specific conditions to be at its best. Phlox can be susceptible to mildew and red spider attacks, needs thinning to help air circulation in and around the plant, and needs frequent division (at least every three years). Phlox does best in really good, rich soil and likes lots of water and to be fertilized regularly. Sometimes it needs staking. Varieties of *P. paniculata* tend to self-seed, with the resultant plants looking like wishy-washy lavender imitations of the original, so you need to weed those little plants out. A. Cort Sinnes, in *All about Perennials*, notes that phlox care is "difficult for a presentable appearance." At this point, you might wonder why anyone grows phlox. Well, it *is* a really beautiful flower, with the shape of its flower heads echoing the fluffy clouds floating lazily above in the summer sky. For some it is *the* flower of high summer, with its sweet pea scent mingling in the air with the green aroma of freshly mown grass. Also, just as some people enjoy pampering and fussing over their poodles, some like coddling phlox, granting it its every thought, wish, and need. In return, it's magnificent for you. And, it's noninvasive and completely hardy.

There are mildew-resistant varieties of phlox. A few summers ago I received a hot pink phlox as part of a Gardenweb.com plant exchange, and it has remarkably clean foliage. It was not named, but I believe it is 'Eva Cullum'. So different varieties do seem to vary markedly as to mildew susceptibility. And I wouldn't get too worked up about the mildew. Usually phlox soldiers on quite well, succumbing only at the end, especially if the summer has been unusually humid. Usually it looks fine. Come early August, lovely drifts of lavender phlox and bright orange daylilies brighten many an Illinois garden, along with tiger lilies, Queen Anne's lace, and stands of bouncing bet (*Saponaria officinalis*).

Phlox benefits greatly from being pinched back in early June. Pinch with your thumbnail against your forefinger, nipping the topmost inch of stem above a leaf pair. If you can stand it, pinch back again in early July. When the double-pinched phlox blooms, finally, it's absolutely spectacular. Put out the lawn chairs, and invite the neighbors over. Of course, you can pinch only once, or don't have to pinch at all, but the pinched phlox will have more branches and flower heads. Pinching is a technique used routinely by greenhouse growers to produce lushly flowering (and expensive) pot plants such as chrysanthemums. You can also use pinching to stagger bloom time for a group of phlox, by pinching some, but not all, buds.

A low-growing, mat-forming phlox, called *P. subulata,* or creeping phlox, can be found in many Midwestern gardens. It's a spring bloomer, flowering in April and May. A Pepto Bismol pink variety is most commonly available at local garden nurseries, with the result that some gardeners have turned against it. I would make an effort to locate a more subtle color, unless, of course, you like Pepto Bismol pink. I have an amethyst color that looks pretty in spring with miniature daffodils. I have noticed that creeping phlox is extremely drought resistant and stays freshly green and presentable through severe drought. So it's quite a useful plant.

Phlox divaricata, a 10-to-20-inch-tall woodland phlox, is a Midwest native and is absolutely lovely with its vibrant lavender blue flowers. Try growing it in among bulbs, as it's a spring bloomer flowering in late April through May. Woodland phlox is mildew resistant. I've also seen woodland phlox grown with prairie smoke (*Geum triflorum*) and snowdrop anemone (*Anemone sylvestris*). These are all in full bloom in late May, and they make a pretty showing.

I grow a short (10-inch) hybrid phlox, *P.* 'Chattahoochee' that becomes severely afflicted with mildew as the season progresses, but is saved from doom every June by its exquisite flowers of amethyst blue with a maroon eye. Put these in a flower arrangement and *everyone* will ask you what they are.

My husband and I were recently at Horlock Prairie, a prairie remnant located about 30 miles west of Chicago. We took a fork in the path that led us into a forest glade filled with woodland phlox. The misty purple of the phlox rose from the forest floor like smoke, and it was one of the most beautiful sights I've ever seen.

PHYSOSTEGIA VIRGINIANA (OBEDIENT PLANT) Physostegia is a North American native wildflower that has found a home in many gardens, and there are more than a few gardeners who have a love/hate relationship with it. Some view physostegia darkly, saying it's invasive. I prefer to notice that physostegia is healthy, pretty, graceful, and long blooming. Because of its strong growth, depending on conditions, you may have to divide it at least every three years or so, if not more often, and I wouldn't put it in with your most delicate perennials. I think it's worth the trouble of dividing and keeping on a leash, though, as physostegia is a striking plant. Variegated physostegia, which sounds like a medical condition, has leaves banded with creamy white. This physostegia is frequently referred to as "spectacular," and I agree, though it's a somewhat busy-looking plant and requires thoughtful siting.

If you're afraid of possible flopping, try *P.* 'Vivid'. It's compact at 24 inches in height. It also blooms later than the other physostegias, from September to frost.

Keep physostegia in ordinary soil in sun, though it can also withstand some dappled shade. Hey, let's be honest—it will like it pretty much wherever you put it, with the exception of dry, dusty soil under a deciduous tree. Its height seems to depend on soil fertility and moistness, but in general, it ranges from two to three feet tall. Its flowers are a rosy lilac shade, and it blooms from July through August and sometimes on through September.

PLATYCODON GRANDIFLORUS (BALLOON FLOWER) I rarely use the word *unique,* but balloon flower buds are just that: unique. The elegant, puffed, balloon-shaped buds open up into star-shaped flowers that bloom from June through August, sometimes through September. Platycodon makes no special demands, just needing good soil, adequate water, and sunshine. It can stand some late afternoon dappled shade. This is a deceptively fragile-looking plant that looks like it could be grown in the most English of English cottage gardens, but it can withstand Midwest weather and is surprisingly tough. It's not made of cast iron, however. Dig good organic matter into its

An unnamed hot pink phlox was pinched back in early summer and is in full bloom here in late August.

planting site, and be sure to water. It will reward you. *P. grandiflorus* is about three feet in height and needs staking, or at least it does in my garden. A dwarf platycodon called *P. apoyama* has become available, if you want to avoid staking. This variety is only 8 inches in height. *P.* 'Mariesii' is 18 inches tall with lovely, big, blue flowers. I've seen it planted with purple coneflowers, with the blue of the 'Mariessii' picking up the blue undertone of the coneflowers for a very pretty combination.

After blooming, cut the whole plant back by two-thirds and water deeply. It will bloom again. Balloon flower plants have thick, fleshy roots, and I have read that they are difficult to transplant. I was faced with a desperate situation this spring, though—a balloon flower plant, grown much too large for its allotted space, had been flopping over a path, and it needed to be transplanted to a roomier spot or my husband would kill me. I dug down as deeply as I could and found a root like a long turnip that went straight down about six inches and then veered off at an angle—it probably ran into a stone. I attempted to keep digging, but the root snapped off, and I wondered if I had just killed it. I transplanted it, however, and it's fine—invigorated actually—and doesn't seem affected by the move at all.

I have since learned in the excellent book *The Well-Tended Perennial Garden*, by Tracy Disabato-Aust, that cutting the plant back by half in late May to early June produces sturdier plants that don't need staking.

Note: For a long time, I had balloon flowers confused with bellflowers, which in turn I had confused with lady bells. As it turns out, they are all in the campanula family, and there's definitely a family resemblance. Bellflowers are more varied in color and height and tend to bloom earlier in the summer than balloon flowers, which in my garden right now are blooming in early August. I like them both.

POLEMONIUM REPTANS (AMERICAN JACOB'S LADDER); P. CAERULEUM (EUROPEAN JACOB'S LADDER) Jacob's ladder is one of those old-fashioned plants that got left behind in the dust by the modern rush to the bright, the big, and the sensational. With pretty blue flowers, its leaves look like little ladders, at least if you use your imagination. Polemonium is a plant of woodland areas and likes partial shade but not deep, deep shade.

There are at least two varieties of Jacob's ladder commonly available. *P. caeruleum* grows to about two feet in height and blooms throughout the summer. *P. reptans* is about a foot in height and blooms for about six weeks starting in April. It's nice planted among the daffodils.

Keep an eye on your polemonium if you have planted it among vigorous ground covers. I lost a plant that was totally overcome by vinca before I noticed it was gone. So it does need its own space.

POLYGONATUM MULTIFLORUM (SOLOMON'S SEAL) If you don't get polygonatum confused with the next entry, polygonum, you're doing better than most of us. But it's only the name that can be confusing, so let's call it by its common name, Solomon's seal. This is an elegant plant, and the longer I have it in my garden, the more I love it. It's really subtle. With rows of little cream- and green-colored flowers dangling like earrings on graceful arching stems, Solomon's seal is perfect for a secluded shady nook in your garden. It doesn't seem to mind being a bit crowded, and in my garden it's jostled by some lily of the valley and hostas. Lily of the valley, hostas, and Solomon's seal are all in the lily family and are a natural combination in the garden. It would probably work well with ferns, too. Dark blue berries (not edible) appear in the fall. When planting, remember that in nature this is a woodland plant, so it likes moist soil rich with leaf mold. A patch of Solomon's seal, with its patterning of rows of flowers and arching stems, is really lovely.

Last year I planted variegated Solomon's seal, and all summer long it did nothing—it didn't get larger, it didn't get smaller. So I'm waiting with interest this spring to see what happens.

Postscript: It came back! Actually, three of them came back, and it looks great. In my sister's garden, which has good soil, her variegated Solomon's seal has increased to a clump and is truly beautiful, with the variegation of the leaves, the arching stems, and the bell-like white flowers creating a lovely patterned effect. Get this plant!

POLYGONUM BISTORTA Polygonum is not exactly a household word in Midwest gardens, but it deserves to be known better. *P. bistorta* 'Superbum' is a low-growing, spreading plant that can be used either as a ground cover or in front of a border. It has upright spikes of tweedy-looking rose and white flowers. It grows in pretty much any soil and in our hot summers likes some dappled shade. 'Superbum' has the showiest flowers of the polygonum group. Other varieties include *P. affine* 'Darjeeling Red' and *P. amplexicaule* 'Firetail'.

The polygonums are members of the buckwheat family, a large group that contains common weeds such as dock and knotweed, as well as food plants such as buckwheat, sorrel, and rhubarb. The variety *P.* 'Superbum', mentioned above, is admittedly a gnat's eyelash away from being an out-and-out weed, and I've heard it described as "horsey." If that makes you nervous,

A cluster of variegated Solomon's seal (*Polygonatum odoratum* 'Variegatum').

you might consider growing *P. amplexicaule*, which is considered noninvasive. Nevertheless, there is a famous photograph of the gardens at Sissinghurst that shows the towers of the estate's gate and, right down in front, a big clump of *P. bistorta* 'Superbum'. As a strong-growing and ornamental plant, it deserves a place in more Midwestern gardens.

Some years back, the genus *Polygonum* was renamed *Persicaria*, and you will sometimes find this plant listed as *Persicaria bistorta*, and I already have referred to *Persicaria virginiana*, above. When they placed some polygonums (large ones with spotted leaves instead of streaks) in the genus *Fallopia*, I became apathetic and continue to call polygonum "polygonum."

I'm also growing *Polygonum virginiana*, the woodland knotweed, by a shady path. It's about a foot and a half tall, has the jointed stems typical of polyganums, and sends out arching stems of tiny flowers in August. A group of blooming woodland knotweed looks like fairies are throwing rice at a fairy wedding, and the effect is charming. A warning: This plant self-seeds and is borderline invasive.

Another member of the *Polygonum* genus is the notorious silver lace vine, *P. auberti*. This is a fast-growing, woody vine that can grow to at least 25 feet in length. I would hesitate before planting a silver lace vine. On the plus side, it grows easily and has pretty silvery flower clusters in August. On the minus side, turn your back on a silver lace vine for a year or two, and like me, you may find it climbing all the way to the top of a 25-foot pine tree, and searching for new vistas to conquer or flagging down a passing airplane. I didn't even know I had a silver lace vine and, as an ignorant young gardener, had cut it down as a weed. This seemed to reinvigorate it, filling it with bursting energy. This brings us to the other negative of silver lace vine, which is that it's hard to get rid of. If you have the space to let it run, this vine is okay, and possibly helpful, because it is pretty. If you have a regular city-lot-sized property, though, it's probably too much.

POTENTILLA (CINQUEFOIL) This member of the rose family thrives in the hot sunshine of the typical Midwestern summer that can be a problem for other perennials. Potentilla doesn't mind dry, ordinary soil, and it's another of those plants that I wouldn't waste good compost on. Most varieties are 18 to 24 inches in height and have flowers in white, yellow, or various shades of red. Potentilla flowers June through July.

I must admit to not jumping up and down with joy over the typical potentilla—there can be something a bit thorny and prosaic about them as they sit all alone, baking in parking lot islands. But as easy and reliable perennials that don't mind Midwestern weather, they can be very useful plants as part of a border ensemble.

I have a love-hate relationship with *P. nepalensis* 'Miss Willmott'. It requires moister soil than the rank-and-file yellow potentillas found at many garden centers. Low growing with loose, relaxed stems, 'Miss Willmott' has cherry red flowers glowing with an undertone of raspberry. It could be considered a sprawler, so I grow it by a wide brick path where it sprawls with impunity, except from the mailman, who doesn't like Miss Willmott. The close relationship of potentillas with roses and strawberries is really apparent in this plant. A local nurserywoman taught me a trick for caring for this potentilla. It blooms through most of midsummer, at which point some of the outer stems become long, dry, and sprawly. The nurserywoman told me to gather up these stems as you would hair for a ponytail and cut them off with shears. Water thoroughly, and the newly compact plant will bloom again.

The problem with *P. nepalensis* is that it is a native of the alpine meadows of the Himalayas, a fact that rightly should fill us with deep foreboding. It may be that both our winter and summer temperatures are too extreme for this plant, and I notice that 'Miss Willmott' is declining. So perhaps the mailman will get a reprieve.

PRIMULA I'm getting more and more interested in primroses, almost against my will. The rather garish, even somewhat awful-looking little primroses (*Primula × polyantha*) I purchase at the local grocery store every April (it's almost impossible to resist these little plants—I guess we're starved for flowers and can't help buying them) and plant once they've faded always come back quite respectably, even strongly, and are very easy to divide. This year I planted an English primrose (*P. vulgaris*) and will see what happens. It apparently prefers acid soil, which concerns me—I'm not sure the organic matter and the Miracid I mixed in the soil will be enough, but we'll see. A local nursery that meticulously trials all its plants for suitability to our climate sells *P. denticulata*, which is said to be one of the easiest, hardiest, and most tolerant of dry soils of all primroses. They are also the earliest primrose to bloom. This nursery also sells *P. elatior* (the oxlip primrose).

I have also started *P. japonica* (Japanese primroses) from seed outside this spring. The seeds germinated very easily. Japanese primroses are also reputed to be the easiest to grow. And I know at some point I'm not going to be able to resist cowslips, *P. veris*. This may be an exercise in futility, but somehow the word "cowslip" calls, or moos, to me, and I have to try.

Even worse, I have heard the siren call of auriculas. As Doretta Klaber says in her charming book *Primroses and Spring*, "These primulas are so decorative, so definitely man made, that there is something not quite real about them, and one feels they must have been designed to illustrate story books and fairy tales." I guess as beautiful as prairie flowers can be, sometimes you lust for something totally different, and auriculas are that. They come in strange colors like morocco brown and Wedgewood blue and are silly-looking little things—the plant equivalent of poodles. My auricula, which bloomed beautifully this spring, is called 'Exhibition Blue' and has a pale green center eye with yellow stamens, a cream-colored center ring, and scalloped burgundy petals fading to white at the edges. I have divided the plant, potting up the divisions. I have heard that there is actually an auricula nursery up in Wisconsin, which I shall track down. Hopefully, this love will not go unrequited.

Postscript: Tracking down the auricula nursery in Wisconsin led me to a Web site: auricula.com, where I found that the nursery had fled to Virginia, a fact that filled me with foreboding regarding the feasibility of raising auriculas in northern Illinois. I did get in touch with the owner, Ken Alston, by e-mail, and asked him if it were possible to grow auriculas here. He said yes, but you have to be very careful about watering in the summer. "Auriculas rot at the carrot very easily so in the summer water enough to keep them alive (and keep them out of full sun in the heat of the afternoon)." He also said he uses clay pots and waters from below and that he kept the pots outside in a cold frame in the winter. This led me to ask him if he usually keeps his plants in pots. He answered, "If you want to be able to shelter them in the spring so that no rain gets on the leaves and flowers you need to be able to put them under cover. You can either keep them in pots and move them to cover or devise some sort of cover for the plants in the ground. Either way works."

I am digesting this information, wondering what happens if water gets on the leaves and flowers in the spring, a situation that would make every other plant I know deliriously happy. Auriculas seem to face peril at every turn. In *Auriculas for Everyone*, Mary A. Robinson warns, "August is one of the most dangerous months in an auricula's life." Apparently excess water is again the culprit, and she advises, "If pots are dust dry, give the plants *no more than one dessertspoon of water*" (my italics). See what I mean when I say auriculas are different from prairie plants? Wondering if my pots were dust dry, I just went out to look at my auriculas, looking nervous in their little pots

The delicate sprays of woodland knotweed *(Polygonum virginiana)*. Pretty, but it's an aggressive self-seeder.

under a bench, knowing that they were in the hands of a duffer. The pots *were* dust dry, so I trickled in a bit of water. Now I'm worrying that their carrots are stewing. *To be continued . . .*

Postscript: I have just learned that the best soil for auriculas is the earth tossed up by tunneling moles. Auriculas look increasingly hopeless for me.

Postscript one year later: In late April, I noticed with astonishment that not only had the auriculas survived the winter, but that one had buds. They are toying with me. Two perfectly respectable flowers have since bloomed. Then one flower was eaten by a rabbit. Who knows what will happen next?

PULMONARIA OFFICINALE (LUNGWORT) Another charming old cottage garden favorite, pulmonaria comes up in spring and is nice grown with daffodils. It looks very English, somehow, as though it would be right at home in a Lady Fernwood-Snoot's Tudor cottage garden in Suffolk. But it does great right here in the Midwest and deserves to be better known here. Its leaves are spotted with silver, and its flowers change from pink to blue as the plant matures. Pulmonaria is in the borage family, and anyone familiar with borage and its pink and blue flowers won't be surprised at this characteristic. (Note:

There are also some white-flowered varieties.) Pulmonaria is low growing, likes shade and moist soil, and is a durable, hardy plant. As a matter of fact, pulmonaria is so eager to grow in the spring that it may get nipped by frost. It recovers from this, though, and goes on to bloom in late April and early May. It can be used as a ground cover. It only has problems when planted in dry soil, so plan to dig plenty of humus into the soil when planting. The spotted foliage holds its own and looks crisp even during hot weather and drought.

Pulmonarias self-seed a bit, but I don't think you'll mind once you become acquainted with the charms of the plant. They do need open space to seed, though, and can't compete with aggressive spreaders such as vinca.

I had long held an irrational prejudice against pulmonaria; to a trauma-tized Midwestern gardener, its spotted leaves at first glance suggest mildew, an all-too-common problem in our gardens. But the longer I grow pulmonarias, the more I like them. They are amazingly hardy, interesting plants and provide a nice contrast to the usual spring bulbs. Pulmonarias grow on you after a while—not literally, of course—and I have to resist the temptation to start collecting them, as there are many varieties. Of course, come to think of it, *why* resist the temptation to collect pulmonarias? It's not like they're fattening or anything. We have to give in to something, right?

One more pulmonaria fact: a bumblebee's nose fits exactly into a pul-monaria flower. I'm sure it's no coincidence.

PULSATILLA VULGARIS (PASQUE FLOWER, ALSO KNOWN AS ANEM-ONE PULSATILLA) If you haven't ever seen a pasque flower, you're in for a treat. With its soft, downy covering of "fur," a pasque flower looks like a chick hatching when it comes up in spring. It is one of the earliest bloom-ing spring flowers, often appearing in March in our area, and often bloom-ing even before the plant's foliage appears. This is a small plant, reaching barely eight inches, and has purple flowers with yellow centers. After it has bloomed, even the seed heads are ornamental, having long feathery tails. Its only request is to have good drainage, and it doesn't like to be crowded by other plants. The pasque flower is the state flower of South Dakota, so we can be pretty sure it's not a weak sister.

RATIBIDA SPP. (PRAIRIE CONEFLOWER) The charm of ratibida is that the entire plant seems to hurtle through space, with its petals, like floppy ears, forced back by the wind, and that the center cone of the flower is very promi-nent, like a nose. Another charm of ratibida is that, as a Midwest native, it's perfectly adapted to our climate and actually likes hot, humid weather.

Ratibida is closely related to black-eyed Susans and coneflowers. There are two species to consider: *R. pinnata* (yellow coneflower) and *R. columnifera* (long-headed coneflower). *R. pinnata* grows to about four to six feet in height and blooms from early July through October. The flowers smell like fresh soap, and the plant like anise. *R. columnaris* is about two to three feet in height and blooms June through September. *R. columnaris* is nearly indestructible and can become aggressive. A variety of *R. columnaris* named 'Pulcherrima,' or Mexican hat, has vivid mahogany flowers.

As plants of the dry, open meadow, ratibidas need full sun and good drainage and will grow in rather poor soil. A gardener could complain that they are floppy, but in the wild, ratibidas are supported by tall grasses, and this should be kept in mind when planting.

RODGERSIA If you have a low-lying boggy area in your garden, instead of bemoaning your fate, consider yourself lucky: you can grow rodgersia. Rodgersia isn't exactly a household name to most gardeners, but if you have a bog, give it a go. They are known for their dramatic, oversized foliage and astilbe-like flowers. Rodgersias are related to astilbe and do well in the same conditions astilbe enjoy: dappled shade and moist soil rich in organic matter. Astilbes like constantly moist soil, but it should be well drained. Rogersias seem to like even wetter, more acidic soil. With my dry soil, I have not grown rodgersia, as it would be an exercise in futility, but I have seen it growing in local gardens.

I was talking about rodgersia today with my sister, who has a low-lying damp area by a small creek in her back yard. Her rodgersia is holding its own, but not thriving, she thinks because her soil is damp clay, which is entirely different from peaty soil. She is much more satisfied with her ligularia, a member of the aster family that is often mentioned in the same breath with rodgersia as a plant for a damp, shady spot. My sister says ligularia is the type of plant that droops in the heat of the day if it's in dryish soil and can thus be constantly annoying. It's in a steadily moist area in her garden, though, and so stays upright and vigorous throughout the day.

RUELLIA HUMILIS (WILD PETUNIA) What a charming flower. A native of the dry, open prairies of Illinois, wild petunia is about one to two feet in height and is covered with pale lavender-blue flowers for much of the sum-mer. Wild petunia is not related to the common garden petunia, but its flow-ers do resemble small petunias. This is a plant that can take heat and drought and thrives in full sun or bright shade. In very poor soil, it grows low enough to be used as a ground cover. It's trouble free and noninvasive. What are you waiting for?

In nature, wild petunias are supported by surrounding short grasses and other low-growing foliage. In our gardens it looks nice with butterfly weed and black-eyed Susan but is no match for tall grasses. I recently saw ruellia flowering and thriving in some very dry soil at the edge of the black-topped parking lot of the Ferson Creek Fen in Saint Charles, Illinois. In our gardens, wild petunias have much the same slightly sprawling habit of garden petunias, so keep this in mind when planting.

RUTA GRAVEOLENS (RUE) Rue is often lumped in with herbs as a quaint oddity, eclipsing its real value as a highly ornamental, easy-to-grow perennial with intensely blue foliage. It likes sun and can tolerate somewhat dry, poor soil and has perfectly decent yellow flowers come midsummer. *And,* it protects you against witches and the plague. What other perennial can say that?

Another rue plus: My sister has mentioned that rue is a host plant for the black swallowtail butterfly. At the local nursery where she works, she sometimes sells rue complete with the butterfly caterpillar—asking the customer not to dislodge or harm it. They have a butterfly bonus!

SAPONARIA OFFICINALIS (BOUNCING BET) Saponaria has a kind of faded, genteel charm that can be so appealing in a cottage garden. Growing to about two feet in height, it has clusters of pale pink or white flowers that bloom in summer. Often, pink and white flowers will appear in the same group of plants. Saponaria has a nice, mild fragrance and was once used with water to wash clothes and hair. Bouncing bet is often found growing wild in alleys and in waste areas, a sure sign that it's a tough plant, well adapted to our climate. I consider it a true Midwestern cottage garden plant.

There's a low-growing saponaria named *S. ocymoides,* which many gardeners love, but I disliked the insipid pink-lavender hue of its flowers the moment I saw it. I'm pretty sure I'm in a minority of one on this matter, but still, you might want to see it in flower before planting it in your garden.

SCABIOSA SPP. (PINCUSHION FLOWER) Poor scabiosa is saddled with an unfortunate name, but don't let that keep you from growing it, as it's an easy-to-grow plant with charming flowers that are frilly and sweet, perfect and long lasting in bouquets. The plants are about two feet tall with neatly mounded foliage, and the flowers come in varying soft, old-fashioned-looking shades of blue, white, lilac, and plum. Any scabiosa, including the annual variety, brings instant cottage garden charm to the garden. All scabiosa needs is a sunny spot,

The serrated foliage of *Ligularia stenocepthala.* Slender spires of yellow flowers will appear later in the summer.

decent soil, and an occasional drink of water. Otherwise, it demands little care as it's pest free and neat looking. Scabiosa begins flowering in July and will persist through September, as long as you keep picking the flowers. Particularly nice is *S. caucasica* 'Blue Perfection'. I also have an unnamed white variety of scabiosa, which is hardy and blooms profusely. I think it's *S. ochroleuca*, though I'm not 100 percent sure. It self-seeds profusely, almost to the point of being annoying, but not quite. It has long spindly stems and needs support from surrounding foliage.

The much-touted *S. columbaria* 'Butterfly Blue' lasted exactly one year in my garden before vanishing. It was beautiful while it lasted, though, covered with intense blue flowers from spring until frost. Maybe it died of exhaustion.

SCUTELLARIA SPP. (SKULLCAP) Scutellaria is perhaps not the first perennial I would think of when planning a garden, but I received a plant in an Internet trade, and I've come to really like it. It has long been grown in herb gardens as a sleep remedy. It's easy to grow, hasn't shown signs of invasiveness, and is flying through a six-week drought without complaint. My plant is next to *Lychnis coronaria*, and the blue and white flowers of the scutellaria and the neon magenta flowers of the lychnis mingle pleasingly. My scutellaria is about three feet in height and started blooming in mid-June. I'm not sure of its exact species.

Scutellaria lateriflora is sold in the Heronswood Nursery catalog, a pretty sure sign that it's gardenworthy. And in *Dream Plants for the Natural Garden*, coauthor Piet Oudolf comments, "There are quite a lot of species [of scutellaria] which could be promoted to the status of garden plants, but until now there is one which has achieved this: *S. incana*."

There are four skullcaps found in the Illinois wild, and Dick Young, in *Kane County Wild Plants and Natural Areas*, uses adjectives such as "fine," "choice," "pleasant," and "lovely" to describe them. *Scutellaria ovata*, the heart-leafed skullcap, comes in for some particularly high praise, with its white and sky blue flowers being deemed "exquisite."

The bottom line is that scutellaria is outgrowing its herbal image and is being discovered by more and more gardeners as a decorative perennial, so perhaps more of us Midwestern gardeners should investigate this interesting genus of plants.

SMILACINA RACEMOSA (FALSE SOLOMON'S SEAL) It's too bad that this is called *false* Solomon's seal, because it gives the impression that it's a kind of *second-rate* Solomon's seal, whereas nothing could be further from the truth—it's a beautiful, elegant plant in its own right. This is a late-spring-blooming woodland plant with soft spikes of creamy white flowers. A drift of smilacina in a shady garden is a lovely sight, as the leaves, the flowers, and later the berries create an attractive patterned effect.

SOLIDAGO SPP. (GOLDENROD) Goldenrod is a glorious native North American perennial that has been ignored by Americans for years as "just a weed." Go figure. Meanwhile, European plant hybridizers have jumped in and developed goldenrod varieties that are perfect for the Midwestern garden. The many goldenrod varieties that grow naturally in our prairies (what's left of them) and waste areas, such as stiff goldenrod, Riddell's goldenrod, grass-leafed goldenrod, zigzag goldenrod, bog goldenrod, showy goldenrod, old-field goldenrod, swamp goldenrod, early goldenrod, Missouri goldenrod, elm-leafed goldenrod, Canada goldenrod, late goldenrod, tall goldenrod, blue-stem goldenrod, sweet goldenrod, and I'm sure there's a medium goldenrod somewhere, tell Midwestern gardeners: Grow goldenrod! If you want to use a "wild" goldenrod, be sure to obtain it from a nursery source. Wild goldenrods can range from two to four feet in height, but in good garden soil they may get much taller. I have one behind my back fence that's nine feet tall, and I've never been able to figure out just which one it is—maybe nine-foot-tall goldenrod. If you have such a tall goldenrod, you can cut it back by half in early June to stimulate more compact growth. I learned this from the excellent book *The Well-Tended Perennial Garden*, by Tracy Disabato-Aust. This might also help curb self-seeding.

For goldenrods that are beautiful, but a bit more predictable in height, try hybrids such as 'Baby Gold', 'Cloth of Gold', 'Crown of Rays', 'Peter Pan', 'Golden Fleece', 'Gold Dwarf', 'Golden Thumb', or 'Goldenmosa'. These represent a variety of heights and flower sizes. I'm growing *S.* 'Golden Baby', a two-foot variety with sprays of green buds expanding into brighter and brighter golden, open flowers. *S.* 'Fireworks' is the rising star among the new goldenrods. Its long, narrow panicles are covered with golden blooms. Apparently it's a sprawler and needs to be planted with ornamental grasses for support.

And there's one more member of the goldenrod tribe that's nice to know about. Goldenrod is in the aster family, and plant hybridizers have made a hybrid between an aster and goldenrod. The result is named *Aster hybridus luteus* × 'Solidaster', a nice plant that I think is almost better looking than the parents. It's about two feet tall and has soft, pale, creamy, fluffy-looking yellow blossoms that appear in summer. It can get slightly mildewed—I think it's the aster side of the plant weighing in. But the mildew is not unsightly, and the plant is definitely worth considering for a spot in your garden.

If you need convincing as to goldenrod's beauty, take a trip to a prairie remnant on some early September day, like my husband and I did just yesterday. We drove to Almon Underwood Nature Preserve, near Sugar Grove, Illinois, and stood on a gravelly hill overlooking a carpet of goldenrod and big blue stem grass (*Andropogon gerardi*) waving slowly in the warm wind. Butterflies, at least five different species that we could count, were everywhere. Am I being sentimental to admit that I had tears in my eyes to see something both so beautiful and so fragile?

STYLOPHORUM DIPHYLLUM (CELANDINE OR WOOD POPPY) A perennial member of the poppy family and a North American native, the celandine poppy thrives in shade, its yellow flowers blooming in late April and May. If you deadhead, it will keep blooming at least through June, and this year after a cool spring, I've had blossoms in July. This is an attractive plant whose oakleaf–shaped leaves stay fresh and untattered right through summer heat, though they will become tinged with gold. *S. diphyllum* self-seeds a bit (actually *ants* carry the seeds around the garden), but you will count yourself lucky when you see the new plants. This is a wonderful plant, and I urge you to try it.

My satisfaction with *S. diphyllum* led me to order *S. lasiocarpum*, a related species from China, from Heronswood Nursery this spring. This plant seems to have the same toughness and drought resistance as *S. diphyllum*. Its leaves are more jagged in shape, and its flower is a bit paler, but so far it's very similar to *S. diphyllum*. I'm happy to have it but am not sure it's different enough from the American native to recommend that anyone rush to buy it.

Postscript: S. lasiocarpum is slowly revealing its charms. The leaves definitely stay fresher and greener looking right through summer and fall than those of the wood poppy. So I'm glad to have both of them.

TANACETUM VULGARE (TANSY) Tansy is an old-fashioned herb with pungent, deep green, ferny leaves and clusters of yellow button flowers. It's sometimes called "button bitters." My plant is almost three feet in height. Tansy can be an untidy plant with invasive tendencies, but it's also cheerful, pest free, and easy to grow. The flowers are neat looking, and the ferny foliage remains attractive in the late summer heat, long after real ferns have dried to a crisp. This is one of those plants that some gardeners dismiss as a weed, and

some, like me, like a lot and would hate to have a garden without it. Admittedly, I grow it behind our back fence near the alley and not in the garden proper, but it would still feel funny to not have tansy. Tansy can benefit from being grown in lean soil and by having old foliage removed at the end of the gardening season. This, and pulling up any runners attempting to escape from the main plant, will keep it presentable.

I like tansy so much that if I had more room I would grow other tansy varieties. The "Companion Plants" catalog lists *Tanacetum niveum* (Silver Tansy) and T. vulgare 'Crispum' (fern-leafed tansy), which has finely cut foliage.

Note: Since writing this, I discovered that I *am* growing another tansy variety—the fern-leafed type. I had purchased the plant, labeled "fern-leafed yarrow," at a garage sale. I guess if you squint your eyes and stand five feet away, yarrow and tansy do look alike. The plant's true identity emerged this summer. It's nice, but not significantly different from plain tansy.

TELLIMA GRANDIFLORA (FRINGECUPS) I am mentioning tellima here to recommend that you *not* grow it. I bought a plant three years ago at a local nursery, attracted by its resemblance to heucheras, which are among my favorite plants. No one could tell me a thing about it. Curiosity got the best of me, and I had money in my pocket—always a dangerous thing—so I bought one. As it happens, it *is* a member of the heuchera family, but it is the branch that lives in cool, moist coniferous woods in California and up north to Alaska. So it's not exactly Uncle Fred. To give it credit, it's still alive, and it looks okay in the spring, but by summer it tells me loud and clear that IT DOESN'T LIKE IT HERE IN THE MIDWEST! SEND ME HOME! I am trying to, via the Internet Gardenweb plant exchange, so we'll see what happens. You can give this plant moisture, you could even give it a conifer, but you can't give it a cool summer. So much for tellima.

THALICTRUM DASYCARPUM (PURPLE MEADOW RUE, MAID-OF-THE-MIST) About three feet in height, purple meadow rue is a native of moist meadows and prairies. Its airy, feathery flowers are actually a cream color and bloom in June through July. The stem is what has the purple color. It likes bright shade with rich, moist soil. The foliage and stems become yellowed and dried after blooming, so they must be cut back pronto. Fresh new foliage will sprout if the plant is watered. Thalictrum self-seeds in my garden, but just a little.

T. DIOICUM (EARLY MEADOW RUE) This is a spring bloomer, about one to two feet tall. I can't add anything to the comments of Dick Young, in *Kane County Wild Plants and Natural Areas*: "These pastel tassel blossoms softly embellish the pristine, ephemeral woodland like lace curtains in a quietly elegant room." Prefers rich, moist soil and some shade.

You'll do fine with meadow rues as long as you remember that they like moisture and a touch of shade. They won't make it in hard, clay soil and blasting sun and don't take kindly to tree roots. Dig plenty of organic matter into the soil and don't fertilize.

THYMUS SPP. I'm sure you're familiar with the common thyme (*Thymus vulgaris*) of the herb garden, but you might also want to investigate lemon thyme (*T. citriodorus*), woolly thyme, and the creeping thymes, which are attractive, long-lived additions to the perennial or herb garden.

Mat- and low mound-forming thymes do very well here in the Midwest. Keep them to the front of a sunny border or edge a path with them—don't crowd them with other plants. The soil should be quite poor and dry, as thyme planted in moist, loamy, "good" soil won't last long. My creeping thymes pour like tiny, determined, emerald green rivers between the paving bricks of our pathway—it seems the more difficult, hot, and stony their prospect, the better they like it. I also have a soft, gray, mounding woolly thyme curled up by the back steps that I often stop to stroke like a cat, and nearby, two very low-growing bright green thymes, one with slightly lighter-colored leaves than the other. These thymes are so old that I have long since lost track of their names, but I suspect they are varieties of *T. serpyllum*. Since planting the woolly thyme, I've come across an "improved" woolly thyme named 'Hall's Woolly Thyme', which has larger, greener leaves than the original.

These humble plants may be small, but they are tenacious and can survive extreme cold, drought, and heat. The creeping thymes in my garden are some of the oldest plants I have, being almost 17 years old. A tiny creeping thyme plant barely visible above the rim of its pot at the nursery may not seem like a great buy, but I recommend that you give it a try.

Lemon thyme smells wonderfully sweet and lemony. It keeps its fresh, green color through the hottest summers. I lost all my seven- and eight-year-old lemon thyme plants during the strange winter of 1995–96, but many otherwise hardy plants had difficulty that winter, and, in general, I think lemon thyme is quite hardy.

I can also recommend a thyme named *T.* 'Wedgewood' that's about eight inches in height and has attractive bluish leaves that stay fresh throughout the summer. This is another mounding thyme, as opposed to the upright bush type. And I have a wonderful lavender thyme, which has tiny leaves, and an oregano thyme, which is excellent for use in cooking. The latter forms fresh green mounds that are quite beautiful and which could be considered for a ground cover in a sunny spot. Oregano thyme is sometimes called "pizza" thyme.

I have found that some of the choice, upright thymes such as silver thyme aren't hardy here, much to my sorrow. I once brought a *T.* 'Caprilands' back from Caprilands Herb Farm in Connecticut only to lose it the first winter. Guess I'll have to go back!

The common culinary thyme is hardy here but can get brown and crispy by the end of the summer and so is not particularly ornamental.

I wish I could be more specific as to exactly which varieties and species of thyme to buy, but given that there are at least 50 different types of thyme, many of them closely, if not incestuously, related and with some having more than one name, this information could be as tangled as thyme itself. Just remember that common thyme, creeping thymes, woolly thyme, and low-mounding lemon thymes are generally hardy, and as for anything else—all bets are off.

TIARELLA SPP. (FOAMFLOWERS) Charming little woodland plants for the shade, foamflowers bloom late May through June and can be used as ground cover. Dig in humus when you plant, but otherwise, tiarella plants are adaptable to some dryness and look good all summer. The basal foliage is neat, almost prim, with stems bearing airy columns of lacy flowers. I have *T. wherryi* and can highly recommend it. *T. cordifolia* is very similar in appearance, and I'm told it spreads through rhizomes and is mat forming. I also have *T.* 'Filigree Lace', purchased at a Morton's Arboretum (Lisle, Illinois) plant sale. It's smaller than *T. wherryi* and is so demure and pretty it could break your heart.

This is a little terrier of a plant, but there are limits to its toughness. As a natural companion to hostas, a tiarella is always in danger of being overgrown by hosta leaves, which can move fast. I have lost some tiarellas this way, so keep an eye on them.

More and more shade gardeners are discovering these wonderful, tough plants, and if you buy one, you'll probably soon want more.

TRADESCANTIA SPP. (SPIDERWORT) I never used to be a fan of tradescantia, until one day I saw it grown properly, in a big, grassy drift. Tradescantia has strappy, grasslike foliage, and just as a few, lone grass plants aren't impressive, trasdescantia can look weedy if grown singly or in small quantities. A mass of tradescantia, though, can look like an attractive grass with the bonus of pretty, three-petaled flowers. Tradescantia flowers bloom in clusters, or "knots," and last only one day. The flower petals seem to vanish, so there's no deadheading.

Tradescantia is very easy to divide, so it doesn't take too long for the gardener to produce a nice drift, though in and of itself, tradescantia is not invasive in average soil.

Once the gardener has seen the light on how to present tradescantia in the garden, this becomes an increasingly attractive plant, as it's adaptable and long blooming. It doesn't like poor, dry soil and can take sun or dappled shade. Some catalogs characterize it as a woodland or shade plant, but I've seen the "wild" tradescantia, *T. ohiensis*, with its beautiful, deep blue flowers, growing under blistering sun along railroad tracks. The tracks were high above a moist ravine, and I suspect that some water was seeping up from the ravine.

TRICYRTIS HIRTA (TOAD LILY) If you have a lightly shaded spot in your garden with rich, humus-y, moist soil, lucky you—you can grow toad lilies. Their speckled, orchidlike blooms look like nothing you would expect to see in a Midwestern garden, but given the right conditions (mulching helps), they will thrive. If their roots are allowed to dry out, though, their stay in your garden will be brief.

VERBENA CANADENSIS (ROSE VERBENA) If wishing would make it so, I would wish that this plant were hardy in our area. But if ever there was a "perennial" that is borderline hardy in our area, this is it. Out of two rose verbena plants in my garden last year, one made it through the winter, one didn't. Some years all of them will survive, some years none. So although I'm sneaking it in here among the perennials, it's what some gardeners call "iffy." But I mention it because it's so pretty, old-fashioned looking, unfussy, and heat and drought tolerant, that if you see plants sold at a nominal price, you might want to take a chance on it.

Rose verbena is a low (about nine inches tall), mat-forming plant for the front of a border. Faithful deadheading will keep it blooming all summer. Its vibrant pink-purple flower color can add depth to a pastel garden or can set off sparks with marigolds and zinnias.

VERBENA HASTATA (BLUE VERVAIN) This is a slender, elegant plant, about three feet tall, holding aloft a candelabra of dark blue-purple spikes in late summer. It needs moist, even wet, soil. If you have that, try them in a group with *Asclepias incarnata* (swamp milkweed) and *Coreopsis palmata* (tickseed).

A toad lily (*Tricyrtis hirta*) blooms in October.

Blooming on this early August prairie are black-eyed Susans, wild bergamot, and the white spikes of Culver's root (*Veronicastrum virginicum*).

VERNONIA FASCICULATA (IRONWEED) Do you want purple in late summer to go with all the yellows and golds? Then try ironweed, native to moist prairies, about three to five feet tall, and with royal purple flowers from mid-July to October. The name refers to the toughness of its stem. Don't be too concerned about the height. It will reach its maximum height in moist soil; in ordinary garden soil, its stays around four feet.

My soil is really too dry for ironweed, but it does the best it can. Its beautiful, deep green leaves range along arching stems, and its attractiveness to butterflies earns it a permanent berth in my garden.

VERONICA SPP. (SPEEDWELL) Most veronicas are fairly low-growing plants, with church spires of flowers that begin blooming in June and go through August if they are cut back periodically. Veronicas need just regular soil, not wonderful soil, and are good at being pretty at the front row of a border. There are many veronica varieties, both short and tall, some sprawling, and all having the distinctive flower spires. Veronicas come in pinks, roses, and whites but are especially famous for their blues. *V. austriaca* 'Crater Lake Blue' is gentian blue, 'Trehane' is deep sky blue, *V. spicata* 'Goodness Grows' has violet-blue flowers, and *V. spicata* 'Nana' is indigo blue.

VERONICASTRUM VIRGINICUM (CULVER'S ROOT) This graceful, elegant native of the tallgrass prairies and woodland meadows is a fine plant for even the most genteel perennial garden. Growing to about four to five feet, the plant holds aloft curving candelabras of small, white flowers that bloom all the way from June through September. Veronicastrum will do well if you dig in plenty of moisture-retentive organic matter and give it light shade. It's effective when planted with Queen-of-the-Prairie (*Filipendula rubra*), gayfeather (*Liatris*), and wood lilies (*Lilium philadelphicum*) or with common garden perennials.

Just the other day I came across a mention of veronicastrum in an article about British gardening great Penelope Hobhouse. She had given a slide show at the Arts Club of Chicago, and one of the slides was of a garden in Holland. It showed a small pond surrounded by masses of *Filipendula rubra* and Culver's root, both bona fide Illinois natives. The article noted that American influences were starting to "flow eastward across the Atlantic."

VINCA MAJOR (PERIWINKLE) Beware of vinca, a common ground cover. Or perhaps I should more kindly say, be *aware* of vinca, both its good and bad points. It's a journeyman ground cover that can tackle just about any dry shade

The graceful blue spires of a veronica adorn this cottage garden in late June.

challenge you throw at it and look good while doing so, with its mounds of immaculate, waxy, dark green leaves and masses of periwinkle purple flowers sparkling in the shade in the spring. Vinca is a gardening cliche but has been one since the Middle Ages, so this doesn't bother me. What does bother me is the inconspicuous, above-ground stems that it sends out, infiltrating other ground covers and choking hostas. It's the kind of plant that could obliterate an entire Mayan ruin with no problem. Last week I rescued a patch of lamium, a 'Sprite' astilbe, squeaking in fright, and some Virginia waterleaf from the clutches of vinca, and before I was finished, I had pulled out half a bushel of the stuff. So while it is a valuable plant for dry shade, as I say . . . be aware.

VIOLA PAPILIONACEA (COMMON BLUE VIOLET) Violets blooming in the springtime are so charming that you may wonder how anyone could be hard-hearted enough to say a single word against them. Well, I'm that hard-hearted, and the single word I'll say about common blue violets is "invasive." Whatever you do, don't *buy* a common violet plant or accept a clump from a neighbor, as they're garden thugs of the first degree. I actually saw violets being sold at a local garden club's plant sale. Shudder. Enjoy them in some-one else's yard, though let's face it, they're probably in yours already. It's not that they're all that difficult to pull out or that they're not pretty, it's just that there are so many of them, and they will grow right up through your perennials, strangling them. Having said that . . .

I was surprised the other day to come across a "Violet Forum" on Gardenweb.com and, after logging on, suddenly found myself floating serenely in the gentle world of violets where gardeners read the *Violet Gazette* and where every question—"Is this a violet?"—sounds like the title of a poem. My heart softened, and I thought of the little violet 'Freckles' that nestles in my backyard, protected by a chest-beating bruiser of a pulmonaria. Totally against my will, I logged on to the americanvioletsociety.org Web site, which is prettiness itself, with each screen wreathed in violets, and where gardeners seriously into violets discuss vining violets and night violets, and where you can explore the world of violets in music, history, and literature, and soon my head was spinning. The world of plants is truly infinite and wonderful. Still, I couldn't see getting into a plant where you would have to spend much of your time on your stomach in order to see them, and one topic at the Web site—Violets in the Lawn—hinted at their dark side, but I can understand their appeal. The photos alone, of bird's foot violets and meadow blue violets, could melt your heart.

A retiring flower, hidden from the eye!
Fair as a star, when only one
Is shining in the sky.

—Anonymous

VIOLA TRICOLOR (JOHNNY-JUMP-UP) Purchase this plant but once, and it will take it from there and reseed every year. I would really miss Johnny-jump-up if it didn't return, as it's an old-fashioned little flower with pretty, purple, cream, and yellow petals. The colors vary from flower to flower, and that's part of the charm. It's only about six inches tall, and you will sometimes find it shyly hiding under other plants. There are many other tempting varieties of *V. tricolor*, but so far I haven't found any that return like Johnny-jump-up.

ZIZIA APTERA (HEART-LEAFED MEADOW PARSNIP) *Zizia aptera* is quite similar to the following *Z. aurea* but will tolerate drier soils and the flowers of the umbel are farther apart than in *Z. aurea*. It flowers from mid-May to mid-June. Its leaves are tipped with yellow, and it is a solid candidate for any sunny garden. I've seen *Z. aptera* grown next to the perennial cornflower, *Centaurea montana*. The golden zizia flowers and the intense blue of the corn-flowers made a striking picture.

ZIZIA AUREA (GOLDEN ALEXANDER) A small, delicate, perennial wild-flower about one to two feet in height, *Z. aurea* has umbels of golden flowers that appear in spring. This native of moist prairies is long blooming, flowering from April through June.

There are a number of members of the wild parsnip family growing in the Midwest, some of them tall, coarse, and weedy, but the golden alexanders are the earliest to bloom and the smallest, most delicate members of that family. The zizias were named in honor of Johann Baptist Ziz, a German botanist of the late eighteenth and early nineteenth centuries. Thank you, Dr. Ziz.

A pink-flowered geranium pairs with blue Lyme grass (*Leymus arenarius*).

Nobody likes to admit to being a snob, but I'll admit that for a while I was a snob about annuals. Grow boring old petunias in my garden? Grow silly little marigolds like Aunt Gladys? No way. I had to have a *perennial* garden to have a real garden, an attitude I had unknowingly absorbed from the English garden tradition. Annuals weren't *tasteful*. They were for gardening philistines who wanted neon yellow marigolds and flowers the size of dinner plates. Master gardeners grow only perennials. Right? Wrong! Annual flowers can be so beautiful, easy to grow, and heat and drought tolerant that they are perfect plants for the Midwestern cottage garden. And you don't *have* to grow boring old petunias, though I've come to deeply respect the toughness of petunias and really like the newer multiflora varieties.

None of this would mean anything, of course, if annuals were all strident in color and boring. But annuals can be gloriously beautiful and wondrously varied. There really is something for every gardener.

Annuals that thrive

Many annuals are easy to start yourself. Some can be sown directly into the soil where they are to flower, and the gardener doesn't have to bother with coddling flats of seedlings indoors. Cosmos, sunflowers, cleome, and four-o'clocks are good examples of easy annuals that can be sown in place and will be blooming before you know it, as long as you water steadily during the germination and seedling stage.

The best way, though, to have access to interesting annuals is to hone your seed-starting skills—then you can grow anything you want. Tender annuals are best started indoors, while hardy annuals can be sown in the fall outside. Read through the "Starting Seeds" section of chapter 9 in this book, and then try some annuals that sound interesting to you. Some of the best seed selections for annuals are found in catalogs, not stores. I recommend the catalogs of Thompson & Morgan and Select Seeds Antique Flowers for their tempting offerings.

Now let's take a look at some pretty, dependable annuals that are at home in Midwestern gardens.

Heat-Loving Annuals

How hot does it get in the Midwest during summer? Some say it gets hotter than a Panamanian pizza parlor. And, as they always say, it's not just the heat, it's the humidity, a one-two punch that can send a weatherman's discomfort index soaring and leave us wilting. A lot of plants don't like the heat-humidity combination, either, and it's in the scorching days of July and August that weak plant sisters are unmasked. This is when the delphiniums throw their stems up in disgust and shrivel. Otherwise healthy plants wilt at high noon, mildew begins creeping stealthily through the garden, and deep, Death Valley–like cracks open in the clay soil.

Luckily for us, many annuals not only don't mind heat and humidity, they thrive in it. It reminds them of their ancestral homes on the baking hot plains of Mexico, southern Italy, Turkey, or for that matter, the plains and prairies of our own Midwest.

Sometimes the heat begins early, in late June. This can be a dangerous time for the garden, as the gardener is lulled by the gentle gardening conditions of late April, May, and early June. An early three- or four-day heat wave can sear and stunt young plants if you're not alert and ready to water profusely. Once stunted, a plant will never grow up to its full potential, no matter how much it is cosseted later on.

Like most plants, annuals have a better chance of getting through the hot weeks and months in good shape in good garden soil. Soil enriched with humus keeps plant roots cool, moist, and healthy. And good soil allows roots to grow down deep to where moisture content is unaffected by the weather up above. Mulching will also help keep the soil cool, prevent moisture loss, and circumvent self-seeding, if the gardener so wishes. Just to keep things interesting for the gardener, though, some plants have evolved to thrive in poor, dry soil. It becomes the gardener's task to determine which plant likes what, and to plant accordingly.

Some desert plants can tolerate extreme heat but are felled by humidity. You may have heard in garden books and magazines of "xeriscaping," which means landscaping and gardening in drought conditions. Take xeriscaping advice with a big grain of salt, as our prairies and woods are totally unlike the deserts of the Southwest or the dry, alkaline plains of the Great West. Though heat and drought resistant, plants from these regions don't necessarily do well in our clay soil and with our humidity.

CELOSIA PLUMOSA (PLUMED COCKSCOMB) Not known for its subtlety, plumed cockscomb looks almost like flames shooting from the earth, which, in our hot months, seems appropriate. I once saw a bouquet made with feverfew, fairy roses, pink zinnias, and raspberry plumed cockscomb, and it was so pretty. Crested celosia look like big brain corals and are not my personal favorites, but I'm sure someone can find a way to spotlight them flatteringly.

CLEOME HASSLERANA (CLEOME OR SPIDER FLOWER) Make way for cleome, a big, airy plant with clouds of flower heads in spectrums of pink, rose, or purple. There's a white variety, too, beautifully cool and lacy looking on a hot summer day. Easy to grow, totally drought resistant, and will self-seed. Brush past a cleome and bruise its leaves, and you will inhale the aroma of a monkey house at a zoo, disconcerting to say the least. Solution? Give it a wide berth. Cleome is pronounced "klee-OH-me."

COREOPSIS TINCTORIA (CALLIOPSIS) Gay, colorful calliopsis likes poor soil, sun, and good drainage. There are different colors of calliopsis: some are bicolored red and yellow, and some are mahogany. Grow calliopsis among other flowers to provide support for its spindly stems.

COSMOS BIPINNATUS (COSMOS) Easy to grow, doesn't mind being neglected, and doesn't mind average soil or some drought, the graceful cosmos gets the Heroine Flower Award of the Summer. Sow cosmos directly into the garden, and barely a month later, it will be dancing in the wind above all the other flowers. I don't recommend buying this flower already started at a nursery, though you may see it there. Tall plants like cosmos can get permanently stunted if they spend a moment too long in small containers.

The money-saving gardener can purchase a 10-cent packet of cosmos at the local grocery store come spring. The variety is always 'Sensation', a pretty mix of white, pink, and red. Scratch the seed into the soil, water, give it space, and you may have cosmos for many summers to come, as it often self-seeds.

GAILLARDIA PULCHELLA (BLANKET FLOWER) This American native (of the central plains, not the Midwest) is heat and drought resistant and doesn't mind poor soil. The flowers are often bicolored red and yellow with touches of orange or purple. They're about as subtle as a bowl of salsa with taco chips. I really hesitated as to whether to include gaillardia here, though, because they don't like heavy clay soil or extreme humidity. So they seem to do fine in some gardens, not so fine in others, and I think drainage has everything to do with it. You might lighten the soil with fine gravel and a bit of coarse sand to help them. Don't fertilize.

GOMPHRENA GLOBOSA (GLOBE AMARANTH) Given that these flowers look dry even when they are fresh, they are perfect plants for the garden under siege of drought. I think the white variety looks a bit dingy, but the violet or strawberry-colored ones are nice.

HELIANTHUS ANNUUS (SUNFLOWER) I guess if I had just 10 bucks and wanted to grow something easy but spectacular in a sunny area in my yard, I would grow a sunflower garden. The Queens of Flowerdom, sunflowers reign over our Midwestern gardens and have no problem at all with heat. Sunflowers couldn't be easier to start—just sow where they are to grow. They're actually unhappy when started indoors, so there are no shenanigans with little pots on windowsills. Up grow the plants into the sky like Jack's giant beanstalk. I lust for big sunflowers, little ones, Van Gogh sunflowers, Italian ones, a troop of gangly sunflowers, anything—but I only have room for a small grove of sunflowers outside the living room window. Cardinals fight over the seeds come late summer. Speaking of birds, check out the Jung Quality Seeds catalog for the seeds for 'Black Oil' sunflower, the "favorite sunflower of seed eating birds."

HELICHRYSUM BRACTEATUM (STRAWFLOWER) Members of the daisy family that like dry heat. Very easy to dry.

HELIOTROPIUM ARBORESCENS (HELIOTROPE) A bona fide English cottage garden favorite that does amazingly well in our climate is heliotrope. The beauty of heliotrope, aside from the fact that it *is* beautiful, is that even during the worst heat waves it remains in pristine condition, with no spots of mildew, fading, or insect problems. Its jewellike violet-colored flowers smell like cherries, which is how it got its common name, cherry pie plant. It blooms for weeks without deadheading.

I keep heliotrope front row, center in the garden, mainly because it's only about a foot tall, but also because the deep violet color of the flowers and the deep green, heavily incised leaves tend to disappear into the shadows if placed farther back. Traditionally, heliotrope is paired with bright red geraniums. This is a striking combination, perhaps a bit too striking for some, and it can also be paired with pale lavender, pale yellow, and cream-colored petunias for a more subtle effect. Heliotrope is also an excellent candidate for use

in container gardens.

IPOMOEA NIL (MORNING GLORY) Sun, sun, sun, sun, sun, sun, sun, sun, more sun. Is there anything else we need to know about growing the morning glory vine? Just soak the seeds overnight before planting. Also, find and plant the variety 'Heavenly Blue' to snare a piece of the sky and tether it in your garden.

LIMONIUM SINUATUM (ANNUAL STATICE) Annual statice tolerates heat, drought, and salt. Clusters of papery flowers come in pretty roses, creams, yellows, lavenders, and sky blues. The plants are more graceful then some everlastings, and I would grow them even if they weren't so easy to dry and useful for flower arrangements.

MIRABILIS JALAPA (FOUR-O'CLOCK) These are the first flowers that I remember seeing as a child. I was fascinated that the flowers only opened in late afternoon. The seeds are large and easily planted by children; they germinate quickly, and soon the flowers appear in their unique, iridescent shades of pale yellow, fluorescent pink, and white. Problem free and growing to about 30 inches in height, a planting of four-o'clocks can make a nice neat little hedge. Plant them near a window so you can smell their haunting fragrance during summer evenings. It's an unforgettable mingling of something sweet, like vanilla, with a lemon note and then something else—almost a medicinal note. There's something other-worldly about this flower, and if there are flowers on Mars, they probably smell like four-o'clocks. Four-o'clocks self-seed, but only in the way every flower would if the world were perfect, replacing themselves every season and not spreading. Once you have these, you'll want them in your garden forever.

PORTULACA GRANDIFORA (MOSS ROSE) Grandma's old reliables, these low-growing succulents don't mind exposed, poor soil and hellish heat. Unfortunately for us, moss roses close up during the overcast conditions not uncommon here. Before I'd plant moss roses, I'd check out the section below that discusses creeping zinnia and Dahlbery daisy, two annuals that absolutely love heat. Grandma didn't have these options.

Personally, I reserve the moss rose for the hottest, most mercilessly sunny spot in my yard, which is a south-facing window box overlooking the side garden. This summer I planted it with *P.* 'Duet Rose', and it was the answer to my prayers; I have now turned this window box over to portulaca in perpetuity. With fuchsia flowers tipped in bright yellow, this is not a subtle plant, but it faces the hottest sun without wilting and its bright colors stand up cheerfully to the bleaching July midday sun. It's not that it doesn't have to be watered, and I do water this window box every other day in very hot weather. But this is nothing like the exhausting two or three times a day other flowers in this spot would require.

SCABIOSA ATROPURPUREA (PINCUSHION FLOWER) This is a graceful and charming flower. The plant is about 18 inches in height, the flowers shades of old-fashioned lavender and blue. I plant the seeds directly in the garden, along with single-petaled zinnias. While I've never read elsewhere that scabiosa are heat lovers, they thrive in my garden on the hottest days.

SENECIO CINERIA (DUSTY MILLER) Silvery little plants used for their foliage. Typically planted with marigolds and salvia, but I hope we can be more imaginative than that. Try with pale purple petunias and blue salvia. A number of different plants are sold under the name of dusty miller, all quite similar, though 'Silver Lace', with its filigreed leaves, is exceptionally pretty.

Dusty miller sometimes overwinters, so you might want to leave it alone in the fall and see if it pulls through.

TAGETES (MARIGOLD) Another Mexican native, the marigold is one of the classic garden flowers of the Midwest. These days, though, marigolds are sometimes felled by earwigs if you are unlucky enough to inhabit an earwig zone. I love the big Inca hybrids, which glow like the sun itself, as well as the delicate little 'Lemon Gems' and the French Vanilla hybrids.

TITHONIA ROTUNDIFOLIA (MEXICAN SUNFLOWER) Big, husky plants sporting hot orange flowers with gold centers—one look and you'll say, *"ole!"* (Sorry, sometimes I get carried away.) Good for the back of a border or for a mercilessly hot spot with decent soil. Tithonia is the biggest annual I know of, growing to six feet or more with sunflowerlike blossoms two and a half to three inches across, and has the presence of a shrub. Butterflies love tithonia. Direct seed tithonia where it is to grow when the soil is warm, as seedlings started indoors are very prone to rot.

VERBENA BONARIENSIS When I first saw *V. bonariensis* at a garden nursery, I wondered why or where anyone would plant it. What *do* you do with a four-foot-tall, slender-stalked plant with little purple pom-poms at the tip? You plant a lot of it, that's what. *V. bonariensis* is a cloud of purple polka dots hovering above the other lower plants among it. A clump of at least a dozen plants can provide a strong and unusual vertical accent in the garden. This plant is a great conversation piece, as many people are not familiar with it. I'm sure that it hasn't grown more quickly in popularity simply because, as

seen at a plant nursery, it's strange looking. It's kind of like that dress that looks awful on the hanger but looks great once it's on—you have to see it in action, so to speak. And it smells good, like carnations.

V. bonariensis, also known as "Brazilian vervain," self-seeds, popping up when the soil is warm, but it's such a useful flower in the garden, and for that matter, such an expensive annual at the nursery, that most of us won't mind. If your self-seeded plants come up in the shade, dig them up and move them to a sunny spot. *V. bonariensis* needs heat and if left in cool shade may not quite reach the point of flowering.

Whatever you do, don't plant just one of these plants, or even just four, for that matter. Think of it in drifts and clouds and in combination with other flowers, and you can't go wrong.

VERBENA HYBRIDA (ANNUAL VERBENA) Clusters of old-fashioned looking little primroselike flowers cover low-growing plants. The parents of annual verbena are native to subtropical and tropical South America. I include annual verbena in this group because, in general, it does tolerate heat and drought. It's a bit more marginal than the others on this list, though, so don't forget to water it on the really hot days.

VINCA ROSEA OR CATHARANTHUS ROSEUS (VINCA) Low mounds of ground-covering, glossy foliage producing pink or rose flowers with contrasting eyes. My vinca never did very well, and I had an inferiority complex about them, until I learned that while they need *poor* soil, which I certainly have, it should be *light* poor soil. Adding some coarse sand makes a big difference.

TWO LOW-GROWING ANNUALS THAT LOVE HEAT

Creeping zinnia and Dahlberg daisy might not be household words in the Midwest, but they do deserve to be better known here. Both are low-growing plants with daisylike flowers about the size of a dime, and both love heat—horrible, baking, sizzling, frying, relentless, record-breaking heat. Sound like our kinds of plants, don't they?

Creeping zinnia (*Santivalia procumbens*) is also commonly known as santivalia. The plant forms a mat that's about eight inches high and is covered with flowers that look like little black-eyed Susans. You can use creeping zinnia as an edging plant, as ground cover, in hanging baskets, or, as Ortho's *All about Annuals* claims, in "cracks in the pavement." It's one tough plant. Creeping zinnia is a native of the hot, dry plains of Mexico, which is probably why it does so well in the Midwest in August. In caring for this plant, think in terms of what not to do. Certainly, don't fertilize it. And don't over-water. It will then proceed to bloom like crazy from June to frost.

Dahlberg daisy (*Dyssodia tenuiloba*) is another option for the hot spots in your garden. Growing to about eight inches, Dahlberg daisy forms a fluffy mat of bright green, finely divided leaves covered with golden flowers. It's a very clean, crisp little plant that reminds me a bit of chamomile, though it's a much tougher character than that herb. As with creeping zinnia, Dahlberg daisy does well in poor to average soil and baking heat.

While both flowers are very drought tolerant, if you're in the throes of a really long, terrible, record-breaking drought, they wouldn't mind a drink or two. If I had to choose between the two, all I can say is that creeping zinnia is very cheerful looking, while Dahlberg daisy is delicate and pretty. Why not try both?

FOUR UNUSUAL ANNUALS

Not, of course, that we should really *care* about impressing the neighbors—at least not *admit* to caring—but the following annuals sound exotic and hard to grow but in fact are easy and make the gardener look good. All of them are robust plants that tolerate heat.

The first is Jewels of Opar (*Talinum paniculatum* 'Aurea'). I didn't know what to expect when I planted these seeds, but the Select Seed Antique Flower catalog spoke so highly of them that I waited with bated breath. I started the seeds in pots indoors, and they germinated easily. I planted them outside in late May. The seedlings were bright chartreuse, and as the plant developed it looked like a strange, Martian form of lettuce. Then the plants sent up skinny stalks and almost overnight sported pretty little magenta pink flowers. *Then*, small, shiny, round, red seeds formed—the "jewels." At this point, I was fascinated—what else would this plant do? The sprays of seeds and flowers expanded to a cloud over the basal foliage to breathtaking effect. I have some plants in sun, and some in partial shade, and while the shaded plants are doing well, these are really sun plants. Thompson & Morgan offers seeds for the "fame flower" (*Talinum calycinum*), whose description sounds very similar to the Jewels of Opar. I'm very curious about the fame flower and will start seed this spring.

The next flower is *Nicotiana langsdorffii*, an old-fashioned flowering tobacco. Tall spikes (about 30 inches) bear little chartreuse bells. The basal leaves are light green and soft in texture. Once you plant this, it will self-seed in your garden reliably every year, and you won't mind. It pops up between the brick pavers of my garden paths, looking pretty and "cottage garden-y." Last year we had an unusually long, cool spring, and *N. langsdorffii* leaves appeared, but no flowers—apparently it needs a long period of warmth to flower.

I never in a million years would have known about the so-called mosquito flower, *Lopezia cordata* 'Pretty Rose', except that it was in a seed mixture from Thompson & Morgan. The plant is about a foot tall, with lax stems and small, dark green leaves. The little pink flowers don't really look like mosquitoes to me, perhaps more like little butterflies. Whatever type of flying creature they resemble, they are pretty and are conversation pieces in the garden because believe me, no one else on your block will be growing them. What's more, mosquito flower germinates easily from seed indoors and will grow on to maturity even under inexpert care. By mid-June, it is firmly established and will flower continuously into fall. A drought last summer didn't faze it. As I write this, I'm aware this plant sounds too good to be true, but do remember that it is not a big, spectacular plant, but rather a charming, eccentric little creature—just the sort of thing for a cottage garden.

The last of this group is blue throatwort (*Trachelium caeruleum*), a member of the bellflower family. The plant is barely two feet in height and has dark green foliage and misty lavender flower heads. It has no problem with heat, and its foliage is clean and unmildewed all summer. It is native to the western Mediterranean area, where it is a tall perennial growing in damp shade. I've grown it in a spot with early morning and late afternoon shade, and it has tolerated heat and drought. There is a white variety available in England called 'White Umbrella', and I can hardly wait until it arrives on our shores. Trachelium, whether seed or plant, is not always easy to find, and you may have to hunt for it. I usually find it at a well-stocked nursery that offers a wide variety of flowers. This is a healthy, sturdy little plant that goes with almost everything. So if you see this at a nursery—grab it!

The best book on annuals I know of is *Discovering Annuals*, by Graham Rice. He really takes annuals to a whole new level. Photo after photo of mixed annual plantings are truly inspiring, and many are easy. A crowd of white cleome, rose cosmos, and *Verbena bonariensis*, for instance, couldn't be easier and would grow beautifully here in the Midwest. White-flowered borage grown with yellow calendulas or white cosmos with pale yellow zinnias and a white annual sage are just two more interesting and easy combinations.

The little lime green flower bells of annual *Nicotiana langsdorffii*.

Gloriosa Daisies
IN A CLASS BY THEMSELVES

I have grown gloriosa daisies for years. They are cheerful-looking, long-flowering (from midsummer through fall), very heat-resistant plants that are easy to start from seed. So I've always grown them and liked them, but it is only recently that they exploded into my consciousness, in the way certain plants sometimes do, and I realized that they are more than just nice: they can be simply spectacular. The oversized, gold-petaled flowers marked with mahogany and maroon glow with the warmth of the summer's sun and look like the flowers in a child's picture of a garden.

The reason that the gloriosa daisy is so glorious is that it is a tetraploid cultivar of the black-eyed Susan (*Rudbeckia hirta*). Tetraploid plants have four sets of chromosomes, instead of the usual two, and tend to have really big flow-

ers: gloriosa daisy flowers may reach seven inches, and some flowers of other *R. hirta* cultivars may reach nine inches across. So a gloriosa is kind of like a black-eyed Susan on steroids.

Additional *R. hirta* cultivars besides the gloriosa have been steadily arriving on the gardening scene in the past few years, and I have liked each one I've tried, though be forewarned that they are all variations on the same theme of big daisylike flowers with warm gold petals—you won't find anything pink, white, or blue in this crew. But you do have *R. hirta* 'Green Eyes', which has an olive green eye; 'Indian Summer', with huge blossoms that may measure nine inches across; 'Chim Chiminee', with its resemblance to a giant aster; the stunning 'Sonora', with a dark mahogany eye; and the gorgeous 'Double Gold' gloriosa daisy, with its fluffy mound of double petals. Burpee offers some varieties, including the 'Double Gold' and 'Sonora', but Thompson & Morgan offers eleven *R. hirta* cultivars, so they have much to choose from. If you just can't decide, their 'All Sorts Mixed', which contains seeds for everything they offer, might be the answer.

Depending on whom you read, *Rudbeckia hirta* and its cultivars are either free-seeding annuals, biennials, or perennials—take your pick. It may be all of the above, with winter conditions determining what actually happens in the garden. *R. hirta* seeds itself around my garden, but gloriosa daisies are short-lived perennials, with the same plants persisting for two or three years. They seem to be a bit sensitive to winter dampness, and this may be what finally does them in. I have heard, however, that in some gardens they do self-seed, so I guess you have to be prepared for anything, and until you determine how they behave in your garden, it's best to treat gloriosa daisies as annuals. Then if they come back, you'll have a pleasant bonus.

This brings us to another reason why gloriosa daisies are so valuable to the Midwestern gardener—not only are they spectacular, but they are very easy to start from seed, so you can have as many as you want in your garden for the cost of a few packets of seed. So if you are a beginning seed starter and have learned to start tomato seeds and are looking for new worlds to conquer, try gloriosa daisies. They germinate quickly indoors (seven to ten days) and can suffer a fair amount of manhandling on the part of the inexperienced gardener and still emerge victorious. Start them in mid- to late March. This is a bit early, but if the spring seems warm, you can ease them into the garden as small plants. If the weather stays cold, gloriosa daisies don't mind sitting in their pots for a while indoors and will not grow spindly.

Gloriosa daisies range in height from 24 to 36 inches and have no problem with clay soil of average fertility. While usually pegged as sun plants, gloriosas get a fair amount of light shade in my garden, and they do fine. They do best on regular waterings but will soldier on manfully through drought.

Rudbeckias are often grown with purple or red salvias, a combination that I find a bit harsh. I prefer to cool the flames with cream-colored zinnias or tall blue ageratum. Rudbeckias have rather stiff stems, so the feathery love-in-a-mist (*Nigella damascena*) would be a nice companion, as would a soft, annual grass like squirrel-tail grass (*Hordeum jubatum*). Hare's-tail grass (*Lagurus ovatus*) could also be pretty.

Zinnias

In *The Book of Annuals*, written in 1928, Alfred C. Hottes observed about the zinnia that "because it is of easy culture and does well for anyone, it has in the past been admired less than it deserves," and I think this still holds true for some gardeners who seem to need a challenge. As I've gotten older, though, I appreciate the easiness of zinnias more and more. Maybe I'm getting not only older, but more simple minded, but the straightforwardness of just planting seed in regular old soil and getting pretty, cheerful flowers not long after is satisfying. Some gardeners raise a hubbub about mildew and zinnias, yet I can honestly say mine get little mildew, and it usually only appears right at the end of summer and is not disfiguring.

Zinnias thrive in rich clay soil and heat. You can directly sow zinnia seed when the soil is warm, or you can start them indoors. If you direct-seed, remember to give them plenty of space to grow, as one zinnia plant of medium height can take up almost one square foot. Water the seeded soil regularly so that the germinating seeds don't dry out in the often warm and windy weather of early summer. Young seedlings are delicacies for sow bugs, but sprinkling crushed eggshell around the seedlings seems to protect them. Keep watering the young zinnias as they grow—they're not drought resistant until fully grown.

There are so many beautiful zinnias to talk about that maybe we should start at the beginning and look at a species zinnia, the narrow-leaf zinnia, *Zinnia angustifolia*, which has given rise to the mounding zinnias. if you're interested in growing "heirloom" flowers, this is the species to have: it was grown by the Aztecs. According to the Select Seed catalog, these zinnias were grown in the gardens of Montezuma along with dahlias, sunflowers, and morning glories. *Z. angustifolia* are orange, daisylike flowers on low mounds of crisp

foliage. Hybridizers have also developed bright white, orange, and gold versions of this flower. The angustifolias are especially drought and mildew resistant and are becoming more and more widely available as gardeners discover their charms.

The flowers of 'Persian Carpet' zinnias come in variegated shades of gold, cream, orange, and terra cotta. The plants are about two feet tall and, for sheer psychedelic richness of flower color and pattern, are fabulous. Two other low-growing varieties are 'Old Mexico', which has a variegated mahogany and gold flower, and 'Chippendale', which has flowers with mahogany centers and yellow tips.

Another antique zinnia is the red peruvian zinnia, *Z. peruviana*. I saw these growing in the heirloom flower garden of Garfield Farm, a local historic landmark in LaFox, Illinois. They are handsome flowers, dark red or mahogany in color. The guide at the farm said they would turn to a lighter rose color later in the summer.

Most of the taller zinnias are in the *Z. elegans* group. My favorites among these are the cut-and-come-again zinnias. About two and a half feet tall with semidouble flowers, the flower colors remind me of ice cream: creamy and cool. There's nothing strident or over the top about these flowers, so if you want a good, old-fashioned, incredibly easy-to-grow zinnia, try them.

The variously variegated 'Peppermint Stick', 'Swirl', and 'Whirligig' zinnias *are* over the top (though not strident) and are so much fun to grow. They satisfy my need for craziness and fantasy in flowers, and I just love them.

A chartreuse green zinnia might sound odd, but *Z.* 'Envy' is quite beautiful and is *the* perfect addition to many a flower arrangement. The Thompson & Morgan people have even come up with 'Envy Double'.

There are zinnias with large, showy flowers, including the giant cactus and dahlia types. One can also find seeds for individual colors of some of the larger zinnias, including lavender, violet, and white. I'm growing a cream-colored zinnia, which is quite elegant and worthy of a spot next to the prettiest perennial.

The bottom line is that zinnias are a lot of fun. Whenever I'm taking gardening too seriously, I walk over to a 'Swirl' zinnia and get a smile. There's usually a bee on it, and even the bee looks like he's having fun.

Geraniums on the Windowsill
. . . AND HOW TO EXPLOIT

Geraniums are so common in Midwestern gardens that it's easy to overlook their charms—you know what they say about familiarity. And for a long time there was pretty much only one geranium: a take-it-or-leave-it, screeching, brick red zonal. Usually, I left it. Geranium hybridizers, luckily for us, have come up with a spectrum of absolutely luscious new colors in the past few years—I'm thinking of an ivy geranium I was given this summer called 'Merlot,' whose velvety petals are the fathomless color of that ruby red wine. And recherché varieties that were once the exclusive province of geranium specialists are now popping up at mass market nurseries. Just this summer I purchased a geranium labeled "tricolor exotica." Its cream- and green-colored leaves are splashed with rusty red. At another nursery I purchased a stellar geranium, whose leaf is the shape of a goose's foot. So there is no reason to moon around unenthusiastically with pedestrian geraniums.

And think about it: geraniums, which are more accurately known as "pelargoniums," grow vigorously and are drought, pest and disease resistant. They seem to actually like heat and humidity. "Throw it at me," they seem to say, "whatever you've got." "Anything?" we ask, smirking. "Yes, anything," say the innocent plants. Mmmm. Maybe we should rethink geraniums and try to see beyond that crooked, dusty geranium baking in a pot on the front porch.

White *Zinnia angustifolia* x *elegans* blooms profusely through a summer of drought.

For starters, let's think about color. Amid the monotonous regiments of red geraniums sold at local nurseries in the summer, you can usually spot some renegade white ones. Swoop them up and bring home an armload. (Pay for them, first, of course.) White geraniums are as cool, crisp, and clean looking as the cumulus clouds of summer. Plant them in big terra cotta pots that you've "whitewashed" with some white acrylic paint thinned with water, and tuck in some trailing vines of ivy to finish it off. This is so inexpensive (especially if you've rooted ivy taken from your own garden) that you could make up a bunch of these pots and place them all through your garden in sunny spots. On those really hot days in August, when everyone else is feverishly watering their planters of lobelia three times a day only to watch them die anyway, you will smile fondly at your geraniums.

Pale pink geraniums are also pretty and are the perfect plant to prettify the patio. How about pale pink geraniums in terra cotta pots painted with giant, pale pink polka dots? Well, maybe not polka dots, but I'm sure you could think of something pretty—perhaps painting the edge of the pot with a white "filet crochet" pattern or a circle of white doves swooping around the rim.

The almost neon, fuchsia red geraniums can, if used judiciously, jolt the dullest planter or window box into life. Or, go for it, and plant amid a blaze of sulfur yellow marigolds, rose pink petunias, and amethyst salvia.

I've been tucking the regular old screeching red geraniums into the vegetable garden to repel pests. It seems to really help. Many garden books recommend using marigolds for this purpose, but earwigs like marigolds, so here in the Midwest we need stronger medicine. Here come geraniums to the rescue! The orangey geranium red that can clash elsewhere in the garden looks cheerful among the green beans, purple basil, and tomatoes.

As for variety, I've already mentioned that we don't have to confine ourselves to the common zonal geraniums, however useful they might be. There is a treasure trove of fancy geraniums panting to be brought into our gardens and admired, including varieties that resemble other, more difficult-to-grow flowers. Some fancy geraniums have flowers with pinked edges like carnations (*P.* 'Skelly's Pride'), and some are cactus flowered like dahlias (*P.* 'Mrs. Salter Bevis'). The rosebud-flowered geraniums look quite convincingly roselike (*P.* 'Plum Rambler'), and the tulip-flowered varieties (*P.* 'Patricia Andrea') look like very small, half-opened tulips. I have a geranium with flowers like pale pink apple blossoms and have seen varieties with azalealike flowers.

So-called angel geraniums include varieties with two-toned petals much like pansies (*P.* 'Captain Starlight'). The original pansy geranium was 'Madam Layal', which first appeared in France in 1870. It has violet-purple top petals and white bottom petals marked with violet-rose. Need I even mention that I am madly lusting for it? Other "angels" have flowers resembling small butterflies (*P.* 'Imperial Butterfly').

What more, really, can we ask for? How about geraniums with two-tone and even tricolor leaves (*P.* 'Mr. Henry Cox')? These multicolor-leafed geraniums have a rich, Victorian feel. And my newest favorite geraniums are the stellars, with their goosefoot leaves and starlike flowers. The stellars are vigorous growers and very heat resistant. I am writing this in December and, having placed a stellar geranium by a south-facing window in October, have watched it shoot up about a foot and become covered with buds.

I've never had much luck with the regal (Martha Washington) geraniums and have only recently discovered why: they need temperatures below 60 degrees to bud. These geraniums, which can look so spectacular at the nursery on sale for Mother's Day, will struggle during the heat of the summer. If you like regals, it would probably be smart to investigate a variety named 'Hartsook's Uniques'. These regal hybrids are supposedly heat and sun resistant.

I've also found that the trailing ivy-leaf geranium really likes cooler weather than we have here in northern Illinois, but if you have the stamina to ply them with copious water and fertilizer, they can be sensational.

Some geraniums can even tolerate a bit of shade. The less green in their leaves, the less noonday sun they can tolerate. Fancy geraniums whose leaves are edged with cream or white or that have golden markings can be grown in bright shade. The more shade, the fewer flowers, but with the really fancy-leafed varieties, you might grow them for the leaves alone.

If you get really into pelargoniums, and I mean really, *really* into them, you might want to investigate species pelargoniums. At two sites on the Internet, both based in South Africa, I have run across at least 80 geranium species, including *P. quinguelobatum*, the village oak geranium. These sites sell seeds. How well any of the species geraniums would do in our climate is anyone's guess, but if you were wondering what to do with the next 50 years of your life—here's your project.

And then, of course, there are the scented geraniums, God's gift to the Midwest. I find myself liking scented geraniums more and more all the time and have amassed quite a collection. My latest is 'Atomic Snowflake', whose

A stellar geranium, its leaves shaped like a goose's foot.

scalloped, lime green leaves are trimmed in white lace. If you've never grown a scented geranium, I recommend trying one this summer. They have all the strong-growing, pest-, heat-, and drought-resistant qualities of regular geraniums, plus deliciously scented foliage. I think you would have to put a scented geranium in a blast furnace to seriously bother it with heat. The old-fashioned rose geranium is perfect to start with, and then you can try the apricot, the lavender, the nutmeg, the peppermint. . . . Scented geraniums vary wildly in size and habit: some, like the nutmeg, are small and delicate, but others, like some of the rose geraniums, are big and husky and can reach five feet, so look at their tags carefully when purchasing, so you'll know what you're getting.

I keep my scented geraniums in pots and try my best to pinch them back during the summer. This keeps them bushy and easy to handle when bringing them inside for the winter as they are not winter hardy. I often take cuttings in February from potted plants, stick them in moist potting soil in yogurt containers, water, and place them by a north window. To keep the soil moist, I put a small plastic sandwich bag over the plant and snug it in with a rubber band. In about six weeks, there's a new plant. Be forewarned: Scented geraniums can become a mania (as if any of us needed another mania), espe-

Scented geranium 'Atomic Snowflake' amid a jumble of pots.

cially when you find out how well they do here. By the way, one of the nicest books about scented geraniums is *The Little Book of Scented Geraniums*, by Adelma Grenier Simmons.

This brings us back to zonals, which are the traditional, bedding plant geraniums. Hybridizers have been working feverishly, it would seem, with zonals, and so now there are silver-leaf zonals (said to do very well in part shade), gold-leaf zonals, dwarf zonals, the even smaller miniature zonals, and even zonals that have been crossed with ivy-leaf geraniums. Somewhere I saw a zonal named 'Jane' whose lime green leaves are ruffled, and 'Jane' showed me that zonals can be among the most beautiful of all geraniums.

Once pelargoniums have you well and truly in their leafy clutches, consider starting a pelargonium society in your community. "A pelargonium society?" you say. "What next?" While surfing the Internet, I ran into the Web site of the Coventry Fuchsia and Geranium Society in Coventry, England. It meets on the first Monday of each month and has such interesting social events as "Special Fuchsia Evenings." This is where the British have so much more fun gardening than we do, with their wonderful, slightly mad-sounding, gardening societies, and it could be fun to follow in their footsteps.

OVERWINTERING GERANIUMS

Even though geraniums are inexpensive, if you like to have a lot of them in your garden, it's both easy and economical to overwinter them and thus "recycle" the same geraniums year after year. Their thick, juicy stems make it possible. (So far, I have only used the following techniques on zonals, not on any of the fancy varieties.) To do this, come fall, dig up your geraniums and shake the soil off their roots. Cut the foliage and stems back to about five inches high. Take the geraniums down into your basement, or up into a cool attic, and hang the geraniums upside down, either on a clothesline or on nails hammered into a wall. Then, forget about them.

Fast-forward to early spring. Plant the geraniums in either a large planter or terra cotta pots. Water. Within a short time, new shoots will appear, and the plants will be ready to go into the garden by planting time.

Geraniums are tough plants and can be recycled for years. I have read of one gardener who has had the same geraniums for 24 years! Almost members of the family! (They are frost sensitive, though, so be sure to take them inside before the first frost. One hard frost can completely zap a geranium, leaving it dead as a doornail.)

More Fine Annuals
FOR THE MIDWESTERN GARDEN

While not quite as drought and heat loving as the previous crew, these are no shrinking violets, either. Most like regular watering and good garden soil amended with organic matter.

AGERATUM HOUSTONIANUM 'BLUE HORIZON' I've never had much luck with the shorter ageratums in my clay-soil garden. The flowers had a dried-out, spotty look. A tall variety, 'Blue Horizon', has came to the rescue and is now one of my favorite annuals. Its pure blue flowers reflect the summer sky above and are vibrant when grown with marigolds, gold and orange cosmos, pale yellow daisies, and tithonia. It blooms all summer right through fall when deadheaded and is drought resistant.

CENTAUREA CYANUS (BACHELOR BUTTONS) Bachelor buttons need a summer a bit cooler than ours, but it would take a harder heart than mine to banish them from the Midwestern garden. There's nothing like that amethyst blue. You can plant the seed early in the spring directly into the soil where they are to grow. They need sun, and the soil can be poor or average. Bachelor buttons usually look good the first half of the summer, but as heat and drought grind on, their fugitive blue fades and they start to swoon. Time to rip them out, though not before you scatter some seed.

CENTAUREA MOSCHATA (SWEET SULTAN) This sweet, fluffy, clover-scented little relative of the bachelor button deserves to be grown in more gardens. You'll need to purchase seeds and sow them yourself in the garden in early spring, as it's not sold as a bedding plant. Grow with other old-fashioned annuals.

COLEUS (PAINTED NETTLE) Coleus used to be a nice, but slightly fuddy-duddy, bedding plant often featured in rather mundane public park plantings. It was hard to get excited over coleus. Sharp-eyed plant hybridizers noticed the plant's potential, however, and a flashy parade of new coleus varieties has appeared lately, each more fabulous than the next. Last spring, at the Flower Show at the Navy Pier in Chicago, the University of Illinois Extension had an inspired exhibit of coleus grown with grasses. New coleus varieties such as 'Flirtin' Skirts' and 'Say Cheese' partnered beautifully with a variety of grasses, including unusual ones like the annual Mexican feather grass (*Stipa tenuissima*), a rush called Fiber Optic grass (*Scirpus cernuus*), and brown sedges. My sister and I walked around and around this exhibit, taking notes, surreptitiously stroking the Mexican feather grass, and generally being bowled over.

The grass/coleus idea is perfectly do-able for the home garden. Have your perennial grasses in place, along with bulbs for spring color. When the weather turns reliably warm (coleus needs temperatures above 50 degrees), swoop in and plant coleus as well as some annual grasses.

I'm not ashamed to say that the moment I came home from the Flower Show, I went on the Internet and found a source for the new varieties of coleus. Before I could stop myself I had ordered 'Solar Shadow', whose green leaves are shaded with purple; 'Trailing Plum Brocade', with leaves like cut velvet; 'Flirtin' Skirts', which almost forms a small shrub; 'Jade Parade', whose scalloped green leaf is edged with purple; the irresistible 'Atlas', in purple and lime green; and 'Japanese Giant', billed not just as a large coleus, but a *very* large coleus. My sister wanted some chartreuse coleus to light up a dark spot in her garden, so I also ordered 'Chartreuse', 'Copasetic Yellow', and 'Pineapple Queen'. It will be a red-letter day when the order arrives.

Coleus are straightforward to grow. Just make sure the weather is warm before putting them out, as they can't take the slightest frost. Pinch back the center stem to create a nice, bushy plant, and pick off the flower stems as they form. I have read that if a coleus goes to seed, it's a dead coleus, having fulfilled its rather limited mission in life. Coleus can be brought in at summer's end and grown as a houseplant. I'm not sure how feasible this is with really large coleus, but I'll find out next fall.

While the new coleus varieties are said to be more sun tolerant than older varieties, I have heard from other gardeners that they are still not plants for blasting noontime sun and prefer bright shade. You may run across coleus under its new botanical name: *Solenostemon scuttillariodes*.

CONSOLIDA AMBIGUA (LARKSPUR) If you yearn to grow delphinium, but find they are not happy with our summers, try a close delphinium relative, larkspur. Give them good soil and sun and water well: you'll never miss the delphiniums. 'Giant Imperial Mix' is a nice mix of blue, pink, lilac, and white, and it's probably what you'll find at the seed rack at your local hardware store. I saw a 10-foot-long border of this in a garden while on a garden walk a few summers ago, and it was absolutely spectacular. Thompson & Morgan has a wonderful assortment of larkspur varieties, including 'Azure Blue' and 'Giant Double Hyacinth Fl. Mixed'. *Consolida* 'Blue Cloud' and 'White Cloud' have columbine-like flowers that seem to float in the air like doves—*really* pretty.

There are two types of larkspur, by the way: the nonbranching and the

'Solar Shadow', a large-leafed coleus.

branching, or field larkspur. The nonbranching, such as the 'Giant Double Hyacinth Fl. Mixed', can look much like the perennial delphinium. But if a neighbor hands you a clump of larkspur over the fence, it's probably the blue field larkspur, a pretty, delicate flower that self-seeds. I love it in my garden with the nearby black-eyed Susans and some purple monarda.

Larkspurs, as kissing cousins to delphiniums, are not all that crazy about heat themselves and can use a touch of shade late in the day.

IBERIS UMBELLATA (CANDYTUFT) I hadn't grown annual candytuft in the past because I had heard that it needed cool summers. I had also heard what a pretty flower it is, though, and I've given it a try. Well, it's beautiful and is thriving even though right now we're in the midst of a heat wave (mid-June). Apparently the secret is to ignore the advice in books to plant in full sun and to give it bright shade. It's flowering heavily in a spot that gets only two or three hours of direct sunlight on and off during the day. The plants are covered with lacy, domed flowers in pale pink, lavender, and creamy white, the color of candy hearts.

July update: Now we're in the midst of a *real* heat wave, and the candytuft is going to seed. I was all set to deadhead, when you know what? I

Self-seeded larkspur (*Consolida ambigua*) in my sister Kathy's garden.

noticed that the light green seed heads are decorative, presenting a different, but still attractive appearance from the flowers themselves. These are interesting plants! Let's see what happens next.

Late August: They're flowering again. I'm collecting some of the dried seed heads: annual candytuft has definitely earned a spot in next year's garden.

Next June: Didn't need to collect seed heads. Candytuft has reseeded and looks great.

IMPATIENS What more can be said of this old trooper, warhorse, and galley slave of the Midwestern garden? Blooming its head off in hot weather, shade, and mediocre soil and not needing deadheading, impatiens is a Rock of Gibraltar, a linchpin, in our gardens. Oh, hail, impatiens! Some critics say that as flowers go, the impatiens flower is not the most interesting in the world and that impatiens are a gardening cliché. I find that I think of impatiens as a color, not a flower. If I need a violet color twinkling in a shady corner with mediocre soil, I think of impatiens. If I want white blobs in the garden—impatiens. Rose blobs—impatiens. And so on. If you can find it, the double-flowered variety is a change of pace and has impressively roselike flowers. I just saw a brick bungalow yesterday ringed with a foaming, scalloped collar of white impatiens.

Planted with hostas and ferns, the look was simple, cool, easy, and clean. I've also seen a number of gardens planted with pink and white impatiens. This is a feminine look—perhaps not for everyone—but very pretty.

My experience with New Guinea impatiens has been inconclusive, so far. To my eyes, their colors are a bit strident, and they also don't seem particularly sun tolerant, though they've been sold as such. I've learned that it's the seemingly "difficult" colors that can be the most striking if used intelligently, however, so I'm not going to give up on them.

Over the years I've tried a number of different color impatiens but keep returning to white. A shade garden can be so . . . dark, and white impatiens light up the dimmest corner.

During a visit to Cantigny Gardens in Wheaton, Illinois, I saw a great idea for using impatiens. Take a large bag of humus (the bag they used looked larger than the usual 40-pound bag) and punch holes evenly in it. Insert young impatiens plants into the holes and water. Their bag was invisible under a solid mass of impatiens. This would be a good idea to bring some color to a spot in the garden with very poor soil.

I've also recently run across *Impatiens* 'Seashells Yellow' and was entranced by the sight of its cream yellow blossoms with cupped petals. Look for it among the "premium annuals" at your local nursery.

LOBULARIA MARITIMA (SWEET ALYSSUM) Inhaling the honey-sweet scent of alyssum floating on warm summer air is one of the pleasures of summer gardening. I mention alyssum here even though it may stop flowering during really hot weather because it performs well for most of the summer and in good soil is a welcome self-seeder.

NICOTIANA ALATA One trick the Midwestern gardener can use to expand the range of appropriate plant material for the garden is to experiment a bit, find one plant that does well, and then investigate the rest of that plant's family tree. Chances are that the good qualities you found in the first plant will also be found in the relatives. This is how I found out about the nicotiana family. I had planted some *N. alata* 'Domino' plants sold as bedding flowers. They thrived in a rather awkward spot in the side garden that spends the first part of the day plunged in shadow, the second part being broiled by sun, and then plunged back into deep shadow. A lot of plants don't like this spot. As it turns out, nicotiana does like some light shade and did well. Encouraged by success, I then tried *N.* 'Nicki', which also performed well.

This led me on a hunting expedition in the Thompson & Morgan catalog to see what else the nicotiana family had up its sleeve. I settled on *N. langsdorffii* and hit the jackpot. As I mentioned in the last chapter, this is a great annual, both pretty and easy to grow. All nicotianas I've grown so far have a gangly look, with the flower-laden stems drooping like the neck of a giraffe, a look I find very appealing. *N. sylvestris* is another interesting and tall member of this family, with the same endearing, gawky look as it hovers in the back of the border. Thompson & Morgan also has seeds for a nicotiana in lime green—a color that works beautifully in many gardens. Look also for the old-fashioned sweet-scented nicotiana (*N. alata*).

PERILLA FRUTESCENS (CHINESE BASIL) Perilla is a bushy plant of about three feet in height, a close relative to coleus. Both are members of the mint family. Perilla is grown mainly for its foliage, which is a striking deep purple-maroon. The leaves are incised, and a mound of perilla has a pleasing patterned effect. As with coleus, perilla likes a touch of shade during the day, and be forewarned that it's a notorious self-seeder.

POGOSTEMON PATCHOULI (PATCHOULI) I have a soft spot in my heart for patchouli and grow it in my garden every summer with other annuals for its scent, even though it's a real sad sack of a plant in appearance. I guess it's the old hippie in me, but I just love the smoky, mellow fragrance, which is so unlike any other. The popularity of patchouli ebbs and flows. Before the hippies, surprisingly, early Victorians were patchouli fans. Shawls woven in India were sent to England packed in wooden crates stuffed with patchouli leaves to provide insect protection, and the scent became fashionable. Patchouli is a distant and exotic cousin of lavender. I've read that patchouli grows to tree size in its natural habitat. Wouldn't it be outta sight to walk through a grove of patchouli trees? Groovy, man.

PETUNIAS HYBRIDA More than any other flower I know, petunias are the Rorschach inkblots of the plant world, with some gardeners feeling they are among the easiest and prettiest of all flowers to grow and with other gardeners mutinously placing them on their "overrated plants" list. I myself have had silent qualms about petunias, noting that they looked bedraggled after rainstorms and that they need lots of pinching back to avoid scraggliness, their besetting sin. "Pro" petunia gardeners note that petunias bloom profusely for months, are frost *and* heat tolerant, are fast growing, and are adaptable for growing in the ground or in containers. You can't deny that when well grown, they are pretty, with a ruffly, all-girl look. I've come to think that growing petunias so they look "just okay" is easy, but having billowing mounds of petunias takes considerable effort.

Their care depends on the variety. Grandiflora petunias, which are the large-flowered petunias of our grandmothers, and which are still popular today, need to be deadheaded regularly. The plants need to be pinched back at least an inch when planting and require regular watering until established. Late in the summer they often become scraggly, despite all efforts, and need to be sheared back by half, watered, and fertilized. They do bounce back, but how quickly depends on how hot and humid the weather is (petunias really like hot, *dry* weather), and so there is a gap in flowering.

The new "spreading" or "trailing" petunias, such as the Wave variety or Supertunias, have become popular for their surging masses of flowers. They grow very rapidly, are resistant to rain damage, don't have to be deadheaded or pinched, and can be used as ground covers or in trailing baskets. These are beautiful petunias and are great for window boxes, but I have heard some murmurs of discontent even with them. They need more water and fertilizing than grandifloras, and a window box or hanging basket will need watering every day and fertilizing at least once a week. One grower I know of recommends *daily* fertilizing, at full strength.

Last summer I tried a petunia relative, *Calibrachoa* 'Millions Bells' and was underwhelmed. The flowers are extremely pretty, like miniature petunias, but the moment I got the plant home, flowering became a struggle. It turns out that, as with the spreading petunias, calibrachoa need lots of water, and I've read that they should be fertilized every time they are watered, at half strength. In their defense, I simply wasn't giving them the care they needed. So, come to think of it, petunias are not really low-maintenance flowers at all, and this may account for their varying reputation among gardeners.

A nurseryman taught me an interesting trick to having a beautiful, full planting of petunias. After preparing the soil, dig a hole big enough to accommodate three petunia root balls, and then plant three petunias in the one hole. Water deeply. Quite quickly you will have a mound of blossoms, and everyone will ask you what kind of fertilizer you use.

Another interesting thing I learned from this same nurseryman is that petunias can be quite cold hardy and can be planted out early in the spring. The cool weather and sometimes frosty conditions of spring "hardens" the petunia, making it healthier later on.

A Few Problem Annuals

Calendula officinalis grows easily when sown in place in spring in the garden and then reseeds itself. It comes in intense shades of orange and yellow. So what's the problem? Midwestern summer heat subdues this flower, and during hot summers it may flower sparingly or not at all. Come the first cool days of fall, though, it springs to life. Growing up through the fallen autumn leaves that naturally collect around it, calendula flowers glow with phosphorescent color, making up for the difficult summer. If you have a small garden where every plant has to pull its own weight all summer, though, you may prefer to not grow it. I have seen calendula sold as early spring flowers, along with pansies.

Fuchsias, whose flowers are like flirtatious dangling earrings, cause agonies among Midwestern gardeners, as they are so beautiful and so intolerant of heat and drought. I felt deep gloom upon reading the following quote from master gardener Joseph F. Williamson: "Fuchsias dislike consistently high temperatures. That makes them difficult to grow wherever sweet corn flourishes, because sweet corn begs for the same hot nights that make fuchsias collapse." Reading this, any hopes I had regarding fuchsias vanished, as I live in an area of the world where sweet corn grows at every bend of the road in summer. Acres and acres and acres of sweet corn. Rank upon rank. Plant scientists have been busy, however (thank goodness), and have come up with the European upright fuchsia (*Fuchsia × hybrida*), which according to the people at the University of Illinois Extension, is not "your typical fuchsia." These are made for Midwestern gardens. Their upright habit and ability to produce flowers all season are legendary. They will tolerate full sun to part shade in a moist soil and exhibit outstanding heat tolerance. The red-bronze foliage adds to their garden appeal. So there is hope for us.

Pansies are cool-weather flowers that are fine for growing in spring or for fall but that don't fare well in hot weather. So there's always a bit of a gamble in purchasing pansies. If the spring or fall is warm and short, the blooming time of the pansies is also short. Pansies are basically irresistible, though, forming an amiable crowd of friendly little faces in the garden. To extend their time in your garden, remember that they can be planted as early as early April or even late March. Even a fairly severe frost will only nip their leaves and petals.

During one year's long, cool spring, I've been growing 'Crystal Bowl True Blue' pansies and 'Crown Azure' pansies along with fragrant white stock in terra cotta pots painted with a trim of white filigree lace. Every time I walk up the back steps I enjoy the extraordinary true blue of these pansies and inhale the fragrance of the stock. But both the pansies and the stock will decline with the coming of the summer's heat.

Note: I repotted the stock and set it out in a shady spot where it surprised me by blooming respectably all summer.

Last fall I planted some 'Icicle' pansies, which have been bred to survive the winter and bloom with spring bulbs. They immediately stopped blooming when I planted them, but by spring, in the first week of April, small, pretty flowers appeared.

Antirrhinum majus (snapdragons) are grown everywhere in the Midwest, but they have their shortcomings. In severe hot weather they may stop blooming and become seedy looking. They do bounce back when cooler weather returns. It pays to dig plenty of moisture-retentive humus into the site where they are to grow, as they don't like poor soil. And, they need to be pinched back hard early in the season to be free flowering later on. Another negative, in my eyes, is that they seem to be most widely available in a six-pack of so-called mixed colors, which are some of the ugliest colors you'll see on a flower—a ghastly mix of musty old theater-curtain red, wincing yellow, creepy pink-rose, and dingy white. And I was disappointed this summer when out of curiosity I purchased some snapdragons labeled "orange." I'm afraid they looked like the same old creepy pink-rose ones. When I can find them, I purchase pure white 'Rocket' snapdragons, which are tall and noble and are a good substitute for the foxgloves that can be difficult to grow here.

On the other hand, snapdragons sometimes survive mild winters, and that's when you get a surge of glorious snapdragons in your garden. These winter survivors bloom beautifully and fully. But you never know.

Other flowers that struggle in our heat include baby blue eyes, wallflowers, clarkia, gerbera, toadflax, nemesia, Livingstone daisies, Iceland poppies, and painted tongue. Lobelia, ubiquitous at garden centers in spring, can—no, will—die out in hot weather. Gazanias don't like humidity, and *Phlox drummondii* just flat out don't like heat. The monkey flower (*Mimulus*) is sold as an early spring flower in our area, and annual sweet peas are also flowers for very early spring. Many of these "problem" flowers need cool nights to flower, and they really prefer to be in California, not Illinois, and there are August days when I guess I can't blame them.

I have read more than once that California poppies (*Eschscholzia californica*) don't do well here in the Midwest, but several blocks from my house a bed of California poppies blooms exuberantly every summer, apparently self-seeded. They are in a big west-facing flower bed with no nearby trees or encroaching shade, and apparently it's what makes them happy. So they are worth a try.

I have found nasturtiums to be a borderline "problem" flower. In a summer of moderate heat they do fine, and I love the variety known as 'Cherry Gleam', whose petals are like rose-colored watered silk, something you would never guess at from the picture on the seed packet. Extreme heat can set them back, however, so they are a gamble.

Miscanthus sinensis 'Little Zebra' with its reddish purple blooms.

Bulbs

For many gardeners, venturing beyond the familiar territory of the usual spring-flowering bulbs—tulips, daffodils, crocuses, and hyacinths—is straying into a true terra incognita. Ixiolirion, sprekelia, zygadenus—their very names seem to spring from the language perhaps spoken long ago at the Hanging Gardens of Babylon. So we may glance briefly at unfamiliar bulbs at the local garden nursery, hesitate, and then reach past them for our familiar bulb friends. But even familiar bulbs have their mysteries. Why do some seem to come back year after year and spread, while others decline rapidly? The common tulip, for instance, blooms gloriously its first spring and then deteriorates into a few tattered leaves as the years go by.

Other useful plants

A bulb, by the way, is a perennial plant that stores its food and over-wintering buds in below-ground structures that are modified stems, roots, or leaves. Bulbs in northern climates evolved in response to long periods of cold and drought. Safely keeping their buds and food supply underground allows them to sail through hard times and then to sprout when conditions are better, as in the warm, wet spring.

Since bulbs come with their bags packed and are ready to go, so to speak, they are tough customers and can work well in our variable climate. I've come to think that bulbs are among the most interesting of all plants and comprise a treasure trove barely explored by many Midwestern gardeners.

Some of the bulbs we'll be looking at here naturalize, often by self-seeding. These bulbs, which are basically wildflowers, spread and thrive for years with little or no help from the gardener. A common bulb that readily naturalizes is scilla (*Scilla siberica*). The indigo blue pools of flowers lapping under trees in early spring are thousands of scilla. Most of those patches started out as just a few bulbs and then self-seeded and naturalized. Naturalizing bulbs often have small flowers, but they make up in beauty and spirit what they lack in stature, especially when planted by the generous handful.

Plant scientists have taken some of the wild bulbs, such as species tulips and hyacinths, and bred them for size and floriferousness, and so we have big, beefy, tulips and hyacinths with the charm of baseball bats. Vigor, as well as charm, was also often lost, especially in tulips.

I have grouped the following bulbs by their families, as I have found it interesting and enlightening to see who is related to whom.

SPRING BULBS

AMARYLLIDACEAE (AMARYLLIS FAMILY)

GALANTHUS NIVALIS (SNOWDROP) Height is four to five inches; late winter–early spring.

If you only select one bulb from this list to grow, let it be this one. Blooming snowdrops are among the first signs of life in most gardens, emerging through the snow as early as February. Those brave little flowers can have more impact on the flower-starved gardener than many of the more spectacular flowers appearing later in the growing year.

IXIOLIRION TATARICUM Height is 12 inches; late May. I must admit to sometimes confusing some of the small spring bulbs with one another, and whether a particular flower is a leucojum or a chionodoxa can seem hazy. Ixiolirion, though, with its grasslike foliage and nodding graceful purple bells, is distinctive and beautiful. Although it is a Siberian native, for some truly mysterious reason it is hardy only through Zone 6. With our recent warm winters, though, I'm taking a chance on growing it this spring and hope it will return.

Postscript, a year later: Today is March 31, and I went out to search for ixiolirion, a quixotic quest if there ever was one, what with other bigger, beefier bulbs vying for my attention. But I found it, its grassy leaves looking pale and shadowed with purple, but alive, and I look forward to seeing its blooms again.

LEUCOJUM VERNUM (SPRING SNOWFLAKE) Height is eight inches; early spring. These little nodding white flowers are delicate and lovely and can be planted in grass.

NARCISSUS SPP. My favorite narcissus is *Narcissus poeticus recurvus* 'Pheasant's Eye'—it contrasts gently with the blaring, beefy yellow of the daffodils, which are just starting to fade as the 'Pheasant's Eye' appears in late spring. The gardenia-scented flower is smaller and more precise in shape than the daffodils, and the inner cup edged with orange sets off the tightly packed stamens. I've been thrilled to find that it self-seeds, and I now have five clumps of 'Pheasant's Eye'. There's an alertness to a clump of these flowers, as though they are surveying the garden with interest. They often seem to be tittering among themselves, disconcerting, to say the least, to the gardener.

I first read of the Tenby daffodil (*Narcissus obvallaris*) in *Cottage Garden Flowers*, by Margery Fish, and it sounded charming. Growing wild on the coast of Wales, it has been grown in English cottage gardens for years. In America it's available from Old House Gardens in Ann Arbor, Michigan. I think it's a perfect daffodil—not diminutive to the point of invisibility, but not big and swaggering, either. It blooms in early April and is about a foot tall with nice, firm foliage. Fish expressed fears that the flower is "perhaps a little too yellow," but I find the yellow color a perfectly nice daffodil yellow and have no qualms about it.

I also have a double daffodil, with a flower almost like a rose. Planted long ago, I've lost the name, but if you see bulbs for a double daffodil, pounce on them immediately because they're beautiful, with petals like chiffon.

My other daffodils are a motley miscellany, purchased when the mood struck me over the years. I am ignorant enough about daffodils to think they all are pretty. Remember that if someone gives you a pot of daffodils as a gift, they can be planted out in the garden when they fade. They will come up next spring. Just plant them in a sunny spot, and wait until the foliage dies down completely to cut it off. The variety 'Tête-à-Tête' is often sold potted up in the spring, and they transplant into the garden perfectly. This works for potted crocus, too, but not for potted tulips, which lack the vigor for such an ordeal.

Daffodils can crowd in upon themselves as the years go by and flowering diminishes. Dig them up, separate, and replant the separated bulbs.

IRIDACEAE (IRIS FAMILY)

CROCUS SPP. Height is two to three inches; spring. There are about 75 different types of spring-flowering crocus. Crocus that naturalize are often labeled as such on their wrapper and may be called "species" crocus. Some of the species crocus are really tiny, and you might want to plant them in clumps at the front of a border and place a marker where you have planted them, or you might run into what's happened to me—I forget where they are, they come up barely poking between last year's autumn leaves, and I miss seeing them entirely. These tiny species crocus bloom very early in the spring, in mid-March. The Dutch took a species named *Crocus vernus* and came up with the larger, hybrid crocus, so familiar in the garden.

IRIS RETICULATA Height is six inches; early May. These charming, miniature irises whose purple petals are touched with white and yellow, bloom in early spring. Their natural habitat is bare and stony, so don't plant where they could get too much water in the summer. Try planting them with rockcress (*Arabis*). They both bloom at the same time and like the same stony soil.

LILIACEAE (LILY FAMILY)

ALLIUM SPP Height varies; late spring through midsummer. The flowering onion family has hundreds of members, some small and graceful, and others tall and statuesque. Alliums bear their flowers in "umbels," which are clusters of flowers sprouting from the same point. If the flowers are densely packed, they form spheres, and if loosely packed, they droop like tassels. A good way to start with alliums is to purchase a mixture of colors and types—White Flower Farm offers its "Big Mix of Little Alliums," which bloom from spring into summer.

I have *A. sphaerocephalon*, drumstick alliums, which are about two feet tall and bloom in early summer. The egg-shaped flower heads are a two-tone burgundy and green in color. The stems are thin, like chive stems, so these alliums need to be planted amid other perennials like black-eyed Susans for support. I have a row of *A. giganteum* growing along the walk by the side of our house. In May, the big, purple spheres float like balloons above the rest of the garden. The purple flower head gradually dries up and fades to a straw color. It still looks interesting, as long as you have other plants around it to hide the fading basal leaves.

Neither the drumstick alliums nor *A. giganteum* have spread in my garden, but they have persisted steadfastly. A lovely native allium, *A. cernuum*, has spread in my garden by self-seeding (though not obnoxiously). I have a small colony of this pretty bulb, which flourishes in dry, dappled shade. Since I've also seen it growing along a river bank in deep shade and have read that it will grow in sun, I have the feeling this is a jack-of-all-trades allium that will grow just about anywhere. I tried another purported allium spreader in my garden called *A. triquetrum*, but it did not return.

This barely scratches the surface of the alliums, and I look forward to trying *A. christophii* (star of Persia), which has large, airy spheres of purple flowers, and *A. caeruleum* with their clear blue flowers. I'll only have about a hundred more alliums to go at that point.

CAMASSIA SCILLOIDES (WILD HYACINTH) Height is 6 to 18 inches; May–June. Wild hyacinth is a pale blue flower of the moist prairie and open woodland. So far I haven't had much luck with camassia, and I think it's because my soil is too dry. I recently saw a beautiful display of camassia at, of all places, the spring flower show at the Navy Pier in Chicago. It's a thoroughbred, delicate and lovely.

CHIONODOXA SPP. (GLORY-OF-THE-SNOW) Height is four to six inches; very early spring flowering. Among the earliest of spring-flowering bulbs, these pretty little starlike flowers come in blue, white, and pink. This is a really charming, elegant little bulb, and it will naturalize. Plant beneath spring-flowing shrubs such as forsythias and magnolias, or let them form colonies in the lawn along with snowdrops, miniature iris, and their relations, the scilla. A classic combination is red tulips grown with chionodoxa. Chionodoxa (pronounced "kye-on-oh-DOX-uh") like sun and good drainage.

Speaking of chionodoxa liking sun, I always wondered what difference it would make to a bulb whether it was planted in sun or shade, when in the leafless days of early spring, most of the garden is in "sun." But I was forgetting that a bulb gathers energy through its leaves after blooming and stores the

In my sister's garden, the daylily *Hemerocallis* 'Caroline Criswell' blooms in late June with the bulb *Allium sphaerocephalon* 'Drumsticks'.

117

energy as food underground. This happens when trees have leafed out, so it does matter to particular bulbs whether they are in sun or shade.

ERYTHRONIUM ALBIDUM (TROUT LILY OR DOG'S TOOTH VIOLET) Height is 6 to 12 inches; April. This North American native is easy to grow, and thrives in dry shade. It is an ephemeral and will disappear completely after blooming. I always wondered how it got the name "dog's tooth" violet, but when you see it in bud, you'll know why—the bud looks exactly like the pointed canine of a dog.

There are other erythronium species, from Asia and Europe, and the English are into erythroniums in a big way. How I wish I could visit the garden of Miss J. B. Lorraine, of Greencombe, in Somerset, England. She maintains the national erythronium collection, which includes 23 species, 10 varieties, 16 hybrids, and 6 cultivars. For a small fee, one can visit her garden in April and May. Light refreshments and talks—even a WC—are available. There is a yearly plant sale. I am at an age where this sounds like paradise.

Erythronium 'Pagoda', with big strappy leaves and lovely yellow flowers, has been recommended in *Horticulture*. It was shown with a blue-flowered pulmonaria, and it looked lovely.

FRITILLARIA MELEAGRIS (CHECKERED LILY) Height is 10 to 12 inches; early spring. I planted this three years ago, as it was recommended to me by several experienced local gardeners as being hardy and simple to grow, only needing decent drainage. The flowers really are checkered and look like something from *Alice in Wonderland*. The bulbs have an unpleasant, skunky odor that you will sometimes smell walking down the bulb aisle at your local nursery, but once in the ground this isn't a problem. A fritillary flower sounds, and looks, so exotic that I had difficulty believing that it would survive the winter in the pedestrian confines of my garden—but it has done so in fine form. Now, emboldened, I am looking at other fritillaries. Perhaps a Siberian native, *F. pallidiflora*, whose blooms are yellow tinted with mint green, will be next.

HYACINTHUS ORIENTALIS Height is 8 to 12 inches; spring. I have never jumped for joy over hyacinths, as their club-shaped flower heads, often in garish colors and listing to one side, never appealed to me. But there always is a moment when you see the light, and a few years ago I was tempted and fell for 'Woodstock', whose deep, purple-red flowers are admittedly utterly gorgeous, and then planted 'King of the Blues', which according to the Old House Gardens bulb catalog, is "one of the oldest available hyacinths." It's a stunning, indigo-purple color. The individual flowers of the flower head are more loosely packed than in modern hyacinths, thus avoiding the dreaded club appearance. And while it does list over to one side after a while, a new stem emerges and another, smaller flower head blooms. Weakened by the beauty of these two varieties, last fall I found myself buying a pale pink hyacinth and have been perusing the Old House Garden catalog again—what next? Perhaps a single variety, or even the 'Queen of the Blues' touted as an "extra-rare hyacinth." Who could resist?

MUSCARI ARMENIACUM (GRAPE HYACINTH) Height is six to seven inches; early spring. Old-fashioned, long lasting, and strong growing, grape hyacinths increase in numbers with each passing year, but I never feel that they're invasive. In early spring they appear with a pyramidal cluster of intense purple-blue flowers that resemble small grapes. Muscari also comes in white and pale blue.

NECTAROSCORDUM SICULUM Height is 24 to 30 inches; May. Nectaroscordum is closely related to alliums and is one of those plants that you have to have once you see it. Its bell-shaped flowers are green and purple, edged with white, and its stems twist around almost like corkscrews. My plants were a bit floppy last spring; I think they got too much shade. This spring I'm supporting them with a peony hoop.

ORNITHOGALUM (STAR-OF-BETHLEHEM) Height is about six to eight inches; late spring/early summer. This bulb was present in the garden when we moved into our house, and basically it's a weed. I say this as a gardener who is often way too softhearted regarding questionable plants, but in this case, I have to say—it's a weed. There's lots of grassy foliage that pops up everywhere, and a few little starlike flowers appear in early summer, if you're lucky. This bulb's other common name—Nap at Noon—hints at some of its problems. There are other ornithogalum species to try, but I will need to be convinced.

PUSCHKINIA (STRIPED SQUILL) Height is four to six inches; early April. One of the hardiest of all bulbs, puschkinia will survive temperatures down to -30° F. It is also one of the nicest of the small spring bulbs—clean and fresh with a perfect little blue stripe drawn down each white petal. The famed English gardener and writer E. A. Bowles said the flower reminded him of "the ghost of a scilla come back to earth." In some ways it's my favorite of the little, early spring bulbs—just so very, very pretty.

SCILLA SIBERICA Height is four to six inches; very early spring. Vivid blue scilla may appear in your garden spontaneously, as their seeds may be dropped through birds' digestive systems.

TRILLIUM SPP Height is 10 to 15 inches; spring. Trilliums are North American natives so beautiful that the gardener might expect them to be temperamental to grow. But I have *Trillium erectum,* the red trillium, growing in dry shade, and it is tough as nails, nobly doing battle with vinca and sweet woodruff. It is holding its own, not even breaking a sweat. So do give trillium a try. Remember that they are spring ephemerals and will vanish completely after blooming.

TULIPA SPP Height is four to six inches; mid- to late spring. Species tulips are the original wild tulips from which hybrids were developed, *T. forsteriana* being *the* original. Many of these diminutive flowers are native to Central Asia, where they grow on stony slopes and dry meadows. I have *Tulipa tarda,* which is considered one of the easiest to grow. The starlike white and yellow flowers are only about four inches tall, but they literally stop viewers in their tracks. I also have the distinctive *T. turkestanica,* which has twelve nodding little flowers on each stem. Each flower is white with a yellow center. If you want an early flowering tulip try a Kaufmanniana variety. I have *T.* 'Fashion', a white-edged light red tulip, that blooms along with grape hyacinths and scilla. Wild tulips can self-sow, and, much to my delight, I find a few more new plants popping up every year, usually a few feet from the original clusters. There are numerous other wild tulips, including *T. clusiana, T. greigii, T. humilis, T. springeri, T. acuminata, T. linifolia,* and *T. sylvestris.*

TULIP CULIVARS I don't like the big garden tulips very much at all, I have to confess. Monotonous regiments of red tulips marching through public parks have inured me to their charms. And the tattered foliage left when they are finished blooming is unsightly and glaring. And if the spring is warm, their blooming time is brief, *and* squirrels love to dig them up. All in all, I pass these tulips by, with one exception. I have a lily-flowered tulip named 'Elegant Lady', which I have found blooms later and longer than most tulips. The flowers are graceful goblets held aloft triumphantly like treasures on tall stems, and the petals are cream tinted with pale lavender. I have enjoyed this tulip so much that I know I'm in danger of being sucked back into liking tulips again and next year hope to try a parrot tulip, which has been recommended to me by my sister-in-law Leah as also being long blooming.

Postscript, the next year: I've been sucked back in! Darn! The tulip that did it is an antique variety (1860) called 'Van der Neer', ordered from the Old House Gardens catalog. They are blooming right now as I write this (April 24), and I have just dashed out into a warm spring rain to take another look.

The flower is an almost translucent deep purple rose—a simply luscious color that makes the petals of the nearby Poet's Eye narcissus look white as snow. The plants are only about 10 inches tall, with rather short, sturdy stems and are my idea of a perfect tulip.

The Old House Gardens catalog notes that "there's a good reason why old varieties often perennialize better in gardens: they were bred for gardens, not for commercial pot-flower and cut-flower uses as most modern tulips have been." All I know is that come fall, I will be planting more antique tulips.

RANUNCULACEAE (BUTTERCUP FAMILY)

ANEMONE BLANDA (GRECIAN WINDFLOWER) Height is four to six inches; early spring. A coworker brought in a limp little handful of these star-like flowers one day in early spring, and they were so pretty I wondered why they aren't planted more. But they are small and delicate and can easily get lost in the shuffle if not sited carefully, right at the front of a border, carefully marked, or in a rock garden setting along with other diminutive plants. The White Flower Farm catalog recommends planting them as a carpet beneath daffodils, tulips, and shrubs.

ERANTHIS HYEMALIS (WINTER ACONITE) Height is three inches; early spring. "Eranthus" is Greek for "flower of spring." This member of the buttercup family blooms very early in the spring. In the words of *Taylor's Encyclopedia of Gardening,* "if mingled with such bulbs as snowdrops, *Scilla sibirica,* chionodoxas, *Crocus imperati* and *Hyacinthus azureus,* a brave show is made for many weeks." These don't do well planted in grass.

I have not yet been able to grow winter aconite, though I've tried. A knowledgeable gardener friend recently said that she saw a huge patch of winter aconite doing beautifully in a local garden—in March. I have heard that aconite bulbs must be fresh in order to sprout, and herein may lie a clue. I purchased my bulbs at a local garden center where the bulbs probably had been stored at room temperature for weeks, drying out.

Fall update: A few weeks ago I was reading the Old House Gardens catalog of antique bulbs, feeling the despair of the gardener with a small garden, when I noticed that they sell winter aconite that has been dipped in agricultural wax to prevent drying. I sent in my order, pronto, and have a feeling that I will have them blooming in my garden next spring.

Next spring: Wrong again! I could see neither hide nor hair of a winter aconite. Perhaps the secret is to find a gardener who is successfully growing

Close-up of the long-blooming *Agapanthus* flowers.

them and to beg a bulb or two.

I've discovered another clue! I've read that winter aconite is native to moist woods and is best planted in damp sites.

SUMMER BULBS

I know little about summer bulbs, having only grown caladium, begonias, dahlias, and acidanthera. Botanists place daylilies, belamcanda, and liatris in this group, but they are so thoroughly at home among the perennials that I am content to leave them there. Caladium have enormous, veined leaves and thrive in rich soil in the shade. They revel in our heat. Start the bulbs indoors in mid-March in a warm spot (they seem to like humid air, so perhaps keeping them in the bathroom would help), keep moist, and plant out in the garden when the weather is consistently warm, usually in early June. Sometimes you can find started plants at nurseries. I'm not a fan of caladium, however fashionable they may be, but find that the white varieties look cool and fabulous.

For huge leaves, try elephant ears (*Colocasia esculentum*), a close caladium relative. Elephant ears come in handsome greens and dark purplish blacks. The leaves can be truly enormous, reaching up to two feet wide and three feet long—so plan accordingly when locating the plant in the garden. They need lots of moisture, whereas caladium seems able to withstand an occasional drought.

For *Acidanthera bicolor* (also called the peacock orchid and sometimes classified as *Gladiolus callianthus*), in April I plant the bulbs indoors in a deep saucer of good potting soil and water. As soon as it gets warm, out they go into the back garden in an inconspicuous spot. Sometimes I remember to water them, sometimes I don't. Either way, in midsummer they take off, with gladiolus-like foliage and then bicolor flowers (white with brown-purple marks) appearing. This is when I bring them to the front garden, where everyone can enjoy them. The foliage stays erect through fall, and the flowers smell wonderful, a bit like four-o'clocks. All in all, they are "easy" and quite spectacular to look at. After a few frosts zap the foliage, dig the bulbs up and shake off the dirt. Cut off most of the foliage, just leaving an inch or two on the bulb. Place in a brown paper grocery bag, and store in a cool, dry place, such as a basement. The bulbs come beautifully through the winter, staying firm and healthy, and are ready to be potted up in April to begin the cycle again.

My sister grows an amethyst blue lily of the Nile (*Agapanthus*) in a big pot by her front steps, and it's a stunner. It even has interesting seedpods when finished blooming.

Come Christmas, you may well be gifted with an amaryllis. Just add water and the bulb takes it from there! The enormous flowers do make a splendid show. But then there is that awkward moment when you wonder what to do next. Since everyone gives me their spent amaryllis bulbs, I sometimes think of my garden as Fran's Home for Aged and Unwanted Amaryllis, and I have been forced to discover what to do next. I've come up with a rough system that seems to work. When the bulb is finished blooming, I cut off the flower stalks (do this in a sink, as water rushes out) and simply put the bulbs in their pots into the basement in a dim corner, allowing the leaves to wither. When the weather is warm I put them out in the garden in an inconspicuous spot and forget about them. This is where the experts would be regularly watering and fertilizing them for enormous flowers in the coming winter, and you can do that, but with so many other things happening in the garden, I leave them to the elements. But this is the time of year when the bulb is "fattening up," so the experts are right. When the weather turns cold, I cut off all withered foliage and bring the bulbs in their pots down into the basement and place them where the light is dim. There they sit until January or early February, when I start watering them again, and at this point I do fertilize with dilute fish emulsion. Leaves shoot up, and by late March, the amaryllis flowers again.

The main thing to remember here is that in January, when the bulbs look dead as a doornail, they are very much alive. Just start watering, and they will quickly send up shoots.

FALL-BLOOMING BULB

I title this section "Fall-Blooming *Bulb*" because so far I am growing only one—the magic lily (*Lycoris squamigera*). Come late August and early September, you see magic lilies popping up in all sorts of unlikely places, including lawns. They are called "magic" because their strappy foliage appears in the spring, dies down completely, and then the lilies themselves appear in early fall.

Magic lilies are fairly easy to grow (they may bloom sparsely after a dry summer), but they do have their own distinctive timetable. I planted some bulbs one fall, and then nothing came up the next spring. I shrugged my shoulders and wondered if the bulbs had died. Nothing appeared that fall, either, and I began to wonder if I had just imagined planting them, which is not outside the realm of possibility. Long, strappy leaves appeared the following spring, by which time I wondered what they were. The long-awaited blooms came that fall. So the plant had skipped an entire year before appearing. And just the other day I was at a seed-starting seminar at a local nursery when in walked a lady with a handful of lycoris leaves. Did anyone know what they were? I said they were magic lily leaves. She looked totally blank for a moment before remembering that, yes, long, long ago, it seemed, she had planted magic lilies. So be sure to mark them!

I have mine planted around a peony bush. Peonies have such nice foliage but are without flowers for such a long time. The magic lily pops up through the peony foliage and looks quite nice.

PLANTING BULBS

The best time to plant spring-flowering bulbs in the Midwest is October and November, up to Thanksgiving. If they are small and you want them to spread, plant them where they can grow undisturbed in a grassy area or in their own planting bed, as opposed to a spot where there's a lot of coming and going of other perennials and annuals.

Gardeners automatically think "bonemeal" when planting bulbs, and bonemeal is often sold right next to bulbs at garden centers. I learned at www.bulb.com, a very informative Web site, that "modern bone meal generally has little value as a bulb fertilizer and often draws rodents and dogs that dig up the bulbs looking for bones!"

Bulbs can also be planted around perennials, so that when the bulb fades, the perennial is leafing out and will hide the tattered bulb foliage. It has been pointed out that tulips, which like dry summer weather, can't take all the watering the typical perennial gets, and this may be another reason why garden tulips fade away with time.

PLANTING EARLY FLOWERING BULBS IN THE LAWN

I recently ran across instructions given by Becky Heath, of Brent and Becky's Bulbs, for planting bulbs in the lawn. By planting drifts of early flowering bulbs such as crocus, dwarf irises, glory-of-the-snow, grape hyacinths, spring starflowers, scilla, or snowdrops right in the lawn, you can bring cheerful color to your garden in late March and April. Becky recommends planting the bulbs after the first fall frost but before the ground freezes hard (a period of about three to six weeks). Use a narrow-blade trowel and plunge it four inches into the ground, pulling the trowel handle back. Pop in a bulb. Repeat the process about two inches away, closing up the first hole as you make the second. Becky recommends planting 15 bulbs per square foot and watering the planting. By the time these early flowering bulbs have finished blooming, the grass will have started growing. Wait until the bulb foliage has turned yellow, and when it's time to mow, set the blade of the mower to its highest setting.

I have seen a lawn simply planted with snowdrops, and the effect was fresh and pretty. I also saw a picture of a lawn planted both with the heirloom hoop petticoat daffodil (*Narcissus bulbocodium*) and the trout lily (*Erthyronium*), giving the appearance of an alpine meadow. These bulbs need good drainage, so don't plant where the grass is soggy.

A good crocus for naturalizing is the species *Crocus tommasinianus*, which is vigorous and easy to grow.

FERTILIZING TO ENCOURAGE BULB RENEWAL

If you still want the big, beefy classic tulips, hyacinths, and daffodils year after year in your garden, you might be interested in the following unusual method for fertilizing bulbs. Some experts feel that scratching bonemeal or bulb fertilizer into the soil *around* the bulb, as is often recommended, does little good. It takes time for these nutrients to break down and be carried down to the bulb by rainwater or soil moisture. Instead, use a liquid fertilizer, such as diluted fish emulsion, to water the *leaves* of the bulb. Do this twice: once in late winter when the leaves are two to four inches above the soil surface, and then again when the bulb is finished flowering and you've cut off the shriveled flowers. Leaves are absorptive and are a direct route straight down to the bulb.

Also, snap off the faded flower heads of tulips and daffodils so they don't form seedpods. Doing so will divert the plant's energy from seed formation down to the bulbs. Be sure to leave the leaves on after the bulb is finished blooming. Only cut them off when they're completely yellow.

Irises

In Greek mythology, Iris (the rainbow) was an attendant of the goddess Juno, serving as a messenger from heaven to earth. The Roman poet Virgil described

her thus: "Iris, of saffron wings, displaying against the sun a robe of a thousand varying colors." Iris flew through the air so quickly that you couldn't see her, only the rainbow she left behind.

This leads us to the special appeal of irises: irises, sometimes called Rainbow Flowers, are unusually beautiful, even for flowers, with the colors having a rain-misted, iridescent quality. Bearded irises, in particular, flower in a spectrum of irresistible hues, and many gardeners fall madly in love with them.

I try very hard to resist irises, though, because I usually like them better in other gardens than my own. Blooming during the often tumultuous weather of late spring, irises seem perpetually battered, sodden, and splashed with mud. There always seems to be an enormous rainstorm that knocks them silly just as they are about to bloom. Even in a calm spring, irises seem to bloom only for two or three weeks. This is not so terrible, except that the foliage they leave behind can get tattered as the summer wears on. I am trying to limit my tall bearded irises to two varieties: a pale lavender and purple bicolor that was in our yard when we moved in, and a bronze and purple variety a neighbor gave me. Neither has the extremely frilly, oversize flower that some of the newer varieties seem to have. I also have a yellow dwarf bearded iris as well as a miniature iris, which I'll describe in a minute. Meanwhile, bearded irises seem to come at me from every quarter—they are determined to be in my garden, and I resist with all my might. It doesn't help, either, that this fall I fell to temptation and planted an iris with variegated foliage, called 'Zebra'.

It also doesn't help that I have found two other plants with irislike foliage that look better than iris foliage itself. There is the blackberry lily (*Belamcanda chinensis*), which is in the iris family and whose foliage remains quite fresh for the entire summer, and there is the summer bulb *Acidanthera* (Abyssinian gladiolus). The foliage of this bulb is a striking fan of tall, swordlike leaves that stay upright right to the bitter end of fall.

IRIS SPP. (BEARDED IRIS)

When we moved into our house and began exploring the garden, I discovered a clump of what looked like irises, though it was so overgrown with weeds it was hard to tell. I managed to weed and to divide the rhizomes and replant, and sure enough, next June, the translucent lavender flowers of a bearded iris unfurled, floating atop tall graceful stems. These irises had abided in the garden for decades, waiting to be renewed by a gardener and given their rightful space. (A rhizome is a specialized portion of the plant's stem that is swollen with starchy food material that sustains the plant when dormant. The rhizomes also have buds that can give rise to new stems. The actual roots of the plant trail off the rhizome.)

After growing some modern bearded irises, I discovered another attribute that heirloom flowers such as this iris often have: disease resistance. Some of the new irises I later planted fell victim to borers, and I realized that the "old" iris growing a few feet away had survived for decades without borer infestation. This is another reason why I love heirloom flowers and hold them in great respect. They often aren't as showy as their modern counterparts, but they are survivors.

IRIS SIBIRICA (SIBERIAN IRIS, ALSO KNOWN AS GRASS IRIS)

Siberian irises are among the easiest perennials to grow, and some gardeners would argue that in many ways the Siberian iris is superior to the bearded iris in hardiness and in the beauty of its clean, grasslike foliage. Most bloom in shades of blues, purples, and whites and grow to about three feet in height. Far be it from me to step into the fray, but if you are a beginner and want "easy," try the Siberians first. They like sun but will perform decently in dappled shade for part of the day. These irises are attractive even in bud, looking streamlined and graceful. Siberians bloom from mid-June (right after the bearded iris) to early July. The grassy foliage stays in good condition after the flowers fade, and the seedpods are decorative against winter snow.

Some popular varieties include the species *I. sibirica* (blue-purple), *I.* 'Caesar's Brother' (deep purple), and *I.* 'Perry's Blue', (blue). *Iris* 'Butter and Sugar' is an unusual yellow Siberian iris, and *I.* 'White Swirl' is a beautiful ruffled white.

As for care, they need little, other than watering. Siberian irises are notoriously difficult to divide, and it's fortunate for us that they spread very slowly and it takes a long, long time for a bare spot to appear in the middle. A clump of Siberian irises can become very tightly matted together, and it's possible to think of this iris as a ground cover—few weeds can penetrate its hard, tangled roots.

At the risk of greatly oversimplifying the appeal of these two major iris groups, bearded irises appeal to those who like frills, and the Siberian to those who like elegance.

IRIS PSEUDACORUS (YELLOW FLAG IRIS)

The spring before last, I joined a group helping to groom the Japanese Garden in the Fabyan Forest Preserve in Batavia, Illinois, for the summer. The beautiful pond with its arching bridge, bullfrogs, and giant goldfish had become overgrown with an iris, *I. pseudacorus*. Someone had innocently planted two or three plants by the water's edge a few years before and it had gone berserk, spreading with lightning speed and threatening to choke the entire pond. Even the frogs looked scared. When the volunteers were finished weeding, they were left with a wet, muddy pile of iris that (in memory, at least) was about eight feet across and five feet tall. The lady from the forest preserve generously said we could take all we wanted. There was a dead silence. Assured that it didn't grow nearly so wildly in dry soil, some of the more foolhardy among us hesitantly took a few plants, and that's how I now have a nice little clump of this iris in my garden. The forest preserve lady was right: in garden soil of average dryness, *I. pseudacorus* grows quite decorously, reaching a height of about three feet while producing pretty yellow flowers through June and July. In or by water, though, it's an unstoppable garden thug growing upwards of five feet tall.

IRIS CRISTATA (CRESTED IRIS)

This is a small (six to eight inches), mat-forming iris that can be used as a ground cover. It needs part shade, and its lavender blue flowers bloom in April and May. The foliage remains in good shape even after the flowers have faded. Part of the beauty of this little plant is in its sheer smallness and the intricate perfection of the jewel-like flower.

A "BITTY LITTLE IRIS"

This spring I exchanged plants with a lady in Montana through Gardenweb.com. She e-mailed that she had loads of a little iris gathered at a nearby abandoned homestead and could send me a "whole passel" of them. How could I resist? How could *anyone* resist an heirloom iris gathered from an abandoned homestead in Montana? I accommodated her request for some purple coneflowers, hoping they wouldn't cause too much trouble in Montana, and waited for the passel of iris. A small envelope, about five by seven inches in size, came in the return mail, and I was stabbed with disappointment. This was what they called a whole passel in Montana? In Illinois we would call it barely a hill of beans. I opened the envelope and out tumbled the smallest iris rhizomes I had ever seen, about as *small* as beans, or in this lady's word, just "bitty little things." I had to agree, she had sent me a passel, and my respect for Montana returned. I have looked through my perennial books and am not sure what type of iris these are, except that they are very, very small. I rushed to plant them, and next spring we'll see what's what.

IRIS CARE

Give irises sun, good soil, and good drainage. In late summer or early fall, trim the leaves back to about six to eight inches in height, and destroy all the cut-off foliage plus any foliage lying on the ground, as they may have borer eggs on them.

These hideous, fat worms lurk in the rhizomes of infected plants. True to their name, they bore through the interior of the rhizome, leaving it hollow and soft. They may do this for some time before you notice that the plant is drooping. If the plant is severely infested, it must be dug up and thrown out. To prevent future problems, when dividing irises (this is done when they are finished flowering in July and August and should be done every three to five years), dust

A white Asiatic lily, blooming in late June.

the rhizomes with a powdered kitchen cleanser containing bleach. And as well as throwing out any suspect pieces of rhizome, clean up any old foliage lying around. To further forestall borers, when replanting, briefly dip the rhizome and its fan of leaves into a solution of one part chlorine bleach and nine parts water. Allow the transplants to dry completely before planting.

IRIS DIVISION

Left undivided for more than three years, iris flowering diminishes noticeably. So they do need division for renewal, as well as for propagation. Irises (except for the Siberian) are easy to divide. Get out a tarp before you start digging so you have something to lay the clumps on as you work. Dig up a clump, and drop it unceremoniously on the tarp, both to shake the soil off and to loosen the rhizomes. I use a pair of old scissors to cut the leaves back to about six inches. A clump of overgrown iris rhizomes is like a three-dimensional jigsaw puzzle, and you may need to shake it a bit and pull at some of the pieces to separate them. Sometimes you can get the process going by pulling rhizomes off from the edge of the clump. Shake the soil off of each "fan" and carefully inspect. The rhizome should be firm. If it's hollow or slimy—throw it out. A hollow rhizome is evidence of borers, and softness and slime is a sign of soft rot. Either way, don't compost this material. Inspect the leaves of each fan as well. If you see abraded areas on the leaf down near the rhizome, look more closely. You may see little white eggs, which are the borer eggs. They will eat their way down into the stem and then into the rhizome.

Lilies

Foolishly, I didn't grow lilies when I first began to garden, under the vague impression that they were difficult. After several years I finally took a deep breath and plunged into lilies and planted a few bulbs of a pinky-salmon Asiatic lily named 'Lorelei'. The plants grew up and up and up—the suspense kills you—and then flowered spectacularly in late June with everything but a drumroll and a fanfare of trumpets. I was instantly hooked, and let me warn you: getting hooked on lilies is at least as serious an addiction as a hosta or daylily addiction, if not worse. I have come to feel that a garden without these glorious flowers, which are among the oldest cultivated plants (*Lilium candidum*, the Madonna lily, is thought to be the oldest garden plant in the world), is not complete. As well as blooming in a rainbow of luscious colors, the plant's height and large, showy flowers contrast dramatically with other garden flowers. (And you don't have to tell new gardeners how easy they are to grow!)

Lilies grow from bulbs and are considered hardy perennials. They are the one perennial I can think of that is perhaps best purchased from mail-order catalogs. Mail-order growers keep the lily bulbs in cold storage until they are shipped out, while bulbs sold at garden centers may have been sitting at room temperature for some time and may have either dried out or started to sprout. If you can see a sprout just emerging from a bulb in its mesh bag, it's okay to purchase, but avoid those with a long, twisting sprout poking its way out of the bag or box. These sprouted lilies may be on sale but are best avoided. The other good thing about mail-order lilies is that I have never seen an ugly or boring lily, and you are almost always going to enjoy the color and form of the lily you purchase, sight unseen. The same can't be said of, for instance, daylilies, though I realize I'm treading on dangerous ground here. Not that any daylilies are ugly, but some come in rather bland apricots, golden-beiges, and pinks, and they are probably best purchased in person. Lilies, though, rarely disappoint.

If you haven't grown a lily and want to try one, start with an Asiatic. Asiatics are considered the easiest lily variety to grow, as well as the earliest to bloom, usually in late June through early July, and some growers and catalogs offer only Asiatics. (I am writing this on July 6, and most of my Asiatics are just finishing up blooming now, having weathered a horrendous heat spell.) The flowers bloom in clusters at the top of the stem and open fully with an almost flat face. Asiatics are not as fragrant as some other lilies, but on the basis of their appearance alone, you'll probably forgive them this. And if you're like me and don't like the rather heavy fragrance of some lilies such as Orientals, you may consider this a plus. (The perception of fragrance is highly subjective. The heavy scent of Oriental lilies reminds me of rotting carnations, but, truthfully, others find it absolutely wonderful.) Asiatics used to be considered slightly coarse looking by some gardeners, but modern hybrids are delicate and attractive. This summer, 'Crimson Pixie' bloomed for the first time in my garden. Its petals, as smooth as heavy satin, glowed in a saturated carmine hue—just a knockout.

Oriental lilies have showier blooms than Asiatics and, as noted above, are highly fragrant. They bloom after the Asiatics, in July and August. Orientals have a deserved reputation as being fussier to grow than Asiatics. They like cooler summers than we usually have, as well as acidic soil. Still,

Here, the Oriental hybrid lily 'Journey's End' blooms in late August with hot pink phlox. The misty seed heads of miniature hollyhocks (*sidalcia*) are in the foreground, and brown-eyed susans are just coming into bloom.

one local grower, after careful trials, offers the Orientals 'Casa Blanca', 'Stargazer', and the ancestor of today's Oriental hybrids, *Lilium speciosum* var. *rubrum*, a native of Japan, as being straightforward to grow in the Midwest. 'Casa Blanca' is tagged as "simply the best" in the White Flower Farm bulb catalog. The size of the blossoms, the gleaming color—all in all, it's an exceptionally beautiful lily. I've also heard 'Black Beauty' recommended. I have 'Journey's End', which has deep, pink streaks and spots on snow white petals. It flowered beautifully and profusely this summer. Many Orientals, however, tend to peter out and disappear after a while in the Midwestern garden, either in response to our soil, hot summers, or perhaps chipmunk depredations, and some gardeners here treat them as annuals.

Aurelians, also known as trumpet lilies, bloom in July. The fragrant flowers are large and trumpet shaped. My sister is the only gardener I know of personally who has grown Aurelians. She grew 'Black Dragon' and found it easy to grow and strikingly beautiful.

One group of lilies that I have no experience with, but which seem worth investigating, are martagons, or Turk's-cap lilies. Natives to a wide swathis of

Self-seeded
tiger lilies
(*Lilium
tigrinum*).

Europe, including Siberia and Mongolia (which makes them perfect for Chicago), they are reputedly extremely long lived and can be grown in woodland gardens. I've read that in the wild they can be found growing amid viburnum. I have seen some miniature Turk's-cap-type lilies growing in dead shade in a garden in Evanston, and it's possible they were martagons. Next on my list of plants to purchase!

Wild lilies that are worthy additions to the garden include *L. philadelphicum* (wood lily or western red lily) *L. michiganense* (Turk's-cap), and *L. tigrinum* (tiger lily). *L. philadelphicum*, in particular, is considered an outstandingly beautiful wild flower. Dick Young, in *Kane County Wild Plants and Natural Areas*, notes that it has adapted to prairie conditions here and so could be more properly referred to as the "prairie lily." He also notes that it is extremely rare. And in the Herronswood Nursery mail-order catalog, one writer rapturously extols *L. philadelphicum* as his favorite plant. At this point, I have only seen pictures of this lily, but the flower's delicacy and coloring are extremely attractive.

So in the big, happy family of lilies, there is something delightful for everyone!

LILY CULTURE

Most lilies need nothing more exotic than sun, regular watering, and good soil to do well. Lily bulbs can be planted either in spring or fall, but bulbs planted in fall have extra time to settle in and send out roots. The one true enemy of the lily is poor drainage: dig deeply to loosen the soil and mound it up when planting the bulbs. Dig in plenty of humus such as compost or leafmold before planting. Poor drainage can lead to bulb rot. After flowering, clip off the top cluster of spent blooms and seedpods. Just as with tulips and daffodils, the foliage of the lily must be left in place to "feed the bulb" for next year's bloom. My sister bends the lily stalk over to make it a bit less conspicuous. Later in autumn, when the foliage and stalk are completely brown, cut it all off at ground level with pruning shears. Dispose of the clippings.

Experts say that lilies should be planted in groups of threes for maximum effect. In old-fashioned gardens, Madonna lilies were often planted in rows along pathways. One of the wonderful things about lilies is that they are tall and skinny and don't mind being shoe-horned in amid other plants and so are especially useful in a small garden. And they actually appreciate having their roots sheltered. If you have the space, masses of lilies are a mind-boggling sight, and some plant catalogs sell lily assortments in bulk. This summer, with my husband, Jim, on a country drive, I saw a weathered old red barn sailing in a sea of lilies, and the sight was wonderful, unforgettable.

One thing that lilies aren't, necessarily, is drought resistant. They can weather some dry weather, up to about two weeks' worth. Beyond that, even if they are finished blooming, remember to water.

One last thing. I seem to remember reading that the great English gardener Gertrude Jekyll fed her lilies with cartloads of rotted donkey manure, thus raising the bar for all of us. Without carts, donkeys, or their manure, we can only do our best.

A STORY ABOUT LILY HARDINESS

When we first moved into our old house, I hardly noticed the funny-looking weed growing by the front steps. It was about one and a half feet tall, had no flowers, and strange black "beads" were wedged between the straplike leaves and the stem. Jostling the interesting weed rudely aside, I'm truly ashamed to say we planted an arborvitae, and the weed vanished in the process of digging. It reappeared in subsequent years, craning its neck out from under the arborvitae in search of light and never flowering. Things went on like this for years, before the light dawned and I belatedly realized the "weed" was a lily, probably planted many, many years ago by a previous owner. In the spring, I eagerly transplanted the lily to a site with good soil and sun, and it shot upward like a rocket. Tiny long buds formed near the top of the stem, as well as the "beads" that I realized were lily bulbils (seeds), and I was gripped with excitement. At that point, a high-jumping chipmunk scarfed down the buds. Sigh. The next year, I watered and watched again as the plant grew upwards of five feet and again developed buds. This time, the chipmunks, probably distracted by the unusual abundance of the nearby Asian pear tree, ignored it, and the buds swelled. To make a long story short, it was an old-fashioned tiger lily, and it bloomed beautifully for many weeks. And some small lily plants appeared, probably from the bulbils scattered the previous summer. Definitely not a weak sister!

One footnote to this story: I have since discovered that tiger lilies are suspected of carrying a virus that they are immune to but that can sicken other lilies. So they are kind of like a lily Typhoid Mary. Oh, great. Opinion on the seriousness of the virus varies, however, and as usual, it's wait and see to look for any ill effects in my garden.

RECYCLING YOUR EASTER LILY

The old-time cottage gardeners treasured each plant that came their way, and a gift plant such as an Easter lily would have been treasured and planted—never thrown onto the compost heap. Easter lilies (*Lilium longifloreum*) come from Japan and are generally hardy in northern climates when well mulched.

After you've enjoyed your Easter lily (indoors) and it has finished flowering, remove the withered leaves. Place it in a sunny window and water. When the danger of frost is past, plant the lily outdoors in a sunny spot with good drainage. Easter lilies are extensively treated with growth regulators by greenhouse growers (you don't think they all flower naturally the week before Easter, do you?), and it will get taller than when it was potted up. This year my Easter lily reached almost three feet and is blooming now in late September.

For further information about lilies, obtain a copy of *Let's Grow Lilies! An Illustrated Handbook of Lily Culture*, by the North American Lily Society. It may be purchased at their Web site: www.lilies.org

Dahlias

I never thought I'd get into dahlias, but this summer I became a convert. It all started with the Internet, as many things seem to now. I had offered purple coneflowers for trade on Gardenweb.com, and a gardener from California asked if I'd take some dahlia tubers in exchange. I hesitated because of a vague notion that there was something funny about dahlias, a notion I had inherited from my mother, who will have nothing to do with them. You had to dig them up when? How? And why? And for that matter, what was a tuber? But in the spirit of adventure, I decided to trade. I sent off a box of three trembling, young coneflowers cushioned in dry oak leaves and in return received a box full of what looked like shriveled potatoes. Each was labeled with a code, and a catalog of code names was in the box, along with planting instructions.

It turns out that I was trading with an owner of Elkhorn Gardens, a dahlia farm in Carmel, California, and I was the luckiest trader in the whole world. The planting instructions sounded easy enough: dig hole, put tuber in hole, fill hole. I could do that. By late August, the plants burst into bloom. And that's when I got into dahlias because they were stunning, beautiful in the Byzantine, slightly artificial sort of way that is peculiar to dahlias. Up came Procyon, a yellow and red bicolor; Twinkletoes, a pastel cactus; Island Flame, a coral semicactus with yellow tipped petals; and Christine, a pink and yellow waterlily variety. A few of the smallest tubers didn't make it, smothered as they were with nearby parsley—I had underestimated how much space the plants needed, which is at least two feet between each plant, and with some varieties even more.

Now that's what I call a flower, I thought, gazing at the dahlias. There's a formality and a richness to them that's a pleasant antidote to the casual goldenrods and billowing asters blooming at the same time, and they offer a rich range of color, including pastels, that look good in a season awash in the many chrome yellow and purple flowers blooming then.

Cold and frost came early this fall, arriving with a screech in the second week of October, and the dahlia leaves blackened and sagged after a week of nighttime temperatures hovering in the 30s. Now, I thought, comes the tricky part of digging up the tubers, the part my mother had warned me about. I cut off the stems about six inches above the ground and gingerly dug the tubers up with a shovel. There's a bit of a surprise when a cluster of five tubers emerges, looking like little bowling pins dangling from a center stem. There's something vaguely indecent looking about a tuber, I must say.

Averting my eyes, I brushed the clusters off and placed them in vermiculite in loosely closed brown paper bags. You can also slice the tubers apart in the spring, each tuber with its own eye, or growing point, but that's getting into Advanced Dahlia Techniques, and I'm still in Beginners. You might also consider not lifting the tubers at all, as dahlia prices are reasonable, and you do get lots of flowers from one tuber, especially if you pinch out the center shoot when the plant is about 20 inches tall so that blooms form on the side shoots. (Be aware that the notion of playing fast and loose with dahlia tubers like this, though, is truly shocking to dahlia lovers, who would never dream of abandoning their tubers to a cruel death in the cold. I have learned that a trick to successful tuber storage is to allow the tubers to dry for a few days and then to store them in a cool, dark place and not let them dry to a point of desiccation.)

So now I'm into dahlias and plan to spend some pleasant hours this winter studying the Elkhorn Gardens catalog, wondering if the lady from Elkhorn needs any more coneflowers. I've also sent away for the catalog of Swan Island Dahlias, another dahlia farm that was recommended by a chorus of dahlia growers on the Internet. Swan Island has a wonderful on-line color catalog, but it's much cosier in January to curl up under an afghan with an actual catalog in one hand and a cup of cocoa in the other. And I'll mull over the possibility of ordering 'Heirloom Border Species' dahlia seed, which includes seed of four different dahlia species, from Thompson & Morgan. Last, but not least, I'll micro-

scopically study the catalog of Old House Gardens, a Michigan firm specializing in heirloom bulbs, an area of gardening that sounds way too interesting. They offer the trendy Bishop of Llandaff dahlia, with its burgundy foliage and scarlet flowers, among other delights. What fun.

I've discovered that dahlias are a big favorite of earwigs, and while cheap beer in a saucer works to attract and drown the unpleasant little creatures, there's another solution. Reading *BBC Gardeners' World* magazine one day, I noticed a photograph of a garden of dahlias that included numerous clay flowerpots, stuffed with straw and placed upside down on stakes driven into the ground. The gardener had made a virtue of a necessity and the pots were part of the overall garden design. Earwigs like to hide in the dark straw, and the gardener has a pleasant time shaking them out and stomping on them. At any rate, the dahlias, the pots, and a row of tall sunflowers made for a cheerful garden.

Grasses

At a plant exchange I attended this spring, amid a long table full of tempting offerings, there was but one representative of *Poaceae*, the grass family, and only one: variegated ribbon grass (*Phalaris arundinacea* 'Picta') in every size container up to and including an enormous five-gallon pot that had once held a tree. No one was alarmed at this evidence of rampageous growth; to the contrary, delighted gardeners spirited every blade away, pleased to have such a pretty grass that was also "easy." Ribbon grass, also known as "gardener's garters," is viewed with utter horror by some experienced gardeners, who know that its rhizomes run amok in good soil but is just the type of plant cottage gardeners with ordinary soil love. I have to admit I have a soft spot in my heart for *Phalaris*, and if I had a lot more space honestly wouldn't mind having more of it in my garden. It's pretty, drought tolerant, enthusiastic, and requires no skill whatsoever to grow.

And there is the variety 'Feesey', which is reputed to be less rampageous. I've seen 'Feesey' attractively paired with *Sedum* 'Autumn Joy'. I do have the comically named 'dwarf's garters', a slower-growing, shorter version of the classic and am confining a clump of the tall variety in a container. This is a wonderful grass as long as you understand down to the marrow of your bones that it's a vigorous spreader. If you have a largish, informal garden, a swath of ribbon grass can serve as a handsome ground cover. If you fear its roots, grow it in a big container as a handsome specimen. Just don't plunk it down into a carefully planned perennial bed with good soil, or I agree, you and your perennials will be in big trouble.

I was at the ribbon-grass level of grass consciousness for quite a while, until six or seven years ago, when I made the quantum leap of falling in love with prairie dropseed *(Sporobolus heterolepis)*. I would almost say it was like getting hit by a bolt of lightning, except that it was on a cloudless, blazingly hot summer's day at a local nursery that I saw low hummocks of this silky grass interplanted with black-eyed Susan and liatris. I've since seen and come to like many other ornamental grasses, but prairie dropseed remains a favorite. It's barely two feet in height and looks like a little fountain of silky threads. Feathery panicles of tiny grass flowers appear in midsummer, and then the whole plant turns to gold in the fall. It will grow in a wide variety of soils and, once established, is extremely drought tolerant. It grows slowly, so that it doesn't need dividing. I've seen it used as a luxurious ground cover, but it can also be interplanted with perennials or bulbs. It has just occurred to me that it might do well planted with tulips, as both need dry soil in the summer. It even smells nice as it basks in the sun, like toast! Prairie dropseed is a true plant of the American Midwest, just waiting for more Midwestern gardeners to bring it into their cottage gardens.

Wild grasses grace a restored prairie area in mid-October.

You may wonder why, if prairie dropseed is so wonderful, more local gardeners aren't already growing it. There are two reasons: I've noticed that in the many books I own on English cottage gardens, there is almost no mention of grasses. There are grasses growing in the English countryside, but they didn't seem to have been cultivated by the old-time cottagers. So there is little to alert us in our inherited gardening tradition that grasses are of interest. It looks like we must make growing grasses, especially prairie grasses, our own Midwestern tradition. The second, more practical reason, is that it is fairly slow to propagate and grow in a nursery, and nursery owners are understandably reluctant to invest time in a plant for which there is little demand. But if we all clamor for it, things will change. It is available at a number of local nurseries, as well as by mail order.

The *Sporobolus* genus has other members that are also possibly of interest. I can't help but be curious about giant dropseed *(S. giganteus)*, and the Plant Delights catalog highly praises alkali dropseed *(S. airoides)*. They feel that it is "one of the least-known and most ornamental of the native grasses." Apparently it's larger than prairie dropseed and has showier panicles.

Calamagrostis acutiflora 'Karl Foerster'.

Peering over low hummocks of prairie dropseed to see what else is available in the world of ornamental grasses, we are confronted with an avalanche of grasses, as there has been an explosion of new varieties in the past decade, and for good reason. Gardeners everywhere are discovering that grasses are easy to grow. They have deep, efficient root systems, are not fussy about soil, and can be extremely drought resistant. They are usually disease and pest free. Above all, they are beautiful, bringing grace and softness to the garden, and offering natural contrast to other garden plants. Grasses can be planted as backdrops for garden flowers or as single specimens. You could almost say that grasses are so attractive and so easy to grow that they are garden "no-brainers." (But I'm not going to say it, because that's tempting fate! A giant earwig might hear me and decide to make grasses his favorite snack!)

Grasses are flowering plants, though the "flowers" are very small and don't have petals. Clusters of these flowers are called "inflorescences," and these are the plumes, spikes, feathers, and clouds of various grasses. Just like perennials, grasses have bloom times and then go to seed. The flowers are wind pollinated. Grasses are among the most highly evolved plants on Earth, and they are found all over the globe, in almost every ecosystem.

Grasses are so "easy" that some, like a few of the plumed *Miscanthus*, have become instant clichés in the suburban landscaping scene. At every golf course and suburban shopping mall, we meet the weary crew of a plumed M. *sinensis*, *Sedum* 'Autumn Joy', *Rudbeckia* 'Goldsturm', and the omnipresent 'Stella de Oro' daylily.

This year *Calamagrostis acutiflora* 'Karl Foerster' has popped up everywhere you turn, though it is a wonderful grass, and I can see why it's used so much. Growing up to five foot in height, it's ramrod straight and tall and is topped with narrow, golden plumes by late summer. If you want a handsome vertical accent in the garden that is neat and tidy and will not sag, flop, or swoon, this is your plant. I just drove past a garden that used two 'Karl Foersters' planted on either side of the front garden path, like sentries, and it was striking—and a bit humorous. But it also looks beautiful planted in groves, with the wind rippling through its golden plumes.

There are so many beautiful grasses available that if you want to try some in your garden, it's best to think carefully about your available space and sun *before* going to a nursery, where you'll be tempted by everything you see. I've come across a simple rule of thumb for spacing: plant grasses as far apart as they will grow tall. Five-foot-tall grasses should be planted five feet apart.

And while most grasses prefer full sun, some, like *Miscanthus*, can be planted in light shade and simply will grow shorter, or might flop somewhat. Also, think about whether you want a grass as an accent or massed. If you have the space and sun, masses of grasses can be simply sensational looking. I was at a nursery yesterday where I saw a grove of a zebra grass (*Miscanthus* 'Strictus'). It looked cool, modern, and not at all busy, even though it is a striped grass.

Be careful with big grasses. A big grass can have the presence of a tree in the garden, and if you have a small garden, it could be overwhelming. And when you cut the grass back in the spring, the void will be glaring. A similar problem arises when using big grasses as a privacy hedge. Again, when you cut it down in the spring—no privacy. The effort involved in cutting back a big grass is another factor to consider—you may need an electric hedge clipper, and dividing the grass might require an axe. As for plumed grasses, observe them at nurseries and in other gardens before planting them in your garden. They are dramatic—so dramatic that it might be possible to get tired of seeing them every day.

Grasses are a great way to add steady-state color to the garden—there are blue, blood red, golden, silver, chartreuse, and variegated grasses. Some turn gold, bronze, and even burgundy in the fall. I especially love blue grasses like blue fescue (*Festuca glauca*). This is a low-growing, fine-textured grass that combines beautifully with *Sedum* 'Vera Jameson' and pink geraniums (a very drought-resistant group of plants). I don't know which variety I have, as it was purchased long ago, but apparently the variety to look for is 'Elijah Blue', which is rated as "bluer" than the species. Blue oat grass (*Helictotrichon sempervirens*) looks like a big blue fescue and grows to about two and a half feet tall. In a nursery grass garden, I saw clumps of this grass grouped together, creating a cool, misty blue spot in the garden, almost like ocean waves. Don't try to shoehorn blue oat grass in among other garden perennials—it needs space and good air circulation. This grass would make a great contrast to the warm green foliage of daylilies and is a classic companion for upright sedums. Blue Lyme grass (*Leymus arenarius*) is another blue grass, but I've been repeatedly warned that it spreads via rhizomes and is extremely aggressive. I can't help but be curious about it, however, because I've read it was a favorite of gardening great Gertrude Jekyll. And I've also seen it used with spectacular effect as a container plant—a big, spiky blue thing bursting from a copper pot.

(Since writing the previous passage, I somehow came into the possession of a big, damp, newspaper-wrapped parcel of blue Lyme grass. I strode purposefully into the garden and planted it in a Spot of Doom, where nothing will grow, and where it is presently cavorting as happily as a rottweiler puppy in his kennel. I have great expectations for it come next spring.)

Postscript, next summer: In its Spot of Doom, the Lyme grass is suspiciously well mannered. Its powdery blueness is striking, and it pairs nicely with the little pink blossoms of a nearby fairy rose. Still, I feel nervous and wonder if next year it will pop out of its closet and scare me.

Continuing in a blue vein, little bluestem (*Schizachyrium scoparium*) is a clump-forming native grass that changes in color from grey-green early in the summer to purple to bronze in the autumn. Bluish coloration at the base of the stem gives it its name. Little bluestem can reach four feet in height and is only little in comparison to big bluestem, which can reach nine feet. In nature, little bluestem is found on well-drained, dry gravel ridges, and in gardens it is not happy with rich, moist soil, where it may flop and decline. It also needs full sun and will flop in light shade, though I have found in my garden that it does so in an attractive manner. From July onward it bears silvery green inflorescences that turn pinky-bronze come fall. Sheaves of this grass can then be used in flamboyant fall flower arrangements. Just yesterday I saw a variety of little bluestem called 'The Blues', which is a striking powdery steel blue. It shoots strongly up from the ground and is about three feet tall. My project for next spring is to seek out the other cultivars, 'Blaze' and 'Taos'.

Big bluestem, also a clump former, likes moderately moist, black soils and was the predominant grass of the tallgrass prairies. It can tolerate heavy clay soil. Unless you are actually re-creating a prairie, though, I think big bluestem may be too tall for the average garden. Visit a local prairie remnant, and if you're lucky, you'll see big bluestem rippling softly in the wind.

The second most common grass of the tallgrass prairie is Indian grass (*Sorghastrum nutans*). This is a tall, graceful grass with feathery, golden bronze flowers. Sometimes it's called "gold plume." The foliage turns yellow-orange in autumn, and I've heard it suggested that it be planted with New England asters. It likes lean, dry soil. I've seen Indian grass in prairie remnants but have not grown it myself. I've heard it described as "aggressive," and I'm assuming it's aggressive as a self-seeder because it is a clumping grass, not a runner. It's also described as drought tolerant and extremely hardy. It's a beautiful grass, but you do need space for it. I ran across the following interesting description of Indian grass in the Oikos Tree Crops catalog:

Indian grass is an excellent cover grass that produces an edible seed relished by many birds. Recommended if you are trying to attract birds and have an open sunny area. A few breeders are trying to develop a large seeded selection to use for human food. Imagine having a perennial wheat field. Height to five feet. Plant two-three feet apart. This is a large clump type grass. Hardy to minus 35 degrees.

The authors of *Gardening with Grasses* recommend that you avoid overfeeding and overwatering Indian grass, as it becomes brittle and breaks in the wind. So just water it until it becomes established, and let the grass take it from there.

Panic grasses (*Panicum* spp.) are among my favorite grasses because of their misty clouds of seeds that float above the grass blades and stems. Switch grass (*Panicum virgatum*) is one of the chief plants of the tallgrass prairie and is truly ornamental. The inflorescences create a purple haze above the foliage. I am lusting after *P.* 'Prairie', a blue switch grass, and it is really *blue*, not greenish blue, and just yesterday I saw the astonishingly beautiful *P.* 'Cloud Nine'. It's a bluish, tall panicum whose individual blades rise up and seem to dissolve into a mist and float at the top of the plant. The mist looks like the vapor that rises above a big waterfall. If I had the sun and the space, I would plant a grove of 'Cloud Nines'.

Another panicum asset is the lovely golden color of the foliage come winter. It's almost as though the elf Rumpelstiltskin has been at work spinning the grass into gold. The soft golden sheaves contrast beautifully with rose bushes adorned with jewel-like rose hips.

Recently seen adorning the concrete islands of the parking lot of my favorite Mexican restaurant is a red switch grass, exact variety unknown, but possibly 'Hanse Herms' or 'Rotbraun' because the seed heads were almost purple. It had been planted and abandoned and was holding its own beautifully against a bunch of weeds, and this was after a two-month drought.

Fountain grasses (*Pennisetum* spp.) are wonderful for their soft seed heads and attractive vase shape. I recently saw *P.* 'Hameln' used as a lovely, soft-looking ground cover. 'Hameln' is one of the smaller pennisetums, reaching three feet in height. It's a sun lover, but I have a 'Hameln' that gets some shade during the late afternoon, and it's doing fine. The irresistibly cute *P.* 'Little Bunny' is a true miniature fountain grass, reaching only 18 inches. 'Little Bunny' is so small that you will need more than one to make an impact.

Pennisetum 'Little Bunny', a miniature fountain grass.

Just the other day I saw a streetside, municipal planting of *P. alopecuroides*, *Sedum* 'Autumn Joy', 'Green Mound' Alpine currant, and a rose, probably 'Carefree Delight'. This is an easy, handsome, drought-resistant planting that was receiving some shade late in the day.

It's too bad that red fountain grass (*Pennisetum setaceum* 'Rubrum') is an annual, but it has become so popular as a container plant that it has become available quite inexpensively. I saw it this summer selling for six dollars a gallon, and considering its drought and heat tolerance, that's not a bad buy. I've also read that it's easy to start from seed.

And I've just run across directions for overwintering annual grasses such as red fountain grass. Lee Randhava of the Chicago Botanic Garden writes in her *Chicago Tribune* "Question and Answer" column:

Wait until we have had a frost before you begin the process. Cut the grass back to 6 inches. If the clump is quite large, dig it up and divide it into smaller sections by cutting through the root ball with a sharp spade or hedge trimmers. Replant each section in an individual pot and store the pots in a dark, cool room that remains consistently around 40 degrees. Water sparingly just to keep the soil moist. You don't want the grass to break dormancy by exposing it to warm temperatures or bright sunlight.

Next spring, resume normal watering, and gradually introduce the pots to warm weather, taking care not to leave them out if frost threatens. Cut the dried grass back to ground level and replant outside when there is no danger of frost.

I've mentioned Japanese silver grass (*Miscanthus* spp.), and all I can say is that there is a miscanthus for every gardener. I gravitate to silky, fine-textured miscanthus varieties such as M. *sinensis* 'Gracillimus'. This is the maiden grass beloved by Victorians, who used it in their gardens. M. *sinensis* 'Morning Light' is similar to 'Gracillimus', but narrow bands of white on the leaf margins give the plant a silvery appearance. I sometimes think 'Morning Light' is one of the most beautiful of all grasses, as its elegant grace seems to shine with an inner light. Another good miscanthus is M. 'Sarabande', which has silky foliage and unobtrusive plumes and a nice, simple vase shape. At four feet in height, it's considered a dwarf miscanthus and would work in many garden schemes. M. *s.* 'Adagio' is a dwarf miscanthus covered with hundreds of narrow tan plumes when it flowers in August and is a compact 30 inches tall and 36 inches wide.

If you're apprehensive about monster grasses lumbering into your garden, try this dwarf miscanthus. Another small miscanthus is M. *s. purpurascens*, which turns wine red in the fall and is only three or four feet tall.

Miscanthus benefits from careful soil preparation and should not be plunked unceremoniously into hard clay. Loosen the soil deep down for good drainage, and enrich with organic matter. For a large *Miscanthus*, this is quite a bit of work, so be forewarned. I've seen *Miscanthus* growing satisfactorily in a wide range of gardens, but apparently, hard, cold, poorly draining clay soil is its nemesis. *Miscanthus* is not quite as drought tolerant as some of the other grasses mentioned here, in that while it grows pretty well in dryish soil, it will be spectacular in rich, moist soil.

Speaking of monster grasses, I just checked out the Web site of Karl Bluemel, Inc., and among their many *Miscanthus* offerings are M. *sinensis* 'Giganteus', M. 'Goliath', and M. 'Giraffe'. The Web site is a bare-bones list of grasses with no descriptions at all, so it's left to your imagination as to how big these grasses are. I'm guessing really, really big.

I've mentioned that *Miscanthus* can take some shade, and only yesterday my sister mentioned that she has M. *sinensis* 'Variegatus' in quite deep shade, and it's growing beautifully.

If you become a connoisseur of prairie grasses, seek out side-oats grama (*Bouteloua curtipendula*), an elegant grass whose seeds dangle from only one side of its curving stems. It supposedly needs full sun and tolerates prolonged drought. I say "supposedly" because this is another grass I'm experimenting with in a spot that is shaded during the late afternoon, and the grass is growing well. So I guess it never hurts to try!

I planted tufted hair grass (*Deschampsia caespitosa* 'Schottland') just this fall after seeing it at a local nursery. Its seed heads float like clouds of gold dust above the neat basal foliage, so it's an extremely pretty grass. 'Schottland' is said to be one of the most robust varieties. I'm not quite sure what to expect of this plant in my garden. In *Kane County Wild Plants and Natural Areas*, by Dick Young, reference is made to the species being a rarity, found locally only at the South Elgin Fen. I've heard elsewhere that it's adaptable, but its home in a fen told me to dig in as much moisture-retentive organic matter as I could shoehorn into its planting hole, which I dug in a spot of dappled shade. I've read that tufted hair grass should be cut back in the fall, as it is not all that ornamental in the winter.

A cottage garden curbside planting of Japanese silver grass (*Miscanthus sinensis* 'Variegatus'), goldenrod (*Solidago* 'Fireworks'), and pink phlox.

133

Clockwise from upper left: Big-leafed aster (*Aster macrophyllus*), bottlebrush grass (*Hystrix patula*), and *Hosta* 'Cheesecake'.

Bottle-brush grass (*Hystrix patula*) is one of the few true grasses that will grow in dry shade. I had heard that the foliage of this grass is not distinguished, but the distinctive, pale yellow seed heads are truly pretty, and the plant taken as a whole looks fine in contrast to big-leafed hostas.

Northern sea oats (*Chasmanthium latifolium*) is another grass that does well in dry shade. I have a two-foot-tall clump in quite deep shade. The foliage and oatlike seed heads are striking. Be forewarned that this can be a rampant self-seeder, and I've heard a few tales of woe about this grass seeding uncontrollably. This is probably true in rich, moist soil, so be careful. In horrible, dry soil, it does fine.

When I worked at a local plant nursery, the grass that seemed to excite the most comment was purple love grass (*Eragrostis spectabilis*). First of all, there is that groovy name with its aura of hippies and the Summer of Peace and Love, and then there is the diminutive grass itself, which from July onward is obscured by beautiful, soft clouds of purple-brown seeds. Purple love grass is a clump-forming grass that is easy to grow if you have full sun, as it will tolerate poor soil.

I haven't grown green moor grass (*Sesleria caerula*) or autumn moor grass (*S. autumnalis*) and haven't even seen them, but I am mentioning them here because I have heard only good things about moor grasses from several reliable quarters. Seslaria is a European native that is said to be easy to grow, cold hardy, extremely drought resistant, and can be used as ground covers. Apparently they can take full sun or considerable shade and grow up to 20 inches in height. I am going to try one as soon as I can track it down at a nursery.

Postscript: Just this July I saw autumn moor grass at Cantigny Gardens in Wheaton, Illinois. The shining, fine-textured grassy mounds were about two feet tall and were growing in full sun. They were strikingly beautiful.

The newest grass in my garden is striped tuber oat grass (*Arrhenatherum elatius bulbosum* 'Variegatum'), a cool-season variegated grass. I couldn't resist it when I saw it at a local nursery. It may go dormant in the summer heat, but I'll give it a try in a shady spot and see what happens. It doesn't really grow from bulbs but has swollen nodes that store water. I've read in *The Color Encyclopedia of Ornamental Grasses*, by Rick Darke, that it "is among the brightest whites of all the grasses."

Postscript: The striped tuber oat grass (a name that lacks music, don't you think?) has sailed through a six-week drought and heat spell without the

spring and often flower in spring or early summer. They are not as heat tolerant as warm-season grasses. Warm-season grasses come up later, when the weather has turned warm. The disadvantage of a warm-season grass is that if you have a long, cool spring, it might emerge quite late. This year we had just such a spring, and *Pennisetum*, a warm-season grass, didn't emerge until early June. I wouldn't let either of these descriptions deter you one way or the other from buying a grass. Blue fescue (*Festuca glauca*) is a cool-season grass that supposedly goes dormant during hot weather. My blue fescue seems totally unaffected by hot weather and is perfectly drought resistant. I do have it in a spot that doesn't get a full six hours of sun, though, so this may be a clue to growing cool-season grasses in our climate.

WHERE TO BEGIN WITH GRASS

As time has passed, three grasses have emerged as my personal favorites: blue fescue (*Festuca glauca*), tufted hairgrass (*Deschampsia caespitosa*), and prairie dropseed (*Sporobolus heterolepsis*). All are on the small side and are clump formers, so they work well in a small garden. And as fairly slow growers, you don't have to worry about dividing them frequently, if ever. They can also

Carex ciliatomarginata 'Island Brocade' (near bottom left, with golden edges) and *Hosta* 'Kabitan'.

slightest problem. I watered it weekly along with some other nearby perennials but otherwise gave it no special attention. It reminds me a bit of a clumping ribbon grass.

In this look at ornamental grasses, I have truly just scratched the surface of what is available. I saw Molinia 'Sky Racer' at a nursery a few weeks ago and was much taken with this tall grass with its airy foliage. Korean feather reed grass (*Calamagrotis brachytrica*), with its silvery plumes, also looked intriguing. And I've heard that a native grass with a rather unpromising name—*Diarrhena americana*—is quite attractive with "handsome clean foliage" and can take shade. The carexes alone could keep us all busy for a long time.

Grasses and roses might seem an unlikely combination but can look great together. The soft casualness of grasses tempers the stiff, prickly quality of some rose bushes. Use a silky grass like *Miscanthus* 'Sarabande' as a foil to the rose 'Carefree Delight' for a pretty and drought-resistant duo.

You may have already read that perennial grasses are either "cool season" or "warm season" and wondered what that meant. It means that some grasses, and *Deschampsia* is an example, come up in the coolness of early

Carex morrowii 'Silver Sceptre'.

take some late-day dappled shade. Blue fescue is flat-out pretty, especially when its golden seed heads appear. Tufted hairgrass forms such a nice, neat, green clump, topped with a cloud of sparkling seed heads. I like it so much that I am plotting to get rid of a nearby perfectly hideous daylily (a chrome yellow and ox-blood bicolor) and replace it with more deschampsia. And the silkiness of prairie dropseed is so attractive and refined. So if you are wondering where to begin with grasses, these would be good ones to try.

ORNAMENTAL SEDGES

As I write this, ornamental sedges (*Carex* spp.) are emerging as the Plants of the Hour, and they are so useful and beautiful that I have gone a bit carex mad. Sedges differ from grasses in ways mainly of interest to botanists: for gardeners they are basically cute little grasses that come in a seeming endless array of foliage colors and forms. They can be used as ground covers, specimen plants, and in containers. They are perfect companions to hostas. They remind me a bit of the grasslike ground cover liriope, but the foliage is more interesting, some being broad and straplike and some fine and grassy. My first carex was *C. pennsylvanica*, whose silky foliage and shade tolerance quickly made it a winner in my garden.

Nearby grows *C. morrowii* 'Ice Dance', whose green blades are edged in white. This is a wonderful plant—utterly drought resistant and clean looking. I also grow the woodbank sedge (*C. cephalophora*) and Bicknell's sedge (*C. bicknelli*), which are shade tolerant. These sedges have persevered in quite dry soil beneath my horse chestnut tree, but this summer I have amended their soil with planting mix, as they really need decent soil, not depleted, dry soil. But 'Ice Dance' has proven extremely drought resistant. There are also sedges for moist, and even wet, areas.

I think the real problem with sedges, and I mean this quite seriously, is that they arouse the collector's instinct. Maybe it's not really a problem, but it's hard to grow one sedge without wanting another, and another . . . *Carex* 'Silk Tassel', with silvery, threadlike foliage, is what I would like to find under the Christmas tree this December, if Santa could arrange it. And 'Sparkler' looks fabulous, too.

CORN

Corn is a member in good standing of the grass family, though we might not think it as such. Most of us drive by endless cornfields shining in the sun every summer but have never seen a corn plant close up. I think all Midwesterners should grow corn in their gardens at least once, as it is an awe-inspiring experience and is not difficult. This plant is so tall that it grows its own props. I grew an heirloom corn with multicolor corn kernels a few years ago. It grew up, and up, and up, and finally, one day, I judged the plump ears ready for picking and decided to have them for dinner the following day. I hauled out the big, blue granite-ware corn-boiling cauldron and checked in the refrigerator to make sure we had a supply of butter. Yum! Remarkably, sharp-eyed raccoons had made exactly the same determination as I had, and I woke the next day to find the stalks ravaged, with gnawed cobs everywhere on the lawn. Oh well.

Corn is actually quite ornamental, and I've heard it suggested that a clump or two can be effective accents in a flower garden. And there are inedible corn varieties with variegated leaves that actually are ornamentals: *Zea mays* 'Quadricolor' from Thompson & Morgan and 'Japonica' from Johnny's Selected Seeds. Victorians used ornamental corn as accent plants in their gardens.

ANNUAL GRASSES

The grasses and sedges we've looked at above are perennials, and it never occurred to me at first to try growing annual grasses. But this spring I inadvertently discovered that annual grasses are extremely easy to grow from seed. I had purchased a seed packet from a Thompson & Morgan sale list called "Shades of Green." As well as containing some very pretty flowers, the mix contained seeds for annual grasses. The grasses germinated easily and survived my usual bungling seed-starting techniques and went on to thrive. The seeds included quaking grass (*Briza maxima*) and hare's tail (*Lagurus ovatus*). I have also heard of two other annual grasses: squirrel tail grass (*Hordeum jubatum*) and foxtail millet (*Setaria italica*) and definitely will be trying them next spring.

Keep in mind that grasses that are this easy to start from seed might be self-seeders. I would keep these out of your best perennial bed until seeing what they do in a more inconspicuous part of the garden.

I was at the Garfield Farm Heirloom Horticultural Show in LaFox, Illinois, today, when I stumbled across another annual grass and got a bit of a shock. I was shocked that I had forgotten about it in this discussion of grasses, and I was shocked at how beautiful it was. The grass is wheat (*Triticum*), in this case, an heirloom variety called Black Knight winter wheat. The seed head looked like finely carved, gray driftwood, and long, black, graceful bristles, called "awns," curved gracefully around the sides. The farmer instructed me to break apart the seed head and plant the seeds on September 15. I look forward to having a patch of wheat next spring in my garden.

Postscript: The wheat sprang up beautifully. Almost three feet in height, the tips of the soft, pale, green grass blades gracefully droop over, and you can't resist running your hands through them to hear the rustling—this is the most tactile of plants. I am looking forward to the next stage, when the wheat heads start developing (called "heading out"), and then when the wheat turns to gold. Suddenly it occurs to me that I might need a scythe, a flail, and then a threshing basket. But my little patch is so small that I will harvest it by hand.

Wheat is so unexpectedly beautiful that I did a search on the Internet for a source for more varieties and came up with www.seedman.com, which has a long list of grain seeds for sale. The Bountiful Gardens catalog (www.bountiful gardens.org) also has modern and ancient wheat varieties. Wheat seed sold at natural health food stores for sprouting can also be used. If you have the space and sun, a patch of wheat, whether ornamental or for food, could be great fun, perhaps grown with a patch of ornamental corn. Just remember the scarecrow.

GRASS CARE

Grasses are touted as being easy care, and they are, but like any garden plant they need monitoring for possible problems. In general, they are free of pests and diseases. Most warm-season grasses hit their peak in late summer and fall, blooming and then turning color. One of the many remarkable things about grasses is that they look as beautiful, if not more beautiful, in winter as they do in the growing season. Snow frosting the feathery grass clumps is ornamental, even sculptural, and the seed heads attract birds. Enjoy this beauty, and wait until February or March (depending on the weather) to cut back the dead grass stalks. I learned from the book *Caring for Perennials,* by Janet Macunovich, that the best way to do this is to cut the dead grass back very hard, "as close to the ground as you can." She describes this as "shaving" the grass and feels that it delays the development of a dead center. Other experts recommend cutting the dead grass back to only three or four inches of stubble. If you've heard that a grass is "iffy" or a bit tender in our area, I wouldn't "shave" it at first, and then experiment in subsequent years.

I read recently that blue-colored grasses should not be cut back as hard

as other grasses, and since I never cut back the little blue fescues, and they grow beautifully, this may be true.

If a clump-forming grass is growing out from the middle and there is a bare spot, it can be divided like any other perennial. After you have cut it back, use a shovel to dig down and divide the grass into manageable clumps. Dig up the clumps and throw away dead material. Then replant the remaining clumps.

As easy as many grasses are to grow, our variable winters are always a "wild card" among the many considerations that determine if a plant lives or dies in our climate. Poor drainage, or an unusually cold or damp winter, might well kill a grass, but if at first you don't succeed . . .

You might question why I have spent so much time on grasses in a book on cottage gardening, as they are not part of the usual cottage gardening tradition, and most will not be handed over the fence by a neighbor. They can be obtained only by going to a nursery and buying them, and the more uncommon varieties are not usually cheap. The answer lies in our conception of the cottage gardener as an ecologist. Whether you bring only native prairie

An Appleblossom Flower Carpet ® rose underplanted with golden marjoram.

Rosa 'Nearly Wild' blooms on and off all summer.

grasses into your garden, or use nonnative grasses as well, once grasses are planted and established, they may need no supplemental watering from you at all. If you put your "thinking cap" on, you'll be able to pair grasses with other drought-resistant perennials and come up with completely drought-resistant gardens—oh, happy days! The ancient Hebrews differentiated between crops grown by irrigation ("schlachin") and crops grown "by the grace of God." Grasses, happily, are in the latter category.

Roses

And here we come to the rose, the flower of fairy tales, the floral siren that calls irresistibly to even the most hard-nosed gardener. I've never thought of myself as a rose lover, certainly not a rosarian, or one wise in the ways of roses, but in preparing to write this chapter I toured my garden and counted 18, enough to cause my husband, Jim, to remark it was "evidence of a mania." There *is* something about roses. Even after you've seen the ugly ones, or reeled from shock at seeing bud worms boring their way into your rose hopes and dreams, or fought off herds of aphids, or screamed with horror at spying the

coppery backs of Japanese beetles folded among the rose petals, there remains something about them. "*Ma rose, ma rose, tu avez voler ma rose,*" cried the dear, sensitive Beast to the brainless Beauty, and as you gaze into the mandala of an opening rose, you understand his anguish. A rose isn't just beautiful, it's Beauty. An unfolding rose draws us down a rabbit hole into the mystery of the universe, or so it seems. The old hippy in me thinks, "Roses are heavy, man." So roses hold me tightly in their thorny, sometimes imperious grip, and I continue grumbling in their servitude.

Rather than have the foolishness to pretend that I know anything about roses (I think the real story of roses of the Midwest is still waiting to be learned and written), I'll lead a rose tour of what's actually in my garden to see what's thriving, what's dwindling, and I'll mention in passing the works in progress.

Draped on the arch that spans the brick path leading to our front door is just such a work in progress—'Zephyrine Drouhin'. There's not much I can really say about Zephyrine since I just planted her two years ago and she is just hitting her stride. A repeat-flowering Bourbon whose mildly fragrant flowers are a deep, clear pink, this rose is unusual in not having thorns—the stem is smooth as silk. A *Nepeta* 'Six Hills Giant' is planted at Zephyrine's knees, just in case they are knobby, though, so far, she has been a perfect lady.

Also near the arch is a polyantha named 'Mothersday'. The shape and color of the scentless flowers is this rose's claim to fame. The small, cupped blossoms are a warm, luscious red with an underlying shadow of blue. This is a pretty little plant that has to be the all-time great Mother's Day gift for Mom.

Walking around to the side path we come to 'Nearly Wild', a floribunda. Today is June 3, and this plant is smothered with blossoms. The petals are a blushing pink paling to white at the center, with a gold froth of stamens. The flowers have the faintest possible scent, and it's possible I'm imagining that they have any scent at all. The value of this rose is that it offers a long-blooming mass of wild-looking roses on a low-growing, compact bush. Real wild roses are often rangy ramblers and may bloom briefly. I notice that my 'Nearly Wild' is leaning rather poignantly forward—I'm sure it wants more sun, though it's doing well with the four hours plus bright shade it's getting.

On the other side of the path lumbers 'Madame Isaac Pereire'. She's absolutely loaded with fat, round buds, but, sadly, I hesitate to recommend Madame. She's had water, sun, compost—what more can she want?—but her buds are so packed with petals they seem exhausted with the struggle of opening. Some have turned slightly brown without opening. Is it a fungus, or is it Madame? I strongly suspect that Madame is innocent and that the culprit is botrytis blight, a fungal disease.

Next year I will apply a lime-sulfur spray early in the spring, as recommended in my favorite rose book, *Tender Roses for Tough Climates*, by Douglas Green. The extra trouble will be worth it, as the flowers that have opened smell and look divine, even *ravisante*. Of course there is the possibility that Madame is a snob and is pouting at being exiled in Illinois, of all places, and is not in Paris at the Opera Bouffe, where she was *someone*.

Now on to a great success: the wonderful David Austin rose 'Graham Thomas'. This primrose yellow rose is illuminated from within by an apricot glow. It smells like raspberries and tea and is so wonderful that I have two Grahams, one planted under a copper rose arch in my side garden, another against the back fence. Heat resistant and with a flawlessly beautiful blossom and shiny dark green leaves, you can't ask for much more in a rose. This is God and David Austin's rose gift to the Midwestern rose gardener.

Speaking of David Austin, several years ago I attended a lecture on heirloom roses given by Debra Phillips, a local garden designer and Master Gardener, who successfully grows a wider range of roses than anyone I know. On a garden tour in England, she met and spoke with David Austin, who told her he uses granular "tomato food" to feed his roses. Mix the tomato food with water according to directions, and use one cup per plant at the root zone when the rose is just starting to bud.

Two Fairy roses blossom near 'Graham Thomas'. Perhaps too routinely planted and overrecommended, it's still a nice rose, a polyantha with little shell pink flowers. It's often touted as extremely low maintenance, but that doesn't mean it should be ignored. It's so much happier with plenty of water and good soil. One overlooked point about the Fairy is that it can become quite large—not tall, but it does send out arching canes, and before you know it, it can quietly cover quite a bit of space.

I'll mention the tea rose by my back steps, not because I know what it is, but because I *don't* know what it is, only that its appearance in my garden is serendipitous. Years ago I had ordered a Fairy rose from Gurney's mail-order catalog and got this coral-colored tea rose instead. So in it went. I've had it for a dozen years now, and while it occasionally suffers the indignity of neglect, it always flowers beautifully. Thank you, Gurney's, for your excellent mistake.

On the other side of the back step climbs 'Climbing Cecile Brunner',

The flower color of *Rosa* 'Graham Thomas' pales as the rose opens.

Rosa multiflora platyphylla 'Seven Sisters'.

a polyantha. It is a tough rose that can take a bit of shade and abuse. Spine-tinglingly perfect little pale pink blooms, exquisite as seashells, materialize in May.

There used to be a Blaze rose in this spot, but the partial shade was too much for it, and it gave up the ghost. Just last week I saw a perfect Blaze—it was lounging luxuriantly against the side of a somewhat dilapidated, white clapboard house trimmed with green. The deep, rather somber, red of the Blaze glowed in perfect contrast.

At this point we enter a Zone of No Roses as we pass under the horse chestnut. While there are quite a few roses that can take some shade, none that I know of will grow in dense shade.

Emerging from the gloom, we come to another nameless rose. Probably most gardeners have at least one of these—I am ashamed to say I have two. It was at a nursery where I was working, and its tag had fallen off. I was able to whisk the rose away for half price. All I know is that it's low growing, enthusiastic, and garish, but in an endearing way. The petals are a vivid pink bordering on red, paling to a yellow bull's-eye center. In some ways, it's really

quite awful, but it's so happy I don't have the heart to get rid of it.

Now we come to my pride and joy, a 'Seven Sisters' rambler (*R. multiflora grevillei* or *R. multiflora platyphylla*, 1816). A waterfall of raspberry-colored blossom clusters, some paler or pinker or more lilac tinted than others, cascades over the back fence and on to the lawn. Its sweet apple and rose scent stews in the warm air as May turns to June, and I am held in its spell.

Nearby is 'Gertrude Jekyll', perhaps my favorite rose, though I can't say why exactly. There are bigger roses, pinker roses, and roses whose scent is as sweet. But there is something about Gertrude. Her pink is a perfect, creamy-clear pink, like a peppermint patty, and the elegant blossom is quartered and a bit flat. The intoxicating scent is that of fresh raspberries stewing in cream. Some complain about the rather wiry, prickly thin stems, but these flexible stems can be used to advantage. I placed a four-foot wire trellis behind Gertrude, tied her stems here and there onto the trellis, and now she is doing a back bend over the trellis, forming a diminutive rose arch. Without this support, I agree, this rose could be a bit rangy. This year there is a mystery about Gertrude: the flower color is paler than it was last year. People say I'm imagining it, but I know that the pink was deeper last year. Then today I found one blossom in the deeper raspberry color (imagine, if you can, eerie rose space music here). It just shows that I have a lot more to learn about roses.

Nearby is 'Betty Prior', an unpretentious, single-petaled pink rose, a floribunda, perfect in the cottage garden. If I had the space, I'd have more Bettys and surround them with simple annuals like bachelor buttons, so they could all sway in the breeze together. As it is, she seems content with the sweet rocket that blooms in the spring and the purple coneflowers blooming in late summer. 'Betty Prior' has withstood a fair amount of abuse in my garden—she's been moved, forgotten, drowned in lavender mint—and she has pulled though. She is a tough, good rose.

Jammed shamefully in a corner is 'Reine des Violettes', a Hybrid Perpetual whose fat, flat blossoms do have a shimmering violet undertone. La Reine is taking matters into her own capable hands and is sending out canes into my vegetable patch. This year I've accepted the fact that I want roses much more than I want tomatoes, and so I'm letting her do her thing. I can just imagine the conversation that La Reine and Madame Isaac Pereire will have if they ever get together: "Zut alors, can you imagine . . . she expected me to hide in zee corner . . . " "Yes," nods Madame vigorously. "She is *un chien mechant* . . ."

We've come to the back fence, but not to the end of the roses. Behind the

fence is a pink 'F. J. Grootendorst', a rugosa hybrid. The pro for this rose is the unusual flowers, whose petals are pinked like carnations. A cluster of these blooms is breathtaking, and when Grootendorst in is bloom, everyone—but everyone—will want to know what it is. A downside is that this rose is not "self-cleaning"—the brown, faded blossoms stay firmly put, right next to the new blossoms. And since this is an incredibly thorny rose, it's not easy to dead-head. By the time the first flush of bloom dwindles, you have a pretty ugly sight. I don my husband's leatherwork gauntlets, as worn cloth garden gloves with holes aren't up to this challenge, and clip off the dead clusters. There is sporadic blooming the rest of the summer. 'F. J. Grootendorst' and the 'Seven Sisters' are on opposite sides of the same fence and have become intermingled. The effect is quite lovely.

I almost forgot the little rose I purchased last week! It followed me home from the nursery. Called *R. arkansana*, it's a wild rose, only a foot or two tall. I saw it in bloom out on the prairie today (June 6) at the West Chicago Prairie Forest Preserve. Its creamy, pale pink flowers, pure as porcelain, were almost hidden among the prairie grasses dotted with the amethyst blue of *Tradescantia ohiensis*, also in bloom. I'm hoping this rose will make a home in my garden.

Well, that's . . . I almost said "it," but had forgotten about two more roses planted just this spring. They are gifts from my wonderful rose friend, Mr. Ralph Putnam. Mr. Putnam truly merits the title "rosarian," so I know that these aren't just any old roses. One rose is 'Tuscany', one of the oldest Gallicas, with deep, crimson-purple blooms. The other is 'Stanwell Perpetual' whose snowy blooms are among the most beautiful roses I've ever seen. Mr. Putnam advised planting these roses rather low in the ground so that the stems could send out suckers, giving rise to a nice bush. The roses are in, snuggling down into their compost, and are doing very nicely. Thank you, Mr. Putnam!

A recent visit to Mr. Putnam's garden brought even more roses to my attention. He has a garden full of shrub roses, including many heirlooms, and it is an enchanted place. But I am running out of space and will only mention a few of the more unusual varieties. One standout was a climbing tea rose named 'Aloha', which had large, fragrant pink flowers with an unusual, coppery underglow. This rose is notable for its glossy, dark green leaves, courtesy of its pollen parent, 'New Dawn'. Mr. Putnam's plant was about four feet tall, but it can get to eight. It's a repeat bloomer, is disease resistant, and tolerates poor soil. If you want a tea rose, but are hesitant because of all the chemical upkeep,

The distinctive flowers of *Rosa* 'F. J. Grootendorst' (Pink). The petal edges are "pinked" like those of the carnation.

141

consider 'Aloha'. 'Golden Wings' was another standout. The flowers have large, softly drooping, creamy yellow petals, and the stamens form a starry, golden patch in the center of the flower. 'Golden Wings' is a repeat-blooming shrub rose, about four feet in height, and has nice clean foliage. The flowers were standouts in a garden full of standouts. A reblooming Bourbon rose, 'Louise Odier', was notable for the sheer number of blooms on one plant. The lilac pink flower petals, which smell of raspberries, are quartered and nestled in a laced ring of outer petals, and the foliage is a nice light green. 'Louise Odier' is about five feet tall. Another standout was a moss rose named 'Salet'. Moss roses have the most elegant buds and stems, covered with little scented prickles. I've heard that most moss roses don't do well in our climate, but repeat-blooming 'Salet' is an exception. It's about four feet tall and has pink flowers.

Back in my garden, I almost forgot another rose! Last year my sister-in-law Leah gave me a start of 'Ballerina', a hybrid musk. It's busily settling down in my garden, coming up along with some oxeye daisies that hitched a ride in the same pot, and I look forward to seeing it bloom next year. It's a per-

Rosa 'Carefree Delight' intertwined with a clematis.

petual bloomer, with trusses of small pink blooms with white centers.

So that's the tour, and I hope you have enjoyed it. I will now bow my head in memory of roses that stopped briefly in my garden and then quickly left: a rose with the mouthwatering name of 'Sissinghurst Castle' dropped dead almost instantly, and 'Heritage', a David Austin rose, lasted only two summers. More confounding, a rugosa rose called 'Blanc Double de Coubert', supposedly cast iron, also seemed to die last year, though I notice some canes have emerged this spring. Since it is a rugosa, it's possible that these canes will bear flowers true to the plant's name. We'll see next year.

I have never yet found the climbing, fragrant, pink polyantha rose that I remember from my grandmother's garden, but perhaps it's an impossible quest, as pursuing all such memories are.

BE ROSE AWARE

Garden writers aren't supposed to admit that they make mistakes, but, believe me, as you've probably noticed from the above, they do, and I'd like to impart a little of what I've learned about roses.

The bottom line is this: never buy a rose on impulse. Never saunter through a nursery looking for a new pair of gardening gloves and walk out with a rose. Never be so seduced by a rose that you fall into a trance and buy it without the slightest idea where it will go in your garden, or worse yet, knowing that there *isn't* any place in your garden for it. Roses are seducers, so beware! Even as you virtuously examine the latest variety of ajuga, stifling a yawn, you'll see the roses out of the corner of your eye, and it's very difficult to refrain from taking a peek, and before you know it you have a new rose.

Begin buying a rose at home in your garden, evaluating different locations for suitability. Where do you have sun? Most roses like sun from dawn to dusk and won't argue with having nine hours of sun a day. Nine hours! And they want good drainage—I don't know of any that can tolerate wet feet.

Once you've determined your spot, measure it with a tape measure—both width and length—and write it down. Carry this with you when you go to a nursery to rose hunt. The roses sitting in three-gallon pots could vary wildly in their ultimate size. A rose can mushroom into a big, hunkering tank of a plant, or could be a climber, or a ground cover. Some are vase shaped, and some could cover your house. *Rosa eglanteria*, the sweet brier rose, shoots twelve feet straight up into the air with canes the size of your wrists. You'll want to know this kind of thing in advance!

Have your soil tested. It may be fine, but if it isn't, many roses take about three years to become established, precious time wasted if your soil is poor and the rose languishes.

Once you've zeroed in on a rose that sounds interesting, research it. Look it up in at least two or three rose books and catalogs to see what different growers have to say about it, or do a search on the Internet. This careful process may sound too time consuming, but it will vastly increase your chance for having a wonderful rose perfect for your garden. Since some roses can easily live fifty years, taking time in their selection for your garden makes sense.

As to what specific types of roses to consider, if you have the room, many of the so-called heirloom or old garden roses are tough as nails, and their flowers are superb, beautiful in both form and color. Most of these roses are largish shrubs that bloom only once in early summer, though there are a few that bloom sporadically all summer. The albas, bourbons, damasks, and gallicas—aristocrats of the rose world—are completely hardy here, and I have seen them flourishing in local gardens.

My top-rated choice from among the old garden roses is R. 'Stanwell Perpetual'. The flowers, with their Damask scent, are so pretty, with a pale blush undertone in the bud and then brightening to cream white as the petals open. The plant is about three to five feet in height and spread and is compact in form, so it's not a suckering monster. Best of all, just as the name would suggest, it blooms all summer long, just pausing occasionally to take a deep breath. And the gray-green, fine-textured foliage is disease resistant. It can even take a bit of shade. And it has interesting red thorns. Just a wonderful rose!

For the stunning beauty of its flowers and their wonderful scent, I love R. 'Charles de Mills'. The shrub is about four to five feet tall and spreads out to about four feet. The flower is a deep violet crimson, and bloom time is from late spring to early summer. The scent is intoxicating. While it has only one rather long bloom period, its foliage is disease resistant and stays presentable for the summer. But the flower—it's a killer.

What if you don't have space to plant shrub roses? Jump at the wonderful "landscape" roses that have appeared on the gardening scene in the last 15 or so years. Most are low-growing, compact, ever-blooming roses that can tolerate challenging conditions, including drought. The Meidiland roses, the Pavement series, and the 'Carefree Wonder' roses are fine roses for the Midwest. I particularly like the pale pink and the white varieties of the Flower Carpet series. The white is snow white, almost wild looking, and the pink is sweet and delicate. Both are very drought resistant and long flowering.

In the 'Carefree Wonder' series, 'Carefree Delight' is a particular favorite of mine. During much of the summer it's a mound about four feet across and three feet tall completely covered with delicate, single-petaled pink flowers. It stays healthy and is highly drought resistant. This is a very easy rose to grow, and it has real charm. If I only had space for one rose, 'Carefree Delight' would definitely be a contender. 'Carefree Wonder' has double roses in a deeper pink.

RUGOSAS

Consider planting a rugosa rose. These dense shrub roses with thick, healthy foliage are tough as nails and will tolerate average soil and take dryer conditions than other roses are happy with. They are also somewhat shade tolerant. The flowers are often fragrant and will appear off and on in successive waves of bloom during the whole summer. Most rugosa roses have showy hips in the fall, a big added plus.

Rosa rugosa, the species, has striking violet red flowers. Just last summer, in August, I saw R. *rugosa* in full bloom at a local nursery, and it was truly lovely, vibrant with health and covered with blossoms. There are many hybrid rugosas, including 'Hansa', with reddish violet double flowers; 'Fru Dagmar Hastrup', with silvery pink, single blossoms; and 'Therese Bugnet', with lilac-pink double flowers. 'Therese' is considered by some to be "one of the easiest and most reliable roses to grow." You're probably thinking that there must be faults to these paragons, and yet, honestly, no, just certain characteristics to keep in mind. They are shrub roses and don't pretend to be small, and most have thorns or prickles. This makes rugosas excellent as hedge roses, and they also work well as part of a perennial border *ensemble*. Some, like 'Hansa' increase in size by suckering, a problem if space is limited. There is a small version of 'Hansa', named 'Dart's Dash', which is about four feet high and wide. Other rugosas on the small size include the modern 'Pavement' series, at only about three by three feet, and the Canadian 'Parkland Series', only two to three feet tall. Rugosas vary in their habit, with some vase shaped, and some mounding, and this could make a difference in your gardening plans. Just because rugosas are tough and hardy doesn't mean they are pedestrian. Consider the lovely 'Belle Poitevine', which debuted in France in 1894, or 'Roseraie de l'Hay', also from France, in 1900. *Ravisante!*

Rosa 'Ballerina', a hybrid musk, blooms in late June.

For a small rose bush with "old rose" appeal, consider 'Rose de Rescht'. It's only about two feet tall, healthy, and easy to grow. The fragrant flowers are fuchsia crimson. This is a very pretty little rose, and I just saw it a few days ago (June 11), in a friend's garden, covered in blossoms.

Rosa 'Sea Foam' is another useful rose in Midwestern gardens. It's a white shrub rose with a trailing habit, good for weaving through a border or training along a fence. Its flowers are sweetly fragrant, and they bloom all summer long. It can take a bit of light shade.

For more ideas for good roses, check out the J. W. Jung Seed Co. catalog, paying special attention to the back cover. For as long as I can remember, the back cover has featured an excellent roundup of roses suited to this area, including roses from the Canadian 'Explorer' series, which are hybrid rugosas. Check inside the catalog for their "Best Climbing Roses"—more good candidates for the Midwestern garden.

Another idea is to shop for roses at a nursery that trials rose varieties and offers only the best for our locality. I'm lucky to live near The Natural Garden, Inc., plant nursery in Saint Charles, Illinois, where they grow and personally evaluate the roses they sell and so offer a select group (along with perennials, herbs, annuals, and native plants). You can check out their website, www.the naturalgardeninc.com, or better yet, visit the nursery.

If you have shade and yet your heart cries out for roses, dab your tears, for all is not lost. Most roses need at least six or more hours of sun, but some will do quite well on as little as four, though they may not flower as heavily. I have seen the climber 'New Dawn' flowering beautifully on a north wall in bright shade. The hybrid musk 'Ballerina', is doing well in my garden in bright shade for most of the day. I have read that another hybrid musk, 'Cornelia', tolerates shade quite well. And the Pickering catalog singles out albas as tolerating shade, and I have heard one rosarian opine that most white shrub roses need protection from hot midafternoon sun. Just today, in *BBC Gardening* magazine, I ran across a recommendation for 'Souvenir du Docteur Jamain' as a rose for shade. Apparently its "dark velvety-red flowers" fade in bright sunlight. A little research revealed that this is a hybrid perpetual rose hardy in our zone. I could find nothing else about its temperament, however, so growing it would be a true experiment for the gardener.

A unique rose to consider for dappled or light shade is *Rosa rubrifolia* (also called *R. glauca*), the redleaf rose. The leaves are an unusual grey-mauve in color, the stems reddish violet, and the flowers, in the words of one catalog, like "little pink butterflies." In the stern words of Phillips and Rix, authors of

Roses, R. rubrifolia is "excessively popular," but a lot of beautiful things are popular, so I wouldn't let it worry you too much. This is a large shrub rose, growing up to six feet tall.

There are limits to the adaptability of roses, and dense shade won't work for them. If there is sun in the morning and dappled or bright shade in the afternoon, it can work. But if you have dense shade—how about double impatiens or frilly begonias instead?

Once you've chosen your roses, give them as much sun as you can if they need it and as good soil as you can muster. Water faithfully. Learn how to prune them and how to fertilize—look in any current book about roses for guidance.

TANTALUS

In late winter, when we are all at a low ebb, a catalog lands on our doorsteps, a catalog overflowing with pictures of such luscious roses as to madden us with rose desire: it's the Wayside Gardens Complete Rose Catalog, featuring the roses of English hybridizer David Austin. There is little use for me to warn you away—I know it's useless to try—as these roses will entice you irresistibly.

Nevertheless, the consensus among a number of Midwestern gardeners I have spoken to is that these beautiful English roses don't quite work here. They are just slightly too tender and too susceptible to black spot to truly prosper. Our damp, cold winters with their unpredictable successions of freezing and thawing seem to knock these roses back, so they look like they are in their first year, every year. This would not in itself be a totally fatal flaw because if you have a sheltered spot in your garden—a microclimate—they might make a go of it. But black spot can strip some of these roses almost bare by September, and it's an ugly sight. I myself have lost Heritage and Mary Rose. But if you have some protected nooks in your garden and are willing to use chemical sprays, especially fungicides, these roses may be possible for you.

The two big exceptions to this tale of woe are 'Graham Thomas' and 'Gertrude Jekyll'. They both get some black spot but otherwise are quite sturdy. But even these two have never grown as large and luscious in my garden as their pictures in English gardening magazines.

BUD WORM

I have one chronic pest problem on my roses, that of bud worm. It's not a catastrophic problem, as I usually lose only a few blossoms on my Tuscany rose,

but it's still annoying, and occasionally the worm will pop up on 'Gertrude Jekyll', who doesn't like it very much, I can tell you. As much as I've researched the problem, I haven't come up with the real name for this little worm, which is pale green, about a third of an inch long, and which eats its way into the flower bud, making a hole. The worm also nibbles on surrounding leaves, leaving ragged brown edges, and some of the year probably flies around in moth form in the garden, undetected. This late May I used Neem-Away™ Insect Spray, ordered from the Gardens Alive catalog. Neem oil comes from the tropical neem tree (*Azadirachta indica*) and has insecticidal properties. It seemed to work, as bud worms were scarce this early summer, certainly not as bad as in William Blake's dire poem.

THE SICK ROSE

O Rose, thou art sick!
The invisible worm
That flies in the night,
In the howling storm,
Has found out thy bed
Of crimson joy:
And his dark secret love
Does thy life destroy.

WE END WITH A FAIRY TALE

Once upon a time, many years ago, a little girl was walking along a pretty path on her way home. She sang as she walked, happy as a meadowlark. All of a sudden she came upon a great rose bush, the most beautiful she had ever seen. It had pink roses, blue roses, green roses—every color of the rainbow. And its leaves shimmered like gold.

"Oh, rosebush," cried the little girl, "you are so beautiful!"

"Thank you, little girl," said the rosebush, her leaves blushing with pleasure. "I'm glad you like my flowers. But I am so thirsty. No one has given me a glass of water for a long time, as this is a lonely lane. And I can't get it myself," she said, gesturing to her roots. "Could you please get me a drink of water?"

The little girl thought for a moment, her brow creasing. "But the only water is in the City of the Wells, ninety leagues back! And I don't have my seven league boots on! Oh, fairest of all roses, please don't be angry with me! But I cannot get you a drink of water!" She trembled, because as she spoke, the rose's leaves had turned black, and the rose bush suddenly towered above her and then, before the little girl's astonished eyes, turned into a witch, whose black robes writhed about her.

Lightning flashed in the darkening sky, and thunder rumbled, and the little girl began to run. "Oh, dear me! Mother, Father, where are you? I have been abandoned." And then she looked down at her hands and saw that her nails had become thorns. And she ran, and she ran.

"Oh, little girl, you ungrateful wretch," screamed the Rose Witch. "For leaving me thirsty, I curse you. For your meanness, I will turn you into a . . ."

I am so glad I woke up at this point. But I think the witch said she would turn me into a hellebore. So I ran, and I ran, and I ran outside and watered my roses.

Vines

Don't forget about vines. Vines are vital in Midwestern gardens, bestowing leafy coolness even during intense heat. And they add height as they clamber up trellises, providing relief to the eye in our flat landscape. They clothe a naked garden and can cover pedestrian garden structures. They also unite different elements in gardens, for instance, connecting a flower bed to a nearby building or fence.

Traditional cottage gardens always had climbers, whether a romantic-looking rose rambling over a doorway, wisteria dripping from the eaves of the cottage roof, or a vigorous clematis, such as *Clematis montana*, climbing through an apple tree. And of course, there was honeysuckle.

Some gardeners can feel a bit apprehensive about vines. Won't they get loose, we wonder, and begin rampaging through the garden uncontrollably? No, not if you choose the right vine. Let's look at a few good ones for the Midwestern gardener to consider, starting with some perennials.

PERENNIAL VINES

AKEBIA QUINATA (FIVELEAF AKEBIA) This is a twining vine with elegantly simple leaves in groups of four and five. I planted akebia some years ago over an arbor in the back of the garden and have watched it take off, its woody stems twining gracefully around the arbor supports. Akebia can be grown in sun or partial shade. It's sometimes called "chocolate vine" because of its chocolate maroon colored flowers that appear in late spring. The flowers are quite small—look closely! While well behaved, this is a strong-growing vine, and this year I found a stealthy tendril creeping under the back fence, four feet

from the arbor. Since I like akebia, I will leave it, interested in seeing what it will do next—but it would be easy enough to lop it off.

AMPELOPSIS BREVIPEDUNCULATA 'ELEGANS' (PORCELAIN VINE) This grows to 20 feet, so you can feel safe that it won't take over the entire garden, only part of it. It needs sun and average soil. It looks great grown over a white picket fence, and I've also seen it looking beautiful on unpainted cedar latticework. Porcelain vine is notable for its unusual berries, smooth little globes in iridescent shades of blue, lavender, and cream. The berries are not poisonous but are not tasty to humans, only birds.

CAMPSIS RADICANS (TRUMPET CREEPER) This one is a magnet for hummingbirds and butterflies. It grows to 20 feet and has orange-red tubular flowers. This is not for a small garden, and you might want to take a look at it in someone else's garden before planting it in your own, as it can get woody and needs strong support. It has been known to crush small sheds. Still, this can be a spectacular vine in the right place in the right garden—I once saw two trumpet creeper vines planted on either side of a garden gate. They met about 10 feet above the gate and intertwined, looking like something from a fairy tale.

CELASTRUS SCANDENS (AMERICAN BITTERSWEET) With woody stems that may grow up to 25 feet long, this is a twining vine for a large woodland garden. It has glossy green foliage in summer and white flowers in June, but it is mainly known for its scarlet-orange berries, which ripen in the fall and are enjoyed by birds. You need to buy a male plant and a female plant to get berries, which appear on the female vine.

EUONYMUS RADICANS (WINTER CREEPER) I mention euonymus though it truly is a plant for which familiarity breeds contempt. It's a workhorse, but a boring workhorse that at one point stealthily attempted to cover my entire house. But it's sturdy, it's green (except for the variegated varieties), and it grows, so there you are.

HUMULUS LUPULUS (HOP VINE) An acquaintance of mine has a hop vine that clambers up a gutter onto her roof. She cuts it right down to the ground in the fall. The leaves resemble three-lobed maple leaves, and after the insignificant green flowers bloom, the decorative, papery hops themselves appear. *H. lupulus* 'Aurea', the golden hop vine, has golden yellow leaves, and according to author David Stuart in *Classic Plant Combinations*, Gertrude Jekyll devised the striking combination of golden hop vine twining amid blue-leaved hostas. Both plants thrive in part shade.

HYDRANGEA ANOMALA PETIOLARIS (CLIMBING HYDRANGEA) This one only *sounds* exotic, as it thrives in Midwestern gardens. It grows to 15 feet, has white flowers that bloom in July and August, and can take partial shade. After two years, my climbing hydrangea had stalled at two feet in height, but having read that it's slow to establish, I didn't panic—much. When it was four years old it really got going and was covered with flowers. This year I notice it is sending out exploratory feelers and has become positively luxuriant looking. So this is a slowly unfolding plant, but one that is worth the wait.

LATHYRUS LATIFOLIUS (PERENNIAL SWEET PEA) If you want sweet peas, here's your plant. A cloud of tendrils, winged stems, and intense purple-pink sweet pea flowers will enthusiastically clamber up anything in its path. My vine is about six feet tall, but it's crowded by other plants, and I have seen it grow taller in other gardens. A perennial sweet pea bush is an airy, wayward thing that needs support, as it's not at all woody. It leans against its support, and its little tendrils cling nervously to anything nearby. It begins blooming in late June and does get knocked back a bit by extreme heat but in my experience not as badly as annual sweet peas. It will bloom on and off all summer, right through early fall. And with its beautiful stems, smooth, twined leaves, and elegant tendrils, it's a pretty plant whether flowering or not. I cut it back in the spring, leaving only about a foot or less of stem. Perennial sweet peas may self-seed, and I usually find two or three new little plants each spring.

LONICERA SPP. (HONEYSUCKLE) The sweet nectar produced by the tubular flowers of honeysuckle is attractive to honeybees and hawk moths, and honeysuckle is a classic choice for an old-fashioned garden, but the ecology-conscious gardener should be careful in honeysuckle selection—not all honeysuckles are created equal. First on the list of questionable honeysuckles is Japanese honeysuckle (*L. japonica*), described as a noxious, choking pest by Dick Young in *Kane County Wild Plants and Natural Areas*. He rates it just slightly above poison ivy in desirability. Tartarian honeysuckle (*L. tatarica*), widely available in major garden catalogs, is described by Young as a "choking, vigorous plant that severely damages many fine woodlands," so it should also be bypassed. He does give three native species—dwarf honeysuckle (*Diervilla lonicera*), red honeysuckle (*L. diocia*), and yellow honeysuckle (*L. prolifera*)—very high marks, but so far I have not seen a commercial source for them. So what's a gardener to do? A local nursery I know to be ecologically aware offers gold flame honeysuckle (*Lonicera heckrotti*), and I have also read recommendations for *Lonicera* x *brownii* 'Dropmore Scarlet'.

PARTHENOCISSUS QUINQUEFOLIA (VIRGINIA CREEPER) See chapter 3, "Perennial Support Players."

POLYGONUM AUBERTII (SILVER LACE VINE) See chapter 4, "Dictionary of Perennials."

VITIS SPP. (GRAPEVINE) A Concord grapevine, planted by a previous owner, grows over a sagging wooden fence in our backyard. It grows absolutely wild—unwatered and unweeded—and every few years produces a remarkable bumper crop, pounds and pounds of grapes from a 16-foot vine. But why, oh, why couldn't the previous owners have planted the grape for a delicious Chateau du Pape Neuf? There are vineyards in Illinois, and in the early 1900s,

The flower of the perennial sweet pea (*Lathyrus latifolius*), a vine.

Illinois produced 25 percent of the nation's wine. Prohibition put an end to the industry, with many vines being destroyed.

Grapevines can be ornamental: I grow *Vitis vinifera* 'Purpurea', a purple-leafed, nonflowering grapevine that has fruit suitable only for the birds.

WISTERIA FLORIBUNDA (CANADIAN WISTERIA) An acquaintance of mine, as well as having a lovely rose garden, has a prodigious wisteria vine that clambers over a pergola and up onto a tree. He doesn't remember what kind it is, but perhaps it is Canadian wisteria, which I have read is hardy here. Gurney's catalog offers two hardy varieties, identified only as purple wisteria and rose wisteria, hardy to zone 4. Either way, this elegant member of the pea family is perfect for the cottage garden. Wisteria needs good soil and sun. Be sure to provide it with firm, heavy-duty support, as wisteria is a heavy, woody vine that can live to a great age. I've heard that the ideal site for a wisteria vine is on an "old, slowly dying tree," which sounds melancholy, but which is probably quite beautiful. At any rate, a slender steel arch or a wobbly little wooden trellis won't be enough support for it.

And don't forget *climbing roses!*

Like any perennial, most perennial vines take at least a year or two to become established. Even a fast grower like the silver lace vine will not seem to be doing much of anything its first year, though if you could peer beneath the soil, you would see its roots developing. The next year, though, it will shoot up like a rocket. And some perennial vines, such as climbing hydrangea and wisteria, are notorious for their slow development. So if you are in a big hurry for vines, annual vines might be the way to go.

ANNUAL VINES

Planting vining annuals is a good way to experiment with vines in the garden without committing to anything big and gnarly. They are inexpensive, fast growing, and need only decent, not rich, soil.

Morning glories (*Ipomoea purpurea* and *tricolor*), moonflowers (*I. alba*), balloon vines (*Cardiospermum halicacabum*), black-eyed Susan vines (*Thunbergia alata*), canary creeper (*Tropaelum peregrinum*—closely related to nasturtiums), and climbing nasturtiums (*T. majus*) are good annual vines. I mention canary creeper even though it's not a plant for hot summers. I tried it this summer in a sunny spot in my garden, and the heat did knock it back. But I'm wondering if some afternoon shade would help it, and since the fringed yellow flowers were so pretty and the foliage so unusual, delicate, and

attractive, I'm going to try again in a different, shadier spot. Moonflowers flower in the evening and are like huge, pristine, otherworldly white morning glories. They are astonishingly beautiful. There are also the quamoclits, members of the morning glory family that have small flowers and finely divided foliage. Quamoclits include the cypress vine (*I. quamoclit*), which has soft, feathery foliage, and a hybrid between the cypress vine and scarlet morning glory (*I. coccinea*) called cardinal climber (*I. multifida*), which has deeply lobed leaves. I have tried the cardinal vine, and it's so pretty and easy to grow I wonder why it's not more popular—perhaps it's simply been overshadowed by the eye-catching beauty of the flowers of its cousin the morning glory. Sweet potato vines (*I. batatas*), are grown for their smooth, attractive foliage and are perfect for container growing. I would love to try purple bell vine (*Rhodochiton atrosanguineum*). If pictures are to be believed, it has purple, bell-like flowers and dark green leaves edged with burgundy. It's a native of Mexico and is versatile in its sun requirements, so it sounds like a possible winner for our region.

Speaking of morning glories, I always used to think of the morning glory 'Heavenly Blue' as *the* morning glory, but that's before I stumbled across a Japanese Web site called Kondoh's Morning Glory Page. The Japanese are into morning glories in a big way and even use them in a special sort of bonsai. Mr. Kondoh is a member of the Osaka Morning Glory Club and grows an astonishing number of that genus. There are double morning glories, star-shaped ones, even a weeping morning glory that doesn't climb. There is also a group of lovely yellow morning glories. So there is a whole world of morning glories just waiting for us to explore.

One annual vine that I have not grown, but that's been recommended by several local gardeners, is Love in a Puff, or Balloon vine (*Cardiospermum halicacabum*). The Select Seeds catalog describes it thus: "The small, white flowers are followed by buoyant, light green, inflated seed capsules. Inside each capsule reside three seeds, each marked with a perfect white heart. The delicate, finely cut leaves are borne on stems that reach 10 ft."

I have just purchased seeds from Underwood Gardens for the heirloom vining petunia. They are "sweetly-scented, white, pink, lavender and purple trailing (4 ft.) petunias. Fragrant clouds of flowers June-frost."

A fun thing to do with annual vines is to grow two together–and to try different combinations, or to grow them intertwined with a climbing rose or ivy. I've also seen seed packets sold that contain half a dozen different types of annual vines mixed together, which seems like an easy, inexpensive way to try a variety of different vines all at once.

Most annual vines should be direct-seeded into decent soil in a sunny spot and left at that. Fertilization can produce lots of leaves and few flowers. They don't like being mulched or kept damp in any way. Morning glories will self-seed if you give them a spot they like.

One of the best sources for annual vines is the Select Seeds catalog, which may be obtained by writing to them at 180 Stickney Hill Road, Union, CT 06076-4617.

VEGETABLE VINES

Gourd vines can be trained over an arbor, and I've heard that the bottle gourd (*Lagenaria*) is good for this. For that matter, cucumbers could be trained up in a decorative manner, and pole beans work, too. Easy-to-grow hyacinth beans (*Lablab purpureus*) have purple flowers like sweet peas that are followed by shiny purple pods. Scarlet runner beans (*Phaseolus coccineus*) have vivid red flowers and emerald green leaves. The pods are mottled in appearance and contain neon purple beans. I have found that any type of purple bean turns green when cooked, which is rather disappointing. Malabar spinach (*Basella rubra*) is a heat-loving, handsome vine with shiny, dark green, edible leaves and purple stems. The crunchy leaves do taste vaguely like spinach, especially if you're really hungry, but I like this vine for its beauty, not its flavor.

Trees and Shrubs

Traditional cottage gardens usually didn't feature shrubs and trees. These small gardens didn't have space for shrubs that were merely ornamental or for trees, unless they were fruit trees. But modern cottage gardeners can afford to be less utilitarian in their approach to gardening and have come to appreciate the beauty of small ornamental trees and shrubs and to enjoy their steady presence in the garden as the seasons go by. For a useful roundup of these woody plants I had only to turn to my sister Kathy, who grows more beautiful small trees and shrubs in her jewel-like cottage garden than would seem humanly possible. These aren't any old trees and shrubs—they represent a lifetime of learning and interest. Here is her list, along with comments on what makes them special. Even Kathy seemed a bit surprised by how many of these wonderful plants she grows in her garden, which is on an average-size city lot.

The shrub bottlebrush buckeye (*Aesculus parviflora*) blooms from early June through early July. A white astilbe (lower right) grows nearby.

Hydrangea paniculata 'Pink Diamond'.

149

ORNAMENTAL TREES

ACER GRISEUM (PAPER BARK MAPLE) Grows in partial shade; beautiful bark.

CARPINUS CAROLINIANA (AMERICAN HORNBEAM) Understory tree; fall color; attracts birds.

CERCIS CANADENSIS (REDBUD) Rose-pink flowers in early spring.

CORNUS ALTERNIFOLIA (PAGODA DOGWOOD) Flowers, fruit; horizontal branching.

CORNUS MAS (CORNELIAN CHERRY DOGWOOD 'AUREA') Golden foliage.

HAMAMELIS VERNALIS (VERNAL WITCHHAZEL) Yellow flowers early in spring; yellow fall color.

MAGNOLIA × LOEBNERI 'LEONARD MESSEL' Pink-purple spring flowers.

MAGNOLIA × SOULANGIANA (SAUCER MAGNOLIA) Pink-purple spring flowers.

MAGNOLIA STELLATA 'ROYAL STAR' (STAR MAGNOLIA) White spring flowers that bloom with early daffodils.

MAGNOLIA ACUMINATA × M. DENUDATA 'ELIZABETH' Yellow spring flowers.

MALUS 'TINA' Ornamental dwarf; white flowers.

Dill dries on an old bench under a grape arbor.

SHRUBS

AESCULUS PARVIFLORA (BOTTLEBRUSH BUCKEYE) Summer flowers.

COTINUS COGGYGRIA 'VELVET CLOAK' (SMOKEBUSH) Purple leaves; feathery panicles (loose clusters of flowers on a stalk) in summer.

WINTERBERRY Red berries.

> ILEX VERTICILLATA 'AFTERGLOW'. Female.
>
> I. VERTICILLATA 'JIM DANDY'. Male.

HYDRANGEA ARBORESCENS 'ANNABELLE' Large clusters of white flowers ("snowballs").

> H. ARBORESCENS 'WHITE DOME'. Dome-shaped lacy blooms.
>
> H. ARBORESCENS 'WHITE SWAN'. Loose habit.

HYDRANGEA PANICULATA 'ZWIJNENBRUG' (LIMELIGHT ™) Long panicles of white flowers.

> H. PANICULATA 'PINK DIAMOND'. Salmon pink blooms.
>
> H. PANICULATA 'UNIQUE'. Large, showy panicles.

OAKLEAF HYDRANGEA

> HYDRANGEA QUERCIFOLIA 'PEE WEE'. Compact; good for small garden.
>
> H. QUERCIFOLIA 'SIKES DWARF'. Very small (24 to 30 inches); hugs ground.
>
> H. QUERCIFOLIA 'SNOW QUEEN'. Abundant, large panicles.

SYMPHORICARPOS ALBUS (SNOWBERRY) White berries.

PHYSOCARPUS OPULIFOLIUS 'DIABLO' (NINEBARK) Purple foliage.

SORBARIA SORBIFOLIA (FALSESPIREA) White flower panicles in July; needs moist soil.

SPIREA × BUMALDA 'COCCINEA' Deep pink flowers.

VIBURNUM × BURKWOODII 'MOHAWK' (BURKWOOD VIBURNUM) Fragrant flowers; glossy foliage.

V. × CARLESII (KOREAN SPICE VIBURNUM) Very fragrant flowers.

V. LANTANA 'MOHICAN' AND 'VARIEGATUM' (WAYFARINGTREE VIBURNUM) Yellow variegated leaves.

V. LENTAGO (NANNYBERRY VIBURNUM) Lustrous leaves; white flowers; black berries.

V. PLICATUM THUNB. VAR. TOMENTOSUM (DOUBLEFILE VIBURNUM) Horizontal branches; white flowers.

V. PRUNIFOLIUM (BLACKHAW VIBURNUM) Pure white flowers; blue-black berries.

Herbs

There is an allure to the idea of an herb garden—images of cowled monks and Elizabethans, *beeskeps* humming with bees, and ourselves, garden trugs slung over our arms as we dally in the lavender are quite delightful. And an herb garden can be inexpensive to plant. In spring many herbs sell for a dollar or so a pot, and some herb seeds—dill is an example—can be purchased for as little as 10 cents a packet. Some herbs, like tarragon, common thyme, oregano, sage, and lemon balm, are easy-care perennials and will faithfully return year after year. *And*, if that weren't enough, most herbs need soil of only average quality, not requiring that you truck in yards of mushroom compost.

HERB GARDEN PITFALLS

Herb gardening does have pitfalls, though—pitfalls that are few, but deep. My first garden years ago was an herb garden, and it was horribly disappointing. It was a very hot summer, and I remember that by August or so, many of the plants had gone to seed and were nondescript and ratty looking. It basically looked like a weed patch, and I was mortified—horrified, actually. Herbs are a disparate group of plants, and while many are genuinely ornamental, a lot of

them either are a hair's breadth from being weeds or actually are weeds. Lemon balm looks fresh, juicy, and green in spring and like seedy hell in August. (Of course you can cut it back before then, but it's the kind of plant that goes to seed quickly, the moment you turn your back.) Lovage, an amazing herb that deserves to be better known for its wonderful herbal celery flavor, also looks good in spring, but it is very tall and may sprawl later in the season. Tarragon is one of the most nondescript plants I can think of, with only its magical flavor saving it from oblivion, and while culinary oregano has its moments, it, too, can be dishwater-dull in appearance. So to avoid these alarming pitfalls, I've come up with some suggestions for gardening with herbs so that they look decent all season, drawing from hard-won experience.

Remember that in the spirit of traditional cottage gardening, herbs can be grown casually amid other flowers, fruits, and vegetables. Dill, for instance, looks pretty grown with tall annuals such as cosmos. And I've seen bronze fennel used beautifully with perennials and green fennel with sunflowers. Still, having a separate little herb garden is great fun, and it can have a serenity and slight formality that offers pleasant contrast to the rest of a garden filled to the brim with flowers.

Dill grows casually amid flowers and vegetables in my friend Susan's garden.

151

MAKE A PLAN

An herb garden needs a strong plan, so that as the plants wax and wane, the general impression of the garden is ordered and attractive. Even simply dividing a square plot into four parts with a mulched pathway, with perhaps a birdbath or sundial at the crossroads, can provide a framework. A low fence woven of willow branches can be an effective border and can be easy to make, provided you have a willow tree. And a feature such as a beeskep can provide an interesting focus, no matter what the plants themselves are doing.

CONTROL SELF-SEEDERS

Some herbs, such as cilantro or dill, can be rampant self-seeders, and you might not want them right in the herb plot itself. I put them at the back of the tomato patch, where they can self-seed without making themselves obnoxious. Chives, also strong self-seeders, I've quarantined in a narrow border below our living room window. The purple pom-poms of their blooms in late spring are truly ornamental.

Speaking of rampant self-seeders, I rue the thyme, er, time, when I planted garlic chives (*Allium tuberosum*). A fresh crop comes up every spring and is difficult to pull—the central core of the stem pulls up out of a rooted sheath. Regular chives (*A. schoenoprasum*) seem more tender and have a better flavor than garlic chives, at least to me.

Other herbal garden thugs to avoid are comfrey and mugwort, which are unstoppable. And keep mint off in its own damp little corner, because placed in a bed with other herbs, it will busily send out underground rhizomes and choke out other plants. A variegated mint I've been growing is a possible exception. Variegated plants are often not as strong growers as the plain varieties, and I find that the variegated mint stays pretty much in bounds. But in general, mints are such strong growers that I'm surprised that the entire planet Earth isn't covered with them. Old-time English cottagers grew *Mentha × gentilis* (ginger mint), and it was sometimes used as a pot plant in cottage windows.

ORNAMENTAL HERBS

I've mentioned that some herbs are truly ornamental, and rue is a good example. I think of it as a perennial whose beautiful blue-green leaves are striking in any number of planting schemes. I recently heard that rue repels Japanese beetles, so I plan to place a few plants by my roses this summer. Multicolored sages bring color to the herb garden and are problem free. Silver thymes, while not usually hardy here, are beautiful and well worth including. Little globe basil plants can be used to edge a sunny border, especially if you find them in six-packs, so that they are inexpensive. Similarly, emerald green parsley is a great edger. Some potted plants, such as scented geraniums, rosemary, or Dittany of Crete, especially when planted in ornate, terra cotta planters, are good accents.

Interplanting with annual flowers such as marigolds and zinnias livens up even the dullest group of herbs. A classic combination planted since medieval times is deep orange calendula flowers grown with blue-flowered borage. Chamomile and old roses are also flowers of an herbal nature. The rose of traditional cottage gardens was the sweet briar (*Rosa eglanteria*).

My own herb garden guru is the late Adelma Simmons, who gardened at Caprilands Herb Farm in Coventry, Connecticut. I recommend everything she's written for the gardener interested in pursuing a beautiful herb garden.

SOME WORDS ABOUT INDIVIDUAL HERBS

BASIL I buy my basil seedlings at a local grocery store. For some inexplicable but wonderful reason, they sell a big pot of seedlings, tightly packed together, for a few dollars. I have only to bring the pot home, upend it, gently pull the seedlings apart, and plant them in good soil in a sunny spot. Water well. Be sure to wait until at least May 15, if not later, before planting the seedlings, as basil is extremely sensitive to frost and cold soil.

CARAWAY (CARUM CARVI) This grows well here, and the seeds may be used in breads and in pound cakes. It is a biennial.

CHERVIL Bring home expensive chervil plant from expensive garden nursery. Plant in herb garden. Water and weed regularly. Watch plant struggle and go downhill. There is hardly enough chervil to make one omelet *à la française*. Watch plant go to seed and keel over with a sigh. In disgust, yank out plant and toss it somewhere near the compost heap, anywhere, you don't care, and wonder why you ever thought you were a gardener. Fast-forward to next spring. Surprise. Chervil plants carpet an area of dappled shade near the compost heap. Watch as wave after wave of chervil springs up all summer right into fall. Think you've learned something, but are not sure exactly what.

LAVENDER Sometimes new gardeners ask if we can grow lavender here in the Midwest, and the answer is a big, loud "yes." *L. angustifolia* 'Hidcote' (about 12 inches tall) and *L. a.* 'Munstead' (about 18 inches tall) are the two hardy varieties sold at local nurseries. And *L. a.* 'Twickel Purple' (about 24 inches tall) has long been a common variety in English cottage gardens. As

A big bunch of sweet Annie (*Artemisia annua*) hung up to dry in the fall. Sweet Annie is pretty, but it's a rampant self-seeder.

long as they are given good drainage, these lavenders will make it through the roughest winters. Even if a plant looks dead come spring, prune it back hard and watch for tiny new green shoots to appear. Lavender here never gets quite as wonderfully bushy as the lavender you see in pictures of lavender farms in Provence in France because it does get set back by our cold. But they do make it. Sadly, some of the other wonderful lavenders, such as *L. stoechas* (Spanish lavender) are tender perennials.

At the Cantigny gardens in Wheaton, Illinois, I recently saw a simple planting of dill and lavender. Both thrive in sun, heat, and dry soil. The scent of these herbs luxuriating in the sun was clean and refreshing. And a nearby carpet of chamomile smelled like a cup of chamomile tea steeping in the sunshine.

OREGANO The trick with oregano is to find real culinary oregano, not a wishy-washy marjoram masquerading as oregano, at the nursery. The two are quite closely related. True sweet marjoram (*Origanum majorna*), is a wonderful herb with a mild, fragrant herbal flavor. Italians know it as *erba da funghi*, "herb for mushrooms." The plot thickens, however, as we try to pin down true oregano. I have seen both *O. vulgare* and *O. heracleoticum* sold as the true oregano, and to my nose they are similar, but *O. heracleoticum* apparently has more and larger oil glands. And since *O. vulgare* is a catchall name for a number of different varieties and subspecies, I'll put my money with *O. heracleoticum*, which is what is stewing in the sun in my garden right now.

There are ornamental oreganos available; I have the pretty *O. laevigatum* 'Herrenhausen', which has purple stems and a midsummer flowering of pale lilac blooms. I also had a low-growing, variegated oregano, which was pretty but only lasted two summers.

PARSLEY This is a biennial, meaning that it is in leaf one year, and then goes to seed the next. Every now and then I hear someone say that their parsley is a perennial, since it has come up again a year after it was first planted. I know that if they wait a few more weeks, a central stalk will appear, and the plant will flower and go to seed. This second-year plant is very strong tasting and needs to be replaced by a new plant. Gastronomes say that Italian parsley is the best flavored, but don't feel bad if you can find only curly parsley—it tastes very good, too.

ROSEMARY Traditional cottage gardens often had a large rosemary bush, usually by a front door or gate. Margery Fish, in her *Cottage Garden Flowers*, says that "in very old cottage gardens the bush reaches the bedroom windows

and melts into the thatch." Our climate prevents us from growing such large specimens, but we can have potted rosemary plants.

When you buy a young rosemary plant, the first thing to do is to put it in a largish pot and keep it there. This same plant, watered and pruned, can spend winter indoors for many years. Digging a rosemary plant up from the ground in the fall to bring it indoors will often kill it, because rosemary simply can't stand having its roots exposed to drying air. If you can keep the root ball well covered with soil, it might make it, but it is rough going for the plant. Rosemary can be kept outside quite late into the fall and can withstand some mild freezes. *Rosemarinus officinalis* 'Arp' is supposed to be one of the hardiest of rosemaries, but my 'Arp' died quite quickly after a series of hard frosts.

SWEET CICELY (MYRRHIS ODORATA) This herb is not all that commonly grown here, but it works beautifully in the herb garden, or as a perennial, with its soft, ferny foliage and lacy white flowers.

TARRAGON The only thing to know about tarragon is to not buy Russian tarragon. I can honestly say it's a complete mystery to me why Russian tarragon is even sold, though it often is. Russian tarragon has no flavor (that I can detect), but has found its way into nurseries where gardeners purchase it, confusing it with French tarragon. So be sure to plant true French tarragon. Just lightly brushing the leaves of a plant will release the wonderful, licorice scent, and you'll know you're getting the real thing.

THYME There is not too much to say about culinary thyme, except that it will grow, that it is essential, and that it is not particularly ornamental, especially as the summer progresses. As long as it has sun it's fine. The soil can be quite poor. I have a plant close to the back steps so that I can retrieve a sprig or two when cooking supper. See chapter 4, "Dictionary of Perennials," for information about ornamental thymes.

The old-time cottagers grew many herbs that are less familiar to us. Lady's bedstraw was used to curdle milk to make cheese, valerian to cure insomnia (its roots are still sold for this purpose), and a plant named "butterbur" was used to wrap butter.

I find, though, that my interest in herbs is taking off like a rocket in a new direction, less historical in nature and more culinary. It all started when I first grew cilantro for making salsa and loved its vivid, green flavor and then learned about two other Mexican herbs, epazote (*Chenopodium ambrosioides*) and papaloquelite (*Porophyllum ruderale*). It occurred to me that our hot summers are ideal for growing Mexican, Asian, Indian, and Middle

Eastern herbs for use in cooking. So I tried *Nigella sativa*, whose seedpods contain the "black cumin" called for in some Middle Eastern recipes. This grew easily, and I have used the seeds to sprinkle on bread dough when making flat bread. Now I'm eager to try cumin (*Cuminum cyminum*). There is also a seed named "ajwain" (*Carum capticum*) used in Indian cooking, similar in flavor to cumin (at least to my taste buds), and a Malaysian culinary herb named "mamang." There is even a monarda with an oregano-like flavor called *Monarda menthifolia* that is used in barbecuing in the Southwest. And I've also learned of herbs such as khella (*Amni visnaga*), whose seeds are used to flavor cheese; fenugreek (*Trigonella foenum*), used in Indian cooking; and zaatar (*Origanum syriacum*), used in Middle Eastern food. So I see new horizons in my herb garden, and I guess that's what makes gardening so much fun, doesn't it?

Sources for these seeds may be located by typing the key words "unusual herb seeds" in an Internet search engine. Some of these herbs require an even longer growing season than we have and will need to be started indoors.

Fruits

For years, fruits hovered somewhere just outside of my gardening consciousness as I focused on flowers, flowers, and more flowers. I had a red currant bush and some rhubarb, and that was about it. With a yard that's more than half shade, tomatoes and flowers hogged the sunny spots. Having once watched a neighbor spray the living bejesus out of his apple tree every year with an apparatus that looked like it could be used to battle fire at nuclear power plants, and having heard tell of my grandfather's bitter, ongoing battles with the neighborhood kids for the cherries on his cherry tree, it somehow didn't seem like a lot of fun. I did finally notice, though, the grapevine growing in back of our garden, its tendrils finally penetrating my consciousness after years of its fruit being the exclusive province of hovering, covetous birds. The vine must have been there for decades and had never been watered, fertilized, or in any way cultivated, yet had produced pounds of grapes every year. Last year, this 16-foot stretch of grapevine produced six pounds of Concord grapes (*Vitus*). I made enough jelly for every man, woman, and child in our immediate family, only later realizing that no one in my immediate family likes grape jelly, including myself. So, this summer—wine. We'll drink just about anything. At any rate, the grapevine was living proof that certain fruits are a snap to grow in the Midwestern garden and that fruit-growing can be lots and lots of fun.

A Manchurian apricot tree laden with fruit.

Our dwarf Asian pear tree in early September.

155

The peach tree my friend Susan grew from a peach pit. Here, it mingles with white hollyhocks.

From the grapes, I progressed to red raspberry bushes (*Rubus idaeus*) with plants given to me by a friend of my mother. Red raspberries are expensive to buy because they are soft and spoil easily, but you can have as many as you want of these voluptuous luxuries if you devote a neglected corner of your garden to the bushes. Raspberry bushes have long, prickly canes and are not particularly ornamental plants, though they are fine in a kitchen garden. They are also somewhat invasive and have tunneled under the brick walk and reemerged in the lawn. We just mow over the shoots, which tells you something about our lawn.

Red currant bushes grow well in our climate, and the berries can be used to make an exquisitely tart, translucent, quivering, ruby red jelly. Currant bushes are quite compact, only being about two feet tall, and are ideal for the small garden. I've had a red currant bush now for about ten years and it's doing fine, with the jewel-like berries going some years to the birds, and some years to the quivering jelly.

In our side yard grows a dwarf Asian pear tree, which staggers under the weight of its drifts of snowy blossoms every spring. "Dwarf," by the way, is a relative term here, as our tree is a good 15 feet tall. By summer its branches are cloaked in glossy, dark green leaves, and by late September we have bowls of pale green, perfectly round fruit. Pear leaves are among the great unsung beauties of the plant world, having a graceful shape, and I sometimes include a branch of pear leaves in a bouquet of flowers. Asian pears are simply delicious with a delicate sweetness. They are also juicy, and you really drink an Asian pear more than you eat it, so be prepared with a napkin. Asian pear trees respond well to having the fruit thinned early in the season, giving the remaining fruit the space and resources to grow large and blemish free.

A rather imposing rhubarb plant is in residence in the back of the garden. It has an impeccable lineage, originally coming from a start from my mother's plant. My mother's plant came from my grandmother's plant, which probably came from a neighbor. It's that kind of plant. Rhubarb is up very early in the spring, and watching its crumpled leaves emerging from the spring earth is like seeing something being born. It has just occurred to me as I write that in these days of mixes and ersatz baked goods from supermarkets, everyone might not know what to do with rhubarb, or even what it is. A rhubarb plant has thick red stalks with big, crinkled, green leaves.

To pick rhubarb, you grasp a stalk close down to the earth and pull. It will come out cleanly. Chop off the leaves and throw them into the compost heap. The stalks then are rinsed and chopped and can be used in pies, cakes, crumbles, and marmalades. It also freezes perfectly. A rhubarb plant can survive a fair amount of neglect but is happiest being fed with compost or aged manure in the fall, having its yellowed leaves removed, and being well watered in the summer.

Heat is rhubarb's main enemy. A hot, dry summer spurs the growth of a tall, central seed stalk, which is quite ornamental, though disconcerting if you don't expect it. Rhubarb is genuinely majestic in appearance, and a number of rhubarb relatives are grown strictly as ornamentals. The Heronswood Nursery mail-order catalog lists four ornamental rhubarbs, including a miniature variety, which I am lusting after, and there is also a giant rhubarb with purplish leaves. But getting back to the variety that is my grandmother's rhubarb, if ever there were a plant of hearth and home, an old-fashioned plant, a plant antidote to life in the fast lane, it's rhubarb, and I urge you to plant it in your garden.

Speaking of old-fashioned plants, I have just planted a large shoot from an elderberry bush (*Sambucus canadensis*) of my mother's. Elderberry bushes are thickets about six feet tall, have lacy, creamy white flowers in summer, and have clusters of purple berries in the fall. If you want birds, plant an elderberry, as it's a bird magnet. You can also make elderberry wine, poison it, and use it to dispatch indigent old men *à la* "Arsenic and Old Lace." Here's a plant with possibilities! And a relative, *S. nigra*, appears in the Heronswood catalog with nine ornamental varieties, including golden elderberry and variegated varieties. This is definitely a genus that Midwesterners should look into closely.

As for mulberries, you don't usually have to buy one to plant it in your garden, as birds are forever dropping mulberry seeds into our gardens. Different mulberries seem to be of varying quality, with some being bland and flavorless, while others are quite sweet and flavorful. But basically, having a mulberry bush is all about attracting birds, which it does in great numbers.

I have tried the cute little alpine strawberry plants but find that our summers are too hot for them. Even with plenty of water, summer heat seems to foster hard, dry, little berries. If you have the space and the light soil, though, regular strawberries grow perfectly well here, almost like weeds.

Long ago, cottage gardens mostly had apple, pear, and sometimes cherry trees. The apples, especially, were a vital part of the cottagers' diet. Early English cottagers grew the costard apple, a large ribbed apple used in cooking, and the Old English Pearmain, a sweet pear-shaped apple. Today, there are hundreds of varieties of apples, some considered to be rareties and "antiques." In an English book called *The Wild Garden*, by Judith Berrisford, I was riveted by her description of a small orchard garden, and if I had the space, I would plant one immediately. Just imagine a grove of heirloom apple trees, underplanted with primroses, pulmonarias, bluebells, and wild roses! And a fresh-picked apple tastes completely different from the apples we buy in stores, which may have been picked months before. Ms. Berrisford also suggests planting some nut trees, such as hazelnuts. Sounds perfect.

So I've gone from being totally clueless about fruit growing to pondering what else I can plant. A friend planted a sprouting peach pit that she found in her compost heap. It grew, and she has had simply delicious peaches for years, now. So the possibilities really do seem infinite, and I'm rarin' to go. There's an 'Illini' Hardy Blackberry, offered by Miller Nurseries, that sounds tempting, as do black currants, white currants, gooseberries, green gage, and damson plums . . . *Oh, for a bigger garden!*

Down to the Nitty Gritty: Soil

If there's one thing I would go back and do differently as a beginning gardener, it would be to pay much, much more attention to soil. I was so love struck with plants themselves that I often didn't look closely enough at where I was planting them. The soil in my garden *looked* good, being an inky black color when wet and a bit grayer when dry. And as a beginner, all soils looked pretty much the same to me. Boy, was I wrong. Soil quality—it's richness, fluffiness, and moisture retentiveness—can make a crucial difference in the appearance and health of the plants grown in it. I will always remember the vegetable garden of my husband's Uncle Charles, out in DeKalb, Illinois. It was planted on the banks of the Kishwaukee River. Innumerable floods had deposited rich, silty soil on the banks, and the vegetables growing in it were vibrantly healthy, almost luminous. There was a sea of zucchini squash with leaves so big and glossy, they looked like lily pads. The zucchini themselves were crisp, flavorful, and had little pith. When we later returned home, only 15 miles away, I was shocked to see the puny plants struggling mightily in our vegetable patch, with its hard, clay soil. That's when I understood, in my guts, the role of soil quality in the garden. Good soil is crucial to successful gardening.

Elements of planting

But what is good soil? Is it loamy black earth? Sometimes. But soil is actually only "good" in relation to its appropriateness to the plant growing in it. Not all plants need loamy, rich soil. Plant common thyme in humus-rich soil and it will decline. Plant it in rather poor, dry soil and it perks up and thrives. My creeping thymes even flow into the cracks between the paver bricks in the sidewalk, seeming to prefer the most inhospitable environment possible. Purple coneflowers like it just fine in our heavy clay soil, while other plants prefer chalky soil littered with pebbles, and still others like sandy soil with sharp drainage. So there is no one "perfect" soil.

With that said, many common garden plants do like soft soil, rich in organic material, and are more resistant to drought and disease than plants struggling in compacted, unimproved soil. Loamy soil retains moisture like a sponge and allows plant roots to penetrate deep into the moist earth. And turning soil over aerates and lightens it, also helping roots grow. I have heard of Midwestern gardeners, possibly mythical, who do very little watering, simply because their soil is so good.

Midwestern soil is clay soil. Technically, it is called "loess," which is a fine-grained, sticky soil covering the central United States. Some of our soil blew in from the West, as the product of the erosion of ancient mountain ranges. Western soil is alkaline because infrequent rains allow the buildup of soil salts. Glaciation in the central United States thousands of years ago also produced soil, as glaciers pulverized rock into dust while scouring the earth. When they melted, tremendous floodwaters surged down the basins of the ancient Mississippi, Illinois, Wabash, and Ohio Rivers. When the glaciers froze up again, the floodwaters abated, leaving silty soil behind. This soil dried up, and some was blown north. And when warm, shallow seas covered this area, millions of years ago, the shells of innumerable sea creatures drifted to the bottom of the sea, eon after eon, resulting in layers of limestone. The Eisenhower Expressway in Chicago cuts right through these ancient limestone formations—you can easily see the layers as you drive past. Because of the limestone, and because of soil blown from the alkaline West, our soil is on the alkaline side, and acid soil–loving plants such as rhododendrons, which flourish in the acid soil of the once heavily forested East, often have problems here.

GOOD NEWS AND BAD NEWS ABOUT SOIL

The good news about Midwestern soil is that it is rich. Just look at our prairies carpeted with waves of lush, silky grasses and sparkling prairie flowers, at the berry-laden bramble patches at forest margins, and at the towering old oaks to be found in what remains of our undisturbed forests. Our native soil is deep and fertile.

The bad news is that clay soil can be waterlogged, cold, dank, and mossy in rainy times and then turn to concrete in heat and drought. Clay soil is composed of very fine, flat particles overlapping each other, and there is little space between the particles for water or air. Most of us know that plants take up water through their roots, but when I first began to garden, I didn't know that the roots also need air. Solid clay soil doesn't have much in the way of air pockets, so some plants can actually drown in the soil, or be gasping for air. The compactness of clay soil can also make it physically difficult for roots to penetrate down through the soil, resulting in stunted plants. Many of our native plants have deep, powerful roots that make short work of firm soil. But many common garden plants that evolved in other ecosystems need help from us, and digging lots of organic matter into the soil increases moisture retentiveness, creates small air pockets, and softens the soil.

DO YOU HAVE CLAY SOIL?

Clay soil is hard as concrete when dry and can be squeezed into a cohesive ball when moist. Rub the soil between your fingertips—clay soil feels smooth. If soil is sandy, you can feel the graininess, and if the soil is gravelly, you can see the gravel. Certain weeds are indicators of heavy clay soil, including thistles, coltsfoot, dandelions, and plantains. Mosses are indicators of compacted, poorly drained clay soil.

HOW TO COPE WITH CLAY SOIL

There are a number of responses to the negatives of clay soil—more, if you include crying. One is to consider clay soil a plus and to select plants that are adapted to it. There are many. With this approach, our soil is a problem only when we try to grow plants not evolved to cope with it. These plants will grow vigorously and happily with little work done by you. There are many plants that fall into this category, as we'll see later. It can be an interesting challenge to track down clay soil–loving plants, thus using more brain power than muscle power to plant your garden.

Hesitate, though, before going wild with natives. The idea of "going native" has deep appeal, as it makes sense that plants that evolved here for thousands of years should be perfect for our gardens. But there is a pitfall. There is nothing particularly "natural" about the soil in many local gardens, and we forget that humans have almost completely altered our environment. Gone are the buffalo, the prairie fires, and most particularly, the rich, dark brown soil that had accumulated over the last 14,000 years. In urban areas, that soil has been plowed up, built on, drained, paved over, grazed on, and in general had the life sucked out of it. There may be lifeless, compacted clay soil in the garden of an older house with long-established plantings.

Or there may be only lifeless subsoil in your yard if you have a new house. Even in the yard of an upscale house with professional plantings, you may be gardening atop heaps of mushroom compost, a problematical growing medium, as we will see. Many native plants would have problems growing in any of these situations. Also remember that our native plants evolved in a broad spectrum of ecosystems, and not all will work in one garden. Some plants evolved on gravelly ridges, some on dry, sandy prairies, and others on moist river bottomland, so they will all have different requirements.

Another approach to the clay soil dilemma is to add organic matter like crazy to your planting beds. Your own compost, ground-up leaves, pine needles, kitchen scraps, horse manure from local riding trails, or bags of commercial compost—everything that you can lay your hands on—dig it into the soil. The usual advice is to spread a three- to four-inch layer of organic matter over the soil and dig it in at least eight inches down. This is good advice as far as it goes but underestimates just how depleted the soil is, in many gardens, and that most of us aren't producing the truckloads of compost that it would take to really rehabilitate our soil. I found that the compost from one average-size compost heap hardly makes a dent in filling the organic matter deficit of my soil, although it does help. It's possible to dig what looks like tons of the stuff into the soil, only for it to seemingly melt away into the bed, leaving you wondering where it went. After spending several years digging in what compost I could produce, along with bags of mushroom compost and cow manure, my soil was still in trouble. I was also concerned about the ecological effects of throwing away the large, plastic bags the compost and cow manure came packaged in, and washing them to recycle used lots of water.

Speaking of mushroom compost, some local gardeners swear by mushroom compost as the secret to their beautiful gardens, while others swear at it. Mushroom compost is rich and light and is a superb soil conditioner: many plants purr like kittens in it. Other gardeners claim that it is loaded with pernicious weed seeds, such as burdock, and that it is high in mineral salts. Years ago I received a birthday gift from my husband, Jim, of three yards of mushroom compost. In a state of ecstasy I dug it in everywhere and have since noticed only one new weed, which I think is golden ragwort (*Senecio aureus*). As weeds go it's almost an amiable little thing, though, and is easy to pull out. Now my husband has moved on to gifts of beautiful antique jewelry, which I like almost as much as the compost, and every early

spring I routinely order three yards of "planting mix," from a local nursery. It contains some mushroom compost plus composted material and sand, and now I can't garden without it: it's one of the best investments I make in the garden. Using a planting mix delivered from a local nursery might be the best alternative to straight mushroom compost and completely sidesteps the issue of what to do with all those plastic bags. Soft planting mixes have only one other drawback, besides possible weeds, that I can think of. They can make soil so soft that during a dry, windy winter, soil can literally blow away, exposing perennial roots. I have lost several ferns this way and am now much more careful about digging the mix deeply into the extant soil. The resultant soil is neither very soft nor very hard, and it stays in place.

However we do it, I've come to regard digging organic matter into the soil as an ongoing activity in the garden. As the seasons go by, it does make a difference.

Some gardeners feel that a form of sheet composting is the best way to improve soil and is much less work than double-digging, which we'll look at in a few moments. Sometimes called "lasagna" gardening, layers of organic material, such as chopped leaves, are spread on soil needing improvement. By the next spring, the organic matter has broken down, and worms are burrowing into the poor soil below, enriching it. If you have really terrible soil, though, I think the lasagna method just isn't fast enough, and really poor, depleted soil can be full of old wiry plant and tree roots that must be removed, so there is still much work to do. It's a worthwhile approach though, and you can learn more from the book *Lasagna Gardening*, by Patricia Lanza, as well as from the classic *How to Have a Green Thumb Without an Aching Back*, by Ruth Stout.

Another solution to clay soil, and one that is quite practical, is to dig a rather large hole for each new plant and to amend the soil just in that hole. In other words, dig a $25 hole for a $5 plant. Or, what with inflation, a $45 hole for a $7.99 plant. This breaks the work up into manageable chunks. This is not as optimal as the system of double-digging an entire plant bed, but it's a realistic way to deal with difficult soil and can yield good results. You do need to dig a really big hole though—no cheating—and I don't recommend this approach for thirsty, greedy plants such as roses. I recently attended a lecture by a local rosarian who said he never digs holes for his roses. He always digs out an entire bed, and then plants. Water can percolate freely throughout the whole bed, and roots can grow deep.

Speaking of double-digging, a beginner might have heard of it and wonder what it is. Double-digging involves turning over and amending the soil to a depth of at least two feet. Double-digging is a gardening method you convert to, almost like a religion. But many gardeners simply don't have the physical stamina or time for it. You might want to double-dig a small, experimental plot to see what it's like, and go on from there. To learn more about double-digging, send for a copy of the Bountiful Gardens nursery catalog (www.bountifulgardens.org). You will find a mother lode of books and pamphlets from the group Ecology Action in this catalog, as well as offerings of heirloom seeds and gardening paraphernalia such as redwood seed flats and special digging tools, including widgers, which are small British tools for transplanting seedlings. Using double-digging, the gardeners of Ecology Action produce bountiful gardens in their home ground of Willits, California, even though *no rain falls there at all in the summer*. They even argue that double-digging is a lazy person's way to garden, because once you've done it, very little digging ever needs to be done again. There is much to be said for this approach. Even if you don't ever actually double-dig anything, after studying this catalog, and reading *How to Grow More Vegetables, Fruits, Nuts, Berries, Grains and Other Crops Than You Ever Thought Possible on Less Land Than You Can Imagine,* by John Jeavons, Ecology Action's founder, you'll never see soil in quite the same way again.

Speaking of digging deeply, I recently heard of a gardener who digs up all his perennials every three years, removes the soil from the deeply dug bed, and then amends it with a product called Profile. He then returns the soil to its bed and replants the perennials. Apparently he has a fabulous garden: his plants are bigger, bushier, and healthier looking than those in other gardens. Profile is a mineral ceramic product that opens up soil structure and helps soil resist compaction. Golf course superintendents use it to maintain their perfect lawns. I'm not endorsing this product, just mentioning it as a possible route to better soil. It's available at "high-end" nurseries.

What if your soil is so full of clay that you can make pottery from it? In the nineteenth century, "Jugtown" was a common name of a number of Illinois towns where potterymaking was the main industry, so to have such extremely heavy clay soil is not unheard of. One solution is to build raised beds and have all new soil trucked in. This solution might sound drastic and expensive, but sometimes being a wise gardener is to spend money wisely, as opposed to not spending any money at all. So if your soil is really hard, mossy, dank, and veined with clay, truckloads of good black earth delivered to your doorstep could be the best gardening investment you'll ever make. But don't just call up any old number and ask for soil to be delivered to your doorstep. Order from a reputable landscaper or nursery owner. Go and look closely at the soil, smell it, crumble it in your hand and make sure it's good and rich, or you might get the kind of "soil" an unfortunate neighbor of mine received last spring—a clay slag heap left over from the building of a suburban development.

However you improve your soil, once it is aerated and full of organic matter, it should not be stepped on. At first I thought gardeners were being a bit fussy to make a big deal out of this, but stepping on soil compacts it and undoes much of your hard work. So as you create your garden, remember to include pathways to or through each planting bed to give access to plants.

An Illinois greenhouse grower told me to add gypsum to clay soil to lighten it. Gypsum binds to the clay particles, causing them to loosen. Chemically, gypsum is known as "sulphate of lime" and provides sulfur and unlocks other soil nutrients. The same grower also recommends adding peat and mushroom compost. He doesn't recommend using wood chips for soil improvement because soil nitrogen is depleted in the process of degrading the chips. I must add, though, that the value of adding gypsum is a bit controversial, with some experts feeling that it does little good. Give it a try and see what you think.

Most of the above information is admittedly general, and I have found that gardening is often a matter of specifics. It's always amazing to me how different the soils of many local gardens are from one another, even ones in close proximity. My soil is certifiably awful, being sucked dry by an enormous horse chestnut tree and his evil assistants, two maples. The soil in the garden of my sister's first house was wonderful, being close to a river, but it was resting on a limestone shelf and was quite shallow in spots. In her new house, the soil is moist clay as her backyard verges on a ravine. A neighbor's soil, just down the street, is surprisingly sandy. Plants that I have received via Internet trades also show just how varied soil can be. A plant from Kentucky showed traces of astonishingly white soil, and a plant from Louisiana came in a clump of reddish clay. Closer to home, I know of one lucky soul who lives in a house where the builders dumped all the topsoil from the rest of the subdivision into his backyard. He has mind-bogglingly fabulous roses, and we should all be so lucky.

HAVE YOUR SOIL TESTED

I didn't have my soil tested until several years after I began gardening, which, in retrospect, was foolish, because I wasted precious time trying to grow plants in poor soil and wondering why they didn't thrive. I just never suspected that the soil was as bad as it turned out to be, a beginner's error. Finally I called the local county cooperative extension service. Each county has its own extension office, and its phone number is in the phone book. They advised me to come in with a large jar filled with soil taken from three different spots in the area I wanted tested. I brought the jar in, paid 20 dollars, and three weeks later received a scathing report on my soil's quality and pH. Recommendations were given for adding nitrogen, potassium, sulfur, and phosphorous. I had to add some of *everything*.

I've learned my lesson and am now rabidly interested in soil. Right now I'm even reading *Secrets of the Soil*, by Tompkins and Bird, a treatise on biodynamic farming that seems to be 90 percent malarkey and 10 percent absolutely fascinating. I'm not buying into burying cow's horns stuffed with manure prior to the winter solstice for use as a soil restorative, but using horsetail tea as a remedy for mildews and rusts sounds possible, and the book's emphasis on the importance of soil microbes seems absolutely valid. So much to learn.

Drainage

Most plants have specific drainage needs, but drainage is a topic that many gardeners, new and old, feel rather fuzzy about. A plant needing "sharp drainage" for instance—what's that? Drainage simply means the movement of excess water down through the soil to the water table, the depth at which there is standing water in the soil. Rock, clay, or compacted soil can stop the downward movement of water, creating the water table.

The ecosystem a plant evolved in determines its drainage needs in your garden. The native habitat of some plants is boggy and moist, as is found near rivers and streams. The roots of these plants, which include astilbes, rogersias, gunnera, and physotegias, among others, are perfectly happy drowning in very moist, even wet, soil. Plant roots need to take in air as well as water, though, and waterlogged soil can actually suffocate plants not adapted to it. Other plants, originating in areas of light, sandy soil, are used to water percolating very quickly down and away from their roots, resulting in sharp drainage. When contemplating the purchase of an unfamiliar, and perhaps expensive, plant, it's wise to do a bit of research on its drainage and soil requirements before laying down money.

Water does percolate steadily down through our clay soil, but at a slower rate than some plants are happy with. I generally pass up plants requiring sharp drainage, as the drainage in my garden is okay, but nothing to write home about. One of the simplest ways to determine where the poor-draining areas of your garden are located is to observe where water pools after a long rain or heavy snow melt. Whether water has percolated from the rest of the garden's soil because the area is low lying or whether there is a naturally high water table, the results are the same: poor drainage.

The simplest way to combat slow-draining soil is to build up the planting beds with plenty of compost or other humus. You can either literally build a raised bed or simply mound the soil to add height. Sometimes an inch or two of extra height can make a surprising difference. Be sure the extra height contains plenty of humus though, as mounded soil dries out quickly.

I suspect problems with drainage are the single greatest factor behind perennial plants that grow for a season or two and then disappear. Without so much as a wave goodbye, expensive plants can vanish from one season to the next. I had a beautiful specimen of *Artemisia* 'Powis Castle' in my garden but had been cautioned by a fellow gardener that it might not do well in our soil. I was feeling so smug as it came back one year, then two years, then—poof—it was gone. I'm pretty sure that the ordinary drainage of my soil was simply not good enough for this plant, and it finally gave up the ghost. Shasta daisies are also notorious for lasting only a season or two before vanishing. Again, our heavy soil and so-so drainage are probably the culprit.

Determining what a plant's drainage requirements are is often as simple as reading the plant nursery's description of its growth requirements, often on a sign or tag accompanying the plant. For others you have to dig deeper, perhaps consulting a garden encyclopedia.

Water

wa • ter: the liquid that descends from the clouds as rain, forms streams, lakes, and seas, and is a major constituent of all living matter and that when pure is an odorless, tasteless, very slightly compressible liquid oxide of hydrogen H_2O which appears bluish in thick layers, freezes at 0° C and boils at 100° C, has a maximum density at 4° C and a high specific heat, is feebly ionized to hydrogen and hydroxyl ions, and is a poor conductor of electricity and a good solvent.

—*Merriam-Webster's Collegiate Dictionary*, 11th edition

What a remarkable, mysterious, magical substance, and we take it so much for granted. But my years of gardening in the Midwest have taught me that water is life. Where there is no water, there is no life, just Death Valley. Gardeners and farmers know this all too well, that their joy and their livelihood depends on this amazing substance that falls from the sky. I innocently planted my first garden in a summer of record drought. Day after day, week after week, no rain fell. The month of July that year seemed to last longer than a normal month. Our clay soil hardened into concrete as it was baked by the sun. It sucked up any water I could give it, but my waterings were no substitute for torrents of real rain. My garden looked so horrible that summer, with its dusty and stunted plants, that at one point I literally broke down and cried after a visitor from England (of all places—why couldn't she have been from Egypt or Mongolia?) burst into uncontrollable snorts of laughter at the sight of my eight-inch-high rosebush. Talk about a low point. It almost discouraged me from gardening again. Almost, but not quite.

I have never taken water for granted again after that summer and have come to a deep appreciation of our native plants and how they thrive even during drought. Some of these plants have long tap roots that plunge deep into the earth, where the soil is moist.

A garden needs at least one good soaking of rain per week, or one inch, as measured in a rain gauge. A simple rain gauge can be made with an empty coffee can. Mark off one inch increments from the bottom of the can (on the inside) using an indelible marker. Check the gauge for water depth after a good rain or after a series of rains—don't wait until it may have evaporated. At the end of the week, note the number of inches—if you're lucky and there's *been* any rain. If it's under an inch, it's time to water.

If still in doubt whether your garden has had enough water, plunge a spade down into the soil about four or five inches and inspect the soil at the bottom of the hole. If the soil is dry all the way down, water.

Drought can sneak up on you. After weeks of spring rains and flooded basements, finally a day dawns when it doesn't rain. You can go out and dig! But as the rainless days mount up, clay soil, which isn't moisture retentive, can dry up in a day or two. So whenever a nongardener complains about rain, I close my mouth and don't say a word.

Praise the large estate, but cultivate a small one.

—Virgil

Garden size should be determined by how much you can water during a drought. If you are a beginning gardener, this can be hard to determine, but it usually means a garden smaller than the lush Hanging Gardens of Babylon that burgeons in our imaginations. Even the Romans knew that it's better to have a small garden that can be well taken care of than to overreach and have a large garden that is overwhelming. In May and early June, when there is rain and temperatures are moderate, gardening can seem like a snap. We have delusions. The rainless heat waves of July and August are the nitty-gritty, though. How much can you water? How much can you weed? That is what determines garden size.

There is an ecological consideration in watering, as well. The sight of automatic sprinklers operating during rainy days, for instance, is disheartening. Vast, heavily fertilized, emerald green corporate lawns guzzle huge amounts of water and I hope will soon go the way of the dinosaurs, to be replaced by native plantings. My own approach in water conservation is to never water our lawn, and to never fertilize it, either, saving the water for flowers. Emerald green this lawn is not, but it soldiers on, and if you don't look too closely it looks okay. I'm also planting more and more drought-tolerant natives, and have an ongoing program to improve my soil with moisture-retentive humus. I rarely water in the spring, as usually spring rains come frequently enough to keep the garden moist. I do pay attention to newly planted seedlings in the spring, though, as they are vulnerable to the occasional warm, windy day. Mulching, of course, can help. Still, many common garden plants need steady water to thrive, especially during the extreme heat of July and August. Some nurseries water two to three times a day during drought to keep their plants looking good.

Aim for consistency in watering, as plants can be stressed by an uneven water supply. Tomatoes are an example. If you've ever grown a tomato with growth cracks ringing the stem end or with "blossom-end rot," it may be because of uneven water supply.

Organic matter, called "humus," dug into the soil renders it spongelike and able to retain moisture. Water falling on hard clay soil runs off and joins the raging torrent surging down into the storm sewer, instead of soaking into your garden. The main problem with this approach is that you can dig what seems like mountains of humus into soil only to have it sink down into it and vanish without a trace. It makes me wonder if somewhere in China big piles of compost aren't appearing in gardens, and while grateful, the Chinese

are puzzled. So if you don't want to dig in yards and yards of humus, focus on using drought-resistant plants.

Educate yourself about rain and your garden. After a rain, go out into your garden and dig a small hole with a trowel to see how far down the rain has soaked. You may get a surprise. Even a fairly steady rain of an hour may only soak down an inch or two. Check the soil this way after a whole day's rain and after several days' rain. Gradually, you'll develop a sense of how much moisture your soil has and whether you need to water.

My sister, who works at a local plant nursery, has noted that far more gardeners *overwater* plants, especially new shrubs and trees, than underwater. She says that it is a common practice to dig a hole for a plant, often in hard clay soil, and then fill the hole with rich, soft soil, thus creating a type of plant bathtub. Then the gardener sets a dribbling hose at the base of the plant. Then the gardener walks away and fires up the barbecue grill, cooks dinner, eats, washes up, hoists a brewsky, laughs, sings, dances, and then comes back to turn the hose off. A few weeks of this, and the shrub or tree has drowned. Worse, the wilting leaves of the dying specimen suggest dryness, causing the gardener to keep watering. My sister advises checking the soil with your hand under the mulch before watering. If it's sopping wet, hold off. Shrubs and trees can bounce back more easily from dryness than from too much water. She also mentions that some perennials, such as Russian sage and coreopsis, need relatively dry soil. If they are planted in rich soil, mulched, and then watered constantly, their roots will rot.

Group potted plants together for ease in watering. This brings us to another watering rule: never have more container plants than you are prepared to water two, or even three times a day in severe heat. The inferno of the Midwestern summer shrivels healthy plants into little withered stalks within a day or two of not being watered. A new gardener might want to try

Phlox 'Old Cellar Hole' is pretty in bloom, but its leaves are prone to mildew later in the season.

just one or two container plantings, a window box, for instance, to see whether they are up to the upkeep. Have a plan for keeping your garden watered when you go on vacation. A nice nongardening neighbor might volunteer to water your potted plants (especially if promised a pan of brownies) but not really believe you when you ask them to water at least twice a day if it's very hot. You could come back to a disaster. It's happened.

I try to use any dribs and drabs of wastewater from our house in the garden. An interesting thing to try is to put a dishpan in the sink during the day and see how much water accumulates as people run water to drink or to wash their hands. This can add up to a surprising amount of water—enough to regularly water a rose by the back steps, for instance.

Another watering tip is to water thoroughly and deeply, soaking the soil, not the plant. Soaker hoses are a good investment if you have big plans for your garden. Plants can develop long, deep roots in thoroughly watered soil and stunted roots in soil that is shallowly watered. And shower wands are much better for watering than are nozzles on hoses. The water spray from a shower wand is soft—almost like a misty rain—and plants don't get knocked over.

Rainwater is much different in nature from tap water. Tap water is usually quite cold and contains chlorine. While it depends on its source, tap water may be "hard" and full of minerals, including iron. Rainwater contains fewer minerals and is "soft" and often tepid. Plants seem to like rainwater much better than tap water, another reason for us to lessen our dependence on the hose. Purchasing a covered rain barrel to capture and store rainwater could be useful. I've seen several different models in garden supply catalogs, and while not cheap, in the long run they could mean lower water bills and happier plants.

One last thing. In my experience, there is *always* some drought during the summer. Usually this is in late July or August. It may vary from year to year in severity and duration, but come it will, so be prepared.

Drought

I am sitting here thinking about drought, perhaps because it is July 11. The temperature is 85 degrees at 8:30 in the evening, and we are heading into the seventh week of no rain to speak of. A few thunderstorms last week barely dampened the surface of the soil, which is setting up into concrete and drying up farther and farther down below the surface. This is not my imagination: statistics on the weather page of the newspaper this morning noted that only 0.24 inch of rain has fallen this month so far, while the equivalent of two inches of moisture is lost weekly to the atmosphere as we broil beneath the July sun. The rain we did get was only enough to keep the hopes of the mildew alive.

Drought can be as stressful for the gardener as for the plants. How often do you want to pull out the hose, or why didn't you install a drip irrigation system last spring, or why isn't your soil better after digging in truckloads of organic matter are questions that nip at the gardener's soul like a giant gnat. And what seemed like a lark in late April—oh, aren't these daffodils pretty?—has become drudgery, exacerbated by mosquitoes in July and August. In our community we are allowed to water every other day. I let the grass go dormant, abandon the sedums, daylilies, hostas, ground covers, and artemisias to their fate, and concentrate on keeping the container plants, roses, and thirsty garden perennials such as phlox well watered. I also water anything planted this year, as even so-called drought-resistant plants need time to send down roots and become established.

At the risk of sounding like Pollyanna, I sincerely believe that an opportunity lies in every difficulty. Just an hour ago I toured the garden with a pencil and the back of an envelope in hand and jotted down the names of plants that are thriving today in the midst of this ever-worsening drought. I also jotted down ideas that haven't worked; for instance, a shallow saucer of plants that dries out twice as quickly as the other containers; an anonymous perennial geranium received as part of an Internet exchange, whose yellowing lower leaves sport holes *and* black spots; and a planting of pale pink nicotiana. The nicotiana are holding their own and don't look bad, but they aren't thriving, either. Note to myself: Next year, nix the annual nicotiana, which do need good soil and steady water to be at their best.

The list of what is thriving is much longer and gives me plenty of ideas for next year. The sedums in the front garden are doing great, and I make a mental note to propagate more new plants for next spring. I know that for some experienced gardeners *Sedum* 'Autumn Joy' is a yawner, but it's bursting with health today, as are the variegated S. 'Frosty Morn', S. 'Matrona', whose green-blue leaves are edged with rose, and the handsome, purple-leafed S. 'Mohrchen'. These sedum look so good, it has occurred to me more than once that it would be possible to have an entire front garden of sedum only. New varieties appear every year, and the range of colors and habits is always expanding. *And you could water them at your own leisure.* Something to think about!

As I tour the garden I am reminded that there is drought, and there is Drought. Many established, drought-resistant perennials can tolerate up to about three weeks of drought without wilting. But by the time a drought has lasted more than three or four weeks, depending on the plant and on your soil, even drought-resistant plants such as pachysandra start sagging. So keep in mind that there are limits even for sturdy, drought-resistant plants. Sedums and grasses can go on for many weeks of drought, though grasses will start turning a straw color near their roots when they hit their limit.

The hostas are soldiering on pretty well, considering that they were shredded by hail this May and coated with concrete dust this July during a sidewalk renovation by the city. All the daylilies, *Rudbeckia hirta* (black-eyed Susan), and *R. laciniata* (cutleaf coneflower) are also doing well. The *R. laciniata* foliage is in great shape—smooth and velvety green. The gloriosa daisies are spectacular, and a new, richly colored annual rudbeckia named 'Sonora' has been blooming beautifully for weeks and shows no sign of letting up. The purple fennel looks fresh and misty, and *Asclepias incarnata* (swamp milkweed), *A. tuberosa* (butterfly weed), and *A. verticillata* (whorled milkweed) are thriving. I am reminded again during my tour of how wonderfully drought resistant many grasses are—the little bluestem (*Andropogon scoparius*), prairie dropseed (*Sporobolus heterolepsis*), blue fescue, the species panicum, and a planting of annual grasses are unfazed by the heat.

Purple coneflowers are just beginning to open and are doing fine, guara is shooting up and out, and the pink centranthus is heading into its second bloom time, with its foliage in perfect, glossy condition. Two new stellar geraniums (pelargoniums) are the surprise of the day, with perfect, clean foliage, and long blooming flowers. Planted along with some large-leafed coleus, they look great. Artemisias 'Valerie Finnis' and 'Silver King', along with lamb's ears cool the garden with their silvery leaves. Among some of the so-called premium annuals I am trying this year in containers, scaevola is the standout, flowering profusely for weeks on end in heat with no deadheading. And both the blue-purple streptocarpus and the metallic purple Persian shield (*Strobilanthes dyeriansus*) are doing beautifully, as is an indigo-violet tropical tradescantia, snaking over the side of its pot. The New Guinea impatiens and the osteospermum are pretty but have needed lots of water to stay in good shape, and the calibrachoa, with their tiny petunia flowers, have been growing by fits and starts, apparently not happy with intermittent shade they receive during the day. I always feel that if you really like a plant, you'll go the extra mile and give it the water it needs. Since I'm not crazy about the acid colors of the New Guinea impatiens, I won't grow it next year. Heliotrope continues to amaze me with its thick green leaves and iridescent purple flowers sailing through the heat. And the annual blue salvia 'Victoria' is growing by leaps and bounds. Among the herbs, rue is thriving, as are the sages, especially the oval-leafed sage 'Berggarten', whose leathery leaves are celadon green shaded with teal.

In the side garden, wild senna (*Cassia hebecarpa*) has clean foliage and is holding itself resolutely upwards, the balloon flower (no flowers yet) is healthy and clean looking, and an unnamed hot pink phlox received as part of an Internet exchange is thriving and has no mildew. After six weeks of drought, *Carex pennsylvanica* is lying fainted on the ground and has had to be revived with good waterings, but the thicker-leafed *Carex morrowii* 'Ice Dance' is flourishing.

In the back garden, the amsonia, the Japanese painted fern (*Athyrium niponicum* 'Pictum'), a woodrush (*Luzula nivea*), and the ferny *Corydalis cheilanthefolia*, as well as the vinca, sweet woodruff, lamium, and the two gingers are doing fine. The corydalis, in particular, is fresh and green and seems to thrive in the heat.

A group of plants at the north end of the front porch is doing better than anything and has had no water to speak of. Lemon lilies and orange ditch lilies, as well as Queen Anne's lace, a violet-flowering spirea, feverfew, and the dreaded *Campanula rapunculoides*, are all blooming like crazy. I think they are coping so well with the drought because they are in very light shade and never receive the harsh afternoon sun. I almost forgot a rather patrician member of this group: *Myrica pennsylvanica*, a bayberry shrub. Planted in the most inhospitable site you could imagine—a very large hole dug into an abandoned gravel driveway—it has thrived. It's about seven feet in height and has glossy leaves. And here it is flourishing, a shrub that evolved on the Atlantic seashore.

Good reading for during a drought is *Dry-Land Gardening*, by Jennifer Bennett. It addresses the formidable problems of gardening in the cold winters and dry summers of central Canada and the Midwestern United States. She includes a valuable list of plants that are virtually self-sustaining in drought, a list that is worthy of careful study: Achillea, artemisia, caragana (Siberian pea shrub), centaurea, hemocrallis, juniperus, paeonia, sedum, sempervivum, yucca.

These stalwarts have soldiered on through a seven-week drought.

loosestrife thriving in a wetlands area told me that it doesn't mind wet feet. So you can pick up all sorts of clues like this simply by reading garden books and magazines. Observing a plant in its native habitat can also be helpful. At a local remnant of prairie this summer, I saw some low hills covered with delicate sprays of the wildflower *Euphorbia corollata* (flowering spurge). The hills bordered on a gravel pit and were dry and gravelly. I couldn't see a single specimen of *E. corollata* in the lower-lying areas, and this told me loud and clear that *E. corollata* needs, wants, and must have sharp drainage.

This doesn't mean that you can't *try* a questionable plant in your garden to see what happens. Some plants do seem to have all sorts of latent capabilities and reservoirs of strength, and you might get a surprise. After all, this is what evolution is all about. But others are specialized in their needs and might not make the transition.

Pests and Diseases

Part of the current gardening ethic lies in understanding our limits. Science used to seem to come to the gardener's rescue, eagerly providing an arsenal of poisons to fight garden pests and diseases, giving the illusion that we could outsmart nature and grow anything we wanted perfectly, thus removing limits. Science seemed to set us free. Most gardeners now are aware that these poisons can poison us, too, and can easily enter our water, air, and food supplies. And ultimately, Mother Nature will always outsmart the cleverest scientist, however strenuously he or she may work to arrange the world to suit our fickle tastes because she has an infinity of time and power to work with. All she has to do is sit and wait. And many of us have become acutely aware of our fellow inhabitants of this beautiful oasis, the planet Earth: the toads, the bees, the foxes, and other innocent creatures whose lives are interwoven with our own, whether we know it or not.

In the following pages I offer earth-friendly remedies for garden pests and diseases, but let me forewarn you: I routinely offer up a small portion of my garden to insects and am at peace with it. I know that some earwigs will pop up in the daylilies and that I will lose some roses to budworm. Last year a plague of pill bugs, of all things, ate my morning glories right down to the roots, and yes, it was frustrating. But that's life in the garden, and I quickly planted climbing nasturtiums that took the morning glory's place. The happy flip side of gardening without pesticides is the butterflies, toads, dragonflies, birds, and moths that live in the garden and that are as important to me as the flowers.

All in all, my census enumerates a surprising number of plants that actually thrive when faced with our drought and Amazonian heat. I make a promise to myself to study this list carefully next March, when I am tempted by those weak sister plants that, like in the words of a country song, first cause the heart to flutter, and then cause the heart to ache.

Right Plant, Wrong Ecosystem

There are a variety of other subtle reasons why a plant might decline and die in a garden. Searing heat, suffocating humidity, summer drought, piercing winter winds, perhaps even a specific atmospheric pressure all can take their toll on plants evolved to thrive in cool summers, low humidity, steady rain, and gentle snows. Researching a plant's original ecosystem can be so illuminating. Plants of alpine or desert origin, or of such "saline" habitats as sea coasts, salt marshes, and salt steppes, are going to have an uphill climb in our Midwestern climate and soil. Sometimes a picture seen in a book or magazine is worth a thousand words. A photo of *Centranthus ruber* flourishing in and around an old, collapsing stone wall showed me that as basically vigorous as this plant is, it prefers a lean, stony soil. A picture of yellow

Every year in late spring, when I am digging in the garden, a clod of earth springs to life and becomes a toad that hops away, and I am delighted. So if an occasional branch wilts or a leaf gets a spot, I say, so be it. I've been gardening long enough to know that stuff happens—not an original sentiment perhaps, but it does sum up life in the garden. But I've also found that good gardening practices go a long way to maintaining a balance between what you want and what the insects want, resulting in a beautiful garden.

TWO LINES OF DEFENSE

The first line of defense against insects and disease is to have your soil tested, as odd as it may sound. Match your plant to the soil, or amend and improve it as necessary. Loosen the soil and dig down deep. Add organic matter. A plant thriving in good soil is usually a healthy plant, and insects seem to zero in on plants struggling in poor or inappropriate soil. So having your soil tested, and amending and improving it, if necessary, gives plants a firm foundation to grow from.

A plant stressed by drought and heat also is vulnerable to pests and disease. Some perennials just naturally need a lot of water and will always be under threat of drought stress, so think about that when choosing plants for your garden. Most roses, for instance, need good soil and plenty of water. Anything less and the door is left open to disease.

Give your plants the space they need to thrive. While some plants, such as clematis and roses, thrive intertwined, plants growing in a jumble not only look unkempt but are a breeding ground for pests and disease. Plants need air circulation and space to stretch their limbs.

The second line of defense is to inspect your plants frequently. Hardly a summer's day goes by when I don't stroll through the garden to have a good look around. I do this to enjoy the garden, of course, and to see what miracles have occurred since the day before. There are always at least a few. Some days I "take the tour" two or three times—it's relaxing. And any gardener can testify that it's surprising how much a garden can change from day to day. As we tour, we can become intimately familiar with the appearance of healthy plants. I've found that pests and diseases can strike quite suddenly: one day a plant is fine, and the next day its stems are orange with aphids, or a Japanese beetle's coppery back glints amid the rose petals. Garden strolls give the gardener a chance to catch disease and pest problems at an early stage. It's easy to wash off a small cluster of aphids from one plant—it gets harder after they've spread to several plants. Sometimes just one portion of a plant will suddenly wilt. If you notice this, you can simply cut off the wilted portion and dispose of it. If unobserved, the wilt might spread and have the entire plant on the ropes before you notice, and then it might be too late. This just happened to a big-leaf coleus flourishing in a pot out front. Several weeks ago I noticed that one branch of the plant had suddenly browned and collapsed. I cut it off and threw it away, and the plant is now fine, much to my relief.

A TOAD-LOVIN' NOTION

The following pest and disease remedies can be surprisingly effective, but you will need to experiment with them, as natural substances vary in their concentration of active principles. And since homemade pesticides tend to be mild in effect, they may have to be applied more often than chemical pesticides, particularly after rain. I recommend starting out with a very dilute solution and increase the concentration in future uses, as opposed to the other way around, until you find out what works for you.

If a particular plant suffers the constant attacks of a pest and earth-friendly remedies don't work, I recommend *not growing that plant*. Yes, this is a radical notion. Maybe even an un-American notion. It is, however, a toad-lovin' notion, and I'm a toad-lovin' gardener. Before giving a plant the heave-ho, though, try moving it to another spot in your garden. It could make a big difference. And if you keep your eyes peeled and regularly read magazines such as *Organic Gardening*, a remedy might still might pop up in the future from some ingenious fellow gardener who has faced the same problem.

Pesticides

WATER It might sound strange to think of water as a pesticide, but sometimes it's one of the best. Aphids, spider mites, and thrips can be rinsed or sprayed off with a gentle stream of tepid water from a watering can. Water may be all you need to get the upper hand with an infestation that affects only a few plants. Pests often lurk on the underside of leaves, so lift individual leaves and lightly rub off the pests as you sluice the area with water. If the plant in question is delicate with soft leaves and stems, experiment with water pressure by washing just a small part of the plant, as a hard stream of water could knock it over and snap a stem. It's possible that this method won't permanently eradicate every last critter, but it could hold the damage to a tolerable level.

Aside from water, there are lots of organic potions that kill pests or knock them back significantly, and I recommend that you consult books on organic gardening for suggestions. Isopropyl alcohol, ammonia, citrus peels, liquified dead bugs, garlic juice, hot pepper sauce . . . the list goes on and on, and some gardeners really swear by them. I have found that a variety of natural substances can work if you have been observing your plants and catch a problem early. Then apply the natural pesticide frequently, as once usually isn't enough. If you're not into the labor-intensive effort of making remedies like garlic sprays, though, I've found that the following pesticides are especially easy to use.

SULFUR As noted in *Common-Sense Pest Control,* by Olkowski and Daar, sulfur "is probably the oldest effective pesticide in use today, and it remains popular because of its low toxicity to humans." Sulfur tends not to be harmful to the beneficial insects and also acts as a fungicide. Lightly dust a plant with sulfur powder, following the instructions on the package.

ALL-PURPOSE BAKING SODA SPRAY A solution of one teaspoon of baking soda in one quart (four cups) of water can be sprayed on plants to render them unpalatable to pests. This solution also fights fungus infections such as mildew, so it's a good all-purpose remedy.

DISHWASHING LIQUID Good for your hands and bad for the bugs, common dishwashing liquid has been shown by researchers at the University of California Cooperative Extension to be as effective as the more expensive commercial insecticidal soap. Use one tablespoon mixed with one gallon of water.

Dr. Bronner's Peppermint 18-in-One Pure Castile Soap, widely available at natural food stores, is an effective pesticide and is my favorite. Mix two tablespoons of soap with one gallon of water, fill up an old Windex bottle, and use as a spray. This is easy to make and inexpensive.

TWO BUG-SPECIFIC REMEDIES

Japanese beetles are here to stay, so we may as well learn to control their presence in the garden. They appear in early July, having been lurking in our lawns as grubs. Because of this, good lawn care could help curb them. Water the lawn deeply but infrequently, just as the experts say, so that it dries out between waterings, as Japanese beetles like damp lawns. And lure all the birds you can to your garden; the common and often despised grackles and starlings, as well as cardinals and meadowlarks, eat Japanese beetles. These beetles seem especially fond of roses, butterfly weeds, and purple coneflowers, in my experience, so inspecting these plants starting in early July can

pay big dividends. Japanese beetles are slow and dim-witted and fairly easy to capture. Carry a little bowl of soapy water with a head of foam on it (a shot of detergent in about a quart of water), and with a tap on the blossom, knock the beetle(s) into the foamy water. The foam holds them under the water and they drown. Be sure there's a head of foam on the water, because the beetles can fly back out of plain water. I've had this happen, and it's unnerving. Or, while the dastardly brute is still in the water, crush it to death against the side of the pail with a stick. Or, while wearing gardening gloves, knock the beetles into your gloved hand and crunch. Nobody said being a gardener was a bed of roses, right? We must be firm.

Japanese beetle traps have a huge drawback in that they will attract not only the beetles in your garden, but also beetles from all around the neighborhood. You can only use these if you live adjacent to some uninhabited land. Place the trap off your property, and beetles will go to it.

Slugs rank right up there with earwigs as objects of some gardeners loathing and frustration. Like earwigs, they come out at night to do their damage. In a bad infestation, slugs can skeletonize hosta plants and decimate a cabbage patch of its young seedlings, though they are not fussy and will eat just about anything.

The bright side of slugs, if their slimy little bodies can be thought of as having a bright side, is that they lend themselves well to nonchemical control methods. A simple way to kill slugs is to get up early in the morning, put on a pair of gloves, and handpick them off plants and then stomp on them. If you feel queasy about stomping on slugs, they can also be dropped into a cup of saltwater in which they will drown, screaming. (Note to new gardeners: just joking!) New gardeners might hesitate to be so cruel, but older, more experienced gardeners have no mercy and will happily engage in slug-icide for the greater good.

Practicing good garden sanitation is the best way, overall, to control slugs. They like to doze during the day under plant litter and debris in cool, dark, damp places. Keeping plants staked up and off the ground, when possible, also helps to discourage slugs. Or, taking advantage of slugs' tendency to skulk under garden debris, leave large rhubarb leaves face down overnight as a trap. Next morning, lift the leaves—and stomp.

The classic antislug remedy is to leave little saucers of beer around the garden. The slugs are drawn by the smell and will climb over the edge of the saucer and drown. This method really does work, but the beer must be changed every day or so to remain fresh and effective.

A tomato stem spray is also said to help. Chop up some tomato stems and leaves and simmer in water for 15 minutes or so. Cool the mixture and strain. Spray on slug-infested plants. Some gardeners swear by placing half a citrus rind in among plants. It seems to attract slugs, who can apparently climb into the peel, but then they can't get out.

And if you can entice a toad or two into your garden, so much the better, as toads love to chow down on a good slug and can decimate the local population. Strips of copper or copper tubing are said to be effective against slugs and snails. Their soft, wet bodies receive an electric shock when they touch the copper. And my sister-in-law highly recommends Escar-Go® Slug & Snail Control from the Gardens Alive! company. She says it's really effective and is not poisonous to other animals such as cats and dogs.

Herbicides

One year's seeding makes seven years' weeding.

Hand weeding is the money-saving, though unpopular, alternative to expensive herbicides. Springtime, when the soil is soft and moist, is the best time of the year to weed. There's often a little bit of leeway during April and early May before the garden is in full swing but you're ready to be outside in the garden. This is the time to pull out the deep, taprooted weeds such as dandelions.

Don't forget about using a hoe to kill weeds. A hoe is so old-fashioned that it's easy to forget what an effective weed killer it can be. There are a number of different types of hoes—most of us need only a fairly lightweight variety, not a so-called grub hoe, which is used for chopping at big, tough weeds. Hold the hoe like a broom, and skim along under the soil surface with the blade.

Mulches are wonderful for keeping down the weeds. Sheets of newspaper can be used as weed-killing mulch in a vegetable garden. It will gradually disintegrate into the soil. I have found that black roofing shingles are inconspicuous in the garden and are really effective in discouraging weeds. I discovered this when our neighbor's house was reroofed, and some of the shingles flew into our garden. You really can't see the shingles at all, and nothing will grow under them. Pulled-up weeds themselves can be used as mulch, as long as they haven't gone to seed. I especially like using the mineral-rich leaves of burdock as a mulch. This is a nasty weed that is difficult to eradicate because of its

tough taproot. Removing the leaves doesn't kill it, but it doesn't help it either.

There is a trend to eating weeds in order to eradicate them. I've tried dandelions with garlic and lemon juice—in the Greek fashion—but could barely choke the slimy mass down. And then there was the retching . . . so dandelions aren't for everyone. The weed purslane, a low-lying succulent plant that grows in disturbed soils, goes beyond being merely edible and is genuinely good tasting. Purslane salads, made with olive oil, lemon juice, and garlic, are eaten in the Middle East, and perhaps we can emulate this practice here in the Middle West.

Boiling water left over from boiling an egg or making a cup of tea can be poured on a weed, especially a big brute of a dandelion coming up in a crack in a sidewalk. It may take several applications of boiling water to kill it, but this does work, and it's so gratifying to see the big weed melting away, like the Wicked Witch of the West.

We all have weeds we especially dislike, and dodder is mine. Dodder is a parasitic vine that clambers over everything from rose bushes to goldenrod. No plant is too big or too small for dodder to pester. By September, whole plants can disappear under tangled masses of reddish dodder stems. This is another weed that's hard to eradicate, but I've noticed that in early summer delicate shoots of dodder can be seen emerging. If you can pull these out, you are ahead of the game. But somehow, when you turn your back in August, just for a moment, the vines go on a rampage.

I've also been experimenting with using household vinegar as a weed killer. I read about this approach in *The Avant Gardener*, a newsletter filled with interesting tips and news items. I have used vinegar on burdock (*Arctium minus*) and *Campanula rapunculoides* with almost miraculous results. I simply dribble the vinegar on the plant leaves, trying to get it right down into the crown of the plant. It seems to have no initial effect, but come back a day or two later, and the weed will be dead. In the case of the *C. rapunculoides* plants I've tried it on, the plants literally vanish. Vinegar works so well that I am still mentally digesting its possible uses. Since it is so effective, it can't just be splashed around with abandon—just carefully dribble it on the weed. And it would probably not work on lawns, because it would kill the grass as well as the weed.

Alas, I'm afraid there are no ingenious or high-tech solutions to the weed problem. It all comes down to the brutal, nitty-gritty of gardener versus weeds, with weeds often winning. Personally, I kind of enjoy weeding—

I wish all of life's problems were as straightforward to solve, and the sight of a neat garden is rewarding.

Soil Amendments and Fertilizers

Many common garden plants enjoy growing in rich, fluffy soil—full of organic material and minerals. But using big bags of chemical fertilizers and the earth's dwindling supply of peat moss doesn't seem like a cottage gardener sort of thing to do. So we need to think of alternatives. There are actually many. Try weeds (plucked from soil) as a mulch/fertilizer. Many weeds draw up trace minerals from deep down in the soil, and as the weed mulch disintegrates, the minerals become available to your plants. Don't use purslane, which can reroot if placed on the soil. Also don't use weeds that have gone to seed.

If you have trees, you have leaves, and shredding them in a shredder or with your lawn mower creates an excellent soil conditioner. Without shredding, leaves become a slimy mess over winter and take a long time to decompose. Try shredding leaves in fall and bagging them in black garbage bags. Store the bags in an inconspicuous spot in the garden. The shredded leaves will partially disintegrate into soft leaf mold by spring. I use this wonderful stuff everywhere in my garden, both as mulch and to dig into the soil.

Grass clippings are best left on the lawn to decompose back into the soil. If you have a lot of clippings, don't pile them on the soil surface around plants as a mulch. Grass clippings can heat up and draw nitrogen from the soil and actually damage plants. Hot grass clippings also give off a powerful "spoiled" aroma. Add them to a compost heap and turn it over to speed up decomposition.

Pine needles, long or short, can be dug into clay soil to help aerate it. One source of needles is your Christmas tree once the holiday season is over. Take the dried tree to an out-of-the-way spot in your yard and shake it hard. This will yield a nice supply of needles for your soil.

Coffee grounds are an excellent soil amendment, containing nitrogen, minerals, and trace elements. Mix grounds with water and pour the slurry near acid-loving plants such as azaleas, primroses, and ferns. Since I rarely brew coffee at home, it occurred to me that the local Starbucks might have used grounds. Or, I *knew* they would have used grounds, but would they give me any, and would I have to haltingly explain to a 19-year-old clerk what I wanted them for? I went to a Starbucks and asked, and instead of giving me a blank stare, a young woman of piercing intelligence said she only had

espresso grounds at the moment and asked with concern if the grounds wouldn't make my soil too acidic. I promised her I would only use the grounds on acid-loving plants and that espresso would be fine. With that she slung a big, moist garbage bag full of grounds over the counter, and it was mine, all mine. It's wonderful stuff: soft, moist, and fine textured. My sister advised giving some to roses, as roses like slightly acidic soil. Some could also go in the compost heap. I don't think the acidity will be a problem, unless I get dump trucks full of the stuff. So now every time I go in for a frozen latte, I casually ask for a bag of wet grounds on the side. Yum.

Save up eggshells and pulverize them in a blender with some water. Pour some of this mixture in the bottom of the planting hole when planting tomato seedlings. Tomatoes appreciate the extra calcium.

Onion and carrot scraps, potato peels, and other such kitchen odds and ends can also be buzzed with water in a blender. Pour the slurry near a lucky plant and lightly dig into the soil with a trowel. This is my favorite method of "composting." As long as the blender has a permanent spot on the kitchen counter, blending the scraps with water takes only a minute, and there is something satisfying about instantly transforming "garbage" into something so good for your garden.

Add magnesium to tomatoes, peppers, and eggplants by mixing two tablespoons of Epsom salts to one gallon of water and water each plant just as bloom begins.

During a drive out in the country, you just might see a "Free Manure" sign out in front of a farm keeping horses. You can usually have all you want, as long as you do the shoveling. Some say that rabbit manure is one of the best fertilizers. If you know someone who has a pet rabbit or two, they would probably be glad to give you the manure for free, or perhaps you can work out a trade of vegetables or flowers for manure.

At an heirloom seed show, I overheard a farmer mentioning that sorghum builds up soil better than anything he knew. He pointed to his display of onions, admittedly wonderful looking, for onions, and said he had grown them on a plot planted with sorghum the previous year. He said the difference in yield from his other plots had been phenomenal. I did some research and found that sorghum is a cornlike grass grown commercially for its sweet syrup and that the flowering portion of the plant is sometimes used to make whisk brooms. While most of us might not have the space to grow such a crop, some of us might want to give it a try. With the memory of the crystalline onion globes glistening in shades of purple, ruby, cream, and snow white still fresh in my mind, I know I would if I had the space. The Baker Creek Heirloom Seed catalog offers three varieties and calls sorghum "an excellent food crop, that should be grown more!"

Corn gluten has been recommended as both a fertilizer and a weed killer. I haven't tried this yet, myself, but it seems as if here in the Midwest, of anywhere in the world, there must be a good source for corn gluten somewhere.

A small amount of manure tea can be made by placing a shovel of manure into an old pillowcase. Tie the pillowcase closed and suspend it in a five-gallon plastic bucket full of water. Allow this to stand for three days in the sun. The resultant liquid should be diluted, using three parts water to one part "tea" for use on plants. Many gardeners swear by this.

If you are allowing a completed compost heap to sit for a year or two to completely break down, plant impatiens on the surface to disguise the heap. I saw this in a garden that was part of a summer garden walk, and it was quite ingenious, truly making a silk purse out of a sow's ear. When fall comes, spade the flowers into the heap.

Shredded paper, sawdust, spoiled hay, cat fur, dryer lint, hair clippings—once you start looking you'll see all kinds of stuff that can be dug into the soil to enrich and condition it. If you work in an office where papers are shredded, perhaps you can take a bag of it home for your compost heap. If you moisten the shredded paper, it breaks down quite quickly. If I see a shredder at a garage sale, I may buy it to shred our own junk mail. Clean out your gutters and use the wonderful, soft, leafy material in the garden. Burdock leaves, used matches, bird feathers, tea bags—I dig it all into the soil, where the cycle of growth begins again.

Light and Shade

One of the trickiest jobs in the garden is to correctly site a plant so that it gets the sun or shade it needs to flourish. If only the task were as easy as some garden books seem to suggest in their neat division of plants into sun plants and shade plants. While there are many plants that either need six hours of sun (sun plants) or must have shade all day (shade plants), many have less obvious requirements. Some shade plants can tolerate gentle morning sun, and some sun plants can make a go of having only afternoon sun or very bright, dappled shade.

If you have a garden with constantly shifting patterns of light and shade,

siting the plant is even more of a challenge. My front garden, which faces west, is in light shade in the morning. Then the sun peeks over the roof, and the garden basks in gentle morning sunlight. Then the sun disappears behind some treetops, and the garden cools off in light dappled shade. By midafternoon, the sun is shining directly and harshly on the front garden, burning it. And then, the sun again disappears behind the trees across the street and light shade returns. Is this a sunny spot or a shady spot? Experience has shown me that shade prevails. It took me several years to abandon my hopes for hosting a riot of annuals in this spot, and then I was floored when hostas got sunburned there. Now I have planted sun-tolerant hostas and adaptable plants such as sedums, grasses, catmints, heucheras, and rudbeckias, and so far, everyone seems happy. But it did take me a while to determine the exact nature of the spot.

Speaking of afternoon sun, I think a site that is shady all morning and then sunny in the afternoon is one of the hardest sites to plant. The afternoon sun of July and August can burn tender plants that have been sitting in cool shade all morning but is not enough sun for truly sun-loving plants. Again, there are adaptable plants for this situation, but sometimes it takes experimentation.

To complicate matters even more, soil moisture can affect a plant's sun tolerance. A plant in moist, loamy soil can "take the heat" much better than a plant in dry soil. This is another reason to keep working on soil quality.

SHADE

I've been gardening for years beneath the sheltering branches of our old horse chestnut in the back garden. It's an imposing tree, 40 feet tall, and its gnarled trunk is 13 feet around. Its roots are everywhere, and I find new ones every spring when I spade over the vegetable patch, which is 60 feet away from the tree's trunk. This big tree is the soul of the back garden, and not only do I not begrudge its hegemony, I find comfort in its primordial, hulking presence. While it's not easy to coax a garden to flourish in the dust-dry soil beneath its branches, what with also battling wiry tree roots and dodging the so-called conkers (which are the horse chestnuts encased in their spiny shells), it's my favorite spot in the garden.

On sweltering summer days my backyard is literally 10 degrees cooler than out on the nearby main street, where the blacktop melts into pools of tar and the heat shimmers as it rises. The shady coolness is a merciful refuge

Hosta sieboldiana 'Elegans' lounges comfortably beneath the branches of the Asian pear tree. The variegated foliage of Persicaria filiforma 'Painter's Palette' can be seen in front, mingling with buttercup leaves.

from the intensity of the sun, and every visitor remarks on the serenity that enfolds us beneath the protecting tree branches. My sister calls this spot "a magic circle." I often sit on the bench beneath those branches and watch the squirrels chase each other up and down the branches at breakneck speed and the blue jays swooping after crows and then the crows swooping after the blue jays. And sometimes at night I hear the high-pitched, unearthly, quavering wail of a screech owl perched in the tree's branches.

Sure, there are moments when I yearn for an enormous garden of sunflowers and morning glories, but I am always surprised when I hear shade spoken of as a gardening liability. In our Midwestern climate with its sweltering summers, I see shade as a huge plus. Other Midwestern gardeners seem to be coming to the same conclusion, and more and more are planting good-sized—even full-sized—trees and shrubs when they landscape, as well as building arbors and pergolas for vines to clamber over to create shade. In the sauna-like heat of July and August, having shade can spell the difference between relaxing outside in a hammock or being cooped up inside in the damp chill, listening to the droning roar of the air conditioner as it changes gears.

Shade gardens can be among the most beautiful of all gardens, and anthropologists think that some of the first gardens were created in groves of trees. The cool, soft mystery of ferns, the sparkling interplay of color between hostas, blue, chartreuse, and warm green, the mist of seed heads floating above a pool of sweet woodruff, and the glossy leaves of hardy ginger can be balm to the overheated soul and a point of reference for contemplation. A shady garden is a refuge, and I wouldn't trade mine for anything. Well, maybe for a sunflower garden, but even then . . . no.

Now that I've sung the praises of shade, though, I'll admit that it has its challenges. If you have shade you probably have trees or overhanging eaves, and if you have trees or overhanging eaves, you may have dry shade, a phrase that causes unpleasant tingling to prickle up and down the spine of the experienced gardener. The very existence of green plants is predicated upon water and light, and many plants, including many shade plants, won't grow in dry shade. To make matters even worse, tree roots deplete soil of nutrients, so not only is the site dry and dark, but the clay soil is poor as dust. Certain trees are worse than others in this regard, with beech, some maple trees, and—wouldn't you know it—horse chestnuts being notorious for having surface roots that suck the life out of soil.

So if you have shade, it forces you to think. A lot. You have to think about the type of shade you have, and above all, you have to decide how much work you want to invest in dealing with dry shade. I've heard of gardeners rototilling between big tree roots and trucking in mounds of compost and watering, and I mean *watering*, all the live-long day. I don't recommend rototilling or digging deep anywhere around a tree. Trees—though they may be tall, possess rock-hard bark, and look imposing—can be sensitive about their roots, many of which are surprisingly close to the ground's surface. Rototilling, or even chopping through roots to create pockets for good soil and plantings, as is sometimes recommended, is terribly risky, and you can lose a tree this way. And you can smother a tree's roots if you pile on too much compost. I have heard experts say that no more than three to six inches of compost or soil should be piled over a tree's root extension and that the whole root area should not be covered. And many trees will be absolutely delighted with your watering and compost, and their roots will grow right up into the new rich, moist soil layer, the better to suck it dry.

So if you want to have a shade garden and are starting from square one, be sure to consult a local nurseryman for tree suggestions. Please do take the time to do this. Trees are just as sensitive to soil pH and drainage conditions as any perennial, and it's one thing to lose $7.95 when a perennial hits the dust, and quite another to remove a dying tree.

Many trees do coexist politely with plantings. Thornless honey locusts, for instance, with their lacy-leafed canopies, provide dappled shade and are easy on the garden. Small fruiting trees such as crabapples, flowering quinces, Asian pears, and even dwarf, heirloom apple trees, provide both fruit and shade. Small ornamental trees such as dogwoods, viburnums, serviceberries, magnolias, and Japanese tree lilacs are also nice, especially if you want some shade but don't want to spend all fall raking.

I'm sorry to say I have a pin oak *(Quercus palustris)* growing in the front parkway. I'm sorry because this is the one oak that experts say you shouldn't plant in our area, and Dick Young, in *Kane County Wild Plants and Natural Areas*, blasts pin oaks: " We commonly see this yellowing, skeletonized, nursery-recommended Oak as a bleak front yard emblem of wasted money and hope." I was shattered to read this, really shattered, though the tree is healthy and shot up two feet this year. Nevertheless, it seems the thing to do

is to plant any oak but a pin oak. If I had the space I would plant a hackberry tree *(Celtis occidentalis)*, which has deep roots and produces reddish purple berries in the fall that attract birds. Another attractive possibility would be the hop hornbeam, sometimes called the ironwood tree *(Ostrya virginiana)*, which is a small, graceful tree that can be planted along with dogwoods and serviceberries. One of my all-time favorite trees is the Kentucky coffee tree *(Gymnocladus dioica)*, which is enormously tall and handsome, and is definitely not for the small garden.

It's too late for me to make a change, I'm afraid, with my horse chestnut, so I grapple with dry shade on an ongoing basis. I prefer to let fall leaves melt back into the soil during the winter, to water and fertilize moderately, to bring in some compost selectively for special plants, and, above all, to seek out plants that don't mind dry shade.

PLANTS FOR DRY SHADE

Before looking at plants that grow in dry shade, let's remind ourselves that there are degrees of awfulness to dry shade, ranging from soil a bit on the dry side in dappled shade (many plants will grow in this) to bone-dry dust moldering in the stygian depths of tomblike darkness (nothing will grow here—give it up). This last worst-case scenario is sometimes found beneath eaves or under big pine trees.

If you do have really dense shade, consider hiring an arborist to cut off some of the lower tree branches to admit more light. Very few plants will grow in unrelieved deep shade. I remember once walking through a closely planted pine forest up in Wisconsin. The forest was dark, chill, and silent on that warm summer's day, and not a single thing grew on the forest floor, which was carpeted with a sterile layer of pine needles. The sad words of a rather mournful folk song droned through my mind: "In the pines, in the pines, where the sun never shines, I shivered the whole day through." I kept looking over my shoulder and walked faster and faster, as though I were in a forest of a bad spirit—there was a real Blair Witch feeling to the place.

I was glad to emerge into the sunlight of a forest glade, where a crowd of plants cheered me up immediately. So there is such a thing as too much shade, and if you have lots of trees with dense canopies of leaves, astute pruning can let in some light and greatly extend the range of what you can plant.

Remember, also, to get your soil tested. This necessary step is sometimes skipped by gardeners in a hurry to plant, but it provides helpful infor-

Ajuga 'Catlin's Giant' still green and growing after weeks of drought.

mation. While the following plants are real troopers, any plant will have trouble with really terrible, compacted, lifeless soil, and a soil analysis can guide you in improving it.

I'm tempted to rush past the four old dry-shade reliables by mentioning them all together in one breath—*pachysandraajugavincaivy*—and moving on, but I think it would be doing these good plant friends a disservice. Let's look at pachysandra (*P. terminalis*) first. Yes, it is boring. Yes, it is everywhere. Yes, almost any other shade ground cover is more interesting than pachysandra. But for sheer insect and disease resistance and Terminator-like ability to soldier on in a presentable manner through the climatic upheavals experienced routinely in the Midwest, we should get down and kiss its glossy, perfect little leaves. Pachysandra is our friend! It blocks weeds and its little white flowers surprise every spring with their prettiness. Perhaps experimenting with some of the pachysandra cultivars that are available would spice up our sullen, almost resentful, relationship with this plant. First is *P.* 'Green Sheen', whose dark green leaves are, in the memorable words of the Heronswood

Nursery catalog, as "glossy as a buffed baby's butt." The leaves really do look as if they were waxed or oiled. *P.* 'Silver Edge', whose light green foliage is edged with white is another good option. Neither of these cultivars spreads as steadily as the species, but they do hold their own and provide an interesting twist to the old pachysandra theme. I have also come across a tantalizing reference to *P. stylosa* (Chinese pachysandra). Supposedly it's "more elegant and less aggressive" than regular pachysandra, but I have not been able to locate a source for it, only a mention on the Internet that it's being grown at an arboretum in North Carolina. I'm mentioning it because if we don't seek out new, useful plant material for our area, we will be stuck with the same old petunias for all eternity. So I will keep looking for a source.

I've already waxed lukewarm elsewhere about *Ajuga reptans* (carpet bugleweed) because, while it can be pretty, especially in the spring with its amethyst flowers, it can grow in a spotty manner and hopscotch right into the lawn and cracks in the sidewalk. Perhaps it needs a bit moister, better soil than I am giving it, but there are still the unsightly, skeletal remains of all those pretty flowers once they finish blooming, moist soil or not. One good trait of ajuga is that it will flow equitably around hostas and other shade perennials, making a mat, and not resenting their presence. I am presently trying *A.* 'Catlin's Giant' to see if it can jump-start my tepid enthusiasm for ajuga.

Postscript: I like 'Catlin's Giant' *much* better than the smaller varieties. It doesn't hop, skip, and jump—it spreads slowly and almost forms a low mound.

Periwinkle (*Vinca minor*) is a good ground cover for dry shade, actually almost too good. Its leaves are clean and shiny, and its periwinkle blue flowers bloom luminously in drifts like the Milky Way in the spring, and it doesn't mind heavy clay soil. Ominously, though, it grows by sending out long, stealthy, trailing stems that root both at their tip and their leaf nodes. Turn your back just a second, and vinca will be everywhere. For such a delicate-looking plant, it has the strength of 10 men. It will choke hosta, smother astilbe, run rampant on lamium, and wrestle ferns to the ground. It might not do this the first year you have it, maybe not even the second. But after that, your garden will be up for grabs. This spring I pulled up a bushel basket of vinca, but not before it had strangled a hosta—the crime scene was terrible, and I almost wept. I come down on the side of vinca, though, because it is a clean-looking plant whose spring flowers are truly beautiful. Try it in a park-

way where nothing else will grow, including grass. It will form a nice, neat mass of foliage. It's also a so-called heirloom plant, having been planted in medieval gardens and monasteries, so it's got a pedigree. But you do have to keep an eye on it.

All I know about ivy is that it seems dark and dusty, and in its fight in my garden with the vinca and ajuga, it never gets very far. I have one variety that I plucked from the alley behind my little sister's garden in Oak Park, Illinois, and it is noticeably larger than the usual English ivy ground cover, so I think of it as Oak Park ivy. And I have yet another ivy variety that clambers over our garage. It's trying to get *into* the garage and reminds me of the time I saw a garage that was completely covered with ivy, both inside and out, like an enormous topiary. At any rate, I find that I have absolutely no further thoughts about ivy whatsoever but feel that someday in the future I will probably be thunderstruck by ivy and wonder why I was so blind to its charms. But for now, it seems dark and dusty.

Not useful in dry shade is *P. procumbens* (Allegheny spurge). This is a fine, tough plant, and I do have it in my garden, but in soil beefed up with compost. (To say "beefed up" seems so wrong here . . . maybe "vegged up" would be better!)

Then, of course, what about bishop's weed (*Aegopodium podagraria* 'Variegatum')? Gardeners tend to feel very strongly one way or the other about bishop's weed. I feel that it has a role in dealing with some of the toughest garden spots, but it is the sort of plant that is a last resort. See more discussion in chapter 4, "Dictionary of Perennials."

TOP-TIER DRY-SHADE PLANTS

Finally we come to some ground covers for dry shade that I can speak of with evangelistic enthusiasm. First of these is *Epimedium* (barrenwort). Its heart-shaped leaves are smooth and glossy, it has panicles of little yellow flowers like jonquils in the spring, it's drought tolerant to an amazing degree, and it simply ignores tree roots, whether big and woody or small and wiry, adroitly growing in among them without a second thought. I wish more plants could

Hostas with a woodrush (*Luzula nivea*) in dry shade.

figure out how to do this. There are many cultivars of epimedium, some with red-rimmed leaves, some mottled, some with lilac flowers, and I plan to spend the next few gardening years pleasantly working my way through all of them.

Wild ginger is another thoroughbred ground cover for dry shade. I can't say enough for this plant, whether it's *Asarum canadense* (Canadian wild ginger) or the glossy *Asarum europaeum* (European wild ginger). Like the above epimedium, these gingers thrive in dry shade with grace and beauty, though I find that the European spreads very slowly. The Heronswood Nursery catalog offers a tempting 14 species of wild ginger. Probably not all of these are suitable for our climate, but I bet some of them are, and it will be fascinating to try them. Wouldn't that make a wonderful Christmas present for an avid Midwestern gardener? All 14 gingers arriving in a wonderful box from Heronswood at the doorstep in the spring? Hint. Hint.

Aster divaricatus (white wood aster) is a decent little aster that will try its hand at whatever shady spot it's confronted with. No flowers the size of dinner plates, but that's okay. I have read that one of Gertrude Jekyll's favorite combinations was wood aster grown with bergenia. I also have *A. macrophyllus* (bigleaf aster), and it's doing well, though since I heard that it's known as "lumberjack's toilet paper" in some parts of the country, I haven't been able to see it in the same light. Another aster that is recommended for dry shade is *A. cordifolius* (heart-leaved aster). Blue stemmed goldenrod (*Solidago caesia*) is also said to be very drought and shade tolerant.

Sweet woodruff (*Galium odoratum*), which we've already praised highly in chapter 4, is another perfect plant for dry shade. It asks for nothing, but the whorls of little dark green leaves of this diminutive plant spill into the spaces between hostas, pulmonaria, ferns, and other shade plants, accompanying them without damaging them. They are easy to pull up if they crowd other plants excessively. The little clean white flowers that bloom in the spring are a joy. Interestingly, sweet woodruff will not flower or thrive in very good, rich soil. It needs lean soil on the dry side.

Another thoroughbred that almost makes you glad you have dry shade, or at least not mind it so very much, is *Polygonatum odoratum* 'Variegatum' (variegated Japanese Solomon's seal). With graceful, arching stems and leaves brushed with cream, this plant is truly lovely. Also check into other species of the genus: *P. commutatum* (great or giant Solomon's seal), *P. biflorum* (small Solomon's seal), and *P. humile* (a miniature Solomon's seal). They are all graceful and beautiful.

Tiarella (foamflowers) are small but tough, like little plant terriers. They sport fluffy flower spikes in the spring. They have interesting, sometimes bicolored leaves, and new cultivars come on the market all the time, as more and more gardeners discover their charms. Foamflowers are tough and vigorous but can be overgrown and killed by hostas, so keep an eye on them.

Geranium macrorrhizum (bigroot geranium). Please see chapter 4 for a description of this wonderful geranium that is so tolerant of dry shade.

Athyrium niponicum 'Pictum'. I can't say enough about this beautiful fern, which on first sight, I thought was ugly. Its color scheme of metallic gray, dark red, and green is different, to say the least. But it contrasts beautifully with hostas and epimedium. This is not a plant for your worst dry shade. Take time to improve its soil and to water during drought. But considering that many ferns demand conditions found only in an Oregon rain forest, this fern copes quite gracefully with dryness. Three new cultivars have appeared on the gardening scene, and I am overjoyed: 'Ursula's Red', 'Silver Falls', and 'Wildwood Twist'.

Woodland knotweed (*Polygonum virginiana*) is a small, subtle plant (12–18 inches tall) whose arching stems beaded with tiny flowers have a magical quality. It's all about grace and airiness, not color and size. I have some planted along a path where the stems form arching patterns. Its height depends on soil richness. Be forewarned: it is a self-seeder and in moist soil could probably be a pest.

Stylophorum diphyllum (native wood poppy). Its butter-yellow flowers bloom for weeks during April and May, and its pale green, oaklike leaves are so pretty. This wonderful plant self-seeds a bit, but I am happy for each new plant. I also have an Asian wood poppy (*Stylophorum lasiocarpum*) that so far is also a winner. Its leaves have stayed a smooth, light green right through a terrible drought, while the leaves of *S. diphyllum* have turned a mottled yellow, green, and brown. Its flowers are a creamier yellow than those of the native wood poppy.

GOOD PLANTS FOR DRY SHADE

These plants are just a notch below wonderful but still well worth planting; each has its charms.

Anemone cylindrica (thimbleweed). This native of open woods will accept dry soil if it's planted in dappled, not deep, shade. Thimbleweed supposedly grows to three feet, but in its dry, shady spot in my garden it reaches barely two. It's still pretty with its thimble-shaped seed heads in late summer, which turn into fluff come fall and fly away. Some of the fluff is used by hummingbirds in their nests.

Allium cernuum (nodding onion). This pretty little allium will grow almost anywhere, including dry shade. Its drooping sprays of light purple flowers appear in June and July. It does self-seed, but not obnoxiously.

Anemonella thalictroides (rue anemone) is an April-flowering spring ephemeral that is tolerant of poor, clay soil. Airy and graceful in appearance, it's a sturdy plant with wiry stems.

Aquilegia canadensis (wild columbine) features clouds of little yellow and rose-colored flowers hovering over the garden in late spring. This will naturalize throughout the dry shade garden, especially if you help it by plucking off the seed heads when brown and dry and shaking the seeds out like salt from a saltcellar in spots where you want plants to grow next spring.

I find that I almost have to apologize for mentioning lily of the valley (*Convallaria majalis*) because it is so common. But its scent is matchless, and a bouquet of these little flowers is spring itself. The leaves can become shabby later in the summer during drought, so be sure to include the plant in your waterings.

Some of the dicentras do really well in dry shade. Cultivars of both *D. eximia* and *D. formosa* can tolerate dry shade if their soil is improved before planting. But they are not happy with week after week of summer drought, and it perks them up to give them extra water during really dry stretches.

The genus *Corydalis* is related to the dicentras and also includes some possibilities for dry shade. Foremost is *C. lutea* (yellow fumitory). This remarkable little plant with lacy leaves and delicate yellow flowers blooms from May through September. I just went outside to look at my plants and found that now, in November, their bluish foliage is fresh and dewy, nestled amid the russet autumn leaves.

And a few years ago I came across a reference to *C. cheilanthifolia* as being very drought tolerant. It was nowhere to be found, until last year, when it seemed to pop up everywhere. I greedily scarfed up two plants at the Morton Arboretum plant sale but then foolishly allowed them to sit in their pots for a week before planting. The weather was cool and rainy, and they both rotted at the crown and died in a matter of days. It was not an auspicious beginning. I purchased another plant at a local plant nursery and planted it immediately. It took off and is a simply wonderful plant, looking almost like a fine-textured fern. It sent up a slender spike of little yellow flowers and has flourished through terrible drought. It is skyrocketing its way to becoming a favorite plant of mine.

Trout lily, sometimes called the dogtooth violet (*Erythronium albidum*), is a spring ephemeral wildflower in the lily family that can tolerate tough, dry shade conditions. Its bloom time is brief, but it's beautiful and always welcome.

Many gardeners instantly think of hostas when confronted with dry shade, but hostas are happiest with a bit of dappled shade and decent soil—they're only human, after all. Really dry soil can kill a hosta, especially a big one. One hosta that I have found to have no problem with shade and dry, poor soil is *H. lancifolia*. This is a common, fast-growing hosta used in mass plantings. Its lavender flowers are very pretty and appear in late summer. I have found that the small, variegated hosta *H.* 'Ginko Craig' copes well with dry shade, and I have also come across references to *H. capitata* as being very tolerant of dry shade.

The lamiums are fine plants for dry shade. *Lamium maculatum* (spotted dead nettle) takes dry shade in its stride and has pretty flowers (pink or white, depending on the cultivar) in the spring. *L.* 'Beedham's White' has striking chartreuse leaves and grows wonderfully in dry shade. It even looks beautiful in the autumn, peeking up through the leaves.

Lamiastrum used to be included with the lamiums but has been given its own genus because its yellow flowers set it apart, in a manner only understandable to botanists. *Lamiastrum galeobdolon* 'Herman's Pride' (yellow archangel) is a busy little plant with metallic foliage that looks nice next to more serene plants, such as hardy ginger. A clump of 'Herman's Pride' looks like a tiny city of futuristic, silvery towers and is striking. *L. galeobdolon* 'Variegatum' (variegated yellow archangel) is a very different-looking plant, with green and silver foliage on long runners. It can self-seed and has pretty, creamy yellow flowers in the spring.

My amsonia plant does very well in the dry, dappled shade under the branch tips of the horse chestnut, as do pulmonaria, Jacob's-ladder (*Polemonium*), thalictrum (meadow rue), joe-pye weed, and cimicifuga. Heucheras can tough it out if they have to but seem happiest with regular watering.

I have heard that *Symphytum grandiflorum* (ornamental comfrey) works in dry shade. This is not to be confused with *S. officinale*, the herbal comfrey that is an unstoppable garden thug. My sister is trying *S. grandiflorum* this year, so I will hear a report soon. (*Postscript:* Works very well.) There are even irises for dry shade: *Iris cristata* (crested iris) and *I. verna* (dwarf iris).

Mertensia virginica (Virginia bluebells) does very well in dry shade and is a good companion to ferns. As the bluebells fade away, the ferns arise to cover the withering bluebell foliage.

Amazingly, trillium is not out of the question for dry shade. I have a thriving colony of purple trillium (*Trillium erectum*), apparently one of the easier trilliums to grow. It won't take any guff even from English ivy.

Astilbes are generally not plants for dry shade. They revel in dappled shade and moist soil. The one astilbe that I have found tolerant of dryness is *Astilbe chinensis* 'Pumila'. This is a very small, tough astilbe that in my garden has been holding its own against vinca.

And let's not forget Virginia creeper (*Parthenocissus quinquefolia*), a vine that is up to anything that is thrown at it. (Read more about it in chapter 3, "Perennial Support Players.")

Heartleaf brunnera (*Brunnera macrophylla*) is a tough plant with dark green, heart-shaped, almost leathery leaves and flowers that resemble forget-

For the woodland garden with moist soil: babeberry *(Actaea pachypoda)*, sometimes called "doll's eyes." Try it with late-blooming white lilies.

me-nots in the spring. I dug in some good soil when I planted it, but otherwise it hasn't had special care, and it's doing fine. I have seen it persisting in some neglected situations, so it seems quite tough.

ANNUALS FOR DRY SHADE

I may face an argument from other gardeners, but as far as I can see, there aren't any annuals that truly do well in dry shade, at least not if they are planted directly in the soil. Even hard-working impatiens need decent soil and regular water, and the usual annuals recommended for shade, such as coleus, begonias, and browallia, are best planted in pots of a good soil mix and kept watered.

GRASSES FOR DRY SHADE

Since I had laboriously dug up a big patch of moth-eaten lawn that was listlessly degenerating under the horse chestnut in order to plant shade-loving perennials, it didn't occur to me at first that any type of grass could grow in such daunting conditions. Then while at a local nursery, I stumbled across a sedge, *Carex pennsylvanica* (common oak sedge), that was recommended for shade. A clump of this silky, fine-textured grass now thrives beneath the horse chestnut. Many sedges derive from woodland habitats and are able to compete with trees. I also have *C. morrowii* 'Ice Dancer', which has wide, striped leaves and has proved impressively drought resistant. At the same nursery I found the wonderful *Luzula nivea* (woodrush), whose thin, straplike blades have a delicate, feathery trim. This is one of my favorite plants, growing with such grace and health in a difficult situation.

I have come across references to two other grasses that thrive in dry shade. One is *Chasmanthium latifolium* (northern sea oats), and the other is *Leymus arenarius* 'Blue Dune' (blue Lyme grass). Both have been described as invasive, with the northern sea oats characterized as a "vicious seeder." I'm betting that they will meet their match in the horse chestnut, though, and I will cautiously try them next year.

I hope the above suggestions cheer you up a bit if you are faced with daunting, dry shade. It's a respectable list of choices, and it doesn't even touch on shrubs and barely grazes the surface of all the possible spring ephemerals, the full range of grasses, and the small understory trees that can grow beneath trees with tall canopies. And then there are the violets, blue phlox (*Phlox divaricata*), may apples (*Podophyllum peltatum*), the wood lily (*Lilium philadelphicum*), and the primulas, which can be surprisingly tough customers in dry shade.

Occasionally I catch a fleeting glimpse, as though on a far horizon, of even more possibilities. I just came across a Web site for the Crug Farm Plants nursery, which specializes in shade-tolerant plants and is located in North Wales, United Kingdom. In a discussion of dry shade plants, they firmly state, "Cacalia, Farfugium, and Miricacalia are of the same ilk as Syneilesis and will vanish if too wet." I am in awe of this extraordinary sentence and wonder if Farfugium would grow in my garden. It seems that there is plenty of plant material out there waiting to be discovered by Midwestern gardeners.

So there's no need to cry in our beer if we have dry shade—quite the opposite, in fact. Let's rest in a hammock in our leafy glade, sipping a gin and tonic with a twist of lime, enjoying the cool.

Cutting Back

So the plant has bloomed gloriously, and you have ooh'd and aah'd, and your friends have been gratifying in their admiration of your green thumb. The expensive hybrid daylily surpassed your wildest dreams, the lily soared, and the snapdragons snapped. But now what? Much attention is paid to planting plants, watering and fertilizing them, and then admiring their blooms. But what comes after? At some point, the show is over, and the daylily flower browns and shrivels, the gay flags of hosta flowers become tattered, and the hollyhocks list to one side, leaves pocked with rust. Since many plants, perennials, especially, will spend at least as much time in our gardens out of bloom as in, we need to take care of them after blooming so they will look good and be healthy. This is where new gardeners start to feel uneasy. What now?

No matter what it's called, lopping off, deadheading, pruning, yanking, hoiking, shearing, whacking, pinching, thinning—in other words, gardening— the process of dealing with plants past bloom seems an art, almost an occult one. A beginner fears nipping off something he or she shouldn't, and then whoops, the plant is dead or Will Never Bloom Again. There are dark visions of an *experienced* gardener, eyes gleaming and armed with arcane knowledge, swooping in with a special knife and expertly slicing off just the right amount of spent foliage at precisely the correct point in its life cycle. I have news for you: there is no arcane knowledge. Well, maybe a little, but basic common sense, your own likes and dislikes about a plant's appearance, and its role in your garden have a lot to do with how a plant is cared for after it blooms.

Above all, don't be afraid to cut back spent foliage. It's truly hard to kill a perennial by whacking it back too far. I think of my husband, having read that grapevines need to be severely pruned to renew them, and then cutting our 16-foot-long grapevine back to two inches. I will admit to feeling odd tremors in my chest when I bent over to look at the stalk. I even felt a bit light-headed. But do you know, by the next year it had sprouted back up several feet, and the year after that it exploded, not literally of course, but it just went wild and we had many pounds of grapes. So the renewal pruning worked—so well, in fact, that I begged him not to do it again. I also think of a local landscaper who confided to me that he ran over his perennial bed with a power mower when the plants were finished blooming. I was interviewing him for a newspaper article. "Don't tell that to your readers," he added hastily. So I'm not really telling it to you—certainly not recommending it—just wanted to illustrate that perennials are tough and can withstand even inexpert cutting back. And I also think of my coworker Jeff, who trims back his gaillardias with a hedge trimmer. He has more of this flower all summer than he knows what to do with.

Before going one step further, though, let's keep the difference between annuals and perennials firmly in mind. Most annuals will bloom all summer if deadheaded and watered. Deadheading means removing spent flowers, cutting back to the next leaf, bud, or stem. Don't leave a little stalk sticking up. You can use your fingers or a pair of clippers or even old scissors. If you deadhead, water, and fertilize an annual, blossoms will keep coming all summer. Most annuals are small plants, at least compared with perennials, and have tender foliage and stems. Cutting them back to the ground *would* kill them. So the following advice pertains to perennials, which are a different kettle of fish entirely from annuals. So you deadhead and water annuals, and this is an ongoing, summer-long process. At the end, you ruthlessly rip them out, unless you want them to self-seed, in which case you ruthlessly leave them in.

Also, let's say a good word for a select group of perennials that don't need any care after blooming, other than watering. I'm thinking of amsonia, whose icy blue flowers, silvery as moonlight, bloom in early summer. As the summer progresses, the petals vanish into thin air, and inconspicuous, bifurcated pods appear. The plant spends the rest of the summer looking graceful, and then its leaves, through the alchemy of time, turn to gold in the fall. And then, come to think of it, I don't do anything with amsonia—I've never done anything to amsonia—but it comes up next year, looking beautiful again. This is the kind of plant beginning gardeners tend to ignore but more experienced gardeners treasure. Sweet woodruff, a ground cover, is another truly low-maintenance perennial. Spangled with pretty little white stars in late spring, the stars turn

Goatsbeard (*Aruncus diocius*) blooming in the shade of a weeping birch.

to a mist that veils the plant for the rest of the summer. And wild ginger also always looks good, shiny and healthy all season, as does epimedium, many ornamental grasses, and most sedums.

Other perennials form ornamental seedpods and heads after blooming and can also be left alone. Some people like the seed heads of perennial candytuft and leave them; others don't like them and lop them off. Blackberry lilies form little purple seedpods that do look exactly like blackberries, and are ornamental. Anise hyssop looks like a candelabra after blooming, and its delicate shape is pleasing, even silhouetted against snow. Berries, including rose hips, and seed heads can also be left especially with the birds in mind. Birds love the seed heads of purple coneflower and rudbeckia, for instance. And I always leave sunflowers for the birds, only pulling out the stalk when the seeds have been plundered. The bottom line is, if you like the way a plant looks after blooming, then leave it be. And if you see birds and bees flocking to its seeds or berries, also leave it be. It's truly up to you.

So, in some cases, just leaving a plant alone after it has flowered is the best course. But also remember that we never truly should leave a plant alone:

always continue to water and observe it for disease. We do this for appearance, of course, as dried, tattered leaves don't look good, and most plants can look green and presentable through most of the year if watered. But we also water to help the plant prepare for the next growing season. For instance, peonies and irises spend time after blooming fattening up their roots. To leave them thirsty would be cruel, and there would also be reduced blooming next year.

With most plants, though, something must be done after blooming. The first reason to cut a plant back is disease prevention.

DISEASE PREVENTION

I've mentioned that peonies are disease free, and, in general, this is true. They are extraordinarily healthy, vigorous plants whose foliage stays in good condition throughout the summer. But even peonies have their limits, and they can become infected by a variety of blights and rots if their foliage is left in place over the winter. So come fall, remove their metal support hoops and cut the plants back to the ground. I leave only about four inches of the stems above ground. Then I whisk away all the foliage and bag it for disposal. Similarly, monarda and phlox can get wilts and mildews, and cutting them back to the ground can control the spread. And iris foliage must be cut back in the fall, and the foliage disposed of, as borer eggs can overwinter in the leaf folds near the ground.

APPEARANCE

The second reason to cut back is for good appearance. The stark stalk of a daylily, with its withered flower hanging like a tattered flag, can look pretty terrible and needs to go. I remove it the moment the stalk starts to turn brown. Some people hate hosta flowers and remove them the moment they appear, while others wait until the flowers become tattered. You can also just leave them, but I have found that when I cut off the dried stalk and water the plant, the whole garden suddenly looks better. Another example is ladies mantle. Towards summer's end, ladies mantle can look dry, limp, and dusty, and the flowers look seedy. Cut the flowers off right down to the main mass of foliage and reach down under the plant and cut off any ragged leaves. Water the plant, and you and it will feel 100 percent better. This brings us to one of my guiding mottoes regarding plant care: if it's ugly, get rid of it. I know it sounds just brutal, but it's such a useful piece of guidance. Withered leaves, brown stalks, anything mildewed, rusted, tattered, nibbled full of holes, pathetic, stark looking, yellowed, shriveled—anything ugly—cut it off or yank it out. (The exception, of course, is bulb foliage, which needs to stay to bring energy down into the bulb for next year.)

But where do you cut? This is where beginners' knees knock. For many plants past flowering, dried stalks and foliage need to be cut back to the basal foliage. What's basal foliage? In a hosta or daylily, for instance, the main mound of foliage from which the stalks and stems grow is the basal foliage. *Basal* means "pertaining to the base, or foundation," and many perennials do have a mass of foliage from which the stalks emerge. A few weeks ago I went around the garden and cut back spent feverfew plants to their basal foliage. It was easy to see what had to be removed: the dry, yellowed stalks and buttonlike seed heads. I cut the stalks right back to the bright, fresh green, basal foliage. Some of these plants are already reflowering. If you look around at a variety of perennials and study their foliage and flower stalks, you'll see that many have basal foliage, and you can use this knowledge when cutting back. Plants don't always have basal foliage, and the stalks seem to come up directly from the soil. Platycodon is an example and can be cut back two-thirds. Speaking of reflowering . . .

CUTTING BACK FOR REBLOOM

The last major reason to cut back perennials is to stimulate them to reflower. A great example of a perennial that will reflower after being cut back is the remarkable peach-leafed bellflower (*Campanula persicifolia*). After its long, early summer flowering, cut it way back down to its basal foliage. Water it thoroughly and fertilize (with fish emulsion or granular fertilizer), and in about three weeks it will be blooming again. I've had three waves of bloom from one plant in some summers—it almost makes me feel guilty for overworking the poor thing, but it doesn't seem to mind. Red Valerian (*Centranthus ruber*), catmint (*Nepeta* sp.), perennial cornflowers (*Centaura montana*), early blooming phloxes such as 'Miss Lingard', early blooming perennial geraniums such as *Geranium sanguineum,* and some members of the lychnis family also will rebloom after being cut back. I'm sure there are many others, but these are ones that I've had success with.

Remember, we're not flogging these plants to death, though, so be sure to water well and fertilize. Also, some plants won't rebloom no matter what you do. I've never had daisies come back, for instance, though it may be more a matter of summer heat repressing them than anything.

HOIKING

Occasionally, an entire plant becomes rusted or wilted, and at that point you must steel yourself and yank the whole thing out. Or, I've noticed, that some gardeners "hoik" plants out. Same thing. If there has been a long, rainy spring, especially, rusts and wilts can be a problem, and yanking out is the only solution.

Neatness

To pontificate on the value of having a neat and tidy garden has a Victorian ring to it, and it's a subject that might not seem to apply to casual cottage gardens. Nevertheless, the best gardens all give evidence of the gardener's "controlling hand" and have an underlying order and structure that is attractive in and of itself, quite aside from whatever spectacular plant material is planted there.

For most of us gardeners with limited money, keeping our gardens well tended is a straightforward way to maximize our assets. This is a rather mundane approach and come August, when we are battling heat and big weeds, perhaps not always possible, but it does pay big dividends. Just yesterday I walked past a neighbor's garden and thought how nice it looked. There was nothing special or exotic planted at all, just an overgrown juniper, a row of nondescript hostas, and some bishop's weed. But the juniper was as carefully trimmed as a giant bonsai; the lush, well-watered hostas formed a neat curve in front of the junipers, and the bishop's weed sprouted in two big fluffy tufts at either end of the hostas. There wasn't a weed in sight, and the lawn was mowed and crisply edged. Junipers, bishop's weed, and hostas are among the dreariest and dustiest of gardening cliches, but sheer neatness here had won the day. Gardener Elsa Bakalar has remarked in her book *A Garden of One's Own: Making and Keeping Your Flower Garden* that if her lawn and edgings aren't neat and groomed she always gets far fewer compliments on her garden than if everything were shipshape, no matter what is flowering. And a local gardener, famous for her fabulous garden has commented that she can't stand it if gardening tools such rakes, hoses, and bushel baskets are left out in the garden and feels that everything needs to be neatly stowed away when work is done.

BE CRUEL (TO BE KIND)

Neatness extends right to the plants themselves, of course. Plants that badly need to be deadheaded, cut back, or staked can seriously detract from a garden's appearance. Be ruthless. Especially with perennials, there's often a stage when a plant is just past flowering and there still are a few perfectly good blooms left. A beginning gardener might hesitate to cut the plant back and lose those flowers. If this really bothers you, see if you can't gather enough of the flowers to use indoors in a bouquet—then cut the plant back. But always look at the big picture. You're not doing your garden any favors if you leave a perennial untouched past its prime to the bitter end, with tattered flowers clinging to it, just because a few "good" flowers are left. It's not always easy, I know. Today I cut back a peach-leafed bellflower that had been flowering gloriously for a month. It had been one of the showpieces of the side garden. But it had gotten to the point where deadheading couldn't keep up with the decline. So I cut it back and gave it a good, thorough watering. If the summer isn't too beastly, it probably will flower again later on. But I did lose a few still-pretty flowers in the process. Believe me, though, the moment you cut that plant back, your garden will look better.

THE "UGLY" RULE OF THUMB

If something is ugly in the garden, get rid of it. This is a draconian piece of advice, but it is so useful. I like to focus on one small section of the garden at a time and see if there isn't something "ugly" going on, and then I step in and remove it. Sometimes all it takes is a bit of weeding, lopping off, or some deadheading, but sometimes a plant obviously isn't thriving and a more radical solution is required. A plant listing to one side might be crying out for more sun and should be moved. Don't hesitate to move it. Some of the best gardeners I know will move a plant two or three times—or more—before the plant is happy. But if a plant is a chronic problem, moping around and always being attacked by insects or disease year after year, don't hesitate to pull it up and throw it out. Gardening great Vita Sackville-West said that a good gardener has to be brutal, and I agree.

Speaking of neatness, one of my own worst faults as a gardener is taking too much pity on volunteers, often leaving them in. Rampant self-seeders or spreaders can clutter up a garden, making it difficult to see and appreciate the other plants. Give the extra plants to other gardeners or compost them, but don't let them get out of control. Of course, this is easy to say if you're talking about lemon balm or feverfew, but what if you're talking about *Nicotiana langsdorffii*, or a pale pink nigella, or a perfectly good spotted joe-pye weed? These are harder to yank out. Sometimes moving them is a good solution. Whatever you do, you be the one who decides what goes where, taking advantage of interesting random effects, but removing plants that are out of place. Even if you decide to have a "wild" area of self-seeding flowers, including natives, be sure you're the one to decide where it goes.

Limiting the number of varieties of plants in your garden can also greatly help its appearance. Jettison plants of marginal interest or robustness, and concentrate on plants that do well for you. Impressive stands of a few well-grown plants look so much better than a scraggly mess of different varieties.

And sometimes I steel myself and get rid of what I call a "Dr. Fell plant." Dr. Fell was the unfortunate subject of the old nursery rhyme:

> *I do not love thee, Dr. Fell,*
> *The reason why I cannot tell;*
> *But this alone I know full well,*
> *I do not love thee, Dr. Fell.*

Some plants are like Dr. Fell—they leave you cold. You've moved them, you've pruned them, you've made up special fertilizer formulae and fed them—and you still don't like them. My advice is to dig the plant up and then ask a neighbor if they would like it. You will never be happy with a Dr. Fell plant. Of course if you're unlucky, the neighbor will plunk the plant into a simply brilliant planting scheme, and you'll suddenly realize the plant isn't a Dr. Fell at all—it's a Paul Newman. Such are the vagaries.

MARKING PLANTS

Becoming a good gardener seems to be an unavoidably long process. We begin by knowing nothing; then for a while, we seem to know a lot; and then the torturous process of shedding misinformation and gaining true knowledge begins. For instance, I have always known that labeling plants in the garden is a good idea, but only time has taught me just how important labels are. I used to rely on my memory quite a bit to remember what plant was where, but my memory has proven shockingly unreliable. But the value of labels goes beyond their usefulness to those of us with poor memories. I have noticed the satisfaction of visitors when they spy the marker of a plant—its presence seems almost more significant than the plant itself. "Ah! *Dianella tasmanica!*" they exclaim with delight, and the plant suddenly assumes a consequence that it wouldn't have, naked and unlabelled. Somehow the plant isn't quite *there* without a marker. Markers are especially important for perennials such as hostas and daylilies that come in many different varieties and have fanciful names. Markers are even more important for plants that emerge late in the spring, like butterfly weed. In that case, it's not a matter of knowing the name so much as remembering there's anything in the spot at all!

I have tried a variety of plant markers and have yet to find one type that is truly satisfactory, though I do keep a supply on hand of what look like large, wooden tongue depressors, purchased at a local nursery. Stuck deep into the ground, they quickly weather to an inconspicuous gray and last for several years. I've also been lucky at garage and rummage sales and have found a variety of nice metal markers, often packaged with their own indelible pens. E-bay, on the Internet, includes a Labels and Markers section under the Plant category, and I have gotten copper plant markers there. For seed starting, strips of foam polystyrene cut from meat trays and incised with a ballpoint pen work well but quickly look tatty in the garden. I even cut out cedar markers on my scroll saw and painted the plant's name and picture on the marker. These cre-

ated a sensation with passersby—again, far more of a sensation then the plants themselves. Where had I gotten them? What were they made of? Alas, even a cedar marker lasts only a bit more than one season out in the Midwestern elements. Quaint, prelabeled terra cotta markers for herbs and vegetables pop up at local nurseries but would seem to have little value since they only come in varieties that everyone already knows. We don't really need a label for dill and carrots—it's the salsify that leaves you wondering. For a wide variety of inexpensive labels, take a look at the Mellinger's catalog—they sell plastic, wood, aluminum, and stainless steel markers and even offer their own brand of fine-tip, indelible marking pen, advertised as water and fade resistant.

Meanwhile, I am lusting for the plant markers available from Alitags, a British firm (www.alitags.com). They sell heavy-duty blank copper labels plus "Character Punches and Jig" to engrave your very own labels. Perhaps this is carrying labeling too far, but when you think of the plants that have gotten lost in the hurly-burly—I hate to say "chaos"—of the garden, perhaps it's not.

A handsome container overflows with cottage garden flowers.

Container gardening

Reading a magazine article or book extolling the joys of container gardening, I am sometimes swept up in the enthusiasm and fantasize about all sorts of cute planting schemes using everything from coal scuttles and old boots to empty olive oil cans and derelict kitchen chairs as planters. In my imagination, pansies, cozily nestled in moist potting soil, peek over boot flaps, fresh green herbs spring from olive oil cans, and coal scuttles and chairs overflow with colorful annuals. Veritable waterfalls of asparagus ferns gush over the rims of Italian terra cotta pots, along with foaming billows of petunias. Then my imagination flies to England and Ireland and to thoughts of little whitewashed cottages adorned with fluffy clouds of impatiens, rainfalls of fuchsias, torrents of geraniums, and tidal waves of lobelia. But then (if I may continue in a pluvial vein), a rain cloud appears in this sunny, imaginary world. Then the rain cloud, smirking, scuds away, and the sun appears, shining mercilessly as the temperature climbs. I hear the faint whine of squadrons of mosquitoes. I have come back to earth, to that portion of it known as the American Midwest, where a pot of lobelia can shrivel to a leafless stick in a single day of heat and drought. I think of past torrid summers when watering a window box three times a day was barely enough to keep the petunias from wilting, and most of all I think of the two little problems Midwesterners face regarding container gardening, two little problems called July and August. Our sizzling summer heat can make container gardening a formidable challenge.

A window box planted with parsley, annual sage, and white geraniums.

Containers

If you are new to container gardening, start with only a couple of pots or a single window box so you can get some idea of how much work is involved. Use large pots, at least 14 inches across, not little quart or even gallon sizes. A small pot has a lot of surface in relation to the interior of the pot and dries out quickly. A large pot has much less surface in relation to the interior and dries out more slowly. (There is probably a mathematical equation that explains this precisely, but I'll be darned if I know what it is.) So the bigger the pot, the more slowly it dries out.

Large pots are heavy, so consider trying some of the new fiberglass pots that look remarkably like stone or terra cotta. Normally I'm a stern purist regarding garden ornament, and I like to use natural substances, but these pots are wonderful. Enormous fiberglass "granite" urns and Italian renaissance "terra cotta" pots can be lifted easily in one hand.

What about the classic terra cotta pot? I love the warm look of terra cotta, whose color is the opposite of dark green on the color wheel, making it a vibrant accent in the garden. But terra cotta, whether cheap quality bought at the local discount store, or good quality imported from Italy, can crack if left outdoors in the winter, leaving us with the chore of hauling it indoors in the fall and then outdoors again in the spring, and this can be heavy work. My sister has mentioned that what really causes terra cotta pots to crack is not cold, but water in the pots that freezes and thaws, thus expanding and contracting and causing cracks. Wrapping the pot in plastic and tying it snugly keeps water out and forestalls breakage.

Soil in plastic pots dries out more slowly than in clay. Plastic pots are light, and they don't break easily, so from a practical standpoint they must be considered for the Midwestern garden. I have found that the best source for interesting plastic pots is usually at neighborhood garage sales. Look for interesting "vintage" pots stacked forgotten in a corner, sometimes coming complete with soil and dead plants. Just last week I bought a large brown plastic pot with a surface molded to look like woven fibers. It has a fifties feel that is good looking and fun. That pot, plus several large self-watering pots, cost a quarter.

If you do use small pots, group them to make watering easier, and place them close to the water source. Even better, have them positioned so that they can be watered by a sprinkler when you are watering the rest of the garden. I don't advise putting any pot, large or small, all by itself in a spot that requires a special trip to hand water, because as the summer progresses, your spirit may be willing, but the rest of you might feel it's just too hot to trudge to that plant with a watering can. I also like to nestle pots right in among the foliage of garden plantings, wherever there is a bare spot that needs color. This is a great way to bring flowers to a spot of poor, hard soil where you don't want to dig.

You might also bring out a tropical-looking houseplant to nestle in the foliage for a dramatic accent. Surrounded with foliage these pots dry out very slowly and sometimes never have to be watered at all. This is a great way to have foxgloves in your garden, if you don't mind a little expense. Purchase young foxglove plants, pot them up, and tuck them into a shady nook.

My sister-in-law Leah gave me a great tip for planting containers—crumple up some empty plastic six-packs that annuals came in, and place them upside down in the bottom of the container you are planting. The six-packs take up space so that you don't have to use up lots of soil, and the finished container is lighter. Since many annuals don't have very deep roots, this really works. I also sometimes place an upended plastic quart-size pot at the bottom of the larger pot, which accomplishes the same thing.

Just this spring I installed two self-watering window boxes, and so far they have worked well, keeping soil consistently moist. They have water reservoirs and a tube at one end of the box where the water is poured. Some pots contain capillary mats that wick water up to plants. I've also seen a "Plant Sitter," which is a reservoir tank that hooks onto the side of a pot and that uses a sensor inserted into the soil to deliver water when needed. So if you like the look of pots, but don't like the frequent hot-weather watering, these pots and tanks could be a big help.

The strawberry jar, which is a columnar terra cotta pot with holes in the sides for planting strawberries, gets my nomination for the Midwestern Planter from Hell. Use it for decoration, but don't seriously expect to grow real plants in it without watering five times a day. Several years ago in an Iowa art museum, I saw a little flower sculpture, a creation of the Iowa artist Grant Wood. He had filled a flowerpot with cement and, using twisted colored wires and painted knobs, had created a fantasy plant. So if you have a strawberry jar, perhaps you could try something like that.

What to Plant in a Container

There are many books on container planting—just make a beeline to your local library or bookstore and dive in. These books are loaded with planting schemes, some of which are totally impractical in our hot summers, but some of which would work well.

Consider using perennials as potted plants. At the local plant nursery where I worked for several summers, they overwintered many of their perennials in pots outdoors. Hostas, heucheras, catmints, sedums, and grasses survived the winter and sprouted again the next spring in their pots. So a dramatic specimen hosta can look quite beautiful in a large pot or urn and doesn't have to be moved inside in the fall or dug up. Try a blue hosta with white impatiens and vinca that you've rooted in water from your own garden. I've also seen gaura used as a spectacular pot plant that can survive extreme heat and drought, and long-blooming dicentras such as *Dicentra eximia* 'Stuart Boothman' can brighten a shady corner.

Grasses grown in containers can be spectacular, and their natural drought resistance makes container growing relatively easy. And invasive grasses like ribbon grass (*Phalaris*) grow well in pots, which keep their roots under control. Containers have a dwarfing effect on grasses, so even quite tall grasses, such as maiden grass (*Miscanthus*), may be potted up. A big container of silky M. 'Morning Light' or a blue fescue in an urn is a dramatic sight. Though I haven't tried it, apparently containers of annual grasses like *Pennisetum setaceum* 'Rubrum' can be overwintered in a cool basement or garage. This is worth trying, as this particular grass is especially beautiful, and buying it anew every spring is costly. In its pot, you could place it near some violet cleome for an easy, drought-resistant planting.

Investigate succulents for pot plantings. Pots filled with hen-and-chickens (*Sempervivum tectorum*) in a variety of colors were featured recently in a lifestyle magazine, and they looked quite chic. Fill the pots with a gravelly cactus mix for good drainage. The large sedums such as 'Autumn Joy' and 'Matrona' can look quite dramatic erupting from a large urn.

So-called houseplants can also come to the rescue. One of my favorites is *Plectranthus*, a diverse genus related to coleus. "Cuban oregano" with its herb-scented leaves is a plectranthus; I have several yellow and green varieties. There is a furry, silver plectranthus called *P. argentus* that is especially striking. And this summer I grew *Plectranthus* 'Nico' and was bowled over. The glossy, incised leaves are green on top and burgundy on the reverse. Sprays of little pale lavender flowers appear as the summer progresses. It is tremendously drought resistant and grew well for me in a shade planter with white impatiens and a yellow coleus. The other big plus for plectranthus is that it can be brought inside and will thrive over winter. In spring, cuttings can be taken for use in outdoor planters. Cuttings root easily in water in about 10 days.

The tradescantia group of houseplants also adapts well to outdoor containers. I have silver and green striped ones, green and purple, and an indigo blue tradescantia. These are incredibly resistant to heat and drought. I found my first tradescantia as a fragment lying on the ground at the Madison, Wisconsin, farmer's market on a day of blast-furnace heat. It had broken off someone's purchase and had lain there until I picked it up. There's something almost abnormal about tradescantia's survival capacities, but abnormal or not, let's take advantage of it. These houseplant tradescantias are related to, but not the same as, the perennial garden tradescantias.

Then there is always portulaca, the moss rose, for really ovenlike conditions. I have a south-facing window box, and nothing else will survive there cheerfully but the moss rose. Moss roses used to be pretty pedestrian, but hybridizers have come up with some pretty new varieties, and they can take punishing heat. Also for heat, consider a planter of lavender, which is highly drought resistant and which could be a knockout in a sunny spot.

One of my favorite annuals for container planting is bidens (*Bidens cernua*). Its little golden, daisylike flowers on long, lax stems make it a perfect hanging basket plant, and making it even more perfect is its tremendous heat and drought resistance. Container gardening also lends itself to the making of a little kitchen garden. A useful crew of kitchen herbs such as rosemary and basil will flourish right to the bitter end of fall.

For an easy and drought-resistant planting, geraniums with licorice plant (helichrysum) is always correct. Or use pots of just one color of geranium all through the garden to pull it all together.

If you have an established garden, self-seeded plants that would otherwise be tossed onto the compost heap can be used for pretty planters. I just looked out my window on this rainy April day and saw self-seeded oxeye daisies, black-eyed Susans, tiger lilies, golden feverfew, white valerian, and plenty of English ivy, lamium, and vinca. These could be used in planters with a lavish hand, and the flowering plants can be featured front-and-center when in bloom. Just seeing the tiger lily seedlings gives me the idea of potting up a crew of them in a wicker basket. People will think you spent a million dollars!

During a recent walk at Cantigny Gardens in Wheaton, Illinois, I was impressed by their beautiful containers, which were imaginatively planted. I noted one easy idea that we could all steal: the ground cover yellow archangel (*Lamiastrum galeobdolon*) was used to trail from the pots. If you have this vigorous ground cover at all, you probably have a lot of it, and it would be easy to root some cuttings in the spring for an inexpensive and striking container accent plant. Vinca and *Lysmachia nummularia* 'Aurea' could also be rooted and used this way.

Spring calls for special baskets of fleeting beauty. Try miniature daffodils, violas, primroses, and ivy. Or pair butter yellow primroses with purple violas in a little wicker basket. The smaller bulbs are not difficult to force. Buy at a garden center as early as they are available, pot up in moist potting soil, water, and set in a warm, brightly lit spot. They'll be up before you know it. Grape hyacinths in a pot also look pretty. And primroses are available so inexpensively in early spring that you can buy a bunch. Cool-weather-loving calendulas, also called "pot marigolds," are traditional cottage garden annuals that look great in a terra cotta pot. These may be purchased in early April at local garden centers, or they are easy to raise under fluorescent tubes.

It has just occurred to me that if you are plagued with ground ivy (*Glecoma hederacea*), perhaps its formidable energies could be pressed into service in a basket. I'm going to try this with a rex begonia this year, for a shady spot.

How about potting up a lemon tree? We've had a Meyers lemon potted up now for years. Out it goes in early summer, and in it comes when fall arrives. The flowers smell wonderful, and every year we get a surprising number of thin-skinned, juicy lemons.

If you feel dazed by all the possibilities, remember that using just one variety of plant in a planter has its own merits. A big pot of self-seeded oxeye daisies, or of single-color annual salvia, or red lettuce allowed to bolt, or heliotrope (*Heliotropium arborescens*), or one big red cabbage, or . . . anything, really.

Of course for the ultimate in easy container plantings, try a beautiful container filled with nothing! If you have something really big and beautiful, you may not need to put anything in it, and think of how it would save on the water bills!

Whatever you plant, remember that cottage gardens are casual and unpretentious, and sometimes all you really need is a pot of pansies by the back door or a big pot of gaily colored geraniums by the front walk—something pretty, cheerful, and easy on you, the gardener.

Planting Mix

Use a premium planting mix for your containers, not soil from your garden, as our hard clay soil is the worse thing I can imagine for a container. Once your container is planted, consider spreading pea gravel or coarse sand over the exposed soil. I have tried this and it really seems to help moisture retention. I got this idea from a wonderful book called *Native Gardens in Miniature: Australian Plants in Containers.* Parts of Australia are literally desert, and it looks like Australians have become the world experts at hot-weather container gardening. They use their own native drought-resistant plants—a fascinating and entirely different palette from ours—and use "topping" sands and gravels as mulch to preserve both moisture and coolness in a pot. By corresponding on the Australian forum of Gardenweb.com, I've found that nowhere in Australia does it get as cold as it does here. I have received heartfelt condolences from Australians hearing of our weather conditions. This constant warmth means that they can install groups of container plantings for year-round growth and that they sometimes install trickle-watering systems into the pots.

Watering and Fertilizing

How do you know when to water? Stick your entire index finger down into the soil—if the soil is dry all the way down, the pot needs watering. If there's moisture, you can wait at least a day.

Container plantings do need fertilizing, as there is a finite amount of soil in the container for the plants to draw on as the weeks go by. While normally I eschew chemical fertilizers, there is nothing particularly natural about container plantings, and I find that an all-purpose 15-30-15 "plant food" fertilizer works.

I have come up with a watering and light-fertilizing scheme that perhaps borders on the eccentric, but it works for me, so I will tell you about it. I place a five-gallon plastic pail beneath a faucet in my backyard. I measure two tablespoons of the dry "plant food" into the bucket and then add two gallons of water and stir to make a basic, liquid fertilizer mixture. I have at hand a two-cup measuring cup. When ready to water, I scoop up two cups of the liquid fertilizer mixture and pour it into a recycled plastic, one-gallon detergent container. Then I fill up the rest of the container with water from the faucet. Then I start to water, pouring around the edge of the planter first, and then down amid the plants. The plants themselves stay dry and are lightly fertilized, and

the process is quick. Just be gentle when you water, or the stream of water could dislodge soil. By August, I stop fertilizing and just water.

When you water your containers, be sure that all the soil is moistened, even way down to the bottom and at the sides. A well-watered large container can stay quite moist this way for days, even during severe heat. If just the surface is watered, the plant is weakened by the heat and repeated drying out.

The bottom line is that we Midwesterners have to think outside the box—the window box containing lobelia and dianthus, that is—and rethink our native resources to create imaginative container plantings.

Self-seeded bachelor buttons (*Centaurea cyanus*) bloom in my friend Susan's cottage garden.

The force that through the green fuse drives the flower
Drives my green age; that blasts the roots of trees
is my destroyer.
And I am dumb to tell the crooked rose
My youth is bent by the same wintry fever . . .
　　　　　　　　　　—Dylan Thomas

One of the hallmarks of a cottage garden is its overflowing abundance of plants—every nook and cranny is sprouting something. Spare and Zen-like it's not. And you've probably heard the following garden design advice before: plant in generous drifts-, always using odd numbers of plants. Start with at least three plants, but five or seven or nine is even better because masses of plants have stronger visual impact than single specimens spotted here and there. James van Sweden and Wolfgang Oehme, two of the preeminent garden designers of our time, sometimes use *hundreds* of a particular plant for rich effect in their planting schemes.

But if you're on a budget, don't own a greenhouse, and are possessed of only a normal amount of physical and mental energy, reading this may make you cringe because you probably already know it. But plants can be expensive, so you're in a bind. I visited a large discount garden center today, where the absolute cheapest gallon perennial was $4.95. Multiply that by nine, and you're spending real money—and what if the plants aren't happy and die? You're left with two large holes: one in the garden, and one in your wallet.

Propagating
plants for your garden

There's a solution to this gap between modest resources and the realities of commercial plant expense, and that is to learn some simple techniques of plant propagation so that your gardening life can be more about gardening and less about driving to the nursery and handing over your credit card. Harness the awesome life force of green, growing things—"The force that through the green fuse drives the flower"—and your trips to the nursery will be fewer but a lot more fun. Just today I set out 11 plants of a lavender columbine, *Aquilegia vulgaris* 'Clematiflora'. If I could even find this plant locally, which I can't, I certainly couldn't afford 11 of them. But I got seeds through a seed exchange, planted them, and ended up with 13 wonderful plants. (I gave two away.) And since columbines tend to be short lived, even if these plants vanish in a few years I'll have meanwhile collected more seed for more plants and will have lost no money at all.

There are at least three straightforward ways that a gardener, even a beginning gardener, can propagate plants: by starting seeds, by rooting plant cuttings, and by dividing perennials. We'll look at these methods in the coming pages.

But let's be honest: building up a bountiful crowd of plants takes a bit of time. Few perennials bloom from seed the first year, and most perennials have to grow for at least two or three years before you can take slips or divide them. If you're in a hurry for a full-looking garden and you have sun, look to quick-growing annuals that are easy to direct-seed into the garden: zinnias, four-o'clocks, sunflowers, cleome, cosmos, and tithonia. With shade, the task is harder, but you can start with some hosta, which multiply like rabbits, and fill in with flats of impatiens. Nothing original here, but it gets you going.

As well as learning to propagate your own plants, learn to take advantage of invasive plants. "Invasive" is definitely a pejorative term, but for the cottage gardener, plants that spread and multiply rapidly, either by underground runners, quick formation of new crowns, or by self-seeding, can be extraordinarily useful as long as you know what you're getting into. One could say that the fuel that powers a cottage garden is invasiveness. This is how we get exuberant drifts, munificent mounds, and showy shoals of plants, even in poor soil. And I prefer to call such plants "enthusiastic" rather than "invasive." Some gardeners loathe invasive plants because in a carefully designed garden they can run amok and upset plans. In the slightly untidy abundance of a cottage garden, though, harnessing the power of an enthusiastic plant can be your route to a full and beautiful garden.

But beware! There are invasive plants, and then there are INVASIVE, MARAUDING, BRAIN-SUCKING PLANTS that I strongly advise against bringing in to the garden. Extremely invasive plants such as wormwood (*Artemisia absinthium*), comfrey, garlic chives, common milkweed, buttercups, and *Campanula rapunculoides* are unstoppable spreaders, and you would quickly regret letting them through your front door.

Starting Seeds

Growing plants from seed would seem the most obvious route to having a wide variety of inexpensive plants for your garden. And this is true . . . to a point. For the dollar or so it costs for a packet of sunflower seeds you can have your own grove of these glorious flowers. And for another dollar, a cascading waterfall of nasturtiums.

Many seeds, though, have exacting requirements for germination. They may need to be chilled or notched before planting to recreate the germinating environment of the parent plant's natural habitat. Or sometimes the seed must be fresh to germinate. These stipulations reflect the fact that the seeds offered so conveniently between the covers of a garden catalog pour into our waiting hands from all corners of the Earth. A flower may have come originally from the Himalayas, or from South Africa, or from Mexico. It may have been discovered blooming on a misty mountainside in China, or on the shores of the Mediterranean. Different climates require different germinating conditions, and the gardener needs to research the specific needs of each plant. Not doing this research can lead to seed-sprouting failures.

There is also the problem of where to germinate those seeds needing heat. Unless you have a south- or west-facing window, porch, or sunroom that receives bright sunlight, you almost have to use artificial light to have healthy, stocky plants ready for the garden by May. The weak, rather listless light of the Midwestern March is barely enough to power up a little row of tomato plants on the windowsill, much less enough plants for a whole garden. A warm, sunny March might help, but our Marches often aren't sunny. And plants grown without enough sun become pale and spindly from their struggle for light. Seedlings can also be buffeted by cold drafts whistling through cracks in uninsulated windows. When it comes time to plant, these frail seedlings will be vulnerable to insects and disease and can be easily knocked over by wind or rain or shriveled by an early heat wave. They also make an especially toothsome treat for rabbits. So artificial light is almost a necessity if you are going to start more than a packet or two of seeds.

The flip side of all this is that many seeds are incredibly easy to germinate and raise. I started some seeds for the perennial *Verbascum phoeniceum* this spring, just to try something new. The seed packet predicted a germination time of 14 to 21 days. My seeds germinated in five days and are doing great. And seeds for *Malva sylvestris*, planted last Friday, are up today, Monday. Some seed companies, such as the venerable Thompson & Morgan, label easy-to-grow varieties as such on the seed packet. The malva I just mentioned was labeled with a banner claiming "Easy to Grow" on the packet. Another malva variety I'm trying is labeled "Very Easy to Grow," and I am really looking forward to that one. I know of one gardener who routinely grows delphinium from seed every spring. The seeds pop up quickly (they do have to be prechilled), and since the plants themselves don't always make it through the winter, it's an inexpensive way to have this flower every summer.

One gardener I know who starts a *lot* of seeds every spring swears by Shepherd's Garden Seeds as being the best quality. And a plant propagator at a local nursery likes herb seed from Richters, a firm in Canada that sells by mail order here in the United States. My own favorite companies include Underwood Gardens, Select Seeds Antique Flowers, and Thompson & Morgan.

Since I have very limited space by my windows (I have an old house with narrow windows) and I'm in direct competition with a cat for this space (and guess who usually wins), I don't start a lot of seeds requiring heat for germination, limiting myself to some unusual zinnias, hot peppers, and an irresistible heirloom tomato or two. I've been leaning more and more toward starting seeds that can be started outside in the cold, and we'll look into that in the next section. But first, let's take a look at seed starting indoors.

SEED STARTING INDOORS

If you are new to seed starting, start small, with just two or three varieties. If you enjoy it, next year you can purchase a light fixture and try more.

Always read the information on the seed packet carefully. It will tell you when to plant and how to plant. Some packets even have a picture of the seedling so that you'll know what to look for when the seed germinates.

MEDIA FOR SEED STARTING

I recommend purchasing a commercial seed-starting mix. I like Jiffy Mix, which is a soil-less mixture. It's light, soft, and fluffy, which makes growing easy for seedling roots. Soil from the garden, especially from our Midwestern gardens, is much too firm and contains soil pathogens. A dense soil can actually impede delicate sprouts trying to emerge from the seed case. While supposedly you can sterilize garden soil by heating it in an oven, the soil still has to be amended with vermiculite to lighten the texture. All in all, I stick with the commercial mix. It's easy to use and usually can be purchased on sale early

in the spring. There are other seed-starting media to investigate, but be sure they are labeled as such, as even commercial potting soil is too heavy.

Several successful gardeners I know make their own mix with equal parts peat moss and vermiculite, and some gardeners add coarse sand to their starting mixes. It really depends on what you're germinating, and that's where a little research can be valuable.

RECYCLED CONTAINERS

Containers to use for starting seeds indoors are everywhere. I've had good success using cardboard tubes from kitchen paper towels and toilet paper. I cut them in half across and jam them together into a small empty flat left over from the previous year. I fill the rolls right to the top with moistened seed-starting mix, and the flat is ready to be seeded. Start collecting the cardboard rolls early, because you need more than you might think to fill a whole flat.

Make a beeline to your recycling bin for other container candidates. Plastic yogurt cups, both eight- and six-ounce, are fine for starting small quantities of seeds. My own favorites include quart-size cottage cheese containers and rectangular foam polystyrene mushroom containers. Whatever type of recycled container you use, be sure to poke holes in the bottom for drainage and water uptake. I like to place these small seeded containers on recycled foam polystyrene trays. For larger quantities of seed, for instance if you want a bunch of one type of impatiens, use a plastic flat—it makes handling easy. Avoid using a jumble of different size containers as it's easy to under- or over-water them.

Compressed peat pellets that are reconstituted by soaking in water work pretty well but only for large seeds, such as for four-o'clocks or sweet peas.

For the actual seed planting, again consult the seed package. Some small seed should be scattered on top of the soil and kept moist. This type of seed needs light to germinate. Speaking of seed size, the larger the seed, the more likely you should plant the seed directly out in the garden. For instance, sunflower seeds do much better when directly sown and may languish if started indoors. When direct seeding, keep in mind this little verse:

One for the rook,
One for the crow,
One to die,
And one to grow.

I like to seed most small seed as thinly as possible. I would rather have seed left over than be faced with a tedious thinning process once the seeds have germinated.

WATER FROM THE BOTTOM

The starting medium must be thoroughly watered once you've finished seeding, even though it's been premoistened. I put my flat or containers into an old jelly roll pan and add water to the pan so that water can be drawn up into the pots. This is a gentle and even way to water, so the seeds near or at the soil surface aren't sloshed around and disturbed. Some people run an inch or less of water into their bathtub and place the flats into the bathtub, letting the water wick up into the soil from the bottom. Or you could use an old plastic kitty-litter pan. If the surface of the medium still seems dry, mist with tepid water from a spray bottle. Whatever you do, don't deluge the seeds or later, the seedlings, with water gushing from a watering can. This can splash small seeds right out of the container and can damage delicate seedlings. And this is where you could get into real trouble if you haven't premoistened the medium, as dry medium will repel water.

MAKE YOUR OWN GREENHOUSE

At this point, if you are starting seeds indoors, you will need to put the flat or containers on their polystyrene trays into a large plastic bag, such as a grocery bag. Make sure the bag isn't drooping on the surface of the flats or containers. Tie the open end loosely with string, and your greenhouse is ready!

One of the best places to germinate seeds, especially for warm-weather crops like tomatoes and marigolds, is on the top of a refrigerator. The low, even heat is perfect for the germination process. It's not necessary at this point to put the seeded flats or containers by the window or under a light. And as long as the flats are within the moist environment of the bag, they probably won't need further watering—but peek in every now and then to be sure. The flats can be misted with plain water from an old Windex bottle, if need be.

Most seed packets indicate the best temperature for germination. If you're a beginner and growing something straightforward, such as tomatoes, a room temperature of 70 degrees or more will work fine, and many other seeds germinate well at normal room temperatures (60° F to 70° F).

As you venture into more exotic territory, though, pay close attention to the recommended germination temperature. Many perennials and hardy annuals actually need chilling, not warmth, to germinate. Flats of these seeds need to be placed outside.

USING LIGHT

Once the seeds germinate, remove the flats or containers from their plastic coverings and place them by a window to get some natural light. Do this even if you know that all the seeds haven't germinated. Give thought to which window you use. Afternoon sun pouring through a south window might actually be too hot. I have found that a bench set by a west window works quite well, as the afternoon sunlight is bright but not broiling. I rarely ever put seedlings actually on a windowsill, as it can get cold and drafty at night and hot during the day. If you choose to use a windowsill for a small group of seedlings, be prepared to move the seedlings to a warmer spot on cold nights.

If you use artificial light, it's not necessary to purchase special "grow lights." Fluorescent tubes, sometimes called shop lights, work fine. You'll need a fixture with two 48-inch tubes, which should be 40-watt cool-white fluorescent. The fixture can be suspended on chains above your table of seedlings, about two inches above the seedlings. This floods them with light, and they grow up stocky, not spindly. If your light is stationary and can't be lowered, find some way to raise the seedlings, even if it's just using old telephone books. You'll also need to purchase an inexpensive timer. Keep your lights on for 18 hours, off for six.

SPINDLINESS

Plants grown indoors by natural springtime light and those grown with intense fluorescent light will be of different quality. Natural-light plants usually are going to be more spindly. This isn't necessarily a disaster, but you will have to take extra special care when hardening them off, something we'll be talking about in a moment. A seedling that's very spindly can sometimes be transplanted more deeply into the soil, burying some of the thin stem underground as well as the roots. This is routinely done with spindly tomato seedlings, and it works with many perennials, as well. Roots will grow from the buried stem, resulting in a stockier plant. I haven't tried this with annual seedlings, and I can't promise it will work with all perennials, but it's worth the try if you're faced with a flat of seriously spindly seedlings. (Sounds like a new syndrome! SSS, Seriously Spindly Seedlings. How awful.)

The first leaves of a germinating seed are called the *seed leaves*. The second set of leaves will be distinctive to that plant type. By the time these leaves appear, you are ready to thin out your seedlings.

THINNING

At this point you can snip off any extra seedlings at the soil surface with a pair of manicure scissors. Or you can transplant the extra seedlings into other pots, if you want. If two seedlings are growing right next to each other, though, I snip one off. Pulling one out can disturb the roots of the other. You might wonder why you don't just plant one seed per pot in the first place instead of sowing *en masse*. The answer is that very few seeds have a 100 percent germination rate. So you could start out with a tremendous number of pots, each containing one seed, and then find that not all the seeds germinated.

Also, seeds can be strangely "social" little things, and some seeds won't germinate if sown all alone in a big pot. How they know they're alone, or among good seed friends, is a very good question.

Some seeds can be sown in clusters and left unthinned. Chives, marjoram, and thyme can be sown thinly in four-inch clay pots and will grow up into nice clumps that go directly out into the garden. I learned this from *Herb Gardening at Its Best*, by Sal Gilbertie. Alyssum can also be started in clumps.

Experience may show you, though, that you can often seed just two or three seeds into, say, a three-inch pot, thin, and transplant right out into the garden. I find that tomatoes, for instance, work well seeded directly into the cardboard tubes. Most seeds, though, are best seeded into a flat, germinated, and then moved to larger pots: this stepwise process "builds the roots."

Professional greenhouse growers, of course, germinate lots of seeds. Seedlings sprouted in long flats are dumped out quite unceremoniously onto a big table. The soil and seedlings fall apart into clumps, and the seedlings are deftly transplanted into their cell packs or subdivided flats for "growing on" and later planting in quart or gallon containers. In the moist, warm air of a greenhouse, the seedlings suffer little damage.

WHAT IF THE SEED DOESN'T GERMINATE?

Take another look at your seed packet. Have you given the seeds the conditions they need? I have found that the seeds of heat-loving annuals, herbs such as basil, and tomato, pepper, and eggplant seeds, especially, need strong, steady warmth. If seeds of those plants haven't germinated in about a week, see if you can't move them to a warmer spot. And some seeds simply take a while to germinate. I started some hosta seeds last year that took six weeks to germinate.

TRANSPLANTING

Seedlings are ready to be transplanted, or "potted up" into their own pot, when they have three true leaves, and once seedlings are at this point, don't delay transplanting. It can take only a few days to go from being ready for transplanting to being crowded and sickly. Transplanting the seedlings is a delicate operation: the less you tug, pull, or otherwise manhandle the seedling, the better. Don't grasp the seedling by its stem—only very lightly by its leaves. The seedling can lose a leaf and still survive, but if its stem is damaged, its vascular system is crushed, and it will die.

A wooden craft stick can be used to gently lever the seedling up out of its soil. I like to transplant the seedlings to plastic four- or six-packs I've saved over the years.

FERTILIZING SEEDLINGS

At this point, I begin watering the plants with water mixed with a tiny amount of fertilizer. A very weak mixture, looking like weak tea, of fish emulsion or seaweed extract, once a week, is all that's needed. One teaspoon of fish emulsion per gallon of water is a good dilution. If the tiny plants look dry any time during the rest of the week, use plain water.

HARDENING OFF

As they grow further and have recovered from being thinned or transplanted, the seedlings need to be introduced into the outside environment in stages to become acclimated or "hardened off." Hardening off is more of an art than a science. I bring the seedlings out just very briefly at first, just for an hour, and lengthen the time spent outside each day. If you were planning to bring the plants out, and it's very windy or cold and damp, wait until the weather improves. Don't put the plants in direct sun, initially, and watch for signs that the plants and their soil are drying out. There are usually some warm, windy days during Midwestern springs when delicate seedlings can become dried out and killed in a flash. The hardening process must take place because the tender seedling is just too delicate to face whole days and nights of wind and sun right away.

PLANTING TIME

May 15 is the average date of the last frost in Zone 5, and it's usually safe to set warm-weather plants such as tomatoes out by that date. Remember, though, that May 15 is the *average* date and is not carved into stone. The last frost could occur earlier, but I have seen a few frosty days in very late May. So if planting out by May 15, always be ready with newspaper or a blanket for your seedlings if frost strikes late. A rule of thumb is to plant out when dandelions are blooming in open fields. And an Illinois greenhouse grower told me he never plants our warm-weather plants such as peppers before May 20.

If you have a choice, transplant your seedlings into the garden on a cool, misty, overcast day. That's the ideal. This way, sun and wind can't speed up transpiration of water from the seedling leaves. The worst kind of day for planting out seedlings is warm and windy.

If you've used the cardboard tubes for germinating and growing on, the plants can be planted out, tube and all, or they can be popped out of their four- or six-packs. I use a pancake spatula to lift the cardboard tube and seedling out of the pan. The cardboard tubes are spiraled, so if you don't want to plant the seedling with the tube, just unwind the cardboard from around the soil and plant. The tube itself can be tossed into the compost heap.

RABBITS

At this point, a bunny might hop into your garden and eat all of your little plants. It could happen, and you will understand why gardeners can be a prematurely gray, philosophical lot. Rabbits seem to be attracted to new plantings of any kind. I have never heard that the usually recommended rabbit repellents such as sprinklings of cayenne pepper actually work—quite the contrary. In my experience, only physical barriers seem to work. Some gardeners take chicken wire and wire cutters and make little cages for new plantings. This is a bit of work, but the cages are reusable. Plastic pint-size strawberry baskets could help, but only for the smallest seedlings, and the baskets must be weighted down. Just last week I planted some seedling clumps of *Agastache* 'Aurea'. These rather unusual seeds had come from a seed exchange and had sprouted quickly in outdoor flats. I planted three clumps in the front garden, and overnight, two disappeared, munched down to the nub. Desperate, I took a clear, plastic takeout container and punched a hole in the bottom for air. I placed the container over the remaining clump and weighted it down with two stones. So far, the rabbits, who are apparently not

very clever with their "hands," have not overturned the bowl, and the seedlings are doing well. I have my fingers crossed.

Absent rabbit incursions, though, usually the seedlings will thrive, and there's a real sense of accomplishment as you watch the plants dig in and really start growing.

STARTING SEED—AN EPIPHANY

Okay, now I have a confession to make. Several years ago I had an epiphany regarding seed starting. This was after I'd been starting seeds for years, always growing a small selection of heirloom tomatoes, exotic hot peppers, and an unusual flower or two. I don't have space in my garden to delve as deeply into seed starting as some gardeners, but I liked the freedom of trying plants not offered at local nurseries. But as much as I loved the plants themselves, I found the germinating and growing-on process rather nerve-racking. I never seemed to have enough light or space, sometimes I started the seeds too early in the season, sometimes too late. There was damping-off, spindliness, feelings of worthlessness. All in all, I felt rather lugubrious about seed starting. Well, perhaps "lugubrious" is too strong a word, but I did wish I had a wonderful little glass greenhouse on the banks of the Thames, ranks of grow-lights, an infinite supply of tepid distilled water, that sort of thing. The year my heirloom French Peach tomato seedlings were knocked off the windowsill by my cat Blackie, in eager pursuit of a robin taunting him from the pear tree just outside the living room window, remains a dark memory. I did *read* a lot about seeds, however, and do remember reading somewhere of seeds that need cold, not heat, to break their dormancy. This information, like a hapless seed landing on concrete, failed to make an impression on me, other than it seemed a rather obscure process, something for advanced gardeners.

Meanwhile, I was struggling with larkspur. Every gardener has some simple thing they can't grow, though it thrives abundantly in gardens all around them, and for me it was larkspur. The moment I planted some purchased plants in my garden they clutched their hearts and keeled over; seeds planted directly in the garden, however early or late in the season, never bothered to appear at all. Seeds started indoors, however early or late, were weak and spindly, and so my larkspur efforts came up zero.

The turning point in this maelstrom of discontent with seed starting and larkspur came one day when I stumbled across a battered old wooden flat at a garage sale. I brought the flat home, envisioning it picturesquely planted with pansies by the back steps. But meanwhile, I was grimly facing the latest packet of larkspur seeds. It was a moment of truth. Since nothing else had worked, I decided to shelve the pansy idea and start the larkspur seeds outside in the wooden flat. I filled the flat with dampened seed-starting mix, sprinkled the seeds lightly over the surface, sprinkled on a dusting more of seed-starting mix, and gently misted the surface. I pressed the surface down lightly, just enough to smooth and compact it. I placed the flat outside at the back of our house, right up against the wall, and, whispering a prayer to St. Fiacre, backed away genuflecting and left it there. Please grow, I begged pathetically. *Please grow.*

This was in February, and as the days passed, the usual inimitable Midwestern weather raged. Snow, drizzle, heat spells, ice storms. Hail, fog, wind, solar flares. Every now and then I peered at the flat, and if it seemed dry, I lightly watered it. Then I forgot about it. It was late April before I took another look, and to my joy and astonishment I found a lush, feathery forest of healthy larkspur seedlings. I nearly fell over. The germination rate, if not 100 percent, was close to it. I was too busy to plant them out instantly, so I stowed the flat under the pear tree, where it looked delightfully pretty and old-fashioned—much better than picturesque pansies. I planted them out all over the garden a few days later, and there they thrived and continue to thrive, taking matters into their own hands by self-seeding. So now I have larkspur, and I had my epiphany, which I guess is a moment when we *really* understand something we only thought we understood. I realized that seeds needing cold to break their dormancy were easier for the home gardener, especially the lazy home gardener like myself, than seeds needing heat for germination. I've never looked back. Where before I studied the Thompson & Morgan catalog seeking "easy" seeds that germinated quickly indoors, now I look for plants whose seeds require cold to germinate. It doesn't really matter how long it takes for them to germinate, since late winter is so interminably long anyway. I just put the flats out and leave them to their own devices. It makes a gardener's life so much easier.

But what about tomatoes, you might ask. *What about tomatoes?* Okay, here is where I confess to a laziness so abysmal, it's quite shocking. I've been growing heirloom tomatoes in the garden for a dozen years, now, and every year they self-seed. I'm a little unclear about how and why they do this, since tomatoes seem to be heat lovers, and you'd think the winter cold would kill the seeds, but self-seed they do. The seedlings pop up all over the garden, and

here is where more evidence of my many gardening failings becomes clear: my compost is pretty good, but it's obviously not really good or it would heat up and kill any seeds in it, which it does not. At any rate, the seedlings come up, and every year I take potluck and replant some in the vegetable patch. It's mostly wild cherry tomato plants that come up, but sometimes it's Mrs. Benson's tomatoes or Eva's Purple Ball. If you are a control freak, this method of growing tomatoes would drive you mad, but I am perfectly satisfied to allow these healthy, stocky tomato plants to pop up all by themselves. I also grow tomatillos this way. These are a bit weedier, almost invasive, but considering how much I like salsa verde made with tomatillos, it's okay with me. So that's my tomato method, again, not for control freaks. It does not work with hybrid tomatoes, of course, which will only revert to their parent's type, and who knows what you'd get. But with heirloom tomatoes, it works fine.

Okay, but what about marigolds, you ask. And zinnias and nicotiana? I am lucky enough to live in an area where I'm surrounded on all sides by plant nurseries, where professionals do an excellent job of growing these plants and selling them at a reasonable price. Anyway, I had found that even when I started my own seeds, I still ended up falling to temptation and buying flats of annuals at these nurseries. Nurseries are becoming more sophisticated and attuned to gardeners' needs with each passing year, and I find that the assortment of plants keeps getting better. Part of the fun of spring is visiting these nurseries and finding treasures.

There is another category of easy seeds, ones that not only *should* be started outdoors after the last frost, but which might fail if started indoors. These include sunflowers, four-o'clocks, nasturtiums, borage—all sorts of large-seeded plants that need heat.

At this point you might wonder if I haul out the grow-lights and start any seeds indoors at all. Yes I do, because starting seeds in the dreary, low days of late winter is one of the great, satisfying rituals of gardening, and I would never miss it. The damp scent of the soil, the soft feel of it between your fingers—the very miraculousness of seeds themselves—are happy portents of the spring days to come. And that first tiny seedling that arches it head up through the soil to greet the light of day is one of the most thrilling sights of the gardener's year.

And there does remain a core of interesting plants that are not found at local nurseries whose seeds do need heat to germinate and that must be started in the warmth of indoors. This spring I'm starting some lime basil seeds and Kashmir hot pepper seeds, and they will need the cozy, moist warmth of the indoors.

A FEW GUIDELINES FOR OUTDOOR SEED STARTING

Germinating perennial and cold-hardy annual seeds outdoors couldn't be easier, but there are a few guidelines to keep in mind to ensure success. Most of the "work" involved in this method lies in choosing the correct seeds and in monitoring the flats, but there are some ins and outs to know about.

To find seeds that need cold to germinate, study seed catalogs or seed packets. Seeds that can be planted in late fall or early spring need cold and will work for this method. Seeds that can be planted outside only when the weather and soil are completely warm will not work. Zinnia or basil seed, for instance, will rot in the soil if planted too early (usually before May 15) and should be started indoors. If your seed comes from a seed exchange, you may have no instructions at all to go by. Perennial seed can usually be started outdoors, but some research in a good garden encyclopedia or on the Internet is worth the time.

For planting containers, I use the square, 11 x 11 inch plastic flats sold for seed starting as well as the 6 x 5 inch foam polystyrene containers that mushrooms are sold in at produce departments, and quart-size cottage cheese containers, are both suitable. Soil in smaller containers dries out too quickly.

February is a good month to ready the flats. December is busy, January cold, and February is early enough to let weather do its job germinating seeds. It depends, though. If late January is mild, you can set out the flats then. And if you are buried under a foot of snow, seeding will have to wait until the snow melts a bit.

When it comes time to seed the flats, be sure to fill the flat to the top with seed-starting mix and to gently pat it down with the flat of your hand. The mix will compact when it's rained on, and you don't want too thin of a layer or seedling roots will touch bottom and be damaged. If seed is very fine, like dust, mix with cornmeal or fine sand before broadcasting over the soil. It's easier to broadcast thinly that way, so there won't be seedling clumps. Try not to let any seeds land up against the side of the flat. Seedlings can get stuck to the side and will be damaged upon removal.

Once the flats are seeded, sprinkle them with very fine sand or vermiculite. This seems to stabilize the soil surface. Think carefully about where to place the flats. The north side of the house is usually recommended, so that

flats aren't dried out by winter sun. Place them way out of the way of downspouts so that they don't get blasted by torrents of water during rainstorms. Aim for at least four feet from a drainpipe. And covering the flats with wire screening can protect the flats from animals that like to dig in flats if given the opportunity. Even the wind can play havoc—a few weeks ago a wicker basket was blown off my back porch and sent rolling over the nearby flats. No harm was done, but it does show that they are vulnerable. Old storm windows can be propped up against the wall over the flats to help protect them, forming a simple cold frame.

In an ideal world, once you've placed the flats outside, it will snow. The soft snow blanket will chill the seeds and keep them moist. When spring comes, the snow melts, and the seeds will germinate as the days get longer and warmer. In a snowy winter, you can pretty much forget about the flats as they slumber beneath the snow, and in areas where there is reliable winter snow cover, seeded flats can be placed out in the fall.

In the real world, the one we live in, it may snow only intermittently, and weather conditions may fluctuate wildly. If there is no snow, patrol the flats at least twice a week, and water if they seem to be drying out. Frozen flats won't need to be watered, but if the temperature goes above freezing on a sunny day, the flats could dry out. Also check for interloper seeds, for instance, elm or maple seeds, that have landed in the flat and have germinated.

Different seeds take varying lengths of time to germinate, so don't panic if some flats seem dead as a doornail, while others are sprouting well. By mid-April, you should see some germination, depending on the seeds you're starting, but some seeds might not germinate until a month later or even in early summer—it all depends on the plant. This spring, a flat of antique perennial candytuft seeds had germinated by the first week of April. By mid-April, up came *Allium tanguticum*, and by April 30, the tiny seedlings of *Primula japonica* had appeared. So all seeds are not on the same timetable.

Be ready for seed germination. When seedlings first emerge, they sport a generic set of leaves called cotyledons or "seed leaves." The second set of leaves is characteristic of the grown plant, and when they appear, it's time to transplant them from the flat into little pots. This spring I tried five-ounce waxed Dixie cups as pots, and they have worked perfectly. I punched four or five holes into the bottom of each cup for drainage using a metal skewer. Then I filled each cup with potting soil (not garden soil—it gets too hard). I made a hole in the soil with my finger. Using a small pancake turner, I lifted up a block of soil with its seedlings and gently let it drop on the table. Then I pulled off a clump of soil with its seedling and planted it in the little pot. After firming the soil gently around the seedling, I placed the pot in a metal jelly roll pan. Proceed in this way until all the seedlings are potted. Bring the pan back outside and water gently with a shower of tepid water. In the coming days, water with a very dilute solution of fish emulsion to fuel the plants for their next stage of growth. Keep them in the shade at this point, but gradually move them out into dappled shade and then to sun if they are sun lovers, and watch like a hawk for signs of drying out.

The seedlings of very tiny, dustlike seeds may be scarcely larger than the head of a pin. I scoop blocks of them up with a teaspoon and repot. Some seedlings are usually lost this way, but don't feel bad. Mother Nature often wastes great quantity of seeds in the hope that one will germinate, and if we gardeners lose a few, it's just part of the process.

At this point, we come to a fork in the road. Some seedlings are slow growers and will be too small to place directly out in the garden. Place their flats in an out-of-the-way spot in the garden and leave them there, right through the next winter. During drought, water them along with the rest of the plants. By next spring they will be mature enough to plant. Some seedlings are fast growers, though, and mature quickly into useful plants by their first spring. These can be planted directly into the garden. This May, I have planted out some small echinops and variegated lunaria plants that were just started in February. Both germinated and grew quickly into stocky plants that will hold their own in the hurly-burly of the garden.

Not many perennials begun from seed will bloom the first year—you'll get young plants that will most likely bloom the next year and reach maturity the year after. This might seem too long to wait, but I have found that time passes quickly, and once you have been starting seeds with this method for a few years, plants will come steadily "on-line" to plant out in the garden every spring.

Some kinds of plants may not bloom for years after germination from seed and are usually best propagated by other methods. Lilies are an example. I received some martagon lily seeds from a seed exchange, only to discover that it might take them from five to eight years to bloom! Of course I planted them immediately.

This finally leads us to an odd pitfall of this method, which is that by late spring you may find yourself overwhelmed by your seed-starting success

and be faced with a sea of seedlings, all waiting to be pricked out and given their own little pot. It's a miracle, really, that what starts out in January looking like a handful of dust becomes dozens, possibly hundreds—even thousands—of seedlings, but it can be a rather alarming miracle for the gardener. Some seed companies indicate a seed count on the seed packet, and it's good to take note of it. If you think there's too much, share some with another gardener, or use only a portion of the seeds, storing the remainder in the refrigerator for next year.

What are other disadvantages of the outdoor approach? Digging animals can uproot seedlings, and hard rain can wash them right out of their pots. And pots can dry out in warm, windy weather, so you do have to keep an eye on them over a matter of months if weather is erratic. Building a cold frame could solve some of these problems, but if you have a small garden, you might not want to devote a spot to a permanent cold frame.

And there is one important advantage to outdoor germination to consider, which is that the seedlings are often very healthy, stocky, and extremely well rooted. The cleansing effect of fresh air and water deter fungal diseases that plague seedlings started indoors. Just this spring I planted out a lavender *Aquilegia clematiflora* that had overwintered. This is a wonderfully beautiful columbine, with petals like crumpled organdy. Because I had started my own seeds, I had thirteen plants, many more than I would have been able to afford from a nursery. When I popped the plants out of their pots, I found a solid webbing of fine roots all through the soil. They were not root-bound, just very well rooted. In the plants went, and they took off without a moment's hesitation or wobbliness.

What if some seeds don't germinate at all? Most seed from reputable seed companies should be fine, but there is always the possibility that the seed was not fresh. I have found that seeds obtained through seed exchanges are the most problematic. Perhaps the seed was gathered too early or too late or was poorly stored. Also, seeds do have variable requirements, and some have specific requirements that make them tough to germinate. Avid seed starters like to sink their teeth into these mysteries and strive to find the key to germination.

This spring I am trying 'Earl Grey' larkspur, as I am curious about their slate gray flower color. Some "easy" perennial seeds that I've had good luck with include alliums, cultivars of *Aqualegia vulgaris* and *A. canadensis*, asclepias, asters, feverfew, liatris, toadflax ('Reverend Bowring'), echinops, variegated lunaria, agastaches, rudbeckias, calamints, skullcaps, euportiums, and primroses. Agastaches are extraordinarily quick and easy to germinate this way, and this spring I started six different varieties, including A. 'Aurea', which has golden leaves, all obtained from a seed exchange. Easy hardy annuals include poppies, calendula, borage, nigella, cleome, balsam, candytuft, and *Nicotiana langsdorffii,* The perennial seedlings won't reach full size for at least two years, but the annuals will bloom the same summer.

Once planted in your garden, some of these plants may self-seed, so be forewarned. We'll see more about self-seeders in the next section. Many gardeners adore the ease of self-seeders, and I'm one of them, though be aware that they can sometimes be too much of a good thing. It depends on the plant.

For more information on starting cold-hardy perennial and annual seeds, visit the Gardenweb Web site (www.gardenweb.com) and go to the "Winter Sowing" forum.

Self-Seeding Plants

Maybe you have read in gardening books and magazines all about starting your own plants from seed. It's so much fun! say the writers. Feel the power! Maybe it is, you think to yourself—but it's too much work. Life is short. You like gardening, but sometimes your attention wanders to cooking, watching TV, having a life, etc. The thought of all those flats under lights down in the basement requiring your tender loving care in April fills you with foreboding. You remember a flatful of seemingly robust tomato seedlings a few springs ago that keeled over one day, looking as if they had been felled by an ax but were actually the victims of damping-off, a fungal disease. Then you glance out the window and notice the many plants, weeds especially, that have planted themselves and are doing just fine, without human intervention. A light bulb switches on: nature has been starting her own seeds for a long time, long before Burpee appeared. Many plants do self-seed, meaning that their seeds ripen, fall to the earth, and then germinate, either in the same season or next spring. Self-seeding plants (and I'm mainly talking about flowering annuals, perennials, and herbs here, though all kinds of plants, including trees, self-seed) are the ultimate in low-cost, low-work plants, and the smart gardener will consider harnessing their awesome productivity for his or her garden. They are one of the keys to having a lush cottage garden, filled to bursting with flowers.

What determines which plant is a self-seeder in a Midwestern garden? Plants that evolved in northern climates often will self-seed here, as they need our cold winters to break seed dormancy. Soil type can also determine whether a plant self-seeds. Moist, acid soil might discourage some seeds from germinating but encourage others. Or, the seeds from a plant evolved in the rainy forests of the Northwest might not get enough moisture in our climate to germinate spontaneously.

Plants that evolved in warm, southern climates, like Mexico, will often not self-seed here, though there are exceptions to this. The seed is not evolved to cope with our cold winters and may rot in the soil. Seeds from these plants can be collected at summer's end, however, and saved over the winter and planted the following spring. Seeds are ripe for collection when you can remove them easily from the plant by gentle tugging or shaking.

Many perennials self-seed, though some increase through spreading roots or crown expansion. The purple coneflower is an example of a perennial self-seeder. Experience, and sometimes a little research in a perennial guide, will show you which ones self-seed. A few plants, like the perennial herb tarragon, have lost their capacity to produce fertile seed at all.

HELPFUL SELF-SEEDER—OR WEED?

Some plants self-seed generously enough that they become annoying. In my garden, borage, balsam, garlic chives, cleome, sweet Annie *(Artemisia annua)*, and nigella fall into this category. Of this group, garlic chives and sweet Annie are the worst offenders, and I recommend omitting them from your garden, especially if you have rich soil. There is also a little woodland plant called woodland knotweed *(Polygonum virginiana)* that is treading on thin ice in my garden. It's not that it's ugly—just that there's an awful lot of it. I think whether a plant is a "noxious" self-seeder or not, though, depends on how much you like the plant. I feel that you can never have too many black-eyed Susans, poppies, and larkspur, and, in fact, there are some years when I feel pathetically grateful for their enthusiastic return. Removing ripe seed heads from plants and mulching the soil around them will greatly reduce unwanted self-seeding.

To encourage self-seeding, don't mulch, as most self-seeders need the bare earth to latch on to. And, of course, when deadheading, leave a few spent flowers to set seed. Also, give a flower you want to self-seed its own space. For instance, a flower such as larkspur seems to have a hard time becoming established if it jostled by other plants. How dependable a self-seeder is depends. Some plants get swamped by other more aggressive plants

A self-seeded rose of Sharon (*Hibiscus syriacus*) peeks over the picket fence.

and vanish. Or weather, especially erratic winter weather, could spell the end of their stay in your garden.

Seeds for self-seeding flowers may be obtained from fellow gardeners and from firms specializing in so-called heirloom, nonhybrid flower seed. Here is a list of useful self-seeding flowers:

AGASTACHE FOENICULUM (ANISE HYSSOP) Every year, anise hyssop seeds itself here and there in my garden, and every year I corral them into one spot in the side garden, where I can watch the bumblebees visit the flowers on warm summer days. I have a white agastache that also self-seeds.

ALCHEMILLA VULGARIS AND ERYTHROPODA (LADY'S MANTLE) These will self-seed in good, moist soil.

ALLIUM TUBEROSUM (GARLIC CHIVES) Garlic chives are rampant self-seeders and unlike some seedlings are hard to pull up, as the grasslike leaf breaks off, leaving the root behind. I recommend removing most of the seed heads, come fall, or your garden will be drowning in garlic chives come spring. Better yet, don't plant garlic chives to begin with.

ANETHUM GRAVEOLENS (DILL) Reserve a sunny area at the rear of a vegetable patch for this tall, feathery herb.

ANTHRISCUS CEREFOLIUM (CHERVIL) I purchased and planted a chervil plant some years back, as only fresh chervil will do for certain delectable French dishes. The plant grew a little but did not thrive. It set a few seeds and then perished. Live and learn, I thought, and tossed the plant somewhere in the direction of the compost heap, which is in dappled shade. You know what happened next. Next spring, a clump of fresh green chervil plants sprang up, and since then, waves of chervil appear every six weeks or so by the compost heap, especially after a good rain. Now there is plenty of chervil for *le bouquet garni, merci.*

AQUILEGIA SPP. (COLUMBINE) Many columbines self-seed, and you can help them along by plucking off the dried seed heads in late summer and shaking them like a salt cellar where you want more plants.

ARTEMISIA ANNUA (SWEET ANNIE) With fragrant, finely divided foliage, this is one of those good news/bad news plants. The good news is that if you like to make herbal wreaths, you will have all the material you'll need once sweet Annie is in your garden. The bad news is, how many wreaths do you need? This is definitely a back-of-the-fence plant, along with tansy, in my garden. Be forewarned that sweet Annie can reach six feet and can develop quite a root system. This spring I had to chop down a treelike specimen of sweet Annie with an axe.

ASCLEPIAS SPP. (MILKWEED FAMILY) Both swamp milkweed (*A. incarnata*) and whorled milkweed (*A. verticillata*) self-seed heavily. Common milkweed (*A. syriaca*) is a rampant self-seeder and shouldn't be allowed in the garden. The asclepias that you wish would self-seed heavily, butterfly weed, self-seeds only occasionally.

BORAGO OFFICINALIS (BORAGE) Borage is a big, gangly puppy of a plant with sky blue, star-shaped flowers. Its leaves and hollow, juicy stems have soft prickles. Borage can be a pest, but the flowers are so pretty, and there's something so friendly and happy about the plant that I haven't banished it (yet).

CALAMINTHA OFFICINALIS (CALAMINT) See the entry in chapter 4, "Dictionary of Perennials." Calamint can be a rampant self-seeder.

CALENDULA OFFICINALIS (POT MARIGOLD) Calendula is a rather odd case in that it's not totally happy in the Midwest—it languishes sulkily during our hot summers. But it springs to life in fall's cool weather, looking like glowing jewels amid the autumn leaves. You'll usually find a few seedlings next spring.

CARYOPTERIS CLANDONENSIS (CARYOPTERIS) Caryopteris is considered a sub-shrub, meaning it's a somewhat woody plant that dies back with cold weather. It should be pruned back hard in early spring. Its misty, amethyst flower heads grace the garden August through frost. I've never heard of caryopteris as being a self-seeder, but it does self-seed in my garden every year. As a matter of fact, the original plant has disappeared, and the three plants I have now resulted from self-seeding. Caryopteris is supposed to be hardy to Zone 4, but I think it's the type of plant that doesn't always survive a damp winter or a punishing cycle of freezing and thawing.

CENTAUREA CYANUS (CORNFLOWER) The matchless bachelor button blue of this flower is bleached white by the heat of midsummer. At that point, you can tear the plants out, leaving a few dried seed heads behind to ensure more plants next spring.

CHRYSANTHEMUM LEUCANTHEMUM (OXEYE DAISY) This will pop up here and there in the garden, though it may take a year or two to dig in. The upside of oxeyes is that they look so pretty in June, but the downside is that they need to be cut back after blooming because they look bedraggled. If they've self-seeded generously, this is a lot of cutting back.

CHRYSANTHEMUM PARTHENIUM (FEVERFEW) Avoid planting this in very rich, soft soil—the seeding could become an annoyance.

CLEOME HASSLERANA (CLEOME) Cleome self-seeds to the point of madness, but the lacy flowers are unique and lovely. Just be prepared to spade over seedlings come mid-June.

CONSOLIDA AMBIGUA (LARKSPUR) Needs space, decent soil, and sun. This is a classic cottage garden flower.

CORIANDRUM SATIVUM (CILANTRO) This self-seeds in ordinary or poor soil, though not rampantly. I usually plant an extra packet of seed to boost the yield so there's plenty for salsa. The seed of cilantro is called coriander and has a distinctive, lemony flavor.

COSMOS BIPINNATUS AND C. SULPHUREUS (COSMOS) Give cosmos average soil and sun. Some of the best cosmos I've seen have been growing in sunny alleys, thriving on neglect. Cosmos seedlings don't transplant well, so if a volunteer does come up where you don't want it, moving it may stunt it.

DATURA (MOONFLOWER) This was a passalong plant that surprises me every year by self-seeding, sometimes in the lawn. I've also seen big clumps of datura blooming in alleys. The flower is simply remarkable, like an elaborately folded umbrella of heavy white silk, and I am amazed and grateful every year it returns.

ECHINACEA PURPUREA (PURPLE CONEFLOWER) In good soil, these can be borderline invasive.

EUPHORBIA POLYCHROMA (CUSHION SPURGE) While I've read that this does not spread, my sister says it self-seeds generously in her garden year after year.

FOENICULUM VULGARE (FENNEL) Bronze fennel is especially attractive.

IBERIS UMBELLATA (ANNUAL CANDYTUFT) Pretty little domed flowers in candy-heart colors, these plants are about eight inches tall. The seed heads are also attractive.

IMPATIENS BALSAMINA (BALSAM) Flowers are as complicated in shape as orchids and hide demurely beneath notched, boat-shaped leaves. The flowers are white, rose, and violet, and the plants are about a foot and a half tall. Balsam likes sun with a touch of shade in the afternoon—they are in the impatiens family, after all. Given rich soil, balsam can become a nuisance, but since the plants have very short, stubby roots, they're not difficult to pull out, if it comes to that.

IPOMOEA IMPERIALIS (MORNING GLORY) If these find a spot they like, blasted with sun, they will happily self-seed.

LINUM SPP. (FLAX) I've mentioned elsewhere what interesting and worthwhile plants the flaxes are. While small and wispy, they are drought tolerant and bloom on and off all summer. I have a self-seeding blue flax and this year planted *Linum grandiflorum rubrum*, the scarlet flax, and am crossing my fingers that it will come back next year, too, because it's really lovely. Thompson & Morgan has an interesting assortment of flaxes that merit investigation.

LOBULARIA MARITIMA (SWEET ALYSSUM) Given a bit of space, sun, and good, soft, fluffy soil, sweet alyssum will return in profusion.

LUNARIA ANNUA (HONESTY) Please see the entry in chapter 4.

MELISSA OFFICINALIS (LEMON BALM) You probably will only want one lemon balm plant, but it will throw off at least three or four seedlings every spring, more in some years. Let the extras grow a bit, and before they go to seed, use the leaves to make lemon balm tea.

MIRABILIS JALAPA (FOUR-O'CLOCKS) If you give them their own sunny spot, they may self-sow. And if you are interested in learning how to collect seeds, this is a good plant to start with. After the flower petals wither, look for the seeds, which look like little black hand grenades, clasped in the papery sepals.

MOLUCCELLA LAEVIS (BELLS-OF-IRELAND) This is also known as pink lady in a bathtub because of the tiny pink flowers that appear at the bottom of the funnel-shaped leaves. This is an unusual but pretty plant that's nice in flower arrangements. The pale green leaf funnels are closely packed together in a spike. I recommend initially purchasing a plant and allowing it to self-seed, though I've read it's easy to grow by sowing the seeds in spring where they are to grow. Bells-of-Ireland needs sun and protection from wind to become established.

MYOSOTIS SYLVATICA (FORGET-ME-NOTS). Requires moist soil and partial shade.

NEPETA SPP. (CATMINT) A few discrete offspring of this pretty plant usually appear every spring.

NICOTIANA ALATA (NICOTIANA) Nicotianas will often self-seed a bit, though they're definitely not rampant, at least not in my garden. *N. langsdorffii* is tall, with soft, drooping leaves, and small, bell-like chartreuse flowers. These will pop up between brick pavers and in cracks in the pavement and are wonderful cottage garden flowers.

NIGELLA DAMASCENA (LOVE-IN-A-MIST). Swaths of soft, grassy foliage pop up every spring with this self-seeder, but it's very easy to rip out what

Self-seeded brown-eyed Susans (*Rudbeckia triloba*) radiantly bloom in the August side garden.

you don't want.

PAPAVAR SPP. (POPPIES) Just give them their own space and plenty of sun, and they'll take it from there. I have a small red field poppy that self-seeds, and a neighbor has a many-petaled carnation-type poppy that comes back faithfully every year.

PETUNIA HYBRIDA (PETUNIAS) For a long time it somehow escaped my attention that petunias can self-seed, and, in fact, they don't self-seed everywhere, just where you don't expect them. Last summer I had a self-seeded petunia growing up in the crack between the concrete back steps of my house and a brick path. I want to ask it if there weren't easier places it could have grown. Petunias are often hybrids, and the self-seeded flowers are usually small and lavender. My sister notes that the 'Wave' petunias are particularly prolific self-seeders.

PULMONARIA SPP Despite this being a shade plant, my sister finds pulmonaria seedlings popping up in sunny areas in her garden. Pulmonaria seedlings can't compete with aggressive ground covers such as vinca or sweet woodruff, so if you want it to self-seed, give it its own space.

RUDBECKIA HIRTA (BLACK-EYED SUSAN) A Midwestern gardener's best friend. Self-seeds *just right*—here and there, never obnoxious. They glow with health and life.

RUDBECKIA HIRTA 'GLORIOSA DAISY' Sometimes these self-seed, sometimes they don't, and I've heard it's damp autumns that inhibit self-seeding. When they do self-seed, some of the flowers will have reverted back to plain black-eyed Susans. So if you want a particular kind of gloriosa daisy, you will have to reseed with purchased seed each spring.

RUDBECKIA TRILOBA (BROWN-EYED SUSANS) See chapter 2, "Six Indispensable Perennials."

SALVIA HORMINIUM (SOMETIMES CALLED S. VIRIDIS) You'll be glad to see this little sage with its multicolored bracts return every year to your garden. It's not aggressive, though, and other bigger, beefier plants may roust it from the garden.

SCABIOSA OCHROLEUCA Pretty little white flowers dance at the end of spindly stems footed by a leafy rosette. That's the good part. The bad part is that this self-seeds relentlessly, to the point of being annoying.

SILENE ARMERIA (CATCHFLY) A little annual whose magenta flowers bloom from May through September. It's very adaptable, and I suppose you really could call it a weed, but it's pretty.

VERBENA BONARIENSIS Very tall (five feet), with purple pom-poms at the tip. Self-seeds profusely, but the plant looks good just about everywhere. Seedlings will appear only when the soil and air are thoroughly warm, in early to midsummer. If the seedlings have appeared in the shade, move to a sunny spot, or they may not flower.

VIOLA TRICOLOR (JOHNNY-JUMP-UPS) This is a faithful reseeder.

Other plants in my garden that have self-seeded include the Japanese tree lilac, soapwort (*Saponaria*), bleeding hearts, pussytoes, dame's rocket, violets, baby's breath, wood poppies (*Stylophorum diphyllum*), a sedum named *Sedum aizoon*, a grass named *Hystrix patula*, and bulbs, including scilla and species tulips.

Slips

When I was a kid, my mother rooted cuttings of a favorite African violet or geranium by taking a "slip" from the plant and rooting it in a jelly jar of water. (A slip is a piece of a plant that's been pulled, or "slipped," from the main plant. It's also called a stem-tip cutting.) Usually within a week, tiny roots appeared and quickly started to tangle. The rooted cutting was then potted up and—voilà—we had a new plant.

Slips are a way that gardeners, probably since the time of Adam and Eve, have "passed along" plants to one another. A stem pulled from the main plant and wrapped in a twist of damp newspaper was often a parting gift to a visiting gardening friend. In times past, many a garden was made entirely of plants grown from slips from friends and were known as "friendship" gardens, which sounds like a nice idea.

Rooting a cutting from a plant is an example of "vegetative" propagation: from a piece of the parent plant, an identical offspring is created. Plants grown from seed often vary from the parent plant.

ROOTING IN WATER

Rooting cuttings in water is an easy way to propagate some plants. While it's possible to root some plants just by taking a leaf with a bit of stem (the African violet is an example), a stem-tip cutting should have a growing point at its end, where you can see new leaves emerging. Simply take a stem-tip cutting that's about four to six inches long, strip off the lower leaves, and place it in a glass of water with some of the plant's leaves hooked over the side of the glass so it doesn't slide in. Keep the cutting in a warm place in bright, but not direct, light, and usually it will root in less than two weeks, depending on the variety. Keep the water level up, and replace it every few days. Cloudy water indicates bacterial growth and should be changed immediately.

Here is a list of plants that can be rooted in water:

agastache

ajuga

basil

begonia

calamint

coleus

English ivy

geranium, including scented geraniums

impatiens

lamium

lavender

lemon verbena

mint

monarda

patchouli

physotegia

pineapple sage

varieties of *Plectranthus* (a coleus relative)

rosemary

tradescantia

Many of these plants are members of the mint family *(Lamiaceae)*, and it's worth trying to root any member of this family in water. One quick way to determine if a plant is in the mint family is to grasp its stem between your fingers: many mints have square stems. To learn more about this remarkable family, go to mintchronicles.itgo.com on the Internet. It has a complete list of mints, plus pictures and cultural information for many of them.

Impatiens that have been displayed as summer pot plants may be brought inside in the fall and overwintered. I know of one gardener who does this and then takes slips and roots them come spring. She pots them up, and out they go again when it gets warm. The same can be done with coleus. Doing this depends, though, on having a sunny, cool spot for the plants to overwinter—a sunny porch is ideal.

I have a variegated ivy that started its life as part of an outdoor container planting. It was so pretty that I potted it up and brought it inside in October. Now it's late February, and I have three stem tips rooting in a little glass jar on the kitchen windowsill. They look fresh and green, and when it comes time to make up new outdoor containers, I'll have four variegated ivy plants to plant, instead of just one.

Tradescantia cuttings are extremely easy to root and are good plants to start with. There are many different varieties of tradescantia, and cuttings will usually root in less than a week. These can be also used as vines in a container planting, in early summer.

Not every plant can be rooted this way, but I think it's worth trying any member of the mint family, or anything with a rather soft, succulent stem.

PROPAGATING SLIPS IN ROOTING MEDIA

Once you've rooted some slips in water, you'll be ready to learn how to root them in a rooting media, which could be potting soil, perlite, or even sand. Garden soil from the outdoors contains pathogens such as bacteria and fungi and is too firm a texture for delicate cuttings.

A good project to begin with is propagating pachysandra. Pachysandra is often derided as a garden cliché, but it's a good little workhorse, and sometimes it's just what you need for a difficult area in the garden. And if you need pachysandra for a landscaping project, you usually need quite a bit, so propagating some of your own could save money.

Begin by filling an empty flat (I have used a black, plastic flat) with moist sand and smooth the surface. From some of your own supply or from a friend or neighbor, cut off stems of pachysandra, making sure there is a node or two on each stem. (A node is a bump on the stem from which new leaves and buds will grow.) Gently push each cutting into the sand. You don't have to space the cuttings very far apart, so you can jam many cuttings into one flat. Leave the flat in a shady spot, checking occasionally to make sure the sand is still damp. Wait for about a month before tugging on a cutting to see if it has rooted. My sister says the ideal time to propagate pachysandra this way is in early spring.

Another easy project is to propagate geranium cuttings. Take a cutting that's about four to five inches long and pull off the lower leaves. Then fill a clean (washed with hot water and soap), eight-ounce yogurt cup with damp potting soil. Be sure to poke some holes in the bottom of the cup for drainage. Take the cutting and press its stem down into the soil. Then place a plastic sandwich bag over the slip and cup and secure with a rubber band. Place this on a bright, north-facing windowsill, but out of direct sun. I do this in early February and have a very high rate of success. This is a great way to propagate a geranium that you really like, to have plenty for the coming summer months.

OTHER TYPES OF CUTTINGS

Plant propagating can feel like magic, and once you get into it, you will want to learn more and more. There are other types of cuttings besides the stem-tips, including cuttings made from leaves, roots, and basal stems, and there are a variety of techniques for propagating them. I direct you to a very good book on the subject, *American Horticultural Society Plant Propagation*, by Alan Toogood. His *Complete Book of Plant Propagation* is also good. Study up, and soon you'll be propagating perennials, shrubs, and even roses, from cuttings. Another good source of info is on the Gardenweb.com, at their Plant Propagation Forum.

The previous explanations make the whole business of cuttings a bit more complicated than it sometimes actually is. Some gardeners just pull off a stem of a plant in the spring, stick it in the soil, and water. There is a ferocious energy in many plants that is aimed at one thing: reproduction. So a surprising number of times, that stem will take root and grow. The better your soil is, and the more you remember to water, the more likely this casual approach will work. It can't hurt to try. I am reminded of the little fence I once made from willow branches bent to form hoops. The willow rooted, and stems shot up. Not wanting eight willow trees by my back door, I pulled them up, but it was a good lesson in just how easy propagation can be.

WATERING

For watering cuttings, try using willow water. Willow stems contain the plant hormone indolebutyric acid (IBA), which stimulates plant growth. To make willow water, take a handful of willow twigs and cut into pieces a few inches long. Cover the twigs in hot water and let soak overnight. This water can be used to water cuttings. I have also heard that water used for rooting ivy cuttings has a similar effect.

DIVIDING PERENNIALS:
THE GARDENER AS SORCERER'S APPRENTICE

While an annual plant blooms for but one brief and glorious season and then dies, a perennial matures over a span of years. Or in the words of a short verse about perennials, "First year they sleep,\second year they creep,\and third year they leap."

It's this ever-evolving quality that alarms new gardeners and gives perennials the undeserved reputation of being "hard." The *when* and the *how* and even the *why* of dividing perennials can seem fuzzy. The *why* is the easiest thing to explain. Many perennials will decline if not divided at some point in their lives, as they may have used up the nutrients in the soil where they are planted. They may crowd in upon themselves and cease to flower, or the flowers may get smaller and smaller, or the plants may grow out from the center, developing an ugly bald spot. So we divide to renew or rejuvenate them. We also divide some perennials to propagate them. Hostas are a good example. You don't *have* to divide them, but you can easily increase your supply of hostas if you do.

Most perennials are extremely tough customers that can withstand a fair amount of bungling, dropping, being trod upon, and generally being manhandled—I speak here from experience—and are straighforward to divide. I've never lost a perennial yet from dividing. All have survived and thrived. For instance, I've just come in from transplanting a boltonia that I had desperately squashed in behind a rose the previous year. As I lifted up the plant in the shovel, it fell apart by itself into individual crowns: the plant had divided itself! (Crowns are the part of the plant where the stems arise from the roots.) The original plant had given rise to about eight new crowns. I replanted these in another, roomier location, where hopefully they (no longer an "it"!) will be more content. Not all perennials are this easy to divide, of course, but I hope this gives you some idea that the process can be easy.

WHEN TO DIVIDE

A general rule is to divide perennials at a time opposite their season of bloom. Plan to divide most summer- and fall-blooming perennials in early spring, when you can just barely see some green shoots above ground. This gives the roots time to recover after division, without having to support extensive aboveground growth. Late March through early April are the best times to divide many perennials, if weather allows. Wait until fall to divide spring and early summer-blooming perennials, such as irises. Dividing them in spring will stop the blooming process in its tracks. Since summer heat stresses newly divided plants, wait until fall when they are dormant to divide.

But how do you know if they need dividing? Many perennials will tell you loud and clear that they need to be divided. For instance, some perennials grow nicely for several years and then, as I've mentioned above, begin to grow outward from the center of the plant, leaving a bare spot: it needs dividing. Or the plant will crowd *in* upon itself and go into a decline, blooming less than in previous years. Again, it needs dividing. As a rule of thumb, many perennials need to be divided after three to five years of growth.

And be sure to use good tools. A sharp set of pruners to cut foliage back and a sharp, heavy-duty spade are needed to divide plants with a minimum of trauma. A tarp or piece of burlap are useful to hold divided plants before replanting.

SLICING UP THE PIE

There are different ways to divide perennials, and which one you use depends on the plant. Begin by cutting the plant's foliage back by at least two-thirds. Some experts advise cutting back to six inches. Then gently dig around the plant to loosen it, digging at least four inches from a visible crown. It's better to dig too deeply around the roots than too shallowly. You might want to deposit the plant onto a tarp to keep the soil from scattering about. At that point, if you're lucky, as with the boltonia I divided, some plants will literally fall apart into natural clumps. Or you might have to tease the roots apart with your fingers. The key is to observe the plant, looking for its natural divisions, and take it from there, making sure that each piece has some roots. Aim for divisions with at least two to four shoots. Just use your judgment, and learn from your mistakes.

The size of each division depends on the plant and what you want to do with the division. Larger divisions recover quickly, but smaller divisions give you more plants. Just be sure that each division, or section of crown, has shoots and roots. Especially in plants that have grown out from the center, discard any dead, woody, or gnarled plant material.

If you are dividing a clump that has deteriorated in the center, newly formed divisions from the outer ring of the clump are healthier and will establish more quickly than divisions taken from near the dying center.

Some plants have tough, hard roots that are hard to divide. Siberian irises, for instance, are notorious for their mats of roots like iron. These irises can go a long time without division, and personally, I've never divided a clump of Siberian iris.

Don't be afraid to divide a perennial. You may feel that you're awkwardly hacking away at some hapless plant, doing it irreparable harm, but leaving a perennial to crowd itself or slowly decline, in the long run, is more harmful to the plant. I've found that once you've gone through the process a few times you can become quite sensitive to the structure of a plant's roots: they dictate to you how they want to be divided. Most perennials recover quickly from the division process. They may seem to be a little under the weather following division, but keep them well watered, and by next spring you'll find they've been rejuvenated.

REPLANTING

Replant your divisions as quickly as possible, as roots don't appreciate being exposed to air. If you can't plant right away, perhaps after being totally exhausted from struggling with digging the plant out of the ground, sprinkle the divisions with water and cover with a tarp or leaves. Be as careful about planting a division as you would with any newly purchased perennial, making sure that the soil is well prepared and watering the division thoroughly. The crowns of most perennials should be set a bit higher than they were originally, because the soil will settle.

DIVIDING SPIDERWORT

Today is March 26, a beautiful but cool spring day, and during a walk through the garden I notice a clump of perennial spiderwort (*Tradescantia*). Spiderwort is about 15 inches tall and is a spreader, but this clump is in some really poor soil. The clump itself is crowded, and I can see many small, purple-green shoots poking about half an inch above the soil. The plant is about four years old. In better soil, it probably would have needed dividing before this. I dig up the clump, inserting the spade four or five inches away from the clump itself to not damage roots. Not to worry: the whole clump comes up easily, with its tangle of gorgonlike roots completely undamaged. As I shake dirt off, the clump falls apart by itself: there are three natural divisions. Pulling gently on each natural division results in each division further untangling and coming apart. I put the six divisions aside and spade the soil, breaking it up and adding some compost. The roots of the plant are about a foot deep, and I try to plant each division in a hole with plenty of legroom. By the time each division is planted, the soil firmed down, and everything deeply watered, I'd spent about 20 minutes on the whole operation. With this particular plant, it wasn't even necessary to use a knife or sharp spade to divide the clump—as with many perennials, the plant was easily teased apart into its natural divisions. I could have made more divisions if I had wanted—as even a division with one shoot and root would grow, eventually forming its own clump—but, being lazy, I didn't want to replant all 16 individual shoots separately. And the smaller clumps are more vulnerable to drying out and other vagaries of weather.

Postscript: It's April 8, and all of the six divisions have recovered and are growing, even after a titanic two-day windstorm and a cold snap with zero degree wind chill. Does this happen in England?

WHAT NOT TO DIVIDE

Not every plant needs to be divided, and some perennials can go for years without division, or shouldn't be divided at all. The first group includes peonies, daylilies, and Siberian iris. Peonies, in particular, can go just about forever without division. Daylilies are usually divided to increase stock but in terms of their health and vigor don't always need to be divided.

At the opposite end of the spectrum are plants that need dividing every year or so to remain presentable. Monarda is an example. A new gardener, harboring doubts about his or her green thumb, might be attracted to such vigorous plants, but when some experienced gardeners look at monarda they think "work," as in "lots of it."

Many perennials take time to get well established and come to full maturity. If you're not sure about whether to divide leave the plant alone. Sometimes in our rush to make new plants, we tend to hurry perennials along. Hostas are an example of this. They are so easy to divide and it is fun to make new plants. But many of them reach their full magnificence only if they are left undisturbed for years. Where there is a will, there is a way, and sometimes even so-called "difficult" perennials can be divided if you study them careful-ly, wait for the right moment, sharpen your tools, water profusely, go into a Zen state, and leap. And whether a perennial should be divided every two years, every three years, or whatever, depends a bit on whether the years have been rainy or drought stricken and whether soil quality is good or poor: use your judgment.

Plant Propogation, by Alan Toogood, sums up division this way: "The secret of successful division at any time is always to have more root than shoot, to cut away excess foliage, and to keep the divisions moist and sheltered until established."

Oh... for a bigger garden!

The side garden in late August after weeks of drought.

Index